SKASE, SPAIN & ME

NEVER A DULL DAY

Harold Antony 'Tony' Larkins

SKASE, SPAIN & ME
Never a Dull Day
Harold Antony 'Tony' Larkins

Publisher: Harold Antony Larkins
skasespainandme.com.au

Cover photo: Tony Larkins (left) and Christopher Skase enjoy a light-hearted moment on Mallorca. For more photos, go to: skasespainandme.com.au

CONTENTS

Prologue . . . 5

Amanda, Charlotte and I dedicate this book to

CHRISTOPHER CHARLES SKASE

(1948–2001)

Skase, Spain & Me

Why have I put this story down on paper?

I am telling it from a unique, close-to-the-action point of view to explain what really happened to Australian businessman Christopher Skase—what he achieved, why he did what he did, the things he did right, the things he did wrong, why and how the tide turned against him. Why he went to Spain after his high-flying corporation Qintex was forced into receivership in 1989, what he did there, what went on behind the walls of the Mallorcan hacienda, the Australian Government's failed Chase for Skase campaign and the real circumstances surrounding his illness and death.

I believe I am in the best position to take you through this for two good reasons:

- I was his right-hand man for the last decade of his life. I worked beside him on Mallorca for fourteen hours a day, seven days a week, designing resort projects, putting plans into operation and sorting out our finances.

- I am family. My wife is Amanda, the eldest daughter of Christopher's wife Pixie from her first marriage. Amanda is Christopher's stepdaughter. Therefore 'step-son-in-law' is technically what I am.

I gave up my happy lifestyle and successful livelihood in Sydney as a film technician to pack everything up, cut all ties and move my family to Mallorca at the Skase family's request to help them rebuild their life. This book gives you an insider's perspective on the plans, the dreams, the parties, the resorts, the yacht, the jet, the Qintex collapse, Christopher and Pixie's relocation to Spain and life on Mallorca. It is an amazing story, almost surreal, and I want to correct the mistruths and lies that were published and republished in the media to the point where they were accepted as gospel.

I was with him all the way as he threw himself into a new series of resort projects while trying to stave off the rare, terminal lung disease and the insidious stomach cancer that eventually killed him, all the while battling with Australian authorities and fighting to regain something of what was lost. As he got sicker and sicker, I attended the business meetings, represented him in court, jousted with the media and handled the flak that daily came our way. It was me who travelled around the world to secure Christopher and Pixie new citizenship and the famous Caribbean passports.

Christopher Skase was not only the stepfather of my wife, but he was a father figure to me. A mentor, advisor, business partner and best mate. I therefore also saw the personal side. Amanda and her three sisters—Kate, Felicity and Alexandra—also adored him as a father figure. Over nearly twenty-five years, he provided them with a stability and focus they had rarely enjoyed in their lives before. Similarly, Christopher adored our only child, Charlotte, who was born into a world like no other.

Most of all, I want to tell you about Christopher Skase, the man, the businessman, the ordinary bloke who came out of Melbourne with a vision and the passion, determination and energy to make it come true. Sadly, events—some of his own making, some out of his control and many manipulated by his opponents—cruelled that vision.

That is why I am telling this story.

- HAROLD ANTONY 'TONY' LARKINS, Melbourne, 2016.

PROLOGUE

*'There are many of them,
Señor Tony,' she said.
'Many. With guns.'*

Very early one morning, Mari-Carmen, our devoted housekeeper and caretaker, came rushing into the casa de pollo, the chicken shed we had converted into a home for Amanda and me and our little baby, so we could live something of a separate life from Christopher and Pixie in the main house at La Noria.

She exclaimed excitedly that a huge squad from Spanish Interpol had turned up and were demanding entry. I realised this was very serious, if only for the fact that while Mari-Carmen was five foot nothing, she was as feisty as they come, fiercely loyal to Christopher and usually very good at despatching unwanted visitors, whether they were toting television cameras or flashing badges. Normally, a mere Interpol officer would have been last seen fleeing down the road, his ears burning, with Mari-Carmen giving him a final serve from the gate with a dismissive wave of her dishcloth and a triumphant

5

swirl of her skirt. But not this time. 'There are many of them, Señor Tony,' she said. 'Many. With guns.'

I quickly threw some clothes on and accompanied her to the back gate to be met by a big group of armed officers. Their lead detective, who looked a dead ringer for Vic Morrow, informed me in his beautiful Spanish that they were there to search for Christopher and that he had another, even larger team waiting at the front gate. Wow, talk about overkill. All this to arrest one man, a harmless, unarmed businessman at that.

He showed me the warrant and accompanied me to the front gate to allow his main team in. They swarmed past and began searching the entire property. But I noticed they did it rather half-heartedly. It was more like a real estate Open For Inspection than a search. It dawned on me that they already knew he wasn't there. Spanish Interpol are far from stupid. If they really wanted him, they could have very easily found him, and I felt sure they understood exactly where he was. They knew I had been hiding Christopher and Pixie in a series of safe houses, apartments rented by me in various parts of Mallorca in different names.

They were nice guys who seemed to know something was not quite right about the whole deal. They had already been lied to once by the Australian Government in the lead-up to the extradition request and they knew it. It looked like they were putting on a big show to keep the Spanish authorities and, more so, the Australian Government happy.

When all was done and nothing was found, the lead detective gave me a shrug and a knowing look as if to say, 'Look, I'm only doing my job. As far as we Spanish are concerned, your boss has done nothing wrong and is of no interest to us. It's just that your Australian authorities keep wanting us to come down here.'

We shook hands, he looked me in the eye, patted me on the shoulder and gave me a little smile. The message was implicit. 'We know you've hidden him. Tell him to keep low and go about his business quietly, and we'll get on with more important things, okay?'

Okay. But if only it were that simple. Would someone like Christopher Skase be able to do that?

ONE

W here to begin a story about big business, high finance, corporate takeovers, glamorous women, sensational headlines, unbelievable parties, French champagne, private yachts, personal jets, courtroom stoushes, crazed conspiracies, glorious triumph and heart-breaking tragedy?

At the Melbourne Cup, of course. Where else?

I had never been to the Cup before. No, wait, I tell a lie. I had. But that had been a fake one, where the result had been predetermined! Where the race had to be run six times over until we were all happy with the finish and the big red horse had won and the extras playing the crowd had gone wild and the director had said 'Cut!' We had produced some fine footage that time back in 1982 at Flemington for the movie *Phar Lap*. I had been part of the film's production crew, working in the art department with the props boss, Karan Monkhouse, a friend of my sister Kate. Our job had been to find, make, build, rent, beg, or borrow items from the 1930s to help authentically reproduce the period of Australia's greatest racehorse and his legendary success.

We had to source everything from cars and horse floats to wallets and money. Working from the back of a truck full of watches, cameras, glasses, pipes, umbrellas, bicycles and clothing, we handed bits and pieces out to cast members and extras each morning and made sure we got them back at the end of the day. It was important to keep track of who held, wore or drove what in which scene so they had the same prop with them in the following one, which might not be shot for another two weeks. It's called continuity, and one error can destroy a film. It was fun, exciting and a great way to make a living.

But this? This was another world entirely. This was three years down the track and the real thing. It was Tuesday, November 5, 1985, and I had come from my hometown Sydney and was about to head out to the racetrack with a vivacious young woman I had met just five months earlier and who was rapidly becoming a serious part of my life. Her name was Amanda, and she was beautiful. We had met by chance in the Northern Territory, where I had been working on the first *Crocodile Dundee* film, the one that made Paul Hogan an international superstar. As an Ansett flight attendant, Amanda regularly came in and out of Darwin from her home base of Melbourne, staying overnight.

I could not help but notice her late one Sunday afternoon as I sat in a Darwin gutter—as you would— eating a much-needed, post-Saturday night recovery hamburger. As she walked past in a group, my initial smooth, opening line, 'Hullo, darlin', drew something approaching a rebuff. 'Fuck off, arsehole,' came the reply. Well, love starts in many strange ways.

But that night we ran into each other again at a nightclub. 'You're the girl in the street!' I said. 'And you're the hamburger guy in the gutter,' she said. Can't remember what I followed that up with, no doubt a different kind of line, but obviously an improvement on my earlier effort. We got talking, had a few drinks, partied all night and connected beautifully. But when I woke up after about thirty minutes of sleep in order to go to work, I discovered she had already left for the airport to catch her return flight home. I was devastated. Until I found a phone number in lipstick on the bathroom mirror.

Better still, I had to front up to work that morning at the same airport! We were scheduled to shoot in the middle of the tarmac what was to become one of the iconic scenes from *Crocodile Dundee*, the Qantas plane in the sunrise. As we were setting up and I was copping just a little bit of stick from my workmates about hooking up with a hostie the night before, who should suddenly come out of the terminal and march across the tarmac to board their plane but Amanda and one of her cabin crew, all dressed up for a day's work. Woo-hoo!!!

She flew back to Melbourne, we shot the scene and then the whole crew was immediately relocated to a mothballed camp on the site of the Pan Continental uranium mine at Jabiluka in the Kakadu National Park. This was to be our home for the next six weeks, and I wondered whether I would ever see Amanda again.

I decided that, yes, I would. I contrived as much as possible to speak to her by phone from location so we could meet up when she was in Darwin. Not an easy thing to do in a world long before mobile phones. Then one day, against production policy and all generally accepted movie-making protocol, I had her smuggled out on the light plane that did the return trip to Darwin each day with the 'dailies,' the rushes, or rough footage of the day. Kerry 'KJ' Jackson, the shoot's runner, met the plane and picked up the rushes—and Amanda—from the runway near the still-operating Jabiru uranium mine and drove her out to the set at the beautiful UDP Falls, now known as Gunlom.

This was madness. Love and lust gone truly blind. 'No Outsiders' is a hard and fast rule on film sets, a law that can lead to instant dismissal for anyone who breaks it.

But Hoges and his co-writer/producer mate John Cornell were not in the least bit fussed. Hoges is an amazing person. He is as you see him, a naturally funny bloke with brilliant observational humour combined with an engaging warmth. They are both great blokes to work with. Extremely professional at making films, they do not put up with shoddy workmanship and will only work with people dedicated to producing a quality product. But they are quite humble and able to make it an enjoyable experience. The sort of guys that due to the respect they have earned along the way, when they said, 'Jump,' you simply replied, 'How high?'

I could not have been happier for their ultimate financial success because the making of both *Dundee* films provided me with some of the best times of my life, linking me with some of the most wonderful people I have ever had the privilege of working with. Both Hoges and Cornell appreciated the work ethic of the grip crew, of which I was one of the assistant grips, because we were very professional, hard working and got on well with everyone else.

So instead of throwing Amanda off the set, they made a great fuss of her. At one stage, they set her up in her own director's chair, sitting her between the two of them as if she was a star in her own right. Not only that, all the grip crew, led by my boss Ray Brown, voluntarily vacated our shared quarters in one of the old mining huts so Amanda and I could have space to ourselves. I was in lust, and they knew it.

After the shoot finished, I went back home to Sydney but things continued to blossom when Amanda would be in town on airline commitments and we would meet at the Regent or Hilton. We talked about family, and I began to get something of a handle on her convoluted background. It turned out that her mother went by the name of Pixie and had been married three times. First, to a Melbourne hotelier and restaurateur, Albert Argenti. Out of that marriage were born Amanda and her sisters Kate and Felicity. After that had ended, Pixie had married hotelier and developer George Frew, who had apparently been a headliner for his involvement in horse racing and his endeavours to spark up Melbourne and boost tourism. Out of that marriage was born Pixie's fourth daughter, Alexandra, often simply known as Alex.

By the time I got to meet Amanda, Pixie was by then married to husband number three, some bloke called Christopher Skase. As I was from Sydney, the name meant absolutely nothing to me. But I started to get a little bit of an inkling of what it might mean when I finally got down to Melbourne and we went out to her parents' place to pick up a few things. Pixie and Christopher were not home, but you didn't need to be Einstein to work out from the location—Toorak—as well as the house, the furniture and the art works, that they were not short of a dollar. Not by any means.

TWO

T he fact that there was a bit of money rolling around the Skase place did not faze me. I had been brought up in pretty well-off circumstances myself, and what I saw was not over the top from my perspective. My father had been a very successful car dealer in Sydney, and my three sisters and my older brother and I had grown up in an idyllic world in a rambling home on an exclusive deep-water frontage at the Woolwich end of Hunters Hill, the peninsula where the Lane Cove River and Parramatta River meet to form the foundation of Sydney Harbour. It was a unique upbringing with a colourful heritage. My grandfather had owned a beautiful house nearby with magnificent gardens called High Cliff, and every morning the family used to row across to go to school at St Ignatius', the Jesuit college at Riverview.

Every family knew every other family on the water's edge, and it was a glorious, free, happy existence. Money was never an issue, and like my father, I loved the water. I grew up mucking around in boats, fishing, water-skiing and sailing. If I wasn't doing that, I was at one of the northern beaches, surfing.

The Larkins family was prominent in Sydney legal and medical circles, producing judges, QCs, doctors and politicians across seven generations. They counted Sir Frank Packer, Kerry Packer and the Fairfax family amongst their clients. But my father, Harry Ogilvie Larkins, better known as 'Mick,' turned his back on a legal or medical career.

Having been a mechanical engineer in World War II, working on Catalina flying boats at Rathmines RAAF base near Newcastle—where he met my mother who had grown up in that city and whose father was a famous criminal defence lawyer there—Harry instead went into the motor trade. He and my mother and his business partner built the operation, Kinsley Motors in Drummoyne, into one of the most successful Volkswagen distributors and service centres in Sydney.

Dad's middle name of Ogilvie came from his mother's side of the family. Albert George Ogilvie was an energetic and forward-thinking Labor Premier of Tasmania from 1934 until 1939 when he suddenly died in office aged just forty-nine. A statue erected in Parliament Gardens in Hobart honours his remarkable policies on education, health, employment and hydroelectricity.

From my Mum's side—Maureen Lamb O'Neill—I am hoping I will get longevity. She died a happy person at ninety-two! And from her only sibling, Neil Owen Lamb O'Neill, I believe that's where I got my live-for-today attitude. He was engaged to be married to Mum's lifelong best friend but sadly was killed by friendly fire right at the very end of World War II and is buried in Labuan War Cemetery, Malaysia. He was apparently a fantastic, give-it-all-you've-got person, and I like that. Neil's death impacted on my mother and her family immeasurably; she told me that it basically killed their father who never got over it.

I also feel I get my sense of adventure from my mother's great-grandfather, James Rixon, a pioneer in the

Illawarra district in the 1880s. He was widely regarded as the greatest white 'black tracker' of his time, saving the lives of many a lost explorer, resulting in a plaque being dedicated to him in Wollongong.

When it came to naming me, a lot of family heritage came into play. My full moniker is Harold Antony Larkins. Harold was the name of both my maternal and paternal grandfathers, and I was also named after Dad's brother, the Honourable Harold Antony Larkins, QC, who became a Judge of the NSW Supreme Court. Keen-eyed readers will note that my father was named Harry and his brother, my uncle, was named Harold. What can I say? That's the Irish for you. Then again, Mum's brother was Neil O'Neill! Crazy.

All this has led me to being known by two different names by various groups of people at different times over the years. My mum wanted to call me Hal, derived from my initials, H. A. Larkins, but from when I was aged about five until I was twenty, I preferred Tony. From twenty to thirty, a lot of people, particularly in the NSW film industry, knew me only as Harold—or 'Arold as my crew boss Ray Brown pronounced it in his heavy pirate-like Devonshire accent. Most still do. In Spain, I used both Harold, which struck a bit of a chord with the locals, and Tony, which rolled off the tongue easily. These days, I am more Tony than anything.

Under the influence of my mother and father, I developed more of Dad's approach to life than the rest of the family. Like Dad, I didn't want to spend my days wandering around a courtroom in legal robes or patrolling a hospital ward with a stethoscope around my neck. Trouble was, I had no real burning ambition either, something that was to deeply frustrate many people over the years, particularly Christopher Skase.

Worse still, when I did take on a four-year motor mechanic apprenticeship, ostensibly to prepare me to take over Dad's business, it all came to a sudden, premature halt. With just a year to go, I was in a horrific motorcycle accident that left me with injuries that I still carry to this day. This was the first time I broke my back. Among other things, two vertebrae in my lower spine were crushed, a finger was totally smashed and one foot was so badly damaged that surgeons had to remove about five centimetres from its middle. Throw in a badly broken femur and this left me with more or less a club foot and one leg two and a half centimetres shorter than the other. They told me I would never walk properly again! But one of the family medicos, Uncle Bill, organised for two specialists to put Humpty Dumpty together again, and with a lot of determination and help, I did.

Spectacular as it was, the accident was typical of my lifestyle. I was always in scrapes, prangs and bizarre accidents, such as the time a Volkswagen Kombi fell on me from the workshop hoist. When I would arrive at Royal North Shore Hospital after another bust-up, the ongoing joke was that it wasn't me that needed to be brought in on the trolley but my medical files.

However, growing up by the waterside meant that by the time I was twenty, I had discovered one thing that I was very good at—sailing. Having spent six months recovering in hospital and still unable to work because of the accident, I started getting out on the water as part of my rehabilitation. I had a natural affinity with any vessel and pretty soon wangled my way into a three-man Dragon Class keelboat sailing out of the prestigious Royal Sydney Yacht Squadron. This was an invaluable experience, not only from the sailing perspective but from the point of view of gaining life skills. I learned to handle all sorts of people from all walks of life, many with vast fortunes, it being the most exclusive club in Sydney at the time. I was encouraged by Tony Tyson, the skipper and owner of the yacht, and by the third man on board, my brother Neil. Finishing seventh in the Australian Championships on Sydney Harbour in January 1981 scored us a trip to Travemunde in Germany for the World Championships in the upcoming European summer. It also secured me membership of the RSYS, one of Australia's most sought after and elite clubs, whose snootiness and misogyny in those days was best exemplified by the ruling, 'No women on the carpeted areas please …'

I am sure they only granted me membership because the international racing rules stipulated that I had to belong to a club in order to represent Australia at the world titles and the RSYS just happened to be the place out of where I was sailing.

A creditable performance in Germany, mixed with our somewhat enthusiastic approach to life, drew invitations to Sweden where we competed in the European Cup at Kullavik, south of Gothenburg, and to Douarnenez on the western coast of France for the Gold Cup, where I celebrated my twenty-first birthday.

There for a good time, we spent most of our money on having fun. At one stage, we were so broke we had to set up camp in a derelict chalet in an apple orchard. For several months, we bunked down on an old yacht. I recall the weekly trips by ferry from Sweden to Denmark, largely to top up hash supplies, and the time Neil and I drove the American team's yacht from Sweden down to Amsterdam on the back of a '66 Chevy flat-bed truck.

Eventually in France, we ran out of cash. And the authorities ran out of patience. Having borrowed $50 each from the Australian Embassy, as no one back home would send us any more dough, we were chucked out of the country with our passports marked 'Destitute Australians.'

Back home I was looking around for a job, and it just happened that two of my sisters, Jane and Kate, were working for film production companies, with Kate then married to Mike Willesee's younger brother, Peter, at that point one of Sydney's top production managers. Through Jane and Kate, I got my first job on a shoot, at the bottom of the ladder as a 'gofer.' I was the messenger boy, at permanent beck and call, doing a lot of running around, locating people, finding things, being yelled at and copping the blame if anything went wrong. From there, I moved on to chauffeuring the stars around during the shooting of the *Love Boat* series, picked up the props assistant role on *Phar Lap*, and got employed as a grip or best boy in films such as *Burke & Wills, Coolangatta Gold* and *Crocodile Dundee, 1 and 2*.

'Grip' and 'best boy' are intriguing titles you see in the credits. So what do they do? The grip crew is responsible for the set up, adjustment, maintenance, safety and movement—up or down, left or right—of the camera. It's an important job and involves a range of equipment including twenty-metre cranes for the camera to swing across the scene or sheets of perfectly balanced flooring for it to run smoothly on or dollies to shift it around or railway tracks for it to glide along. You might also have to attach the camera to something like a helicopter for a spectacular overhead view or to a car for high-speed chases and stunts.

It's a vital part of the production, giving the movie the stable, smooth result that the filmgoer takes for granted. Without the equipment and professionalism of the grip crew, the camera would be bouncing all over the place, and the film would look amateurish. The boss of the crew is known as the 'key grip' and the second-in-command is the 'best boy.' I was lucky because I got to work under Ray Brown, acknowledged within the industry as the doyen of key grips.

Now, here I was, on Melbourne Cup morning at a flash beachfront house in Middle Park, preparing for a fun day. My beautiful girlfriend was upstairs getting ready. I was twenty-five, she was twenty-three, and I was thinking, 'Larkins, you lucky bastard, life's pretty fuckin' good right now.'

THREE

Amanda had taken me shopping in upmarket Chapel Street the previous day to kit me out for the Cup, and as I looked in the mirror, I thought to myself that for a knockabout film technician, I wasn't looking too bad in my brand new suit and shirt. Although, in keeping with the fashion of the time, no tie.

It was important, Amanda had said, for me to look good at Flemington. 'Everyone dresses up for the Cup,' she said, 'and don't forget that you'll be meeting my parents there, too.'

She was sharing the place with one of her sisters, Felicity, and two other gorgeous young ladies, Samm Hetrel and Jenny Munster. The doorbell rang, and a voice called down from upstairs and asked me to answer it. I put down my hangover-repair coffee, the legacy of a massive night out at the Underground—the coolest nightclub in Australia in those days—and I opened the door.

If I thought things had been pretty good up until then, they were about to ramp right up. Standing very formally was this bloke in the snappiest limousine driver's outfit I'd ever seen with a flash dark-blue hat and all. Behind him I could see a white stretch limo. Not a tricked-up Fairlane, either. The genuine article. A Rolls-

Royce. I thought to myself, 'This just keeps getting better and better.'

'The Argenti party?' he enquired politely, using Amanda's original family name. I called them all down and away we went. It was the first time I'd been in a Roller, and we had a hoot as we meandered through the streets of Melbourne, enjoying the sights and getting into the drinks bar. At Flemington we turned into the racecourse, silently slipped down the tree-lined road past the members' car park and edged our way through the crowd. My feeling of being a wanker in a limo was outweighed by the thought, 'Hey, I really am doing this shit! This is fucking brilliant!'

I was still getting used to it all when, instead of us heading for the car park or drop-off point, the security gates parted like the Red Sea, and the Roller went straight inside the main gate. We cruised up to the edge of the track and stopped right in the middle of the Birdcage, the focal point of Flemington action on Cup Day! The place was jumping with the beautiful people.

'What a world!' I was thinking to myself as the limo door was opened by a polite young waiter cheerily offering me a glass of champagne. Someone rushed over to Amanda, and suddenly we were having a quick introduction to a group of smiling, chatting, energetic people, including a standout glamorous couple. The woman of the duo looked spectacular, the epitome of the fashionable racecourse image, with piled-high hair and a brilliant dress. Her other half was quite a bit younger than her, dressed in a hand-made suit, bespoke shirt and expensive tie, his longish hair impeccably groomed. They were polite, confident, full of life. It dawned on me I was meeting Christopher Skase and his wife Pixie.

Unbeknown to me, a long, long journey was about to begin.

Pixie could not have been more welcoming. She made me feel important, feel great, feel a natural part of this extraordinary scene, feel as if I had known her for years. I knew straight away that she was a class act. Christopher shook my hand, gave me the once over, smiled, said he was glad to meet me and hoped I would have a great day. What a great combination. She exuded the wealth; he exuded the power. In a sea of beautiful people, they were the standout couple. The ultimate duo. Passers-by could not help but stop and stare. I was thinking to myself, 'I wonder what the fuck they think of me? A film technician? Is that what they would want for Amanda?'

I didn't have time to ponder that anymore as Amanda grabbed my hand and we plunged into the Cup scene. The name Birdcage came from the old English tradition of gentlemen racegoers walking through the area to show off their lady friends—their 'birds.' Now the sponsor marquees had taken over, and it was buzzing. They were like mini restaurants or clubs, with mind-boggling floor-coverings, drapes, furniture, water-features, grand pianos, ice sculptures, whatever the designer could dream up to make it look better than last year and more impressive than next door's. There were chefs and maître d's, MCs, hand-shakers and glad-handers everywhere. Models in extraordinary dresses, fashion designers, television reporters and newspaper scribes. Waiters and waitresses rushed everywhere, dishing out free booze and five-star food. The big corporate names were plastered all over the place—Tooheys, Tabcorp, Saab, Canon, Moet & Chandon—with their staff doing everything they could to impress their clients.

I could see that an invitation to one of these places was pure gold. Firm but polite security guards were intercepting would-be interlopers, while the anointed ones—the sports stars, television starlets, politicians, businessmen and socialites—were noshing into the food and slurping down the grog. There was much air-kissing, inane chatter and serious selection of tips. These amazing, temporary palaces of luxury overlooked the track, but there were big screens everywhere so guests did not even have to go outside to watch the races much less mix with the hoi polloi.

Just light a cigar, Larkins, take a glass of Bolly off the tray going past, grab a canapé and enjoy.

And then … it all went into a blur, actually.

Drink, food, people, drink, tips, bets, races, drink. More drink. At one point, somebody invited us up to the Members Stand and who were we to say no? But an attendant was not going to let me in because I was not wearing a tie with my trendy new suit. Not on, old man.

Wait! Not a problem. The smiling bloke who had opened the limo door a couple of hours earlier appeared out of nowhere and offered me his work tie and in we went. I thought to myself, 'This day cannot get any better.'

It did. After touring the stand, we headed out to the Members' Car Park where little islands of people dressed to the hilt were consuming chicken and champagne from picnic settings out of the boot of the Roller, the Mercedes and the Jaguar. All the while I was being introduced to lots of Amanda's mates. And drinking more champagne. And supplementing things with the odd line or three of 'Colombian courage.'

Suddenly, the big race was on, the place became electrified, the horses charged around the track, the crowd went wild, the winner crossed the line and the jockey brought him back to the presentation yard. Bugger me, there is Christopher up on stage presenting the Cup! What is going on?

There was wild applause as he made his speech and handed the gleaming gold trophy to the owners of the 15/1 winner—Melbourne developer Lloyd Williams and former used car millionaire turned restaurateur turned art aficionado, Denis Gowing. The story went that the horse, What A Nuisance, had been named after Gowing's daughter, Samantha.

As Christopher stood on the rostrum, speaking, smiling, shaking hands and taking in the applause, I looked around at this amazing scene—exactly 79,126 people, many of them dressed to the hilt, others in nuns' habits over footy shorts or as The Pope or as an Arab sheik or as Superman or a ballerina or Fred Flintstone— all pouring beer and champagne down their throats and going nuts.

They told me this was the race that stopped a nation and it had. The thing was this bloke named Skase, who I had never heard of before in my life, was right at the centre of the action. I had to ask.

'Amanda?' I said.

'Yes?'

'Just who the fuck *are* your parents ..?'

She weighed things up for a moment and said, 'Well, amongst other things, Christopher owns Hardy Brothers, the jewellers.'

'So? What's that got to do with the Cup?'

'Darling, they *make* the Cup ...'

Next morning, I woke up with the mother of all hangovers. My shirt was spattered in champagne, my flash suit had taken such a battering it would barely raise

27

five bucks at an Op Shop, and oh shit, I've still got that poor bastard's tie!

But if I had survived just a sample of what life would be like in SkaseWorld, I reckoned I might be able to handle it.

FOUR

A manda had introduced me to her world of French champagne, flashy nightclubs and the Melbourne Cup. Time to show her my world—Frenchs Forest, movie equipment and the Swamp.

The Swamp was my bachelor shack, a permanent party pad, the film techo's flophouse. Ray Brown, my boss and mentor—later to be the best man at our nuptials, where I became probably the only groom in recorded marital history to be actually asked to leave his own wedding reception—had encouraged me to buy the place when he spotted it one day. It was nothing fancy. A one-bedroom brick cottage that I converted to a two-bedroom home when I encased the back veranda with a couple of old window frames, pieces of timber and bits of board I found.

It was in Frenchs Forest, an environmentally friendly suburb about twenty kilometres north of Sydney, a location that suited me perfectly. Manly and the surf were just seven kilometres away. Its rural setting was pretty cool, too. It was surrounded by Garigal National Park, two thousand hectares of bush, sandstone and all sorts of wild life, including the Striped Marsh Frog, pygmy possums and lyrebirds.

Forget the animals, Brownie's main reasoning for suggesting it was that the house had a huge backyard, perfect for storing the trucks and equipment we were accumulating as our careers in the movie business grew. With the help of my parents, I put the deposit together, took out a mortgage and bought it. The only problem was that when it rained, the big front yard flooded. After a heavy downpour, you would look out the front door onto a small lake and so that was why we named it the Swamp. In the five years I lived there, I don't think it was ever dry underneath the house; there was always a foot of water lurking beneath the floorboards.

The property's appearance was not helped much by our carefree, young blokes' approach to domestic management. To get rid of any shit we didn't want anymore, we would simply open the back door and chuck it into the metre-high grass that grew right up to the veranda. We had all the windows covered over with black velvet, like a wartime blackout, so no one could see in. None of us inside ever wanted to see out, anyway.

Film sets were a prime source of paraphernalia for decoration, especially one-off props that no one wanted after the commercial or film had been shot. Pride of place in the lounge was taken up by a giant, fake electric power plug and lead, about three metres by two metres, which had been made for a Big M commercial. Three half-sized Aborigines and a kangaroo occupied the front yard. Left over from the movie *Stanley,* the figures were beautifully crafted from latex, had flexible limbs and carried spears. We used to move them around at night, locals being greeted by a new hunting scenario as they headed off to work in the morning.

The Swamp was the sort of place where renovations were done on a whim. Like the time we were doing a bikini shoot up on Sydney's northern beaches. It was freezing and the attractive model had to bare her flesh in the cold for hours on end. As we were finishing up, she chattered, 'G-g-g-god, I could k-k-kill for a bath.'

Ever the opportunist, I chirped up, 'I've got a bath at my place, darlin'.'

I raced home in the truck ahead of her, emptied the bath of a pile of refuse that had developed in it over the months, gave it a quick clean and began to fill it with hot water. I then set about making the rest of the house warm. The Swamp was always cold because the oil heater in the lounge never worked. Not a problem. My housemate Max and I jemmied it out of the lounge-room wall with a crowbar, revealing the original fireplace, and threw it in the jungle out the back. I then chopped up a couple of four-by-six pieces of wood I had in the back of the truck, threw them plus some wood wedges and other bits in the fireplace, doused the lot with petrol, and whoosh, instant fire and warm house to welcome a very grateful model.

That was the Swamp. A crazy, twenty-four hour party place with a barbecue always running, Eskies full of M&Ms, snacks and drinks we would get from shoots, and a fridge permanently stocked with beer and a very nice champagne made by Laurent Perrier and sold by the Royal Sydney Yacht Squadron under its own label. Oh yes, don't worry, I might have been the man from the Swamp, but I was not going to let my RSYS membership go by. It had one of the most extensive bars in Sydney. Hey, a man has to have what a girl wants! The bonus was that it had a 24/7 'honour bar' where you just signed for what you took, any time of the day or night.

There were trucks and cars arriving and leaving at all hours, cook-ups going at the oddest of times and vast quantities of booze and illicit substances consumed. The carpet ended up like that of a dock-side pub, soaked with booze, making a squelching sound and generating the fragrance of stale Tooheys when you walked across it. The house was close to the main roads leading to the northern beaches, and although locals warned us about the need for security, the front door was never locked. Guys driving past would simply stop in as if it was a halfway house, and so it was always alive with a passing parade of oddball characters that lived, propped or flaked there over the years—some dossing down for a few days until the chill winds of domestic acrimony blew themselves out on the home front; some because they had turned up for a party and liked it so much they didn't want to move on; some because they were incapable of movement.

All the neighbours ever saw were trucks coming and going, guys loading up the vehicles or emptying them and blokes getting slaughtered around the barbie. Despite all the movement, we never caused much friction with the locals. I think they were more bemused than anything. On one side was Harry, a fishmonger who had sold us the house, and his wife Dee. Whenever he met Amanda, Harry's opening line was, 'G'day darl, wanna beer? Or how about a prawn?' On the other side was a Persian family, very strict and quiet. They were a lovely couple, although I detected a smidgin of anxiety lurking beneath their otherwise placid Middle Eastern exterior.

For all the madness, we tried to keep things as sane as possible. Starting a twenty-tonne truck with air brakes at four o'clock in the morning is not the best way to befriend the neighbours, especially as you had to let it warm up. The brakes wouldn't come off until the motor had heated, so you would just have to sit there and wait as it chugged away and hope that not too many people were lying in bed cursing.

In the early days, I shared the Swamp with a bloke who at the time was one of Australia's top props operators. His name was Max Manton, a great guy, part Aboriginal, brilliant at his art department role on any set and one of the funniest human beings I have ever met. He became the worldwide expert for products such as Guinness and Coca-Cola, flying around the globe, all expenses paid, to make sure the products were up to spec in all their international campaigns. Among other things now, he does a breakfast show on Bay FM in Byron Bay.

I worked odd hours in those days, usually six days a week, often sixteen to eighteen hours a day. Sometimes Max and I worked together on a shoot and at other times we didn't and so we would be constantly crossing paths at the house.

I came home one night, and there was a huge slab of black glass smashed on the kitchen floor. I thought Max had dropped a plate or bowl and had not picked it up, so I just stepped over it. For a couple of days, I just kept stepping over it. I thought, 'I am not cleaning up his shit.' You know, the defensive thinking that develops in a share house situation. 'You did it, so you fix it'.

Finally, I looked around the rest of the kitchen and realised that the black glass was in fact the oven door. And that the oven had been blown to the shithouse. Max had apparently come home at three in the morning feeling a bit hungry. To fix the munchies, he had whacked some frozen chicken legs in the oven, turned it up as high as possible and promptly gone to sleep. The ensuing explosion had blown the door off the oven, sprayed glass everywhere and melted the knobs.

Max was like that. If he burnt something when he was cooking in the tiny little kitchen, to get rid of it he would simply kick the back door open with a deft little flick of his foot and turf the lot out into the back yard jungle, pot and all. Anything he didn't want, dishes, cups, you name it, they went out the door to disappear forever in the long grass.

As well as Max, a variety of people spent time at the Swamp over the years, including Jamie Egan—a gaffer and a very cool, funny guy—who I often played golf with, and Kerry 'KJ' Jackson, who I regularly used as my assistant grip. The late KJ was one of my dearest friends, a groomsman at our wedding and the man who smuggled Amanda out to Kakadu for me. RIP, my friend.

Not forgetting the Fridge, Michael Adcock, given that nickname due to his size and his love of food and grog. As you would anticipate, the Fridge always had a slab of beer in … the fridge.

Then there was Kazmer.

Kazmer Harangozo moved in when Max moved out. He was of Hungarian stock, somewhat eccentric in a wonderful kind of way, a bit like Kramer in *Seinfeld*. He looked and sounded like Jack Nicholson, and when he was up for a bit of fun, he loved playing the Samurai from a well-known *Saturday Night Live* sketch or doing the scary axe-at-the-door routine from *The Shining*. You know the one, 'Wendy, I'm home.' At three o'clock one morning, he turned up laughing maniacally at my bedroom door with the axe and jumped into my bed. Right between me and Amanda! This was one of her first visits to the Swamp. Welcome to the mad house, babe.

Amanda and me? Initially we simply loved each other's company, got along well, enjoyed getting wasted and liked having fun, although I don't think either of us at that stage thought it was going to be a life-changing experience. Certainly not an odyssey into the corporate world of money, drama, headlines and tragedy.

But after the Cup experience, she began to reorganise her Ansett schedules and bid for more flights to Sydney in order to spend more time with me. One of the perks in those days was that airlines would put their overnight flight crew and cabin staff up in pretty swank hotels like the Regent or the Hilton. I didn't mind meeting up with her in the five-star surroundings and giving the spa and the mini-bar a going over. Amanda started to meet my family and friends, and before we knew it, the knockabout film bloke and the beautiful flight attendant trying to find her way in life were both thinking that this could be the real thing.

I was attracted to Amanda because physically and mentally we connected. She was stunning when I first saw her. Still is. She combined beauty with brains and a sense of fun tempered by pragmatism and independence. While she laughed at my one-liners, I soon found out she was very much a loner who preferred her own company. After all, she was the oldest of Pixie's four girls and therefore had had to shepherd the others through three marriages and a lot of comings and goings in between. She enjoyed any opportunity to get away from all that and have some time for herself. Guiding her sisters through all that dislocation and change had toughened her up, turning her into a determined decision maker who loved setting the administrative agenda. We made a good team. She would organise what was going on, and I would turn up ready to enjoy it.

But while a flight attendant's life was a bit hectic, Amanda discovered that the day-to-day existence of a film grip was like nothing else she had seen. It's a great job in that you are at the centre of the action, standing right next to the cameraman all the time as his minder. You get the best seat in the house, the unique perspective of the director. But your role is to ensure that nothing happens that will compromise, damage or de-rail the camera or endanger, distract or injure the cameraman. To do that, you have to be on your toes all the time and to work with the best equipment available.

The experienced grip buys and assembles his own equipment, plus a truck to transport it, so he can turn up at any set as required, ready to shoot anything and handle any contingency. While films are based on careful pre-planning and scheduling, there are still plenty of 'ifs' and 'buts,' so you have to be ready to be anywhere, anytime with any possible range of solutions. The phone call can come at any moment, the demands are high and the hours are punishing. You could be required for a shoot at eleven o'clock at night or at three o'clock in the morning. You could do a four-hour stint or work forty-eight hours straight. Your success hinges on your approach, commitment and having all the right gear. Ray Brown, the gun of grips, had already amassed a fair slab of equipment, and with my help had expanded the business to another level with an impressive cache that we took to the shoots using his trucks.

On set, we were the A Team, a dedicated group with top equipment, excellent morale and a professional approach. After hours, party-time, we were the Animals, or as we preferred in a deliberate form of dyslexia, the Aminals. Play up and stay up all night. Drink like there was no tomorrow. Shag anything that moved. Trash the occasional hotel room, like a rock band on tour, often as not as to provide entertainment for everyone else. The rest of the crew almost expected the grip boys to be the party boys.

It was a great lifestyle, especially on international productions. We always stayed in five star hotels with all expenses paid. I would pull two to three thousand dollars a week when the average weekly wage was five hundred bucks. Good productions did that in the 1980s. They looked after their people.

We also knew that mistakes cost money and so we made sure we delivered. We were freelance, and the attitude was that the film producers didn't have to necessarily employ us and we didn't necessarily have to work for them. But they did, and we did, because we all respected each other. They got what they expected from us and invariably made the A Team their first choice for the job.

We also knew that we were only as good as our last job. Gossip ripped through the industry like a mid-summer bush fire through the Blue Mountains, so you would not want to do anything to ruin your reputation. News of any balls-up that had cost money and delayed filming would soon get around the traps and producers would be very wary of employing the perpetrators next time around. If you slowed the production by an hour because of something you had done wrong, it could cost them as much as a day in time and therefore many, many thousands of dollars. Do it a couple of times and you would be dead in the water. Especially in the Australian industry, which was tight and close-knit; a bunch of small groups chasing elite jobs, working hard and feasting on gossip.

While I was always the first in line for a party, I was totally committed to my profession. I always did a good job and went that extra mile to make it a quality result. If you ask around the industry, people will tell you that I always turned up on time, fully prepared, ready to go—admittedly, heavily hung-over at times—and did my job well. You'd have two hours sleep and then go and do another eighteen hours work and not let the crew down. 'You cannot lose a camera; you cannot lose a cameraman.' That was the credo. And I never did. Well, okay, there might have been one or two times when I fucked up and someone saved my arse. But by and large I was pretty good at my job.

I had been trained by the best in the business and was in awe of the talent of the people I was having the privilege of working with. I aspired to be like the greats such as Russell Boyd, Academy Award winning director of photography for *Master & Commander* and Brian Bansgrove the award-winning gaffer, who died mysteriously in Thailand after finishing the *Lord of the Rings* trilogy. Among others there was writer/director/producer Alex Proyas, whose work includes *I, Robot*, *The Crow* and the new film *Gods of Egypt*, and Stephen Hopkins who went on to produce *24* with Kiefer Sutherland and direct *Blown Away*, starring Jeff Bridges and Tommy Lee Jones.

Through a combination of Brownie's influence and my determination, I not only did a lot of the top jobs in Australia but also the cream of the international work, such as the much-envied Coca-Cola and Sprite commercials, which were made for world-wide release. Year after year, the McCann Erickson advertising agency would come across from New York to shoot those commercials and would always use the A Team. We'd spend ten days on an island or a week in New Zealand or five nights in a Pacific beach resort, and they used to pay us huge amounts of money. In turn, we not only delivered professionally, but they liked us. A lot of the film industry was about personality. If you were good at your job, well, that was a given, a necessity, but an engaging approach and people actually wanting to have you on the set, particularly from a grip and a gaffer's point of view, was also important. And with the uber-talented director/director of photography, John Ashenhurst, we also did the memorable Nescafe Gold commercials, shot in places such as Kenya, Morocco and Brazil, and the famous, ground-breaking Singapore Airlines 'Singapore Girl' campaigns, filmed all over the world.

Out of all this, I suppose I got cocky. I had been trained by the best, I was good at what I did, I was doing a lot of the top work and I was one of the hardest after-hours players. I loved to play, always have, always will. So, a lot of people would have loved me to have screwed something up. They couldn't wait for me to make an error and get my job. They're still waiting.

Whatever Amanda thought of me and my weird profession and my crazy friends and my strange little house, she must have seen something that she liked. Because one day, after just a few months of knowing me, she moved in. Up until then, I had enjoyed sleeping in the window-encased veranda. I know that sounds odd. I was the owner yet I used to sleep in this funny-shaped room, only ten centimetres wider than the bed but twice as long, while the main bedroom was occupied by the lodger of the day. At that point it was Kazmer, the axe-wielding Hungarian. But he proved no match for Amanda.

After a few months of sleeping on the veranda, she said that she did not share my love of being able to look at the stars because the room was claustrophobic. She desired the main bedroom and set about making Kazmer feel so uncomfortable that he eventually succumbed. Kazmer shifted out to the veranda and stayed on for quite a while, practicing his Jack Nicholson routines in the moonlight, before eventually leaving us.

Then the feminine touch really kicked in, and we started cleaning the place up. The squishy carpet was pulled up to reveal really nice floorboards, which we sanded and varnished. The waist-deep grass was cut and several trailer loads of rubbish were despatched to the dump, including the oil heater, Max's burnt pots, the Aboriginal figures and the kangaroo. By the time we had finished and put a fence around the place, I discovered that it was quite a nice little house that I had bought. Harry and the other neighbours were impressed, and the Persian couple started to look upon us more kindly.

With Amanda taking up residence and the house now a sparkling example of suburban domesticity, another regime developed—watching the news and reading the papers each day about the growth of Qintex. At that stage, I was not seeing Christopher as a significant part of my life other than he was Amanda's stepfather who just happened to be a businessman.

How all that was about to change.

FIVE

S o who was Christopher Skase, this bloke in the sharp suit who kept popping up on our television screen most nights, the reports usually about him buying up another company or building a new resort?

In the twelve months after meeting him and Pixie at the Cup, as the relationship between Amanda and I hotted up, I began to get to know Christopher a bit better, mainly through meeting him at family get-togethers in Queensland. I soon discovered that quite frankly he was a bit of a dag. In fact, that's how the rest of the family used to describe him, a real dag.

While his public image was one of Italian suits, tailored shirts and power ties, at the end of the day he would change into a pair of Converse trakky daks, a loose-fitting shirt and thongs. He would then mix up his favourite drink, Jack Daniels Black Label with soda and ice, fire up the barbecue and put on Meatloaf's *Bat Out of Hell* followed by Roy Orbison's *16 Biggest Hits*. Pretty daggy, hey?

I also found out there was an ulterior motive behind the barbecue. For all his involvement in big business, Christopher Skase's ultimate aim was to cook the perfect hamburger—a genuine ten out of ten. Sure, he had the capacity and wherewithal to consume the best culinary creations in top eateries around the world. And very often

41

he did, especially if it meant stitching up a new deal or pushing an already established project forward. He could dine on cuisine nouvelle or Japanese-European fusion or traditional French with the best of them.

However, he was fascinated by the hamburger as the ultimate meal. For Christopher, an evening with family and friends cooking up a stack of burgers on the barbecue was what it was all about. Over the years, he investigated dozens of types of meat patties, tried new salads and tested out different buns. Pixie, who was an excellent cook, was always offering him advice on how to prepare them. Hosting a barbecue in the glorious Queensland sun, he would engage some poor unwitting guest in a lengthy conversation about the beauties of the hamburger, going into detailed discussion about the preparation of the beetroot, carrot or pineapple to garnish the ultimate version.

His fascination didn't stop there. He ate them in restaurants and hotels around the world, seeking the best. 'Is this the perfect ten?' he would ask himself. I also discovered that he would turn up at his own resorts unannounced and order a hamburger to see if it stood up to his high standards. And if it didn't, he wanted to know why. After years of research, he declared the winner of the world's best hamburger, a perfect ten out of ten, was a toss-up between those on offer at the Kahala Hilton and the Princeville Hotel, both in Hawaii.

I also discovered that this daggy persona was fostered around the dinner table. Christopher had a natural, easy charm and a style of humour inspired by movies such as his all-time favourite, *Dirty Rotten Scoundrels,* the Michael Caine/Steve Martin comedy about two con men working over a French town. He never cracked jokes so much himself but loved hearing people tell really basic gags or coming up with terrible one-liners. Like the time I told him the one about the two blokes who come across a dog lying in the street licking itself, and one bloke says, 'Wish I could do that.' And the other feller says, 'Yeah, but if I was you, I'd pat him first.'

He would think that very funny. I had the pleasure of spending some time with his father Charles wandering around Paris, and I realised that Christopher had inherited his father's sense of humour.

As soon as the jokes were over and dinner was finished, what would be on the agenda? Intense discussion between Christopher and Pixie about what they would have for breakfast the following morning! Or the composition of the next night's dinner. It became apparent that both of them had a fixation on good food. It didn't necessarily have to be expensive, just good.

As I was coming on the scene, Christopher abandoned Melbourne as his business base and set up his headquarters in Queensland, after more than ten years operating successfully in his hometown. From what he told me and what I could work out, at Caulfield Grammar he was in the high-achiever group but always marched to the beat of his own drum, annoying the teachers no end. Part of his post-school, early work years was to take the somewhat unusual step, for those days, of leaving his job, getting in a car and driving around Australia taking whatever work he could. Deep down, he probably knew what he wanted. After starting as a clerk with J. B. Were in Melbourne in 1968, he worked as a stockbroker and then joined Australia's biggest circulation newspaper, *The Sun News-Pictorial*, as a finance journalist, and then at the *Australian Financial Review* in its Melbourne office. He saw all this experience as a means of learning what big business and high finance was all about. He then started out in 1974 as a partner with three others in a tiny finance group called Takeovers, Equities & Management Securities (TEAM). Four years later, in the break-up of that partnership, he took up 34 per cent and control of the major asset, a little Tasmanian-based company called Qintex. That is where it all began.

The following year he increased his ownership to 42 per cent, sold its Launceston property and directed the company into acquisition of specialist retail assets. Qintex bought Lustre Jewellery, Hardy Brothers—the ones who made the Melbourne Cup—and Leonda Reception Centre on the banks of the Yarra. He also had his first foray into the media, buying and later selling a stake in the Victorian Broadcasting Network, which owned BCV-8 in Bendigo and GLV-10 in Traralgon.

Then his talents as a brilliant multi-tasker—that's what used to amaze me about him, his ability to do many things at the one time—came into play. He went into property development, starting with the Victoria Hotel in Melbourne's CBD. He told me later that this was a pivotal moment. 'That made me my first million,' he used to say with pride.

This fired up his vision for expansion into property. He had successfully transformed a genteel, dry hotel, the sleepover spot for many a country visitor to the big smoke, into an upmarket set of apartments. He figured if he could make that sort of money out of a project like that, then there must be plenty of other opportunities out there. And if you wanted to be a serious kingpin in property development in those days, Queensland was the place to be.

It was the era of the White Shoe Brigade with entrepreneurs like Keith Williams at Hamilton Island and

Mike Gore at Sanctuary Cove buying up vast tracts of land, plonking buildings on them and chasing the overseas tourism and investment dollar. Their object was not only to make money but also help make the dream of the Premier, Sir Joh Bjelke-Petersen, come true—that Queensland would become the number one tourism and development state in the nation. Bjelke-Petersen loved to flaunt his patch, getting up the noses of southern state governments by inviting 'Mexicans' from Victoria, NSW and Tasmania to migrate north.

Bjelke-Petersen offered Christopher some irresistible financial incentives to shift headquarters from Melbourne to Brisbane. But Joh was notorious for mangling his words, and at a welcoming dinner, he warmly introduced Christopher as, 'My good friend, Mr *Skates* ...'

Christopher ignored the typical Joh malapropism, replying that he admired the premier for what he did to promote and encourage tourism in the Sunshine State.

The move north made sense on two fronts. First, after dabbling in the Victorian Broadcasting Network and then purchasing Radio 2SM in Sydney, Qintex had invested in Queensland television, buying stations at Mackay, Mt Isa and TVQ-0 Brisbane. Second, Qintex had secured land for the creation of two visionary, upmarket Queensland resorts. One was the $85 million Mirage at Port Douglas, in those days a tiny, sleepy beachside village in Far North Queensland, seventy kilometres north of Cairns. The other was the $50 million Mirage Gold Coast on the Southport Broadwater. They were designed to set new standards in luxury accommodation, appealing especially to wealthy international tourists and investors. A significant part of the projects was the sale of units to overseas buyers, particularly Japanese purchasers.

Christopher was also negotiating for TVQ-0 to get the exclusive coverage rights to upcoming Expo '88, a world's fair of products, services, lifestyle and culture, to be staged on a newly constructed site on the riverside in Brisbane. The $625 million fair, the biggest event of Australia's 1988 Bicentennial Celebrations, was to be opened by the Queen, run for six months, and focus on the theme of *Leisure in The Age of Technology*. As a follow-up to this, Gold Coast-based architect Des Brooks was influential in the master plan of Brisbane's stunning Southbank Precinct.

While all this was going ahead, I was still living in Frenchs Forest and working full-time in the movie industry, so family holidays were really the only time Amanda and I spent with Christopher and Pixie. On occasions like that, he and I would spend time together discussing hamburgers and his love of Essendon Football Club, golf and cricket, especially his idol, Don Bradman. His prized possession was a cricket bat autographed by Bradman, who set batting records never likely to be broken. But he mainly talked about business. Typical of many high-powered people whose main game was the pursuit of a dollar, he displayed an extraordinary lack of knowledge of the major news events of the day. No matter how big the headlines, if it was not business related, the story really didn't interest him that much. He would not read newspapers on a daily basis. Rather, he would methodically collect them during the week and then sit down at the weekend, either in the lounge or out in the sunshine, and quietly go through them, marking business stories, clipping them out and filing them in very large scrapbooks for reference later.

Neatness was important. He was a classic anal-retentive, almost bordering on autistic, an element of his

Virgo star sign. Everything had to be neat. The pens on his desk, his knife and fork on the table, the paperwork in his folders, they all had to be aligned and straight. Everything had to be put in a box and ticked off. Even people had to be put in boxes. I drove him nuts, because he couldn't find a suitable box to place me.

'Tony,' he'd say, 'what's your ambition in life?'

'To find,' I would reply, 'an ambition ...'

He found that so frustrating because he prided himself on spotting everyone's potential, drawing it out and maximizing it. We had the same conversation regularly until the day he died. It confused him further when he found out I was also a Virgo, born on September 9, 1960. As his birth date was September 18, 1948, he noted we had entered the world twelve years and nine days apart, making us both born in the Chinese Year of the Rat and thus 'ambitious and honest, but prone to spend freely.'

While critics saw him as being aloof, he wasn't entirely insular. People who inspected the resorts with him were always impressed with his ability to know everyone on the staff by name and have a good knowledge of their family, their hobbies, their footy team and so on. As he walked through the property, he could strike up a meaningful conversation with anyone and everyone, from gardeners to general managers, from carpenters to marketers. In situations like that, his grasp of detail was almost Forrest Gump-like.

That is why he drew such enormous support from most of his staff, even when things got tough. They loved him because he took an interest in their daily lives and treated them with respect, even though he was the big boss and wore the power suit. Indeed, it was fascinating to talk to Christopher or observe him dealing with people. When he was talking to you, he worked you over with his eyes. If you started a conversation, his brown eyes would lock on you, and he would give you his full, undivided attention. They had a burning intensity that drilled into you.

Medical tests had shown he also had a high degree of spatial awareness; that is, knowing where his body's position was in relation to the space, objects and people around him. A well-developed level of spatial awareness is often found amongst sports champions, mathematicians, artists and those who use their visual imagination to organise abstract thought. While he was initially prepared to give you his undivided attention, it had to be a riveting topic or an excellent idea to keep that attention. Otherwise, he would very soon drop off.

The clue was in his hands. If you were losing him, he would start to wave his hands around. While still apparently listening or responding to you, he was visualizing other things. Experienced associates soon learned that once the hands started to move, you'd lost him, and it was time to stop and walk away.

All this proved a dangerous formula if he was behind the wheel of a car. Quite frankly, Christopher Skase was the worst driver in the world. It was terrifying to be a passenger with him. If you started to talk to him, he would look across and concentrate solely on what you were saying. Consequently, the actual driving of the vehicle became of no interest to him at all. He would keep looking at you and not where he was driving. You'd scream at him, 'For Chrissake, look at the road! You're going to hit that truck.' Or he would answer the mobile phone, get really interested in the conversation and stop concentrating on his driving. If you were in a car behind him, you would know he had answered the phone because his car would start swerving all over the place.

I don't know how many times I got out of a car shaking and feeling lucky I had survived. But he would stride off as if nothing had happened, people in awe of the power image he exuded as he marched into a building or strode onto a property.

Pixie was instrumental in the creation and design of that image. When it came to clothes, Christopher did not have a clue what to buy. She always went with him and selected the suits, shirts, ties and shoes. He relied on her skill and taste, which was obvious in her interior designs, and on her knowing both instinctively and through observation what people were wearing in the right circles at the time. Over the years, Pixie groomed and moulded the raw Christopher Skase into the image of the well-dressed, astute, go-ahead businessman.

He was a willing subject because he had grown up in the world of media, communication and entertainment, recognising that a cultivated image was part of the game and a key to success. His father, Charles Skase, had been a successful and much-loved singer and broadcaster in Melbourne, especially during the 1950s, and so there was an element of the entertainer in Christopher that was maximised by Pixie. They were a powerful combination, glued together by love, a mutual determination to succeed and contrasting talents that, when combined, created a formidable formula. He had the vision; she had the taste. He had the ideas; she had the creativity. He had the persona; she had the wherewithal to create the image. Nevertheless, he was definitely in charge of one defining Skase motif. His hair.

Throughout his career, no matter how fashion changed, Christopher never wavered from having long hair. It was a look that some people loved, some people loathed and some people never thought much about. It made him stand out from the traditional, clean-cut look of the businessmen of the time such as Robert Holmes a Court, Alan Bond and John Elliott. He stuck with it despite the fact that by the mid-80s, the long-haired look had been replaced by the slicked-back gelled style, best illustrated by Michael Douglas' ruthless character Gordon 'Greed is Good' Gecko in the film *Wall Street*.

Christopher would have none of that. Maybe because he thought it made him look younger; his object was to keep his hair as long as he could whenever he could get away with it. Every now and then, I would hear Pixie bark, 'Christopher, get a hair cut.' In response, he would either go to ground and keep out of her way until she became distracted with something else or head off to a salon and get the merest snip done to keep her happy. In Melbourne, he would have it trimmed at only one place, a salon called Queens Hairdressing, and he searched Brisbane to find someone that could do a similar style. Eventually both resorts had a Queens franchise in them.

I saw from the day I met her at the Melbourne Cup, that Pixie was a shrewd operator, a believer in displaying the right image. She was the perfect hostess, very adept in any social situation, with an ability to put anyone who met her for the first time at ease. She and Christopher recognized that in those heady times creating a high profile, throwing lavish parties and indulging in excess was good for publicity and therefore good for business.

SIX

D id I just say excess? There are few better displays of excess than a yacht. And what a boat Mirage III was. At 33.5 metres long or 110 foot in the old measure, it cost $6 million to build then, probably $60 million now.

I had grown up around boats, sailed at Royal Sydney Yacht Squadron, competed in world competitions and was used to expensive craft for commercial shoots. But Mirage III topped the lot. It was a beautiful creation, a long, sleek white apparition on the waves, with the latest hi-tech navigation, communication and safety devices. It was so big that it had two other boats stowed on board, a full size tender and a runabout. With four double staterooms plus en-suites, a fully equipped kitchen, dining room, lounge and an outdoor eating area where guests had breakfast while watching the world go by, it was a brilliant design.

It had comfortable crew quarters for six, and I think it was one of the first boats where the whole teak-inlaid stern folded down to make a platform for water sports, packed with all the essential boys' toys such as windsurfers and jet skis. There was also a spa at sea level, where the wall opened up so you could look out across the water while enjoying the hot bubbling water and a cold glass of bubbling champagne.

It was such a knockout that wherever it went people would gather to gawk at it, and ask, 'Who owns that?' Which was exactly what Christopher wanted. To him, it was a corporate advertising device, and that is why he named it Mirage III, continuing the sequence of Mirage Port Douglas and Mirage Gold Coast. So, how do you run a thing like this? With a permanent crew of five in crisp white uniforms named Brooke, Graham, Michael, Flossy and Rachel.

Brooke McCabe was the skipper, with Graham as his first mate, best mate, some times bed mate and right hand man. I have never seen a more capable ship's captain than Brooke. I once witnessed him turn the boat around a full one hundred and eighty degrees in a confined stretch of water at the Port Douglas marina with just four metres each side to play with. It was such a brilliant manoeuvre, completed with no fuss, that he got an ovation from the crowd on the nearby Quicksilver pier waiting to go out for a day's snorkelling on the Great Barrier Reef.

The finish, panelling and furnishings were superbly done to the highest standards by Pixie and interior designer Barry Peters, very much at the forefront of fashion at the time. Barry, along with Pixie, helped create the look that was symbolic of the Skase empire, doing all the designs for the resorts, the yacht, the homes Christopher and Pixie lived in, and any significant Qintex building. Barry was blessed with an incredible ability for decoration. He had started out aged fourteen at Myer in Melbourne as a trainee, ultimately becoming master dresser of its window displays. He had an ability to make something out of nothing or see potential in a situation that no one else could envisage. With either a few scraps of spare material or operating on Pixie's unlimited budget, he would make great things happen. The fact that all three major figures associated with the boat—Brooke, Graham and Barry—were as camp as a row of tents did not matter one bit to either Christopher or Pixie.

As an example of the way things were going so brilliantly for Christopher in those times, an unexpected bonus came along with Mirage III—the boat-builder. He had commissioned Brisbane shipwrights Lloyd's to build it for Qintex, but while it was under construction, Lloyd's got into financial difficulty and was about to enter bankruptcy. Qintex ended up taking over the company as well.

On one end-of-year holiday, the whole family was invited to spend Christmas Day with Christopher and Pixie in Brisbane as a preliminary to a week-long cruise up to Port Douglas. True to Pixie's style, the Christmas lunch at home was exquisite with brilliant food, a fantastic setting and a hell of a lot of good booze. Everyone got trashed, and the next day, Boxing Day, we all crawled aboard the boat with deathly hangovers. Things were very, very quiet for the first day at sea. However, as we cruised our way up the coast toward Port Douglas, the following few days were some of the most memorable, happy times we would ever spend as a family.

Pixie got into some good old-fashioned fishing action on that journey. One evening she and Graham were running a couple of hand lines off the back deck while we were all sitting around the dinner table chatting and drinking. Suddenly, there was a scream, followed by Graham standing in the doorway with a metre-long reef shark that Pixie had caught and which he had proudly brought in to show us, not realising that the fish was leaking blood and dropping little baby sharks all over Pixie's carefully selected and very expensive white shag-pile carpet!

Amanda, Felicity and I were in hysterics. Kate was screaming, 'What about the babies? Her babies! Every mother loves her babies.' And Christopher? He was more concerned about the state of the carpet. Eventually Kate and one of the crew installed the shark in the spa bath on the back of the boat and things calmed down.

Another night we struck a severe storm, and the boat was lashed by some of the wildest wind and water I had ever seen. A windscreen was smashed when a huge wave crashed over the bow and onto the bridge, where we were all huddling, but Brooke calmly navigated us to safety. Whatever the situation, Christopher and Pixie loved it all. They were probably at their happiest when they were on Mirage III, out of the public eye and away from all the pressures of running the business, although as it turned out, Amanda and I probably spent more time on Mirage III than they ever did.

As we cruised up past Moreton Island, beyond Fraser Island and into the gap between the Great Barrier Reef and the coast, Christopher and I spent a lot of time together. He said he had dreams of building a resort on one of the Whitsunday Islands, an area that he adored. He particularly wanted to build on Whitehaven Beach, five kilometres of dazzling white sand. They used to say the sand was so pristine, 99.89 per cent pure, you could polish your jewellery with it.

The view from a resort constructed on Whitehaven Beach would have been mind-boggling, but he knew he would never be able to achieve it because it was located on Whitsunday Island, a National Park. Nevertheless, that's the sort of idea he kept coming up with. His view was to always reach for the stars, because you never know, you might just grab one of them.

There were many great things about Mirage Port Douglas. The two hundred and ninety-four luxury guest rooms, the fabulous dining facilities, the exquisitely maintained one hundred and thirty hectares of award-winning tropical landscaped gardens, the two hectares of swimmable saltwater lagoons with white sand beaches at the edges. I think it was the largest resort pool in the southern hemisphere at the time.

Guests entered via a roadway flanked on each side by five hundred giant oil palms which cost Christopher $4 million to transplant from Cape Tribulation and which to this day cost the local council thousands of dollars a year to maintain. They were going to knock them down once because of the expense, but under public pressure decided they were such an icon and tourism draw that they could not part with them.

Even the resort's location was unparalleled, sitting right on Four Mile Beach, a focal point being the championship golf course designed by renowned golf architect and five times British Open winner Peter Thomson. It was, and still is, a magnificent track, ground-breaking in many ways, with some of the holes running along the beach providing uninterrupted views of the Coral Sea. Australia's first ever Skins competition was held there, featuring Greg Norman and Vijay Singh. It also hosted the first professional tournament where players were allowed to break from tradition and wear shorts in the tropical heat instead of the usual bad-taste plaid pants.

During the voyage up there, Christopher had convinced me to try the new course with him when we reached Port Douglas. I had never played golf before at all. While growing up, I might have smacked a couple of balls into neighbours' houses—that was the sort of kid I was—but I had never been on a course, much less had a lesson. Still, I was a reasonable ball-sports person, so I thought, 'This can't be too hard.'

We got up a foursome of Christopher, Brooke, Graham and me. Christopher got the booking all sorted out, and we hired our clubs from the pro shop. Everyone was excited with people saying to me, 'Wow, lucky thing, you're playing with Mr Skase!'

Pumped with adrenalin on the first hole, I stepped up for my opening tee shot with my playing partners standing opposite, as is the custom, watching my every move.

I pulled out the driver, had a few practice swings, lined everything up and let rip. In my mind, it was going to fly off the centre of the club like a rocket and split the beautifully manicured fairway. Instead, it flew off the toe of the club like a Scud missile and split the narrow gap between the heads of Christopher and Brooke.

I can still see it now. The ball left me at an angle of ninety degrees and headed straight for the pair of them at blinding speed. Both leapt out of the way, but I can tell you that the ball had long gone past them before they had reacted. If it had struck Christopher, it would have taken him out. What an illustrious start to my golfing career and my romance with his stepdaughter. First hole, first shot, and I have killed The Man.

Well, what do you do in a situation like that? We all got the giggles. And laughed ourselves senseless at that moment and for the rest of the game. While Christopher was able to keep the ball more or less in play, Graham, Brooke and I were all a pretty similar calibre of golfer—shithouse—and so there were shrieks of laughter as balls disappeared into the rough, cannoned into trees and plunged into the water. Christopher said later he was just pleased to have survived. I might point out that despite his love of the game, the man who was able to attract the Great White Shark to Port Douglas was an absolute hacker.

Despite this disastrous start, we went on to play quite a lot of golf together. Whenever I was at the resorts at Port Douglas or the Gold Coast, even if Christopher was not available, Brooke and I would have a game. I even lashed out and bought a set of Mirage Resort Golf Clubs, complete with classy monogram, which proved pretty impressive on my local Frenchs Forest public course. I ended up playing a lot of golf there with my mates, including KJ and Jamie. None of us were any good, but we would love to get up at six in the morning when we had a day off, jump onto the course, have a lot of fun— you have never heard so much laughter as balls flew all over the place—and race back to the Swamp for post-golf amusement.

But I noticed that no one ever again stood opposite me when I teed off.

SEVEN

T hen I woke up one morning, engaged. To this day, I'm not exactly sure how it happened. It was mid-1986, and Amanda had flown up to the Greenmount Resort on the Gold Coast, where I was staying while shooting a Coca-Cola commercial. We went out to dinner one night, and the next morning I discovered the engagement was a done deal!

There had been no discussion. Not that I can remember anyway. I don't know who had asked who, I don't remember getting down on one knee, and wasn't there supposed to be some sort of ring thing to mark an occasion like this? Nevertheless, I was a happy man. This was a good thing. Amanda and I had been madly in love for a year, and while I was a little sad to be saying goodbye to my rather unusual bachelor life, even I knew it was time to move on.

By now, Christopher's name was becoming more and more prominent in the media. The Mirage resorts were under way, his media interests were growing and he was trying to take over Amalgamated Wireless Australasia Limited (AWA). Nowadays it is mainly an information and communication technology services company with a fairly low profile. But in those days AWA was a household name, Australia's largest manufacturer of radio, telecommunications and audio equipment. Because of its size and history, a takeover by Qintex was big news. Any potential purchaser had to get vetted because AWA also held Defence Department contracts, and although Christopher passed that examination, the company proved to be a very reluctant target for a hostile bid. The board moved to block the acquisition.

All this did was drive the share price up. Through diligent purchasing, Christopher was sitting on a good slab of them. When he realised he wasn't going to be able to buy the place, he sold the lot at a top price, picked up a nice profit and stashed it all in the bank. A few weeks later, the stock market crashed.

On October 19, 1987, Black Monday struck and the arse not only fell out of Wall Street but stock markets all around the world. The Dow lost $500 billion or 23 per cent, dropping by five hundred points to 1739, its worst collapse in history. The European and Asian markets fell a similar amount, with Australia being one of the hardest hit, dropping 42 per cent at one stage and closing at 25 per cent down. But Christopher was walking on water. While other investors and businessmen had done their dough, he was all cashed up. The profit he had made from the sale of the AWA shares, and which he had put in the bank and not back into the market, meant he survived the aftermath of the collapse that had ruined so many others. By knocking him back, AWA had done him a favour.

Pragmatically speaking, he was plain lucky. But contrary to what a lot of people believe, Christopher Skase was not a stock market jockey. Unlike many of the other businessmen of the time, he did not gamble on the exchange. He was not a paper-chaser. He did not have a portfolio of blue chip and speculative investments, nor spend his days working out what to buy and sell. The only time he purchased shares in a company was when he wanted to buy that company. That was when all the reading of the finance pages and the meticulous clipping out of news stories would come to the fore. He would spot a likely target, do his homework, consider its potential, see if it fitted into the Qintex philosophy, determine whether he would be able to do something with it and then go after it.

He usually tried to work to the Skase 51 Per Cent Rule. That is, he had to have control. He didn't want less than 50 per cent because that meant he would not be in charge. He didn't want exactly 50 per cent because that meant he would have to share the decision making with someone else. And he didn't necessarily want 60 or 70 or 80 or even 100 per cent, unless it absolutely fell into his hands, because that meant using up capital that could be put to better use elsewhere. So he would buy up shares until he had a minimum 51 per cent. Whoever held the other 49 per cent never worried him.

He also worked on the basis that any profits that came out of a company went back into it, to make it even better. Sure, he had the toys and the trappings, no doubt about that. He liked to live the good life, and he would put money into something like Mirage III if it offered promotional benefits to his operations. But the majority of the money went straight back into the companies. He did not squirrel it away or buy up on the stock market.

People would later ask him, 'Why didn't you have trust funds or offshore accounts?' He would reply, 'I never stacked money away. I needed every cent to take control of the companies and then make things better in them.'

At this stage, none of this was doing anything to change my life or that of Amanda. I was still a grip and going to work each day, and Amanda was still a flight attendant, although she was turning up to work less and less and calling in sick more and more. One day the airline got sick of her and she got sick of them and she never went back. It was never going to be her be-all and end-all career anyway and so she was happy to look after the house and think about her next step.

I was pleased that she was spending more and more time at home, knowing that we had plenty of money to cover it through my work. After years of coming home from work to find some bloke pissed and slumped in the lounge room or a couple of fellers crashing around in the kitchen or a gang hanging around a barbie raging in the backyard amid crap everywhere, it was an amazing feeling to be greeted by a welcoming kiss from my fiancée, a clean home and a meal in an oven with an actual door on it.

Meanwhile, I would see Christopher once or twice a year at a family function or holiday. I didn't have much contact with him, but when I did, I always got on well with him. For me and Amanda, our main involvement was observing the media reports showing that he was on the way up. At that point, from what I could see, all was rosy on the business front, and Qintex was doing quite well, to the point that even a young merchant banker who later went on to become Prime Minister, Malcolm Turnbull, praised Christopher for his achievements in a television interview.

Having become engaged, preparations were set in motion for our wedding. I was twenty-five when I met Amanda, twenty-six when I got engaged and twenty-seven when I got married at the Wedding That Reduced The Groom To A Shambles.

EIGHT

T he minute our engagement was announced, Pixie went into overdrive, getting very excited about planning the wedding, particularly as Amanda was the first daughter in the family to get married.

I figured the best approach was that of the typical Aussie groom, 'Tell me the time and date, and I'll rock up in the dinner suit.' After all, Amanda knew what she wanted and Pixie was always going to be the creative influence, so what value would I be in the preparations? Besides, I was busy working five, if not six days a week. Long days, lots of jobs out of town, interstate and overseas, and even when I was working from home, I was on set for hours. So the wedding was constructed around me.

But I did not count on the media picking it up as a newsworthy event. They linked it with the ever-rising star of Christopher, his company Qintex and his socialite wife. Before I knew it, more and more press articles started appearing about the wedding of the stepdaughter of the emerging business entrepreneur.

Christopher didn't mind the momentum because it pushed the company name, so bits of news were leaked, such as when Pixie commissioned costume designer Christopher Essex to create a wedding dress that was 'something special' for Amanda. He was renowned for the design, materials and craftsmanship of his creations, particularly his work on theatre productions, movies and the Gay Mardi Gras. Fortunately, the media was not too intrusive. It was more gossip snippets rather than full-on interviews with pictures of Amanda and Pixie 'seen shopping for the wedding dress' and that sort of thing. In the articles, I was referred to as 'film technician Tony Larkins,' and there were plenty of references to *Crocodile Dundee* as being the place where our romance blossomed.

Nevertheless, under Pixie's direction the wedding just got bigger and bigger, a bonus being that her relationship with Amanda, who had been a difficult, troublesome child and had repeatedly clashed with her mother, was probably the best it had ever been.

How did I fit in to all this? Well, I always got along well with Pixie. From the day I met her at the Cup, she made me feel very welcome. As well, Christopher and I had a good relationship; we had things such as the film industry and the hotel game as common ground to talk about. But let's be frank. I'm certain that deep down I was not their first choice as husband material for Amanda. I'm sure Pixie would have had other potential suitors in mind. The son of an old-money aristocrat or an aspiring horseracing identity or a cashed-up yuppie or a Liberal Party hopeful, or someone like that, not a film technician. But on the other hand, I believe they were pleased that at last Amanda was happy and that she was providing them with the least trouble she had done in a long time. Pixie later realised she had underestimated me all along and that I was the right person for Amanda.

Later, when we got to Mallorca, Pixie and I had a lot of fun together, and in front of the girls she used to jokingly say to me, 'You know, Tony, I love you more than my daughter.' Besides, she realised she could not change things, no matter what she did. She knew we were in love and that Amanda was happy to be with me. So, the wedding plans went on full tilt.

Originally we were going to have it at the old Hydro Majestic Hotel at Medlow Bath in the Blue Mountains. It's a spectacular art deco building right on a cliff face, and I had loved it since I was a child. With that location in mind and seeing as I was in the film industry, Amanda and I decided it should be a movie themed wedding, a glory days of Hollywood bash with a Glen Miller Orchestra swing feel to it.

But then Paul Hogan and John Cornell suddenly changed the production dates of the second *Crocodile Dundee* film, which I was contracted to work on. So we had to get married two months earlier than planned. The Majestic was not available at the new time, August 22, 1987, and we had to find somewhere else and consider a new theme.

After casting around for locations, we ultimately settled on my local church, with the reception at an upmarket place in North Ryde. The Catholic Church in Woolwich, a beautiful old Sydney sandstone building, was where I had gone to Mass every Sunday as a kid and quite often during the week. It was named after St Peter Chanel, a French-born missionary who met his death via wooden clubs wielded by angry natives in the New Hebrides. It epitomised the Gallic flavour of Woolwich, a focal point for wealthy French traders who settled in Sydney in the early days.

The reception was booked at Curzon Hall in North Ryde, close to Macquarie University. The beautiful old building featured a banquet hall specialising in big weddings, which we needed because after Amanda and Pixie had achieved the right balance of family, friends and business and entertainment associates, the guest list totalled more than two hundred. Day by day, the project kept getting bigger and bigger. Kevin O'Neill, Australia's best-known, high-society florist, was commissioned to provide the styling and look of the wedding, including the flowers, from his shop in Toorak Road, South Yarra. Kevin and his partner John Graham were the acknowledged specialists in supplying flowers for big parties thrown around the nation by high rollers such as Alan Bond, the Packers and Rupert Murdoch. Pixie knew Kevin and John very well, and as they had done a lot of work for her over the years, they were the obvious choice. There was no problem about Kevin's business being in Melbourne and the wedding in Sydney. Any issues of transporting flowers or personnel could simply be resolved by using the Qintex jet.

The planning surrounding Amanda's dress, the bridesmaids' dresses, the theme, the colour scheme, the cake, the photography and the transport kept changing, expanding and getting more elaborate by the day. It was a big bridal party, with Amanda having four bridesmaids— her three sisters, Kate, Felicity and Alex, and one of her best friends, Katrina Farrow.

I would come home from filming, get filled in on with what was happening, say 'Uh-huh, sounds good' and promptly disappear again. I had a bit of input into the composition of the invitation list, but that was about it. I wasn't that interested in the details and happily stayed out of things while Amanda and Pixie kept organising and reorganising. They hired twenty limousines to move the different parties and celebrities around, and unbeknown to me, Pixie engaged a French heralding horn group to play us into the banquet hall.

Ultimately, about half of the guests were from Amanda's side and half from mine. There were people from Amanda's school days, friends of Pixie, old school mates of mine, plenty of family, most of the crew from the original *Crocodile Dundee* film and some well-known faces in movies and television. A group from McCann Erickson could not make it, nor could Paul Hogan and John Cornell who sent their apologies and best wishes. They were involved in pre-production of *Crocodile Dundee 2*, which I was scheduled to head off to as soon as the honeymoon was over.

The core group, from my point of view anyway, was my mates from the Swamp. The team was led by Brownie as my best man, along with Max, my former house-mate; KJ, a pal for many years; and Roy Mico, probably my oldest friend, as groomsmen. Roy and I had hung around a lot together. Once, when I got a job as a driver on the production of *The Love Boat* series in Australia—which included appearances by Morgan Fairchild, Jim Nabors, Donna Dixon, Delvene Delaney and Bernie Kopell who also played Siegfried in *Get Smart*—they needed further staff, so I got Roy into it and he stayed in the film game for thirty years.

Being a knockabout band of groomsmen, we were keen to add our own individual style. Over a few drinks one night, the conversation got around to how Brownie never worked in sleeves on any of his tee-shirts or shirts, even when he was wearing a tie. The others also felt that sleeves were not very comfortable for hard physical work. And having grown up surfing and sailing, I wasn't a big fan of them either. So we decided to turn up at the church with the sleeves cut out of our extremely expensive hired 'tails' suits!

We were going to hack them off with knives, calmly get out of the wedding cars and stroll into the church as if this was all perfectly routine. The night we dreamed this scheme up over many schooners it seemed an absolute ball-tearer. Talk about roll on the floor laughing. But Amanda got wind of it and, believe me, the concept was very quickly put to rest in no uncertain terms. Funny about that.

Come the day, after a couple of nerve-settling drinks, a little bit of Colombian courage and the usual pre-ceremony joking and laughing, we were otherwise on our very best behaviour when we arrived at the church and throughout the service.

Albert Argenti, Amanda's father and Pixie's first husband, sang at the ceremony. He was known in Melbourne as the Singing Waiter, a nickname he privately said he hated, but everybody there that day appreciated that at least the 'singing' part of the moniker was absolutely spot on. He had started as a boy tenor at fifteen, sang with the other waiters at Mario's restaurant at its Sunday night music sessions, appeared on radio, was a finalist in the Sun Aria, made recordings and sang overseas including London, before returning to Melbourne to get into the restaurant game. He told me he had sung with Pavarotti when he was younger and you could believe it. His voice was beautiful. It filled the church. The memory of him singing *Ave Maria* still to this day sends shivers down my spine.

It was a wonderful ceremony. Pixie and Amanda had done a great job in pulling it together; Amanda looked absolutely gorgeous and the actual moment of the vows was meaningful and quite moving. But then …

As we left the church, rather than my friends throwing rice at the limos, they threw little sniffer bullets of marching powder through the open windows. And this pretty much set the tone for the rest of the day.

By the time we got to the reception, Amanda and I were happy. Very happy. Very, very, very happy. When I got out of the car, to be played into the reception by the band of extraordinarily loud French heralding horn players all done up in medieval costume, I thought, 'Oh my god, what the fuck is this?' Then to walk into the gigantic banquet hall, which Pixie had had decorated in all white, and I mean purest white, with chilled bottles of vintage Moet gleaming on the tables, I thought, 'Young 'Arold, this is going to be better than the Melbourne Cup!' So I pinned the ears back and went for it.

The women's mags were hanging around, because the build-up had been so spectacular, and there were photos being taken everywhere and people chasing around for bits of gossip. Amid this heady environment, I kept getting more and more wasted, drinking lots and lots of champagne and doing lots and lots of coke. I was not alone. Well, it was the 80s, it was a media/film industry wedding, we all had plenty of money and there was a lot of cocaine around at the time. It was part of the scene, particularly the world I inhabited in those days. I reckon probably more than half of the guests from my side at the function that day were doing drugs in one form or another—on coke or stoned or even doing a bit of acid.

Christopher certainly wasn't using drugs, but he was no idiot and so he adopted a humorous approach. In his speech, he said that he was not so much concerned about the bill for the French bubbly but more the cost of the 'chewing gum' for the groom and his mates. 'They are such a caring, sharing groom's party. I see them in the toilets, four to a cubicle, sharing the facilities ...'

In between, Ignatius Jones, the former front man for new wave band Jimmy & The Boys, and his sister Monica Trapaga, a fabulous jazz singer and a kids' favourite on *Playschool*, led a dynamic swing band called Pardon Me Boys. They were absolutely brilliant.

Thus the evening went on. The music played, the booze flowed, a lot of food came, a lot of food went. Up on the bridal table, people were pushing these delicious meals around their plates but not actually eating much. So by the time it came for a few well-chosen words from the groom, the main thing I had consumed was a sizeable block of hash that someone had stuffed into my mouth and I had duly swallowed. Whooo-hooo! Amid a drug and booze-fuelled feeling of indestructibility, I manfully went to rise to make my speech and couldn't stand up.

I just could not get out of my chair. After much urging, I eventually managed to make it somehow to the podium, muttered a few indecipherable words and started to stagger back to my seat. The MC, Peter Sawyer, Christopher's public relations executive, showed why he was one of the best in the business by stepping up to the microphone and graciously saying what I had meant to say. What a genius, he was fabulous, doing it with style and humour. He then came over and delicately eased me back to the lectern, whispering in my ear the names of people who I should be thanking. I kept thinking, 'Get me out of here,' and so by the time I said 'Thangz' to everyone I was supposed to and made it to the bridal waltz, I was fucking ga-ga. It was all I could do to hang off Amanda like a jibbering idiot.

Then it all went a bit downhill from there …

I came to the realisation that eating hash is never a good idea if you have to do anything apart from staring at a wall for the next twelve hours. More grog was consumed, drugs kept appearing from nowhere and as time progressed I might have got just a smidgin messy. To the point when someone tapped me on the shoulder and discreetly whispered in my ear, 'Harold, we think it's time you left.'

'Me?' I slurred, astonished. 'Why?'

'It's not a good look ...'

Now let's be fair, I had put in a pretty good innings. Starting at something like six in the morning, I had done the right thing all day, stood up to all the pressures of a celebrity wedding, single-handedly consumed half the Australian annual quota of French champagne and did more drugs in one evening than John Belushi could manage in a week. But it was late in the evening, I had run my race and it was time to go. ''Arold,' I thought to myself, 'there is someone disgracing himself at your wedding reception. And that person is you.'

So I shuffled—no, wait, I got shuffled, by a team of expert, sympathetic handlers—down to the limo with Amanda, who wasn't very impressed at being thrown out of her own wedding reception, and we got driven to the Intercontinental Hotel at Circular Quay for our first romantic night together as the new Mr & Mrs Harold Antony Larkins. I was delicately manhandled through the lobby, herded past the slightly bemused reception staff, hustled into the lift and led up to the honeymoon suite. Where, before the eyes of his disbelieving wife, the super stud immediately hit the bed and went out like a light. Bang. Gone. Absolutely ratshit. Fuckin' comatose.

Amanda, unimpressed with the appalling collapse of her husband on their first night of marital bliss, thought, 'Bugger this,' and decided she'd go and party at the Swamp with her mates who were staying there. Much to the amusement of the hotel staff, down to the foyer she went, still in her wedding dress and ordered a taxi. She jumped in, headed off to Frenchs Forest and partied all night, leaving me in the suite to sleep it off. Amanda only recently confided in me that another reason why she had done the runner to the Swamp was that she had had a panic attack about being stuck on our upcoming honeymoon boat journey for ten days without a bong, so she went over there to retrieve it.

I woke up the next day, and oh Christ, what a hangover. I recollect that of all the typical results from such a session—shocking headache, roiling stomach, bleary eyes—the worst was how my tongue seemed to be permanently stuck to the roof of my mouth. It was all I could do to prise it down and somehow make it speak. I was not at all well. And I felt even more aggrieved with Amanda having arrived back feeling much chirpier than me. The thing was, we had to be down at the lobby early to be picked up by the limo, to be driven to the airport, to get on the private jet, to fly off to the yacht, to sail up to the Whitsundays. And Pixie and Christopher had organised a deluxe, cooked breakfast, which some cheery bloody waiter had delivered to our room.

Oh, be still my churning stomach.

For Christopher, there was always work to do, even the morning after a family wedding. He needed to get back to Brisbane for business, and the plane's itinerary was to first fly north from Sydney to Gladstone, where Amanda and I were to be dropped off to board Mirage III for our honeymoon, and then turn around and head south to take Pixie and Christopher back to Brisbane. Jeezus, couldn't we do that tomorrow? I kept thinking, 'You've done enough damage, Larkins. Don't make things worse by throwing up in front of everyone.'

After we arrived at the private jet terminal at Sydney, I fully expected to get a bit of a going over by Christopher and Pixie about my glorious, uninhibited attempt at gaining international wedding reception notoriety. But as it turned out, the discussion quickly turned to what had happened to all the limousines the night before. I had no idea what they were talking about.

As it turned out, towards the end of the evening, my ex-housemate Max had taken it upon himself to distribute the twenty limousines waiting outside Curzon Hall to whichever guests he thought deserved one. So he allotted the limos to all our mates and sent them off to Brownie's place, the scene of a mighty after-party. By the time Christopher and Pixie and all the esteemed guests came out the front for transport, almost all the limos had gone. People were not happy.

What had made things worse was that as each car arrived at Brownie's place, people were getting out and saying to the driver, 'Just wait there.' So the limos, instead of going back and ferrying the dignitaries home, sat outside the after-party until seven o'clock in the morning, clocks ticking. Meanwhile, everyone else was stranded outside the reception centre at North Ryde! Christopher was not exactly totally upset but certainly not overly impressed by that. While all this was being vigorously discussed on the plane, all I could do was sit agonizingly in my seat and battle hard to not redecorate the interior.

Now, I was good at handling hangovers. Seven years in the film industry had taught me that you get up the next morning and you function, no matter what. But I was struggling. It was all I could do not to throw up. Don't forget we were on the Qintex private plane, a Dassault Falcon 20 business jet once owned by King

Hussein of Jordan. Depending on the configuration, up to nine could be seated in it, and while it was luxurious, we were in very close proximity to each other. No matter how discreet I could try to be, there'd be no way of disguising the unsettling sound of 'Rrrrralppphhhhh!' into a sick bag.

I couldn't answer questions, I couldn't talk to anyone, I couldn't even think straight. All I could do was concentrate on not getting ill and making a total idiot of myself. It was one of the longest journeys of my life, but to my eternal credit and thanks to my many years of training, I hung in there, and did not upgrade the Falcon's decor. We got off at Gladstone, and I wobbled out into the boiling North Queensland heat and lurched down to the wharf, where we both spotted Mirage III for the first time. There was the crew standing crisply and professionally in their gleaming white uniforms, waiting for the arrival of the Great Son-In-Law, the New Husband, the Man of the Moment.

You could see them looking down and thinking, 'Christ, that's him?' as I staggered, ashen-faced and silent up the plank. It was painful; absolutely, horrendously painful. There were only two good things about it. First, Amanda by now wasn't feeling much better than I was. She had had a wonderful thirty-six hours partying and fuck-all sleep and I knew that she was suffering too. Second, she didn't give me too much of a going over about my dazzling performance at the wedding.

It wasn't as if it was the first time I'd done something like that. She'd come along to film shoots and knew that I liked to play hard, always being one of the biggest drinkers and usually being the last one to leave but always able to get up next morning and do my job. I liked to party, so it was not a huge surprise to her. But this?

Believe me, the first day of the rest of our lives together was spent down below decks of Mirage III in total darkness.

In fact, we didn't drink much on the trip either. It was water, juice and chocolate milkshakes pretty much all the way. There was a full bar and we could have had anything that we wanted, but we didn't. In typical style, Christopher and Pixie had laid on everything from gourmet food to Krug champagne, but we pretty much ate steaks, burgers, and bacon and eggs and drank juice, although it was nice to know the booze was there anyway. I think we had one bottle of Krug as we approached Port Douglas on the last day. But I will admit that Amanda had managed to smuggle the bong on board, and I had brought enough dope to cover us for the ten days. I had always been a big dope smoker since I was thirteen and still am. Alas, these days I use it more for chronic pain management than recreation, due to some serious damage I have done to my spine and other parts of my body over the years.

I don't back away from it. Coke, too. If someone put a line in front of me right now, and it was decent quality, I'd probably still have it. As Pablo Escobar, the Colombian drug lord, once famously said, 'Mi coca es tu coca.'

Amanda has never been a real drinker, and despite the lurid picture I have painted so far, I was not an everyday drinker back then, rather a binge drinker. Until I got to Spain, I never drank at home. Very seldom would I have anything in the house. Even if the fridge was fully stocked, I would never think of having a drink. I would have a water or a juice or simply light up a spliff. But if somebody pops in and I start, then I don't stop. Suddenly, fuck me, it's two days later, where's the time gone? I'll go out to get a packet of cigarettes and I get talked into one drink, and before I know it, hours have elapsed. There have been many times over the years where I've been standing in a bar at four o'clock in the morning and someone will say, 'Who's that outside banging on the window?' and it's Amanda. She has had to put up with a lot over the years.

So we spent ten glorious days sailing up through the Whitsundays, stopping here and there, and having an almost grog-free journey. A first-ever trip in a private jet is a pretty amazing way to start a honeymoon, but initially Amanda and I were feeling sceptical about being stuck on a boat for ten days. 'What are we going to do for all that time?' we kept asking ourselves. Well, we had the master suite, which was spectacular. Plus, a crew that, after a rather stiff and formal start, turned out to be just fantastic. Ultimately, the whole journey was brilliant.

On the second day, we came back to the room and found that our carefully smuggled bong had been located, cleaned and put back in the cupboard, so we realised that our game plan had been tumbled and that they didn't care what we did. We stopped padding around the boat quietly, soon became the best of friends with the crew, and they looked after us superbly. Every night after we had gone to sleep, Brooke would move Mirage III to a new location, and we would wake up somewhere else that was equally as fantastic, on shimmering water, a breathtaking island jutting out in the distance, a beautiful breakfast laid out on the stern.

While we were having breakfast one morning, Flossie mentioned that we were not far from Hamilton Island, developer Keith Williams' five-star Whitsundays resort, where amongst other owners, George Harrison of The Beatles once had a place. Flossie and Rachel had both worked on Hamilton at various times over the years and had lots of friends there, while Brooke had some boating mates on it. I had worked on the island on many film shoots and had fantastic memories, so after a unanimous vote, we headed for Hamilton to pull in for the evening. It was like arriving on an ocean liner, with everyone on the wharves staring up at Mirage III coming in to anchor. People were knocked out by its size and luxury and came down to the jetty to have a look.

With a different breakfast view every day and just about anything on board you could think of—we really loved the spa bath, which opened onto the ocean—we enjoyed every single moment of a fantastic ten days. But all good things must come to an end, and when we docked in Port Douglas, I grabbed my bags, got off and jumped straight into a car to be driven to Cairns airport to get a flight to Darwin, where I was picked up at the airport and taken to Kakadu for day one of shooting *Crocodile Dundee 2* and two months of living in a dog box. In one leap, I had gone from the penthouse to the outhouse. The crew had already been there for a couple of weeks doing pre-production, which I had managed to avoid because of the honeymoon, but I could stay away no longer and it was a very sad day. Amanda wasn't working at that stage, so she stayed on the boat for the return trip to Brisbane. We had become such good friends with the crew so she couldn't pass up the opportunity of a free ride back.

So what was the eventual follow-up to my inglorious departure from my own wedding reception? When I returned from filming nearly three months later, there were a few barbs thrown my way by Christopher and Pixie. He knew it was no secret that my mates and I were wild boys. I think he had also seen enough of Amanda to know that she was capable of causing some damage, too. So there were a few double-edged comments but nothing ever sharp; both of them were pretty good about it. As far as they were concerned, the wedding had been a great success.

It was Max's hijacking of the limos that was the big issue. Having brought in all these important guests from interstate and overseas, Christopher and Pixie expected a little more than having most of the twenty flash cars being parked outside Brownie's place for an all nighter.

All I could say was, 'How would I know, Christopher? I wasn't there, mate. In more ways than one!'

NINE

I t was a beautiful, warm, sunny Queensland day, and Pixie was heading up the Bruce Highway in the Rolls-Royce.

No ordinary Roller, either. A Corniche convertible, the ultimate symbol of open-top motoring. The same as the one then being driven by Engelbert Humperdinck and Michael Edgley. Pixie's was a beautiful deep blue with a big aluminium V8 and glistening white fold-back roof, and it suited her perfectly. Its model name Corniche came from La Grande Corniche, the road twisting along the French Cote d'Azure that takes in Cannes and Saint-Tropez. On this day, she was heading from Brisbane to Noosa with the sparkling blue Pacific Ocean on her right and the shimmering green Great Dividing Range on her left. With the wind in her hair, it was yet another drive that was symbolic of her extraordinary life. What better car to do that in than a Rolls-Royce?

Pixie was born Jo-Anne Nanette, the daughter of Keith and Nan Dixon. Keith was a senior executive with *The Age*, Melbourne's morning broadsheet, and the family had a lovely house in Kew, one of city's most exclusive suburbs. East of the CBD and bordering the banks of the Yarra River, Kew features big Edwardian, Victorian and art deco homes on large, leafy blocks. Medical professionals live there, business executives and tertiary educators. The price of a house in Kew is twice that of the Melbourne average.

Over the years, Keith held positions such as night manager and human resources manager at *The Age*, often working nights and coming home at six in the morning. Nan Dixon was before her time, making her own yoghurt and promoting an organic approach to living. She got involved in her local community, including book clubs, parent groups and school committees. They were a devoted couple and between them had built something pretty special in Melbourne's leafy green east, providing the best they could for Pixie and her sister Di. But well off as she was, Pixie wanted something better. Her eyes were drawn closer toward the city, where the real money lay. Toorak.

Also draped along the Yarra, Toorak is Melbourne's true suburb of the rich. Its sprawling mansions come from a mix of old money—the long-established investment, banking and retail families—and new cash injected by the property developers, businessmen and industry leaders. In those days, the familiar names included the Myers, the Baillieus, the Fox family, the Lews, the Walkers and the Smorgons, plus developers, sports stars, entertainers, entrepreneurs and celebrities. As soon as she finished at Methodist Ladies College, Pixie set about finding the man who would provide the avenue.

She thought she had found him in Albert Argenti, fifteen years older than her. A class act, a restaurateur and a very talented singer, his magnificent tenor voice first thrilled clientele at his family's Italian restaurant and later took him to concert halls around the world. Over the years, he had developed a media and social profile in Melbourne hosting receptions at the Savoy Plaza, the Pickwick and Le Chateau. He was polite and charming, his Italian heritage providing him with a sophisticated Mediterranean air.

When they met, Pixie was barely out of school, and she was swept off her feet by his suave, mature approach and impeccable, gentlemanly manners. He treated Pixie extremely well, and within a year they were married. Pretty soon Amanda was born, followed the next year by Kate and the year after that by Felicity. By the time she was twenty-four, Pixie was well down the track of motherhood, having had three daughters in three years. With Albert working long, hard hours, the pressure of having a young family within the constraints of the hospitality game, where the timeframe runs contrary to everyone else's schedule, started to tell.

Amanda points out that despite the lack of a big income, Albert did great things for her and her sisters, providing them with a good education, helping them develop a strong connection to their heritage and instigating a love of everything Italian. He gave them as much of his time as he could, introducing them to Melbourne's unique dining and entertainment culture, including lunch on Sundays at restaurants in St Kilda's colourful Acland Street or Carlton's trendy Lygon Street. The girls developed a love of him they never lost. But the marriage ended in divorce when the couple grew apart, and it became obvious that for all his talents, Albert did not have the necessary drive to create the environment that Pixie craved. She felt she saw the required energy, capacity and ambition in her next husband, George Frew.

Starting with Australia's first self-service supermarket, Frew's Superette in the NSW mountain town of Cooma, George had built an enviable property portfolio in tourism and hospitality with his Commodore chain of motels, hotels and restaurants in Australia and

Asia. Among his many properties were the Old Melbourne Inn on Flemington Road and the Pusan Commodore in South Korea. He also owned Melbourne's premier King Street nightclubs, Inflation and, in partnership with Brian 'Mr Nightlife' Goldsmith, The Underground, where Amanda worked sometimes as the supreme door bitch. Giving him plenty of Town Hall credibility were his enthusiastic ideas for developing tourism for Melbourne. Engaging him with the sporting public was his involvement in horse racing, including being part owner, along with property developer Lloyd Williams and Queensland racing identity Tom Pettiona, of Just A Dash, winner of the 1981 Melbourne Cup. With his good looks, self-assuredness and a capacity to offer a headline-grabbing opinion, George was rarely out of the news.

They married and soon became one of Melbourne's glamour couples, and there are photos of Pixie, titled as was custom in those days as 'Mrs George Frew of Toorak', dressed to the hilt, attending the races in the early 1970s. Amanda always liked George and the role he played in the family. He was the clearly-defined head of the tribe, and she particularly remembers how he taught her chess. But whereas Albert was a gentle dad, George was a hard taskmaster, underlined by the title of his autobiography he released in 2003 after he had recovered from declaring himself bankrupt, *Someday I'll Have Money*.

Amanda's two younger sisters, Felicity and Kate, were not so enamoured with his tough approach, and even though George and Pixie had their own child, Alexandra, the relationship started to sour. Pixie and the girls were moved from Frew's inner-east suburban home to the Old Melbourne Inn. Pixie took up the presidential suite while the girls shared a separate room. Being the big sister, Amanda spent a lot of time mothering the others, acting as either peacemaker or big boss. Having four girls cooped up like that, there was plenty of noise. George would bang on the door when the shouting or giggling got too loud, and Amanda would calm him down by saying, 'It's all right, Daddy George; it's all okay.'

A permanent fracture split the relationship, and the couple headed for the divorce courts. Amanda says that life for all four girls was very difficult in those days, being pulled from pillar to post and being separated during their mother's two marriages, with other relationships in between.

Then it happened. Having met her earlier at a business function and been bowled over by her beauty and charm, a smitten Christopher called on Pixie at the Old Melbourne one day, ready to turn on the charm. But despite the flowers, the suit, the coiffured hair and the MG out front, he soon found out that pursuing Pixie was not going to be easy. When eleven-year-old Felicity opened the door and he said, 'Hello, I'm Chris Skase,' she thought that he'd said, 'Hello, I'm Bruce Skoose'!

And when she came back to the door, after informing her mother that there was a man there to see her, she innocently let the cat out of the bag by saying to Christopher, 'Mum says she's not home ...'

But 'Bruce'—it was a name that became an in-house joke we used to bring up just to embarrass him—refused to go away. Pixie eventually came to the door and a unique romantic, social and business partnership, one that was to last more than two decades and grab headlines around the world, got off to a shaky start.

Pixie was by now thirty-five years old, twice married, and with four girls aged thirteen, twelve, eleven and four, while Christopher was twenty-seven. He had been married before, too, but he and his wife Elizabeth had had no kids, and she had left not long after they were wed, taking the dog with her. By the time he first met Pixie, Christopher was sharing a place with a mate.

Christopher did all the chasing in the initial stages. Perhaps concerned about the eight-year gap between them, Pixie took a while to be convinced. Eventually his determination paid off and after about a year, the pair of them and the girls moved to a three-story, single-fronted terrace house in Clara Street, South Yarra. They certainly weren't awash with cash, making up beds and cupboards with boards balanced on Besser bricks. A sports car was hardly the best family vehicle either, requiring the four girls to be squeezed in the back with Pixie in the front. To compound matters, after the divorce from George, Pixie had to fight a huge custody battle with Albert. He didn't think that the children were living in appropriate circumstances and were at risk.

Coming from limited marital and family experiences, Christopher took on a big challenge. I think his was a pretty amazing achievement, gradually becoming the figurehead of a family of four girls, with the three older ones as different as chalk and cheese and going through those shithouse teenage years when they consider every adult the enemy. Amanda was the loudmouth head of the tribe, determined to get her own way and clashing with anyone who stood in her way. Kate was more the hippie, under-the-radar type. Felicity, initially very shy and quiet, became the let's-party night clubber. Even with one child, it would have been seriously hard work, but with these three disparate characters, plus the fourth little one, Alex, trying to find her position in the family, it was a big, big challenge.

I sort of know how he must have felt. I was a stepfather when I was young to three-year-old twins. The little ones were the kids of actress Katy Manning, who starred in *Dr Who* alongside John Pertwee and later was the partner of entertainer Barry Crocker. At the time, she was thirty-six and I was twenty-one. Katy was wonderful and the twins, Georgina and Jay Jay, were fantastic, but it was a rapid learning curve for me. Ultimately, the age gap and the trials of being a father figure proved too much for me and we parted amicably. But Christopher survived his baptism of fire and hung in there, which is something that has always amazed me. The secret to his success was that he didn't try and buy the girls' respect. He earned it.

He would help them out if they needed something. Or if they were in trouble, they knew that they could go to him for assistance. But there were never any handouts; the girls were far from spoilt. They were never given cars or money as such. Maybe a bit of furniture or something if they really needed it, and even then he and Pixie would get it for them. I think that over the years, the only car handed out was to Alex, a second-hand BMW, one of Pixie's old cars. As with all families, it is the youngest that usually gets the fruits of the hard work, and once the business was really flourishing, it was Alex who was sent to off to finishing school in England.

Rather than give them money or gifts, Christopher would provide them with a job within one of the companies he owned. It was made clear they had to work harder than anyone else in the business. If they were employed in the same building as him, he would expressly not give them a lift to work. He expected them to get on public transport and find their own way there and be at their desk half an hour before he arrived. He was persistent and patient, always trying to provide a balance.

If they came home after a party and he was up, he would let them have a glass of champagne and get them to sit down and tell him about how it all went.

To his credit, 'Bruce Skoose' did a great job in uniting a fractured family. As anyone who has tried to be a stepfather can tell you, it's a difficult role at the best of times much less with four girls who had witnessed two divorces already. The attraction between Pixie and Christopher, whether it was based on love or simply on the fact that they could see they were good for each other, was strong enough for him to stick it out through some very tough times.

Family folklore says that the turning point in Christopher's acceptance into the fold was Amanda's fourteenth birthday party. They did not have the money to create the massive super-cool bash that she had yearned for and dreamt about. So he decked out the garage with Pirelli tyre-tread matting, tricked it up with lights and streamers and turned it into a disco. The guests, all girls, had a ball. That won Amanda and her sisters over. They thought, 'He's not so bad after all,' and grew to love him, not only for the stability and security he provided but for the genuine love that he gave them in return and for being the person he was. It was a love and a respect that continued until the day he died.

Running parallel with the unification of the family was a surge in business activities. Christopher and Pixie used to sit around the kitchen table—their 'business office' as they called it—and make plans. They scraped together $20,000, their ideas were put into action, the dollars started to roll in and, bingo, he had made his first million by the time he was thirty. They had been together three years.

People ask me, 'Were they in love?' The answer to that is this: I think Christopher fell in lust with Pixie at first and then in love. Then he continued to love her with his whole heart in every way, shape and form until the day he died.

Pixie has quite an intellect, is very perceptive and has a great sense of humour, although she is very forthright. She has great people skills and in those days was ambitious, energetic and determined. She was a tough, formidable force and even to this day is one of those rare people that when she walks into a room, all heads turn. It was the perfect mix of Christopher, being a bit socially uncomfortable, and Pixie, having brilliant social abilities.

To jump into that situation, Christopher must have been keen because Pixie was the only person I ever came across who he could not control, govern, manipulate or say no to. Everyone else, no matter who they were—financiers, businessmen, government people, managers, staff, family—he could work around, coerce, direct or persuade into giving him what he wanted. Only Pixie could get her own way. As they say, happy wife, happy life.

As with a lot of successful businessmen, while he dealt day-to-day in huge, almost mind-bending sums of money, he was always prudent with his cash. 'We gotta tighten the drum,' he would say. Or, 'We have to zip the purse.' But she was a bit of a shopaholic and spent money like it was water on food, clothes, jewellery, furniture, decorations. You name it, if Pixie liked it, she bought it. And why not? She could afford it.

Occasionally, he would have a look through the bills and have a go at her. 'Pixie, for Christ's sake,' he would say, staring at the credit card charges. But he never tried to stop her. That's because she was his world. He loved her unconditionally. He was infatuated.

Did Pixie love Christopher in return? Yes, I think she did. Maybe she did not love him with the same passion as he had for her, but she loved him in Pixie's way. After two failed marriages, I think the concept of unconditional love had lost a lot of its shine for her, but history shows that she was certainly devoted to him and they made a great partnership. Once the relationship was cemented, she certainly did not look for anyone else. They had a lot of fun together, they genuinely enjoyed each other's company and in the fifteen years I knew them as a couple, they were very rarely apart.

One thing that surprised me when I returned to live in Australia was the number of people who, on hearing of my association with Christopher, would ask, 'Was Skase gay?' Up until then, I'd never, ever, ever considered that as an issue. I guess people would think there were some classic pointers—his first marriage ended quickly; his second marriage was to a very strong, older woman; he never had any kids; he preferred the long-haired, slightly effete look to the traditional clean-cut business image; he was certainly not your standard macho homophobic; he enjoyed the company of gay friends, associates and staff. But then again, he got along well with practically everybody and treated everyone he met with respect. He was often surrounded by gay people providing the artistic design input for Pixie and this never caused him to be uncomfortable or antagonistic. They all had a wonderful relationship based on mutual respect for each other's professional ethic and sheer talent, and so a great friendship existed outside of work as well.

I was surprised when the gay thing became a regular question; because in all the time that I was with

Christopher—and, don't forget, we worked side-by-side for more than a decade—I never saw any indication of him having closet tendencies or any evidence of him having clandestine relationships. And from what I saw, if something outside the marriage were to ever occur I am sure it would have been with a female. Over the years I simply did not see anything that would give the slightest credence to that notion. It was never an issue, never on anyone's radar, never at the back of anyone's mind. His sole devotion was to Pixie. And at the end of the day, the pair of them could not have been a better match. She had what he lacked—the poise, confidence and wherewithal to play the social and corporate game at the very top level. In turn, he had what she knew she could mould into something very special—the vision, business acumen, endurance and ambition to succeed.

That is why on this beautiful, warm, sunny Queensland day, Pixie was loving the trip up the Bruce Highway in the Roller. By now, the days of everyone being shoe-horned into the little Melbourne terrace were long gone, they were living in a mansion they had built in Brisbane, Qintex was expanding in the Sunshine State, the Mirage projects were well under way and the cash was flowing.

Having just spent four weeks shooting the first part of a commercial on Hayman Island, my film crew had all been relocated to Noosa for the next segment, and Amanda had joined me. So Pixie had figured it would be good to head north and bring along Alex, then fifteen, to have some nice family time together. I think also it was because she wanted Amanda to have a sisterly chat to Alex about her increasingly difficult teenager behaviour.

But if Pixie was ever going to get a glimpse of the enormous contrast between her lifestyle and mine, then this was the moment. I always thought that one of the great ironies was that while Pixie and I got along famously together, we were obviously heading in different directions. I was lucky enough to be born with the proverbial silver spoon in my mouth. Yet, I never pursued the money and power and trappings of my medical and legal forebears. I was just happy to rock along in the film world, make a few quid and hang out in places like Noosa.

Ah, Noosa. That was my kinda town! It was the place where we filmed international, beach-based commercials, and on this occasion, we were working on a huge Sprite shoot. It was massive, something like twelve weeks. We'd done four weeks on Hayman, were in the middle of four weeks in Noosa and were scheduled to then go onto New Zealand and finally Los Angeles. We were staying, all expenses paid, at the five-star Noosa International Resort. Hey, it was a tough job, but somebody had to do it.

Even though Amanda had flown up to be with me for a few days, my devotion to the film crew philosophy had not flagged. The Aminals were hard at work and play—getting belted, getting an hour's sleep, getting up, putting in a sixteen-to seventeen-hour day, then going straight back to the bar and doing it all over again. Amanda was aware that this was par for the course in the profession and could handle pretty much any excess, so long as she and I had some time together to have dinner and a bit of fun.

Then one morning I woke up, hung over, lying naked on top of the bed, with no blankets, sheets or pillows, just the bare mattress, and her standing, fully clothed at the end, with her bags packed, glaring at me.

Now, I had pushed the envelope many times, but even I thought to myself, 'This can't be good.'

My mind started to race. What had I done? Where had I been? How much damage had I caused? She'd seen me in full flight many times before and had been fairly forgiving but obviously this one was an epic incident and I had really crossed the line. She continued to stand there, bag in hand, foot tapping, saying nothing.

'Christ,' I thought, 'how long has she been standing there waiting for me to wake up? Oh, 'Arold, this cannot be good.'

After what seemed an age, especially for me feeling as crook as a dog, she finally stopped fuming enough to relate what had happened. She had found me in a spa bath with one of the female producers.

'I was right,' I thought. 'This definitely is not good.'

At least, she allowed, I had been in the spa fully clothed—cowboy boots, leather jacket, jeans, wallet, the lot. Fortunately, the young producer was still dressed, too. 'Thank Christ,' I thought, 'I might wiggle out of this yet.' But she was pissed off with the likelihood of what might have eventuated.

She told me she had dragged me out of the spa by the hair and taken me back to our room and flung me on the bed and then had packed her bags and waited for me to wake up to tell me that she was leaving.

How come I was now totally naked still had me a bit puzzled.

Nevertheless, after she had torn strips off me, common sense prevailed and she agreed to stay on. This proved to be a wise decision, because a couple of days later, young Alex disappeared into the darkness with one of the Aminals. A teenage girl with a couple of drinks in her and a wasted film technician is never a good formula.

Worse still, Amanda and I had organised for her to stay with us for a night in our suite, so Pixie was going to be very, very annoyed with our dereliction of duty. I put the word out, and the search began. Our man obviously did not know that Alex was only fifteen, because she certainly didn't look it, and I could see the whole thing was going to end in very serious tears.

We searched all over the place, through the resort, in the pubs and clubs and along the main Noosa drag. I thought, 'Boy, am I going to be in the shit.' My pleas were passed along the crew lines and eventually reached the right ears. Amanda rescued Alex in time and all was saved. We judiciously decided not to tell Pixie; she only found out about it much later in life.

I think that had Pixie found out that night, Amanda and I would have been in the doghouse forever and Alex would never have been allowed out of the house again until she was thirty-five.

TEN

Rolls-Royces, yachts, jets, resorts—the Christopher & Pixie Show was in full flight. It was time to party.

Pixie loved to entertain and positively sparkled amongst the glitz and glamour of a big occasion. Having been tried and tested in the Toorak set, she had developed and finessed a great ability to socialise in any given situation. She could make anyone she was introduced to feel good about themselves no matter what they did or where they came from, as she had done for me on that day of our first meeting at Flemington. On the other hand, Christopher was not all that fussed about parties. He much preferred a quiet Jack Daniels and a hamburger around the barbie. He was a very unpretentious bloke without an ostentatious bone in his body. Even though he had plenty of money, he never spent it to personally show off. He would prefer to pour it all back into Qintex. Behind the headlines, he was a pretty normal, ordinary bloke, trying to make his dream come true.

But being media savvy—don't forget, he was once a journalist—he recognised that a headline grabbing bash was always good for business. The more spent on it, the better the coverage. Besides, if Pixie enjoyed putting on parties, then why not? Christopher expected his people to work fourteen to sixteen hours a day, six days a week, without too many 'thank yous' dished out along the way. So for fifteen years, a big Qintex dinner was held at the end of the year to show appreciation to everyone who had put so much into the company over the previous twelve months. It was the only thing the executives, staff and other associates were given. He worked hard himself, he expected his people to work at the same level, and out of that a mutual respect and a tremendous sense of loyalty had developed that went both ways.

I went to a few of these parties held at places like the Brisbane Hilton. They were huge, newsworthy affairs, one of them estimated to have cost more than $400,000. But for Christopher and Pixie, it was work. While they were always fun events for the guests, I never heard either of them talking about getting real enjoyment out of them other than the genuine pleasure of seeing people being acknowledged and appreciated for their efforts during the year. For the two at the top, these were still corporate events—meeting, greeting and lots of 'thank yous.' No getting pissed and making idiots of themselves. He played the benevolent, grateful boss; she played the perfect, supportive wife. It was probably a more personally enjoyable time for them when they held a Welcome to Queensland Dinner in 1987 to mark their move up from Melbourne to Brisbane.

But in 1988, they really set new standards with a massive party on Mirage III in Sydney Harbour for the Australia Day Bicentennial Celebrations. Part of Channel 7's live broadcast of the celebrations, guests included Glenn Wheatley and his wife Gaynor, and Derryn Hinch, who had been signed by Christopher to head up an evening current affairs show on the network. Moored off Mrs Macquarie's Chair, it was a fabulous moment in history, an awesome experience floating amongst the tall ships and hundreds of other boats as we watched the fireworks and raised a glass of champers to our great nation and anyone else we could think of at the time, which seemed quite a few, as I vaguely remember.

Another of the headline grabbing bashes was the official opening of the Mirage Resorts. While the projects were actually up and running by late 1987, two big parties, one at Mirage Gold Coast and one at Mirage Port Douglas, were held across ten days in September 1988 to make things official. Local and international guests were flown in from around Australia and the world, accommodated, ferried between the two properties, and wined and dined. Limos, planes, helicopters and yachts ripped around everywhere, the champagne flowed and nothing was overlooked in an endeavour to please the guests. The Hollywood crew featured the original Hotlips from the *M.A.S.H.* movie, Sally Kellerman, the voluptuous Raquel Welch, and the ever-smiling George Hamilton, who was becoming quite a friend of Christopher's.

It was a media frenzy as the daily papers and women's magazines rushed everywhere, gorging on photos and stories of celebs, business people, politicians, financiers, tourism executives and assorted wannabees noshing into the food and sloshing down the grog. In support, Qintex created a series of eye-catching events such as releasing a thousand blue and white helium balloons containing accommodation and dine-out vouchers.

Knowing the value of publicity, Pixie and Christopher always invited the media and the resultant stories were generally positive. Even during construction, the Qintex jet used to leave Brisbane every Tuesday loaded with businessmen, journalists and potential buyers and fly up to Cairns, where they would be put on board the Qintex chopper to Port Douglas to see the resort unfolding. Sometimes the company would lease Australian Airlines planes to ferry finance and travel writers up.

Typically, Pixie was with Christopher all the way, and the pair used to combine beautifully to make everyone welcome and to sell the Mirage story. It was interesting to note that later, when some of the press were no longer invited to events, those journalists turned on them. They started to declare that the Skase group were all 'corporate wankers' whereas before, when they were all enjoying the free food and piss, they loved it and wrote very positive things. I guess that is the typical press mentality.

Mike Gore had earlier that year flown in Frank Sinatra and Whitney Houston to perform at the opening of Sanctuary Cove, so Christopher looked around for a similar quality entertainer to head up the Mirage launches. Indicative of how high he aimed, his first choice was the Beach Boys. Well, he liked them, and even though they were pretty passé at that point, as they had not been in the charts for ages, he figured their surf image would mix nicely with the Queensland lifestyle. Unfortunately, they were already booked and couldn't do it. As it turned out, Christopher was on the money. A few months after the launch, the Beach Boys released *Kokomo*, and it went on to be their first number one hit in more than twenty years.

Ultimately, while Whitney was a guest at one of the parties, I think Christopher settled on local talent to perform at the actual launches. You could not blame him chasing a top liner to mark the opening of the resorts. He had done a great job pulling the whole thing together and wanted to make the celebrations special. The famous story goes that when Pixie discovered the dress she wanted to wear for the Port Douglas opening was back in Melbourne, the Qintex jet was despatched to get it. Hmmm, not sure that that is true. But, you know, a girl has to feel comfortable on the big night.

The two resort projects—they cost $330 million all up—were massive challenges and for a guy that started virtually from nothing, to create the biggest and best resorts in Australia and set a then international quality benchmark for this type of development, was a tremendous effort. What Christopher had achieved up until this point was tiny by comparison, so this put him on the international stage. How good was he? Mirage Port Douglas and Mirage Gold Coast won practically every Australian and international tourism, hospitality and media award around that time for their excellence and unsurpassed quality. This included the ultimate accolade, being voted Best Resorts in the World in 1990 by *Resorts & Great Hotels* magazine, the premier upmarket accommodation publication aimed at the true travel connoisseur. Not only were both resorts chosen to appear in the magazine's annual 'best of' edition but Port Douglas scored the much sought-after spot on the cover. Later, the Mirage was chosen by US President Bill Clinton and his wife Hillary to stay at when they visited Port Douglas on their 1996 Australian tour.

Why did Christopher select Port Douglas in the first place? He told me that its selection stemmed back to the time when he was about twenty or so and he quit his job in Melbourne and set off around Australia in a car, taking on whatever jobs he could pick up along the way. Doing anything from cleaning trains to working in mines, he happened to go through Port Douglas. He was so impressed with its potential that he decided there and then that one day he would come back and do something special with it, even making a sketch in the sand of what he planned to do there. At that point, Port Douglas was just a little coastal fishing village that had slipped into obscurity after being a vigorous port when gold, tin and copper mining, sugar production and vegetable farming were flourishing in the surrounding area.

To start with, he did something on a far less dramatic scale at Port Douglas with a small apartment complex. When this succeeded and the Mirage projects came up, he tendered for both because he knew that this was his chance to fulfil his dream.

Of course I had invitations to both the Mirage parties, but I couldn't go because of work commitments! I was very busy at the time, and if I wasn't shooting a commercial somewhere in Australia, I would be overseas on a job. At different times in that period, I was in the US, New Zealand, Kenya, Morocco and Brazil. But the big bash that I did get to attend, the one that really caught the public's imagination and grabbed the headlines, was held on September 19, 1988. To this day, people still say to me, 'Skase? Didn't he have a big party for his fortieth? I remember reading about it. Wasn't that on the yacht?'

Actually it was not on the yacht but at an equally exotic location, their fabulous Brisbane mansion, Bromley, which was then still relatively new. When Christopher and Pixie had decided to move north in 1986, they sold their Toorak home and first rented a place in Willesmere Road in Brisbane while they looked around for somewhere suitable to live. Eventually they bought two adjoining properties on top of a hill in the well-to-do suburb of Hamilton. They demolished the two homes, merged the properties and built a home they named after Bromley Court, the Toorak street they had formerly lived in. There was some local outrage about them knocking down two old Queenslanders to build a contemporary mansion but that was like water off a duck's back to them.

The thing was, Pixie never wanted to live in Queensland. She hated the idea. After establishing a lovely family home and a social presence in Toorak as the fortunes of Qintex had skyrocketed, the last thing she wanted to do was head north to what she considered the unsophisticated back blocks of Brisbane. She did not want to sell the house in Melbourne. She wanted to keep it.

Christopher's approach was based on the philosophy of always putting your money back into your business to keep it expanding. He told me that he was never sentimental about homes. To him, keeping the Toorak place was unnecessary. As far as he was concerned, you would sell it and the new Brisbane house would simply be another investment. Money being used to make more money. Any property investor knows that technique.

To her credit Pixie was loyal to her husband and accepted the move despite her misgivings. But she insisted that if she was going to have to start all over again, she wanted to live in something pretty special. As they were then personally worth something of the order of $50 million, she figured that the first thing that any woman in her right mind with access to money like that would be to create a great house, a brilliant home, the grand palace of her dreams. So she did.

Bromley was a massive house, set on three levels overlooking the city of Brisbane and the river. It had fifteen hundred square metres of living space, four bedrooms, a fully kitted-out office and a library panelled in maple. Pixie and Barry Peters, the former Myer decorator and now part of the family, did the interior designs, as they had done for the resorts and the yacht. Quite frankly, the themes and styles in all those locations could have quite easily crossed over; they were very much out of *Vogue* at the time. A lot of the furniture in the house was Pixie's via her previous marriage to George plus other bits and pieces she had collected along the way, supplemented by new stuff she and Barry bought. Christopher let them come up with whatever they thought would work. Design and decoration was definitely not his department. He wouldn't have known if a piece of furniture was a Louis XV original, a Queen Anne reproduction or an Ikea knock-together.

Sitting atop an underground car park that accommodated six cars, Bromley was an amazing mix of tasteful ideas, over-the-top notions and hi-tech wizardry. The whole back wall was done in a spectacular trompe d'oleil—a Tuscany scene in soft pastel—while at the other end of the scale there was a secret, impenetrable safe room, required by the insurance policy, that everyone could hide in if something went wrong. There was marble everywhere, a huge pool, a full tennis court and an eight-person lift. With a view to catering for big parties, the kitchen had four commercial-sized ovens, plus walk-in fridges and freezers.

It also had its own inbuilt cinema, which was relatively rare in those days. By the time the house was nearly finished, Qintex not only owned a television network but Christopher was attracted to the idea of getting into Hollywood, so he had a big screen installed on the basis that as a network executive he would be able to view new films, evaluate rushes and assess pilots.

All in all, it was a beautiful home, a great property. It was later valued at $4 million, but the generally accepted opinion was that they spent nearly double that amount constructing it and fitting it out. Whatever, it was just perfect for Christopher's fortieth birthday party. In typical style, they jetted in three hundred people from Australia and overseas, with guests including Robert Holmes a Court, Hollywood stars, local celebrities, business people and politicians. To accommodate them the whole tennis court was covered by a massive marquee. No expense was spared, and once again the spectacular setting was complemented by flowers supplied by Pixie's great friend Kevin O'Neill and catering managed by his partner John Graham.

Inspired by the trompe d'oleil, the theme was Tuscany with lots of blue and white lights everywhere, making the swimming pool shimmer. Nothing was left to chance, with Pixie ensuring that the catering, seating and entertainment was just right. If there was one thing Pixie was good at, it was being able to produce a party with flair, sophistication and military precision. She knew what she wanted, and she made sure the suppliers and the staff provided it.

A memorable moment was the keynote speech honouring Christopher by businessman Robert Holmes a Court, Australia's first billionaire. Holmes a Court had a distinctive way of speaking, very quiet, very measured, yet he silenced the rowdy crowd. You could have heard a pin drop. He spoke very highly of Christopher, praising him for his ability to spot an opportunity and to maximise its potential through hard work and good decision making. Whether you liked him or not, Holmes a Court, variously described as a 'corporate raider' and 'WA entrepreneur,' was one of the real gentlemen of the Australian business scene, and he and Christopher had a very strong bond. Whenever and wherever they would meet, they would go to a corner somewhere and sit quietly and talk about business for ages, very often over a balloon or three of Remy Martin Louis XIII Cognac.

Christopher was a bit embarrassed with the glowing praise heaped upon him by Holmes a Court, who was similarly involved in the media. As well as having a diversified resources portfolio, he had made bravado takeover attempts of Australian institutions such as BHP and the Herald & Weekly Times, bids that may well have failed but had resulted in him walking away smiling from the table a much wealthier man.

Christopher only had to look around that night and listen to the roar of applause that followed the Holmes a Court speech to realise that perhaps the accolades were well deserved. He had come a long way from his days as a stockbroker's clerk and was at the top of his game. The resorts, the media and the other investments were flourishing, Hollywood was beckoning, the future looked bright and every one of the three hundred people in the marquee was there because they genuinely appreciated him.

What a star-studded crowd it was, too. Turn one way and there would be actress Catherine Oxenberg, New York born, of Serbo-Yugoslav royalty, star of *Dynasty* and who had twice played the role of Princess Diana, her real-life distant cousin. Turn another way and there would be Linda Evans, star of *Dynasty*, a former Golden Globe winner, two-time *Playboy* centrefold girl and who later was a guest at the wedding of Prince Charles and Camilla Parker-Bowles. Turn again and there would be

Christopher's newfound mate, legendary Hollywood actor George Hamilton, all golden suntan and sparkling teeth. And who's that over there? Why, that's Diane Lane, star of *The Outsiders, Rumble Fish* and *The Cotton Club*. Who's that with her? That's her husband, Christopher Lambert, of *Greystoke* and *Highlander* fame. In one corner was Queensland Premier Mike Ahern, a great believer in bringing quality resorts to the state and therefore thrilled with the Qintex contribution, and in another, just to balance things out was Opposition Leader Wayne Goss.

And me? Well, as parties go, I gave it my best shot, with the Krug coming by on every passing waiter's tray. I remember a pregnant Amanda coming down to drag me off to bed a couple of times and me replying, 'Hey, plenty of champagne, a lot of Hollywood actresses walking around, I'm not going anywhere. I'm here to play.'

The music rocked, the food was terrific and the booze first class. It was a typical balmy Queensland night and at least one person jumped into the pool. Eventually the neighbours across the road went ballistic and called the police so we must have had a good time.

At that moment, I think everybody in SkaseWorld was thinking they were pretty much bulletproof.

ELEVEN

A s experienced media moguls used to say, owning a television station was 'a licence to print money.' I'm not sure if that was the main reason that Christopher went after the Seven Network. After all, the Fairfax group had purchased Melbourne's Channel 7 from Rupert Murdoch and had made a mess of things. It chopped local shows and at one stage, the reaction from Melbourne viewers to a Sydney group taking over their beloved station resulted in its news bulletin heavily engaged in a ratings battle with the SBS test pattern.

But he saw it as an opportunity because he had the media in his veins and in his heart. He had not only worked in it as a daily newspaper reporter but he had been brought up in a household absorbed by it. His father Charles Skase was synonymous with 3DB, the Melbourne radio station that also had strong links with Channel 7 and *The Sun,* the paper Christopher started out on. In terms of Christopher's big picture approach, it's interesting to note that when 3DB began in 1927 it was described as 'the first in Australia to carry out the American idea of making revenue from advertisements.' That's the sort of thinking and opportunity Christopher loved and aspired to achieve. From that point on, 3DB worked an eclectic mix of music, drama and sport into one of Melbourne's top-rating stations, creating talent such as Ron Casey, Ernie Sigley, Bill Collins, Brian Naylor and Lou Richards.

Charles, having been educated at Melbourne Boys High School, came to the station via his wonderful singing talent. This included winning The Sun Aria in 1948, the year Christopher was born. That's the same young operatic talent contest won by Joan Sutherland and Kiri Te Kanawa and in which Albert Argenti competed. Charles' talent and genial personality sparked the interest of 3DB executives, and he joined as a performer, starring in one of its biggest ever programs, *The Happy Gang*. His understanding of the medium was so innate that he eventually became the station's general manager. Charles and his wife Audrey, who lived in Geelong in later life, were a lovely couple—intelligent, genteel, warm—and I thoroughly enjoyed the times I got to see them and have a chat. They were a class act. From what I could see, Christopher had a great relationship with his parents and his sister Robyn, and they were all justifiably proud of his achievements.

Growing up and working in that environment, it is not surprising Christopher pursued media interests. From the late 1970s on, Qintex held either minor or controlling interests in Telecasters North Queensland, Mackay & Mt Isa Television and the Victorian Broadcasting Network, which owned GLV-10 in Traralgon and BCV-8 in Bendigo. In 1984, Qintex moved from rural television into the metropolitan market with the purchase of TVQ-0 in Brisbane. Qintex bought it via a timber company it owned, Wilkinson, Day & Grimes, for $34 million from Ampol, and in the deal not only got the station but also picked up Sydney radio station 2SM.

Christopher felt there were more opportunities out there. He was quite taken by the endeavours of entrepreneur Alan Bond, who was chasing the Nine Network. Whenever I used to talk with Christopher on family holidays about his plans, he would say he wanted to get his hands on a genuine network. 'I've been eyeing them off,' he said one day. 'But something like the Nine Network is too expensive for what they are selling.'

Alan Bond became more and more a topic of conversation around the Skase table, and even though the Brisbane station proved to be a very profitable buy for Qintex, Christopher still sought a group of stations. When Bond made his move on Nine, Christopher felt he was paying way too much. In a celebrated deal in 1987, Bond paid Kerry Packer more than a billion dollars for just two Channel Nine stations—Melbourne and Sydney—to gain control of the Nine Network. It was a huge deal and became even more celebrated three years later. As Bond's fortunes crumbled, Packer bought the stations back from him for virtually a quarter of the original price. Bond's original payment of $1.184 billion had been structured as $984 million in cash and $200 million in redeemable preference shares.

Packer redeemed his preference shares and seized back the Melbourne and Sydney stations as well as QTQ 9, Brisbane, and STW 9, Perth. At the end of the day, he famously stated, 'You only get one Alan Bond in your lifetime, and I've had mine.'

Meanwhile, Christopher, having sold TVQ-0 to Darling Downs Television in 1986, saw the opportunity to get into major league in 1987 in the form of the Seven Network. The process started early that year when Rupert Murdoch's News Limited spent $1.8 billion on a share buy-up to gain control of the Herald & Weekly Times, whose portfolio included *The Sun, The Herald, The Weekly Times,* Channel 7 Melbourne and 3DB.

For Murdoch this was a sort of coming home. His father, Sir Keith Murdoch, had been a significant figure in the history and growth of the Herald & Weekly Times as an admired war correspondent, managing editor, managing director and chairman. It was always held around the traps that Rupert, driven by sentiment or revenge or both, would one day come back to restore the Murdoch name to the board. An earlier takeover attempt in 1979 had failed. This time round, the bid succeeded but came just as government legislation was being prepared to limit print/broadcasting ownership in capital cities. This was the first opening of the door for Christopher. Having regained the newspapers that had been synonymous with the Murdoch name, Rupert had to off-load Channel 7 a month later.

Then followed one of the nastiest episodes in Australian television history. Murdoch sold the station for $320 million to John Fairfax & Sons, the family-owned Sydney-based publishers of the *Sydney Morning Herald, Financial Review* and the Melbourne *Age.* Fairfax knew all about television, having started ATN-7 in Sydney in 1957. So it linked its new Melbourne purchase with Sydney and Brisbane and set about developing a mini-network with a three-state link, plus affiliates. But if there was ever an example of the differences between Sydney and Melbourne, this was it. The story goes that the Fairfax executives were overheard on the plane coming down from Sydney laughing about how they were going to pull Channel 7 Melbourne apart and show those conservative Melburnians how a television station should really be run. They did. Into the ground.

They hung on to it for just six months. As well as the disastrous viewer backlash, they also had to sell because the new media cross-ownership regulations prevented monopolies dominating one market. Fairfax had to decide whether to keep the newspapers or the television stations and concluded it was better to stick with what it was good at, print. It was into this dogfight of media change, government regulation and viewer anxiety that Christopher plunged.

He confided in me one day that he could get the finance, that he had the backing of the Seven board and that he had the support of Warwick Fairfax, the young chairman of the owners, John Fairfax & Sons. It was at a time when newspapers, radio stations, television channels and even entire networks were being bought, sold and traded like swap cards, and that's what happened. Qintex bought the Channel Seven stations in Melbourne, Sydney and Brisbane from Fairfax for a reported $780 million. To round out a mainland network, ADS-7 in Adelaide changed to ADS-10 and joined the 10 Network, while SAS-10 swapped and became SAS-7 and joined the Seven Network. Qintex then purchased SAS-7 and TVW-7 in Perth from Holmes a Court for $130 million.

Christopher always used to say that the Seven Network purchase was probably the best of his career and that behind the inflated numbers the press reported there was another story entirely. He was said to have paid as high as $910 million, but he used to say privately that the gross purchase price was $780 million, reduced by $263 million to $517 million. This was achieved via six separate financial strategies led by the discounting of residual debt, Fairfax investment in Qintex and Fairfax underwriting the sale of TVQ0. The figure of $517 million represented a discount of about 50 per cent of the then market value. Shortly after, the publicly listed value of the network was given as $1.2 billion, showing that it was an excellent deal.

The whole thing was one of Christopher's classic structured deals. Fairfax had gotten under pressure, Warwick wanted to get out, and he liked Christopher's concept. There were a lot of people circling around Fairfax at the time, chasing the network, including the now owner Kerry Stokes. But I think Fairfax wanted Qintex to have it, so between Warwick and Christopher they worked it out, bit by bit. It was a very good deal, a brilliant piece of work on Christopher's part. I don't think anyone ever truly appreciated how clever it was.

It's a good example of what brings success and is a lesson for anyone with aspirations to succeed in business: the diligence of studying, stalking and taking down a target. All successful people do it.

Under Christopher's hands-on direction, the Qintex management team set about building up the network and in particular restoring the Melbourne station's fortunes. The Fairfax-devised *Seven National News* was changed to *Seven Nightly News* and focused more on local events. Christopher also reinstituted local programs, hired a parade of new and old personalities that viewers accepted and made a decision that has stuck with us to this very day—launching *Home & Away*. Yes, it was Christopher Skase who gave devoted viewers their nightly fix of love, rebellion, anxiety, births, deaths, marriages, car crashes, pregnancies, fires and mine collapses, played out by characters such as Pippa, Sally, Irene, Colleen and, flamin' heck, the one and only Alf Stewart. Christopher used to call the show his 'baby' and would tune in every night to ensure it was up to scratch.

This was simply mind-boggling stuff to Amanda and me. While all this boardroom wheeler dealing was happening, we were at home at Frenchs Forest getting on with life and loving it. We never thought in a million years we would get swept up in it.

TWELVE

Not content with success in Australia, Christopher now looked to expanding overseas, aiming his sights at the biggest market of them all, the US. Little did he know he was virtually signing his death warrant.

His first port of call was Hawaii. Christopher adored the island paradise. He loved staying there whenever his schedule allowed, especially at the Kahala Hilton, which he reckoned was one of the best hotels in the world and sold the greatest hamburger on the planet—a ten out of ten.

He discovered the opportunity to get into Hawaii almost by accident. He was going through a local newspaper when he spotted a story about a resort for sale called the Princeville. It was massive, around about 2800 hectares, including a hotel, two golf courses, dozens of apartments and thousands of housing plots and commercial sites. Not only did it have its own utilities company, which managed the resort's water and sewerage, it had its own airline and its own airport! But the grand scheme was nowhere near finished, and what had been done already needed a lot of work to bring it up to date. The hotel, while grandiose, was not really up to scratch and required refurbishment. Some apartments needed to be renovated, others had to be finished and planned ones were waiting to be built. As well, there were

113

thousands of housing blocks that had yet to be developed. It was a huge undertaking.

The owner, Harry Trueblood, had run out of enthusiasm and was looking to get out, but Christopher could see the possibilities. To begin with, it was in a great location. It was on Kauai, the fourth biggest island of the Hawaiian group, and known as the Garden Island. Although only thirty minutes by air from Honolulu, it was a world away from the hustle and bustle of Waikiki Beach. It was also acknowledged for the more laid-back approach of its locals.

It had some of the best mountain scenery of the Hawaiian Islands, too. The cliffs on the eastern coast rose a thousand metres from the water, and the view from the air as you flew in was breathtaking. The three *Jurassic Park* movies were filmed on Kauai as well as *South Pacific, King Kong* and Elvis in *Blue Hawaii*. What also set it apart at that time was its strict planning regulations. No building was allowed to be more than four storeys high and the resorts were not to be jammed together, fitting in with the philosophy that Christopher had developed in Australia.

Christopher couldn't wait. He bought the Princeville property in two deals—40 per cent for US$57 million in 1987 and 53 per cent the following year for US$59 million. One of his first decisions was sell its air offshoot, Princeville Airlines. While there was something pretty cool about owning your own airline, Christopher realised this was not really his forte. He was very good at making decisions like that.

The key to success on Kauai was to call on the services of his good friend, Des Brooks, one of the world's great hotel architects, who had designed the Mirage resorts. A brilliant designer and operator, as well as a charming, delightful and funny man, Des knew what Christopher wanted. He started to convert the half-done mess into a first-class resort, retitled Mirage Princeville. Plans included a new golf course and residential subdivision on five hundred vacant hectares, tripling the existing shopping centre, building a $17 million tennis complex and refurbishing the hotel, highlighted by a huge fountain at its spectacular entrance.

Des maximised the property's fantastic views across Bali Hai, Mount Namalakoma and the Pacific. He used lots of black marble, brass and glass to recreate the hotel and the golf course clubhouse. The man who had worked on some redesigning of the Mirage Port Douglas golf course, Mac Hunter—a head golf pro from Los Angeles and who had taught Howard Hughes how to play the game—became involved in building the Princeville course.

At the same time, Qintex began another American project, redeveloping a property at Dana Point, in Orange County, California, about sixty kilometres south of Los Angeles. It was a real waterside haven with boating, sports fishing, parasailing and shopping. Qintex planned to spend US$245 million on a resort, the development including a golf and tennis club, spa and shopping facilities. This is now the home of the Ritz-Carlton, Laguna Niguel, resort.

These two moves into America encouraged Christopher to look at investing in communications in the US. Why not? It's the home of entertainment. After shopping around, he bought Hal Roach Studios, not one of the biggest players but one with a fascinating history. It was one of the first to get into sound and colour production and into early television with *Abbott & Costello*. By the 1980s, it was known for networked movies and the long-running series *Kids Incorporated*, which gave a start to Jennifer Love Hewitt, Martika and Stacy Ferguson of the Black Eyed Peas.

The purchase included a film library of a thousand titles, a prize being the original *Laurel & Hardy* movies. The company also included a film distribution network, an interest in two television stations, plus Colorisation Inc, which made digital coloured versions of black and white films. But what Christopher had noticed with great interest was how the Roach studio had recognised the value of renting out its back catalogue for television and home movies. He had also observed how a valued part of Rupert Murdoch's purchase of 20th Century-Fox was its movie library.

While it was a significant buy for Qintex, it was still not a huge investment in a massive market such as the US. But it allowed Christopher to get his foot in the door in his typical style—test the water, learn the ropes and then jump in and go hard. Then the real opportunity came up. If you're going to get into the big time, you can't get much bigger than MGM and United Artists.

My career was in the film business, I had been involved in internationally released movies and series, and I had travelled all over the world to work on million-dollar commercials. But when Christopher told me he was going to bid for the now combined MGM-United Artists, I was blown away by the size of what he was taking on. MGM had produced *The Wizard of Oz* and *Gone With The Wind*, both versions of *Ben Hur*, musicals such as *Singin' In The Rain*, all the Tom & Jerry cartoons and films ranging from *Gigi* to *Doctor Zhivago* to *How The West Was Won*. United Artists, formed in 1919 by four Hollywood legends—Mary Pickford, Douglas Fairbanks Senior, Charlie Chaplin and director D. W. Griffith—had produced franchises such as *Rocky, The Pink Panther, James Bond* and the Spaghetti Westerns. Films included *African Queen, West Side Story* and *In the Heat of the Night.* Its television offshoot, Ziv Television Programs, was responsible for *Gilligan's Island, The Patty Duke Show* and *The Fugitive.*

These were all solid gold, legendary productions.

But while Hollywood studios create dreams, in real life they are also cesspits of backstabbing, creative clashes, ego showdowns and complex deals. By the time Christopher got to MGM/UA, it was practically bankrupt.

Its owner was a tough operator named Kirk Kerkorian, a billionaire Nevada property developer. The son of Armenian immigrants, he didn't let being a high school dropout get in the way of him becoming one of the world's richest men, amassing a fortune in airlines, hotels, casinos and studios. Dubbed the Father of the Mega-Resort, he changed the face of Las Vegas by building the International Hotel with more than fifteen hundred rooms. How 'mega' was it? The opening night line-up featured Barbra Streisand in the showroom, *Hair* in the theatre and Ike & Tina Turner in the lounge. When Streisand finished her contract, she was replaced by Elvis.

Although the studio was struggling, Kerkorian figured the MGM name would add a Hollywood touch to his Las Vegas empire while he would also pick up a huge chunk of real estate. The land was sold, the props, sets and furnishings, including Judy Garland's ruby *Wizard of Oz* slippers, were flogged off and film production was cut back. Kerkorian opened his new hotel, named the MGM Grand, in Las Vegas in 1973 and

117

a few years later announced he was buying United Artists and merging the two into MGM/UA Entertainment Co.

In 1986, he sold MGM/UA to Ted Turner, owner of the CNN Network. Curiously, Turner sold most of it back to Kerkorian ten weeks later, retaining some of the MGM film library, which he later began to run on Turner Network Television. It was into this crazy scenario that Christopher jumped in 1989. He put to Kerkorian an offer for MGM/UA of US$1.2 billion.

It was a big call, but he could see great possibilities. Despite the part buy-back deal from Turner, there was still plenty left in MGM/UA, boasting a wonderful pedigree, a viable studio and a significant film catalogue. He told me it was the movie library that appealed to him most. The Hal Roach Studio had proved the value of renting out material, and he could see the same possibilities with MGM/UA but on a much bigger scale.

However, as we all know, movies are the stuff of dreams. Sometimes things don't turn out the way we expect.

THIRTEEN

I n the middle of all these American adventures, Christopher started playing football. Not actually kicking the ball, I might add, but getting involved in a daring project by the then Victorian Football League to take Australian Rules into Queensland, a fanatical Rugby League stronghold.

Being a Melbourne boy, Christopher was attracted to this idea. He was an absolutely mad passionate Aussie Rules fan and a lifelong supporter of one of its founding clubs, Essendon. He loved the game and he loved the Bombers almost as much as he loved his Don Bradman cricket bat, and that is saying something. He would chat on for hours about how Essendon was going, who they were recruiting, who was playing well and what their chances were of winning another premiership. It meant bugger all to me. As a Sydney boy, brought up on sailing, surfing and League, Aussie Rules was another world entirely. All those blokes in little shorts running around catching the ball did not excite me that much.

There had always been a bit of an Aussie Rules movement up in Queensland. A few ex-VFL players had retired there, including Essendon legend Dick Reynolds and former Essendon and St Kilda ruckman, Ted Rippon, who ran a Gold Coast motel. Even in those days, the local league was a pretty vigorous organization with one of its key teams, Southport, on its way to becoming one of the strongest, most successful clubs outside Victoria. But for the VFL (now the AFL), the decision to enter Queensland was more a matter of pragmatism. While many Victorian fans were not enthused with the idea of interstate teams wrecking their cosy twelve-team suburban set-up, the VFL's view was that a national league was essential for the game's survival. Cynics pointed out that the licence fee would also be a handy boost to the league's bank account, which by all reports was fairly empty.

But its first interstate venture, sending South Melbourne up to NSW in 1982 and converting them into the Sydney Swans, had been a highly emotional, expensive and difficult process. By the time Christopher turned his attention towards footy in Queensland, the Swans had racked up millions in debt and were now being funded by a consortium fronted by my sister Kate's then brother-in-law, Mike Willesee, the current affairs superstar and owner of 2Day FM. In the Sunshine State, it would prove to be an even rockier road. From a handful of hopefuls, the choice boiled down to two consortiums. One was headed by former Australian Open Tennis promoter John Brown and the other by actor Paul Cronin, best known as Dave in *The Sullivans*.

Raised in footy-mad South Australia, Cronin said he had always felt that one day Aussie Rules would expand into a national league. Although he had said that struggling Fitzroy should be relocated to Brisbane, his submission was bolstered by his partnership with the Queensland Australian Football League. Eventually his group got the nod over Brown's.

With Cronin as chairman, the next aim was to raise $4 million to secure the VFL licence to enter the competition. But over succeeding weeks, the group struggled to get the money and fragmented. On hearing this, Christopher rang Cronin and suggested they go into it together. He underwrote the funding, becoming Cronin's deputy chairman. Why? Well, apart from his great love of the game, he had two things in mind: the Mirage Gold Coast, which could bounce off the publicity, and the Seven Network, which could cover the games.

As luck would have it, although the team was called Brisbane, they could not locate a ground in the city big enough to accommodate the Aussie Rules style of game. The preferred choice, the 'Gabba, still had a greyhound track around it. This could not have been better for Christopher, who suggested, 'How about we play on the Gold Coast?' Over summer, a field at Carrara was secured, which just happened to be not all that far from the Mirage Gold Coast.

Temporary stands, clubrooms and catering facilities were whacked up, and banks of floodlights constructed with night matches and television in mind. Peter Knights, a likeable ex-Hawthorn champion, was appointed coach. They set his office up in a demountable shed, the sort of thing you see on a building site.

The plan lost a little traction when the full name and colours of the new club were unveiled. They were called the Brisbane Bears, but in a public relations disaster, the koala was announced as the team mascot, even though it is not a bear but a marsupial and the jumper was a maroon and yellow shocker. It featured the initials BB and a logo of a pissed-off looking koala, presumably to give the notion that they weren't a team to be messed with. It did not look angry, so much as comical.

With no local talent to speak of, the Bears had to recruit from interstate, the Victorian teams reluctantly following a VFL directive that they each give up three players from their list. Most of the clubs played hard ball, offering the Bears fringe players, would-be heroes, blokes on one leg, retirees and delisted troublemakers.

With a bag of oddball talent supplemented by enthusiastic players from all over Australia and the whole thing flung together in a matter of weeks, it was assumed by observers, fans and critics alike that the Cronin-Skase Brisbane Koala Bears would be the easiest of easy-beats. To everyone's astonishment, they won their first game in the opening round of 1987, beating North Melbourne by 33 points at the MCG, having run through a pre-match banner reading, *History In The Making.*

Mark Williams, later to coach Port Adelaide to its first AFL premiership, was best on ground, supported by sterling performances from ex-South Australian Mark Mickan and former Collingwood/Richmond wingman Phillip Walsh, later appointed Adelaide Crows coach only to be killed in horrific circumstances. Young ex-Bomber Brenton Phillips booted five goals. The following week they flew down to play Geelong on the Cats' home turf, always a difficult place to play, even for the best of teams. But they won again.

The Brisbane Bears were a revelation. The VFL was thrilled that its new baby was so competitive, and amid all his heady business dealings, this was an exciting diversion for Christopher. He'd done it again. He'd picked a winner! Don't know whether Pixie was all that interested in thirty-six blokes running around a paddock chasing a bag of wind, but she was the perfect hostess in any given situation and the president's lunches, complete with typically excellent food and wine, became the hottest ticket in town.

After two rounds, it all went down hill. A fifty-point hiding by St Kilda, the customary crap side of those times, set Brisbane on a slippery path. By season's end, they had won only six games of twenty-two and had been dubbed the *Bad News Bears* after a movie about a hopeless baseball team. Christopher said it was not the finish that he had wanted. Undaunted and under instructions to chase the best talent, the Bears recruited tough man Roger Merrett from Essendon, who added strength, skill and professionalism and who went on to become a club legend. But the headline grabbing coup was the high-flying glamour full-forward Warwick Capper. The Sydney Swans, desperate for cash, off-loaded 'Wokka' over the summer, and with his golden locks, white boots and ball-cracking shorts, he looked the perfect Gold Coast beach boy Bear.

Despite Merrett putting the frighteners on the opposition while getting a lot of the ball and motor-mouth Capper kicking goals and dragging the fans through the gates, the Bears won only one more game than the previous season and again finished second last.

Over the summer, while the club considered its next move, Christopher's football participation broadened on another front. He was up at Port Douglas watching Greg Norman play in a Skins match when a bloke approached him and explained that he had just been elected president of the newly formed Port Douglas Football Club and was looking for financial support.

Christopher bought a major sponsorship, and it proved to be a good link. Some of the new team, many of them expatriate Victorians, had either worked on the construction of Mirage Port Douglas or were now working around the resort or on the golf course. That first season, Port Douglas made the finals. The following year they were runners-up, and in 1991 they won the flag.

But season 1989 saw only more problems for the Bears. Coach Knights was sacked near the end of yet another poor year. Under his replacement, former North Melbourne utility Paul Feltham, the Bears won five of their last seven games to scramble up to tenth of fourteen teams.

There were still years of heartache and agony to come before a bankrupt Fitzroy would be forced into a merger with the Bears. Out of that, the Brisbane Lions were formed, relocated to an upgraded 'Gabba Stadium, and triple-premiership triumph came in 2001-3.

But how about this? In 2011 the AFL introduced the Gold Coast Suns and set them up at the old home of the Bears! The Carrara stadium was transformed into a first-class 25,000 seater venue with a massive $126 million renovation. This to me shows once again that when it came to spotting the right place and the right opportunity, Christopher was always on the money.

However, back in 1989, the poor form of the Brisbane Bears was quickly becoming the least of his concerns, and he had to get out.

Some very dangerous problems had suddenly appeared on the horizon.

FOURTEEN

S o, while all this high-level, high-energy activity was swirling around at a frenetic pace, what was I doing?

Well, amongst other things, becoming a dad. That's right, the serious notion of fatherhood had been bestowed upon Larkins, the knockabout film guy, hack golfer, enthusiastic lover of the odd glass of champagne and sometime involuntary participant in the occasional misadventure which might have produced disturbing consequences but where no actual physical harm was occasioned to innocent bystanders.

Charlotte Caroline Larkins was born on April 8, 1989, at Manly Public Hospital. So many floral tributes turned up from Christopher and Pixie and family and friends that the other new mum sharing the room with Amanda had to be moved out to make space for the gorgeous displays.

We could not have been happier. Charlotte was and still is our beautiful treasure. She symbolised the state of domestic bliss we had achieved. Although Qintex was roaring ahead and Christopher and Pixie were living an accelerated, upmarket, international lifestyle, we were still not part of it. We were simply living at my modest little one-and-half bedroom, single-brick house in Frenchs Forest which, through a bit of renovation and eviction of some of its more outrageous tenants, guests, visitors and dossers, we had turned into our happy family home.

The Swamp was no longer the party place that it used to be. Amanda had shut the regulars out, the front door having an actual lock on it by now. Blokes would knock on the door with a slab, and if she was on her own, she would just sit there quietly and not answer it. She'd think, 'Nah!!'

Meanwhile much of the yard, which used to get flooded, had been concreted to facilitate the two large film trucks, three camera tracking vehicles and six-car garage full of tools and equipment that Brownie and I were amassing as the A-Team expanded its influence on the freelance grips world. So, its nick-name, the Swamp, had lost all its meaning.

As any mum will tell you, having that first baby is a huge challenge, and this was even more so for Amanda, having come up from Melbourne to make a new life in a new city. It was not helped by us doing renovations, including installing a new kitchen, while she was pregnant. God bless her for putting up with all the disruption and crap all over the place. You know how a fit-out goes. It takes twice as long as you think and costs four times as much.

The kitchen renovation was a 'first grandchild' present from Christopher and Pixie, but over the years we never took, nor were we offered, anything from them other than this and the honeymoon aboard Mirage III. They lived their high-flying life; we always supported our own relatively modest lifestyle.

There was only one up-market symbol that turned up at the Swamp—an emerald green Rolls-Royce. It arrived at our place when Christopher and Pixie, now at their very peak, left Australia to take up residence in Los

Angeles. They could not see much value in taking the right-hand drive car to the US and so kept it on with the lease company. Exotic as it was, it was little more than an amusing, impractical ornament for us. We never once took it out of the garage and onto the streets for fear of causing more damage than we could ever hope to pay for. All we ever did was sit in it and have drinks on the foldout tables in the back seat until it was shipped offshore and sold.

At this stage, I was still not working for Christopher. I'm sure by the time I had married his stepdaughter, it had crossed his mind many times that I would be better off employed by Qintex and that he would be able to slot me into the business somewhere. But in all that time, I don't think he ever actually asked me to come and work for him.

My link with Christopher, however, was well known throughout the film industry. Sometimes on a set, if a director was having a go at me over something, a voice would pipe up out of the darkness: 'Hey, 'Arold, you don't have to take any shit from him. Tell him you'll get the old man to buy him out.'

It was mostly done in a light-hearted way, not with jealousy. There were a few people in the industry who were a bit envious of me, but that was always going to be the case because there were a handful who didn't like who I was, where I had come from, how I went about my business and what I had achieved in the game.

I was very happy working in the industry as a technician. In fact, I was having a ball making a lot of money in comparison to people on average salaries, so it was not a consideration for me to work with Christopher. I also had no desire to be the boss's son. I had been in that position working with Dad in the car industry, and after all the shit I went through, I never wanted to be in that situation again.

Amanda and I had our own lives. We were perfectly happy. We had a good lifestyle, we had heaps of money, we had lots of fun, we stayed in five-star hotels, we ate in flash restaurants, we lived very well. I was always busy, working five or six days a week, fifty weeks a year, and when I got home, I kept on improving our house.

Amanda was also happy in her own career although, and I think this was fair enough, she had taken up the Qintex option. She had joined the resurgent Seven Network in 1988 as a research assistant under the guidance of the fabulous Jon 'Vibes' Vidler on a new show called *Saturday Morning Live*. The show was hosted by the mercurial duo Jonno & Dano—Jonathan Coleman and Ian Rogerson—and was another one of Christopher's pet projects aimed at getting the Seven Network back up the ratings ladder. It was a fast moving, wacky combination of current affairs, pop culture and music directly aimed at the Saturday morning audience of cynical teens and hung-over adults.

Quite frankly, it was a position they had created for her as they didn't know what she was capable of and were obviously under pressure, perceived or otherwise, to employ her. She did not let them down. It turned out to be the perfect job for her. She loved the music and the interviews and the craziness. It was a small crew, too, so while her job was mainly research, developing the questions to ask, photo sourcing and playing parts as an extra, she did a bit of everything, including looking after the guests and helping out on the set.

Jonno and Dano were the perfect foil for each other, with Jonno, never short of chatter, info and gossip, and Dano, the more laconic, laid-back type. They had worked very successfully on Triple J together and this was their first attempt at television and it did well for a Saturday morning show. One of its strengths was that it was produced by Kris Noble, who became a good friend of Amanda's and who went on to a stellar television production career, including becoming executive producer of *Big Brother*.

Amanda loved her time at Seven. She and the two hosts and the production team got along like a house on fire and we all became mates. As it turned out, Ian Rogerson and his first wife Maria Perrigñon lived just around the corner, and the four of us spent enjoyable times socialising. Amanda was Maria's bridesmaid when she married Ian, with entertainment guru and Channel 9 celebrity Richard Wilkins as Ian's best man.

We were having good times in Sydney and socialising with some very good people, old friends and new friends. Through the young mums' groups, Amanda developed a support structure in Frenchs Forest and Dee Why, where there are a lot of defence force wives. All this was interspersed with regular visits from Pixie. During the pregnancy, Pixie took quite an interest in the baby and Amanda's health. She would turn up, in typical style, having just flown in from New York, London or Paris with gifts of Baby Dior or Nina Ricci baby clothing.

So, with our house in good shape and us both enjoying what we were doing, the arrival of Charlotte topped things off beautifully. I might point out, however, that on the day she was born, I still played golf with two good mates—Jamie Egan, a gaffer, and Kerry 'KJ' Jackson, my assistant grip, and who had been one of my groomsmen. On this day, we went to the course in the morning with the heavily pregnant Amanda complaining about having pains. In my inimitable style, I showed my concern and devotion to the cause, 'Yeah, whatever. We're off to have a bit of a hack around.' We got back about midday to find her well and truly into labour. So we all sat around for the afternoon keeping a close eye on things—a bit of old post-game amusement—when she finally decided it was time to go to hospital. We took her over there at about five o'clock, and she gave birth about seven, which was pretty quick.

I loved parenthood. My fatherly duties included getting up on Sunday mornings when Charlotte woke up and loading her in our old Honda Civic and driving up to Whale Beach where I had spent a lot of time surfing as a kid—by which time she would be asleep again—stopping, having a coffee and reading the paper. When she woke up, I would make the return drive via McDonalds in the Forest Way Mall to pick up a Big Breakfast so as to give Amanda at least one day of sleeping in with breakfast in bed.

We did fun things like getting my brother Neil to help me construct a fake 'jungle' outside Charlotte's room by covering the whole back paved area in shade cloth and filling it with palms and ferns. It was like our own private piece of rainforest and a spectacular backdrop to Charlotte's nursery, formerly my old, narrow-sided bedroom on the back veranda of the house.

Pixie and Christopher had been setting up house in Los Angeles and had arrived back in Australia the day after Charlotte was born. When they came to the hospital to see our new pride and joy, Christopher, after showing his pleasure, went and lay on the other bed and turned on the telly to check out his own baby, *Home & Away*. He was also keen on watching his upgraded news service as well as *Hinch,* another of his projects, the current affairs program hosted by the 'human headline' Derryn Hinch, who Christopher had lured away from radio 3AW in 1988. The former newspaper editor and talkback radio host had translated well to the small screen and was building a solid viewing audience with his tough, no-nonsense approach. I never thought he would one day morph into Senator Hinch.

Other shows that came on board or were developed included *Saturday Morning Live* that Amanda worked on, *Newsworld* hosted by the ever grumpy Clive Robertson, *Tonight Live With Steve Vizard*, *The D-Generation*, and *Fast Forward*, a comedy sketch program which featured Vizard sending up the network's current affairs superstar via a bearded character called Hunch.

As he stretched back on the bed, watching an ever-improving Seven on the hospital screen, Christopher could not have been happier. The network was looking great, the resorts were busy, the new developments were coming along nicely, the share price was solid, the media was loving him, the investors were happy. And as for the movie studio he was buying in Los Angeles from Kirk Kerkorian, it was going to be a cracker.

Not long after Charlotte had been born, we drove up from Sydney to the Gold Coast in my old V12 Jaguar for a long weekend at Easter and had a great time with Christopher and Pixie. Charlotte was the first grandchild in the family and they were obviously very excited and it was great to watch Christopher with the baby. He had never had his own children, but here was the astute businessman showing a loving, tender side that was never on display when he was in the public eye. A wonderful warmth and relationship developed between him and Charlotte in those early days. It was a bond that was to remain unbroken to the day he died and which Charlotte still cherishes.

When Christopher and Pixie returned to the US, where they were now living, we remained in regular contact. They were obviously keen to get the latest on how Charlotte was doing, how we were coping with a new baby, how the house was shaping up and so on. There was probably more communication from Pixie than Christopher, because he was so involved with the MGM/UA deal. We were reading in the newspapers every day about how Qintex was getting into the movie business and how well that was all going.

So there we were, two arms of the family, separated by the Pacific Ocean but united, optimistic, with plenty to celebrate and a lot to look forward to.

If only it had stayed that way. Instead we were all about to jump onto a horrific one-way journey that was to see us end up in Spain.

FIFTEEN

O ne of the great ironies of this saga is that just before he plunged into the MGM/UA bid, Christopher told me he had begun planning to sell up everything and get out.

He figured by then he would be forty-one, that he had done the hard yards to build things up over nearly two decades, and that it would be a great way to release himself from all the pressure. He would be in a position to do what he wanted to do, rather than what he had to do. He had done his sums, too, estimating that once everything was paid up and sorted out, he would walk away with $150 million in his pocket. Just on inflation rates that would be worth about $325 million these days. A handy retirement figure.

This was no idle chatter or post-dinner cognac rambling, either. He had instructed the accountants to prepare an official Proposal for the Sale of Qintex. I saw the big black books with all the details, listing the companies and properties, the income and outgoings, the profit and loss. The proposal had been prepared by one of the big firms—Price Waterhouse or Ernst & Young, one of those, I can't remember which—to be touted around to potential buyers, both local and overseas. What an impressive portfolio it was, too, with properties in Australia, the Pacific and the US, plus media interests and assorted firms, underpinned by fifteen years of continuous profit, growth and healthy shareholder returns.

At this point, the company was rock-solid, its shares highly recommended as a buy by stockbrokers and financial advisers. He was the golden-haired boy, he could do no wrong, he'd created the resorts, he'd done all the things he wanted, there was no more to do. 'I'm going to take my hundred and fifty million and walk away,' he told me.

Then the MGM/UA opportunity came up.

I guess that is what defines guys like Christopher and makes them different from people like you and me. It's not the money so much as the challenge. Sure, they enjoy the trappings the dough can give them, they love living in a world where cash is no problem, and they enjoy being able to buy what they want when they want or what their partners want.

But at the end of the day, business is what it's all about, and it's the love of the chase and the thrill of the kill that provides the appeal. The research on a company that might be worth buying, the preparation of the bid, the bargaining over the deal, the exhilaration of beating all the others to it. Then there is the joy of taking over the business, reorganising it and making it work successfully to a proven formula, perhaps even to on-sell it.

You and me? We'd probably take the cash. At a present day valuation of $350,000,000, even at today's low interest figures of say 3 per cent, you would be eking out an existence on an income of $10,500,000 a year. I think I could handle that. Might even buy a new oven door for the Swamp.

But when the chance came up to buy MGM/UA, the whiff of battle proved too strong. Sell out and retire at forty-one? Bloody hell, this was too good an opportunity to let slip. 'However,' he told me, 'this will be my last project.'

As well as his own determination to score another success, it's my opinion that Christopher also went ahead on the MGM/UA deal with plenty of Pixie's pushing. I think she loved the Hollywood lifestyle. I reckon that the glitz and glamour of Tinsel Town suited her approach, and having conquered Toorak, why not move on to LA?

The proposal he structured was brilliant. It would have turned out to have been the deal of the decade in terms of the price he negotiated, what he actually paid, and what he was principally after—the film library, the back catalogue of some of the finest, best known films ever made with an enormous market opening up for them.

He and I discussed the purchase a lot. But he only ever said he was doing it for 'the girls'—for Pixie, who he loved more than anything in life, and for her four daughters, who he considered were his and who he loved unconditionally. He had never bought them anything or lavished gifts on them or given them money. Now, this was his way of looking after them, big time.

This was not sentimental dialogue that passed only between him and me either. It was a theme he pursued at family discussions or when I heard him talking to anyone else about why he did what he did. He would always say, 'Everything is for the girls.'

On the other hand, Kirk Kerkorian, the man selling MGM/UA, hadn't become one of the world's richest men through sentiment. A former amateur boxer who had trained as a pilot during World War II, the foundation of his fortune had been established by him taking on a war-time suicide run where pilots flew fighter bombers from

Canada over the North Atlantic to the Royal Air Force at a thousand dollars a time.

Kerkorian had had MGM/UA up for sale for about eighteen months when Christopher offered US$1.2 billion. That was the highest bid that had come along, including that of Rupert Murdoch's News Corporation, which had dropped out of negotiations. Christopher's figure was accepted, and it was a done deal.

Now, you have to take on board what Christopher was buying and also appreciate that these guys do things on a completely different level to what we consider 'buying.' Your concept and my concept of buying something is to go to the retailer, select a television or a dishwasher or whatever, negotiate a figure and pay. The payment might be cash there and then or on credit card or by putting down a deposit and paying the rest off in regular instalments. You might get a deal of no deposit and no repayments until a certain set date. But by and large it's fairly straightforward.

These guys, they buy with cash, they buy with borrowings, they buy with share swaps, they buy with leveraged debt, they buy with bonds. Sometimes they buy debt as part of the package. Sometimes they buy a particular element as part of the deal and then sell it back to the original owner. Amazing. These deals are never simple.

Basically, Qintex made an offer of $20 a share, for a total of $1.2 billion. For that, Qintex was buying MGM/UA assets including the United Artists studio and its library of more than a thousand films, plus the rights to the MGM name and its lion trademark, plus the MGM television and film production operations, which included any films made after 1986, plus the company's Beverly Hills headquarters.

Then, for $250 million, Kerkorian would buy back the rights to the MGM name and lion trademark, the MGM television and film production operations, which included any MGM films made since 1986, plus the company's Beverly Hills headquarters. This would leave Qintex essentially with the United Artists arm of the business. Under the agreement, Kerkorian would then invest $75 million in the new, separate United Artists. There was also something like $150 million cash on the books. Sounds complicated, but there was a reason. MGM was not in great shape.

After all these swings and roundabouts, the effective cost to Qintex would be about $600 million for the greatest film and television software buy-up in history. In retrospect, proven by the huge amounts other studios and libraries subsequently sold for, it would have been the media deal of the 20th century.

The offer sparked plenty of media interest on both sides of the Pacific. In Australia, while the technical ins and outs of it were assessed in the financial sections, the celebrity of it also hit the front pages. It was the classic story of Aussie bravado that the media loves so much, the determined Down Under company taking on the might of Tinsel Town. In the US, however, the financial aspect was the main theme, with a lot of Wall Street commentators suggesting Qintex was paying an inflated price for a business that, after all, had lost a lot of money in the previous year. Some were cautiously optimistic, saying that they could see merit in Christopher's view that the movie library would bring in excellent revenue and that things would be okay down the track. They commented on Christopher's foresight in spotting the burgeoning Pay TV, home video and syndication markets opening up, made all the more attractive with the European segment soon to be de-regulated.

The day after Charlotte was born and Christopher and Pixie arrived at Manly Hospital, he had stitched up the loose ends. Most people probably do not know that after he went back to the US, Christopher actually took over the studio, sitting in the chief executive's desk and running the place on a day-to-day basis and starting to turn the business around. As far as everyone was concerned, it was a done deal. He and Pixie began spending most of their time in Hollywood with Pixie looking around for a suitable house to buy in classic LA locations such as Bel Air.

Then, re-enter Rupert Murdoch.

Suddenly, on September 10, five months after the deal was done and dusted, Murdoch reappeared and offered Kerkorian $23 a share or $1.5 billion for more or less the same package. This was $300 million more than the Qintex offer that had already been accepted.

This confounds me to this day. In Australia, my understanding is that once a deal is done, it's done. If another potential buyer arrives with a cheque after the contract is signed, he's told, 'Too late, mate; it's all tied up.' But in America—ah, only in America—under their regulatory rules a counter bidder can come in with a higher offer up to a certain point in time, even well after the deal has been closed. I reckon that in a backhanded compliment, Murdoch had shown that Christopher had increased the value of his acquisition by $300 million in less then six months, underlining his vision, management skills and business acumen.

By this point, Christopher and Pixie were so ensconced in the film business they were flying around in the studio jet, complete with its own kitchen, attending movie premieres all over the US. He was loving it so much he even managed to cause an on-board barbecue fire! True, he set fire to his hamburger in the plane's kitchen and nearly brought the whole thing down.

As well, they were buying the former home of Louis B. Mayer, one of the original and greatest movie moguls who had guided MGM through its halcyon days. The lavish mansion was in ultra-exclusive Holmby Hills, not as well known as Bel Air or Beverly Hills but containing some of Los Angeles' priciest housing, including Hugh Hefner's Playboy Mansion and television producer Aaron Spelling's 123-room Manor, which was just beginning to be constructed.

Christopher and his management team were over in Paris finalising the funding for the purchase when they heard about the Murdoch bid. After the initial shock was absorbed, they went into full-throttle mode, working all night to come up with a new financial plan.

He figured it was best to kill off the Murdoch challenge there and then. So, he came up with a revised figure of $1.9 billion for the whole lot—not only the UA library, but also the MGM logo, studio, library and anything else in the stable. He flew back to the US and after some fairly robust discussions with Kerkorian—I would love to have been a fly on the wall as those two went at each other—he announced he was going for everything.

Kerkorian didn't mind. He obviously knew that Murdoch not only owned the world's biggest media company, News Corporation, but also 20th Century Fox, one of the great studios, about to launch a cartoon series called *The Simpsons*. He also knew that Murdoch had the cash up front, while, in the period after the 1987 stock crash, a lot of other people were still suffering. Sure, there might have been anti-trust issues for Murdoch to consider—US authorities might not agree on a company owning two major studios—but what the heck?

Did Kerkorian deliberately bring Murdoch back in to crank up the bid, anticipating Christopher would then counter-bid for the whole lot? I don't know, but Christopher certainly went for the knockout blow. He had no other choice. The challenge was to now find the extra $700 million.

Now, around this time, 1988/1989, Australian interest rates had taken off. It was the build-up to 'the recession we had to have,' as the Treasurer Paul Keating so blithely put it a couple of years later, matching his earlier, famed 1986 reference to Australia bordering on becoming a 'banana republic.' When your business is highly leveraged, as so many of them were in those days—and still are, I'm sure—every percentage point increase in interest severely impacts on loan repayments.

When the standard variable home loan interest rate under Keating rocketed from 12.5 per cent in March 1983 up to a peak of 17 per cent in June 1989, with business loans anything up to 6 per cent higher, many businesses were forced into bankruptcy, especially in Queensland. It was a tough time for everybody, from the man in the street looking for a job up to small business owners and large corporations desperate to get cash in to meet their spiralling loan repayments. The whole economy was struggling, and for a high-end business like Qintex, it was tough times.

Then, for all those heavily involved in the tourist/hospitality trade, as Qintex was, there came a second blow. Suddenly, the planes stopped flying.

SIXTEEN

T o this day, many pilots will tell you that they, technically speaking, never went on strike in 1989. That they had put a log of claims on the table that were rejected by their employers, which led to a stand-off and that it flared from there. They will say that they were never really given any further chance to settle on a deal and were kicked out of their jobs. A 'dispute' is how they put it. But the pilots' strike is how many people saw it, and that was the commonly-used term to describe it.

On July 26, 1989, the Australian Federation of Air Pilots served a pay demand of 29.4 per cent, saying that its pay rates for captains and first officers had slipped behind inflation. The situation was muddied by the fact that the pilots were negotiating with two different bodies—Ansett Airlines, a commercially owned operation, and Australian Airlines, owned by the Federal Government, whose members ironically had granted themselves a 36 per cent pay rise a few months before during the pre-Christmas media black hole.

On August 15, three days prior to the commencement of the pilots working nine-to-five only, a meeting was held in Prime Minister Bob Hawke's office between key players from the Government, the airlines and the unions. Attending were Mr Hawke; Sir Peter Abeles, the joint managing director of Ansett, representing both the 50 per cent stake held by TNT and the 50 per cent owned by News Ltd; Ted Harris, the chairman of Australian Airlines and a Qintex board member; Ralph Willis and Bill Morris, both Government Ministers; and Bill Kelty, ACTU Secretary, who contributed via phone.

Former Ansett pilot Alex Paterson, who subsequently wrote a pilots' perspective of the dispute, says minutes of the meeting were taken by Dr D. S. Harrison, a public servant in the Department of Prime Minister and Cabinet. These were later tendered in a Federal Court action instigated by the pilot's federation over changes to the immigration act to allow overseas pilots to take up jobs in Australia. In the minutes, Abeles is noted as saying how they should 'stick together' so that they can 'really take them on,' adding that 'we won't give them anything.' Later he says that he has 'no sympathy' for the pilots, as they 'don't compare themselves with others in the airline industry.'

The Government declared a national emergency on August 23, 1989, and called in military aircraft to carry holidaymakers and business people across the nation. Travellers lucky enough to get a ride were bucketed across the nation in metal-and-canvas seats, wearing earplugs to try and drown out the roaring noise of a converted troop carrier, eating what appeared to be glorified military rations. It dramatically showed where the Government and the airlines were coming from, creating an image of bravado in the face of challenge.

The trouble was, the RAAF planes could carry only a fraction of Australia's daily air traffic, and when the commercial planes stopped flying, people were no longer coming in from overseas or moving around interstate in their thousands. Five-star resorts such as the Qintex-developed Mirages, at that point the benchmark in the luxury field and dependent almost totally on customers flying in, began rapidly running out of guests. Cancellations flowed and bookings dried up. Pretty soon the occupancy rate had flopped to less than 40 per cent, well below the 55 per cent break-even point. From then on, they kept dropping, getting down to as low as 10 per cent.

The knock-on effect was that it not only endangered the viability of the Mirage resorts at the time, but destabilised the projections on which the Qintex group's financing and ultimately its future was dependent. That is, no cash coming in in Queensland, therefore no money to keep all the balls in the air, including the moves into the US.

To rub salt into the wounds, Qintex was blindsided by another attack, this one coming from the Federal Investment Review Board. The FIRB examines proposals by foreign interests intent on undertaking direct investment in Australia and makes recommendations to the Government as to whether those proposals are suitable for approval under its policy. An area of scrutiny at the time was the sale of rural property in Queensland. A lot of sugarcane farms were being sold off to overseas companies and being turned into golf courses.

The FIRB came up with a ruling that insisted that for every property sold to an overseas buyer, one would have to be sold to local interests. This also had a serious effect on Qintex's fortunes. One of the keys to success of the Mirage projects was the ability to sell apartments to overseas buyers. Christopher said that often they would have up to a dozen foreign buyers ready to purchase properties. But now they had to put them on hold while they found the equivalent number of local buyers. It was difficult enough attracting local buyers on a one-for-one basis, much less having to find a dozen at a time. If they had have been allowed to sell properties as they liked, they would have been able to develop crucial income. Instead, sales slowed to a trickle.

Here's the crucial point, the heart of the matter. Christopher regularly told me later that he could have faced and successfully overcome any two of those three situations—the crippling interest rates or the pilots' strike or the FIRB ruling—at the one time, even in the midst of the MGM/UA bid.

If he only had to find extra cash to cover the increased interest on his loan repayments, he would have found a way of doing that. If he only had to concentrate on finding ways of coping with the reduced cash flow from the Mirages, again he would have been okay. One option would have been to concentrate on the local market rather than the overseas clientele. He might have had to slash room tariffs but at least he would have kept occupancy rates up. And if the sole problem had just been to concentrate on selling apartments locally as well as overseas, well, they would have hopped into it.

But when all three situations happened at the same time while trying to finance the MGM/UA deal, it was a triple barrel strain on Qintex's finances that was too much to cope with. He found himself stuck in an economic Bermuda Triangle—the perfect financial storm.

The big question is: why didn't Christopher just let the movie deal go, cut his losses, go back to Australia and focus on the operations that had been so good for him?

Well, the answer is—and this is what he would tell me later in one of those cool-light-of-day 'if only' moments we all have—he had to admit that for once he had made a fatal error in his battle planning. He stupidly hadn't written in a suitable back-out clause, where he could have withdrawn by paying a reasonable exit fee, thus keeping his losses to a minimum. Because of that omission, it was going to cost him a lot of dough to stay in, and a lot of dough—in fact, everything he had put in so far—to get out. He realised he had locked himself in. He was up the proverbial creek without a paddle.

As well, right from the start of his foray into Tinsel Town, a recurring media comment, both in the US and in Australia, was that Christopher was a 'Hollywood outsider' and that this might well cause him a lot of grief. Christopher didn't mind that comment. He was used to that sort of putdown. He considered himself an outsider even in hometown Melbourne, the city of his birth and upbringing, where he felt the old establishment money never welcomed him into the club and, if anything, did its best to freeze him out and bring him down.

In fact, whether the financial establishment put the word out, who knows, but try as he did, Christopher just couldn't get the extra funding together to fully seal the Hollywood deal. He and his Qintex team went around and around the world in the jet chasing the funds, trying to get people to put up the extra money, asking them to help him through a period he knew he could survive if he was just given a bit of support.

In this chase for money, trying to keep it all together, he did some things that were, let's say, 'out there.' Innovative, different, on the edge, but still legal, trying all sorts of financial sources, some well-known establishment operations and others not quite the household name. Not exactly meeting blokes offering a cardboard suitcase full of cash in the back room of a restaurant but certainly avenues he had not tried before. He was just doing his best to keep his company going, but investors simply wouldn't come at it.

With his resorts not producing income, the Qintex stock price buckling, the value of his assets going through the floor and his loan repayments escalating, people did not want to take the risk. Even those that had once backed him to the hilt. They were saying, 'Christopher, sorry, mate, we can't help. We'd love to, but look at the figures; we can't lend you money on the basis of those. We just can't do it.'

To frustrate matters, there was a lot of backwards and forwards discussion between Christopher and Kerkorian at this time, much of it proving inconclusive. Christopher reported to the shareholders that one of the big problems was that Kerkorian was proving difficult to pin down as to exactly what he wanted. Christopher described him as a 'moving target' orchestrating a deal that 'shifted daily.' One minute Kerkorian was happy with an agreed $50 million deposit, the next he wanted $200 million and then he would go back to $50 million.

At one stage, the French banker, Crédit Lyonnais, looked like it would pitch in and solve it all, save everything, but at the last moment, it backed away. Christopher woke up one morning to the sickening realisation that there was no way out. He could not get the money to fund the purchase. He had gone one financial bridge too far.

On October 11, 1989, the MGM/UA deal collapsed when Qintex did not come up with the scheduled $50 million letter-of-credit deposit. Legal letters immediately flew from both sides, with Kerkorian suing Qintex for $50 million and Qintex counter-suing for damages. But that soon was to become a sideshow because a whole lot worse was to come.

Eight days later, on October 19, the company missed a scheduled payment on another deal. Qintex Entertainment Inc, the US arm that had been at the forefront of expansion into America, now strapped for cash and unable to get funds from its Australian parent company, could not come up with an agreed $5.9 million payment to entertainment group MCA Inc. This was part of a deal to finance the planned production of, would you believe, *The New Leave It To Beaver Show*. The next day, Qintex Entertainment Inc filed in the US courts for bankruptcy and the whole lot blew up, the ripple effect crashing across the Pacific and blasting a hole in the company's stocks.

Shares in Qintex Australia Ltd (QAL), $4.70 before the 1987 crash, had already slid to 35 cents, while Qintex Ltd (QNT), the holding company for more than a hundred firms including a 53 per cent stake in Qintex Australia Ltd, had gone from a high of $5.20 before Black Monday to $3.05.

On October 23, in the first hour of trading, Qintex Australia Ltd dropped from 33 cents to 16 cents while Qintex Ltd fell from $3.05 to $1.05 on a turnover of just 200 shares. On that basis, the stock exchange stepped in and suspended trading of both. It was all over bar the shouting.

Ironically, by now the planes were back in the air again. But when the voice over the intercom saying, 'This is your Captain speaking,' came with rounded British vowels or an American twang, passengers realised that flying had changed forever. And for Christopher and Qintex, it was all too late; the damage had been done.

About thirteen hundred local pilots also knew that the game was up as some of them would remark from their crop-dusting, charter work or short-haul passenger work overseas, where eight hundred of them had to flee to find work.

How many thousands of small people also lost their livelihoods, life savings, homes, businesses and sanity during this saga? A hell of a lot of the smaller operators involved directly in the tourism and allied industries got hurt badly. The collateral damage was that many other companies also went under. You rarely heard their stories. The crash of the big names like Qintex, Bond Corporation, Elders and others kept those tales out of the press. The Treasury has since calculated that the pilots' dispute was the costliest decision of any Australian Government other than the Vietnam War.

Christopher formed the view that the effects of what the Government and others did at the time cruelly impacted on Qintex and him. But he never whinged and said that it was a direct attack on him. 'That's business,' he concluded. 'It's a tough game.'

But to think, just a few months earlier, he was going to sell it all up and walk away with $150 million in his pocket.

SEVENTEEN

B ack in Frenchs Forest, Amanda and I were getting on with our lives and had absolutely no inkling, not even the slightest hint, that things were going wrong. As far as we knew, everything was running beautifully— Christopher and Pixie were living in LA and he was sitting at the big desk running the place.

From what we saw, the pair of them were having a great time, loving the role of the new kids on the block— the powerful new studio head and his glamorous wife being seen at the right places, making the invitation A List, attending the premieres and parties and zig-zagging all over the place in the studio jet. If ever there was a town in which Pixie could really strut her stuff, Los Angeles was it. The feedback we were getting was all good news. Things were booming, and it was all going well.

Not only that, during the year Christopher had embarked on several other initiatives to bring more cash in, including restructuring the group's finances, to ensure the future would be rosy. In January of 1989, with him personally making the $40 million bid, the Seven Network had won the television rights for the 1992 Olympic Games to be held in Barcelona, setting the network on course for an advertising and ratings bonanza, and snaring a franchise that Seven has to this day. Seven was already starting to eat into Nine's ratings and was even starting to win some significant time slots.

In March, a month before he signed up for the MGM/UA deal, he had sold 49 per cent of the three Mirage resorts, Port Douglas, the Gold Coast and Princeville, Hawaii, to Japanese interests—Mitsui & Co Ltd and Nippon Shinpan—for $433 million. This was in keeping with his '51 per cent philosophy' of always holding a majority interest in any project while freeing up capital. He used the money to repay loans to providers including Tricontinental, State Bank of NSW, ANZ, Chase AMP, Amatil Ltd and Hong Kong Bank.

In April, the $400 million redevelopment of the Princeville project in Hawaii had begun, with finance being provided by a then relatively new merchant bank, Whitlam Turnbull & Co. This was headed up by three familiar names—former State Bank of NSW head Nick Whitlam, lawyer turned financier and later Prime Minister Malcolm Turnbull and ex-NSW premier Neville Wran.

So, up until October it was business as usual, with Christopher working hard to make everything happen and looking ahead to expansion. And even when the MGM/UA deal fell though, well, from our naïve point of view that seemed to be extraordinary bad luck, a great opportunity unfairly taken out of his hands and a lot of hard work gone down the drain. We figured he would no doubt cop it on the chin, bounce back up and move on to other things. To be honest, we really didn't know. We had no clue about big business. Suddenly the local media were full of stories about how the MGM/UA deal had fallen apart, that the resorts were suffering and that the whole empire was on the verge of collapse. We just couldn't believe what we were reading!

Pixie's tone in phone conversations changed from sparkling happiness to muted concern, and we hardly heard from Christopher at all because he was up to his nuts feverishly working to find a solution. Interestingly, on the rare times we spoke to him, he never really gave us any bad news. It wasn't in him to do it.

He was trying to keep things on the track in the States, while watching it all go horribly wrong in Australia. Experienced as he was, and calm as he could be under pressure, he just did not know which way to turn—whether to come back to Australia and endeavour to shore things up or stay in the US and see if he could pull things out of the fire. I just think Christopher finally realised at a certain point that he would never get the funding for MGM/UA because his asset backing had gone so horribly wrong and that his endeavours to trump the News Corporation bid was killing him.

Other situations over which Christopher had no control did not help either. In September, Westfield Capital Corporation, the inexperienced media operations owner of the Ten Network, sold it off at a bargain basement price, shareholders losing $450 million in the process. This fire sale only served to diminish the value of the Qintex-owned Seven Network on which a high valuation had been placed to provide assurance for the MGM/UA loan.

Meanwhile, Hover Mirage, set up to run a hovercraft service for guests from Cairns Airport to Port Douglas Mirage and from Brisbane Airport to Gold Coast Mirage, was shut down. This was also because of a decline in customers due to the pilots' dispute with Qintex looking to sell the hovercraft overseas. It was not a big operation by any means, but its fancy concept, Mirage name and sudden demise only further battered the crumbling company image.

We could only imagine what was going through Christopher and Pixie's minds. Their whole world was being turned totally upside down. Things that had been so important were now meaningless. For example, Christopher had started a legal battle to get the business name Mirage registered in the US. It was something he had overlooked earlier, and the name had been registered in the meantime by a company headed up by Steve Wynn, a major player in casinos and hotels. Overnight, this issue suddenly became no longer relevant, and the case simply dissolved.

I had never worked for Qintex, and Amanda's involvement had been simply with Channel 7 and therefore very distant from the central focus. As well, she had left there when she fell pregnant with Charlotte and had never gone back. So we had no real insider knowledge of what was happening. All we knew was what we read in the papers. Christopher had no time to get on the phone and relate all the background detail to us and besides we wouldn't have understood much of it anyway. By and large, big business was all a mystery to us, and we were in the dark as much as anyone else.

But that didn't stop the media. They soon worked out who we were and what our link with Christopher was. We awoke to find them camping out on our nature strip, waiting like vultures for us to appear in public and say something, anything, that would add fuel to the fire. Amanda was freaking out, nurturing a baby just seven months old while trying to avoid the pack out the front of the house and endeavouring to cope with an unmitigated family disaster at the same time. But we were savvy enough to realise one thing. We kept the Rolls-Royce well out of sight.

Suddenly my job, which had always been such an enjoyable part of my life and which had provided us with our independence, started turning sour. On film sets, some people rejoiced in the irony of Christopher being brought undone because he had tried to get into the movie business, 'their' game, the toughest of all. Whereas they had once been supportive of him and therefore of me, they now turned on me, and I copped a lot of crap, both to my face and behind my back.

The business brawl of the decade had enveloped us. We had been dragged into a living nightmare. Yet we had very little to do with it, so we could only guess at how much worse it must have been for Christopher and Pixie. Fifteen years of hard work was going down the drain before their very eyes, and they were copping beatings in the press left, right and centre as the shit continually hit the fan. They were both absolutely shattered by the experience. We felt so sorry for them.

Christopher told me that it was the worst moment in his life; how a sinking, numbing sensation, a clutching, nauseous feeling gripped his entire body when it dawned on him that one day he had been worth hundreds of millions of dollars and then the next absolutely nothing. Worse still, the shareholders had lost their money too, and he was on the way to becoming one of the most despised figures of the 1980s, the failed entrepreneur.

EIGHTEEN

A lot of things happened during that period in late 1989 when Qintex was being put to the sword. Some comical, some farcical, many deadly serious and a lot that simply left everyone, particularly Amanda and I, wondering what on earth was going on.

There were at least two high-speed car chases when Christopher was followed and hounded by the press. One was in Brisbane, where he was off to see Jim Kennedy, then chairman of the Queensland Treasury Corporation, the state's main financial authority, and one was in Sydney, when he was on his way to talk to the banks. At one stage, Christopher went into smoke and sought sanctuary from the media horde at Mirage Gold Coast.

Meanwhile, superstar golfer Greg Norman, banker Nick Whitlam and television host Derryn Hinch led a group of prominent Australians showing their backing for him by running an advertisement in the *Financial Review* under the banner 'Australians Supporting Qintex.' But payments on the company debt were either being not made or slow in coming, and the Australian Ratings System slashed the company's credit rating from B B Minus, still good for an entrepreneurial stock, to the second lowest rating of C C C.

On October 22 a meeting of the Qintex board at the Intercontinental Hotel in Sydney proved pivotal. During discussions, tempers flared over what should have been routine agreement on a payment of $79.5 million to Qintex Group Management Services, the group company that serviced all the debts. Of that amount, $13.5 million was scheduled to go to Kahmea, the Skase family company set up to run the family's interests, as many entities did in those days, looking after any payments for, payments against, office running expenses, loans, leases, financing costs, management fees and so on. This is how Christopher had run the operation for over fourteen years. He had never taken a salary; rather management fees had been paid into Kahmea. While Christopher was backed on this issue by one of Qintex's most experienced directors, ex-Qantas chairman Sir Lenox Hewitt, two other directors, lawyer Fred Davey and former Ampol chief Ted Harris, refused to okay the payment.

Instead of passing the payments and getting the interest bills paid on the borrowings such as a State Bank of NSW bridging loan that was funding the Princeville project—which would have kept the company alive and given it time to organise a rescue package—the meeting dissolved into a stand-off. As I understand it, Christopher was asked to leave the room while the directors considered creating a salary package for him rather than him being reimbursed by payments into Kahmea. When he came back into the meeting, Christopher said he did not like that idea but that he would run the company for a salary of $5 million a year. The directors suggested $1.5 million.

The meeting ended in a very unhappy mood. The $79.5 million payment to Qintex Group Management Services was not okayed, so it could not do the job it had been set up to do. That is, service the debt, which had reached a monthly interest bill of about $25 million. By not paying its debts, Qintex had slipped into default.

Harris contacted Henry Bosch, chairman of the National Companies & Securities Commission, and in early November, Bosch said on ABC radio that the Qintex situation needed to be investigated, as the method of payment of directors was 'probably unethical and probably illegal.' He said the commission believed that the 'law should be interpreted as saying that directors' remuneration should be approved by others, other than themselves.' That is, it was usual for shareholders to approve the total quantum of directors' remuneration. 'Within that total quantum, it is reasonable for the independent directors to approve the salaries of the executive directors and if that had been done, we would have no difficulty,' he said.

The Attorney-General, Lionel Bowen, said that as Christopher was the subject of an NCSC investigation, the comments 'pre-empted legal action or investigations.' Christopher pointed out on Channel 7 that Qintex Management Services and its predecessors had been operating for fourteen years, during which time 'management fees paid to that company and charged by that company had never been treated as a secret.'

'They have been disclosed to banks, they have been disclosed in Australian ratings reports, they have been disclosed in the annual reports and they have always been approved, and in the case of the year under review, they have been independently assessed,' he said.

As it turned out, exhaustive hearings concluded that what Christopher was doing via Qintex Group Management Services and Kahmea was not wrong or illegal but standard practice for those times. A financial columnist noted that the amounts alleged to have been improperly authorised to go to the management company 'would not have even paid the interest on the $1 billion that Alan Bond and his cohorts allegedly hijacked from Bell Resources.'

Christopher told me later: 'Irrespective of right and wrong, the bottom line, the truth, was that I walked out with nothing. Zero. Then Government authorities seized upon it as a phantom issue on which to hang me and my company.

'In the aftermath of the 80s, it was used skilfully to mask the real reason for the failure of the Qintex group. This had nothing to do with management fees or other payouts to any person. It was solely due to an unprecedented rise in interest rates in 1989 from 11 per cent to a net cost of 23 per cent.

'The Government screwed the entrepreneurs and waged a propaganda war to blame the entrepreneurs for failure of their economic policies.'

Now, because of the outcome of the October 22 board meeting, the proposed $400 million refinancing of the Princeville resort development in Hawaii via the Whitlam Turnbull merchant bank had been torpedoed. On October 31, Qintex failed to meet a repayment on the $85 million bridging loan from the State Bank of NSW. Four days later, the bank told Qintex it had fourteen days to pay up or it would lose the resort. Eighteen days later, work stopped on the project, and the three hundred employees on the building site were sent home.

With similar defaults on other loans, numerous meetings were held between Christopher and his financial team with bankers, merchant bankers, debtors, creditors, shareholders and government officials to try and find a solution. The crucial element was that there were thirty-two banks or financial institutions involved that had lent Qintex money, and the task was to persuade all of these to agree to a rescue strategy. These included the Commonwealth Bank, the State Bank of NSW, the State Bank of Victoria/Tricontinental, the Bank of New Zealand, Chase AMP and Hong Kong-owned Wardley Australia Ltd, among others.

Christopher pointed out that the problems were caused by four identifiable factors—the ultra-high interest rates, the drop in resort custom due to the pilots' dispute, the collapse of the MGM/UA deal destabilising the US arm of Qintex and sending it into bankruptcy, and the collapse of a planned sale of two regional Queensland television stations, one of which was SEQ-8. He was confident that it could all be turned around by a proposed rescue package, a $1.2 billion sell-off. That is, he proposed, sell off the remaining 51 per cent in the two Mirage properties, sell the two regional television stations, sell all other properties such as the Marina Mirage shopping centre, keep the cash cow of the Seven Network, restructure the debt, batten down the hatches and weather the storm.

It made sense to most people. But in the business world, the standard format of these debt restructure plans is that all the lenders have to agree to it. Every bank has to say yes. It has to be one in, all in, or it doesn't happen. Only one bank has to say no, and the whole thing collapses like a house of cards.

For example, only a year after Qintex collapsed, News Ltd was to nearly slide down the same slippery slope. In 1990, a few months after Qintex succumbed, News Ltd found itself owing $7.6 billion to a total of one hundred and forty-six lenders, and much time and effort was spent in negotiating a restructuring of the loans. If one bank had said no, the result would have been that the mighty News Ltd organization would have gone into liquidation.

One bank nearly did. The Pittsburgh National Bank stalled in rolling over a loan of $10 million, a fairly trifling amount compared to other borrowings and the size of News Ltd. It took a well-prepared phone call to the bank manager from Rupert Murdoch himself to get everything back on the rails.

A year earlier, and if only Christopher had similarly been able to get someone to listen to him. When the banks sat down after studying the proposed Qintex restructuring, thirty-one said yes. One said no.

Which bank?

The Commonwealth. The bank then owned by the Australian Government. The bank you would think would show some faith in an Australian company as the other thirty-one national and international banks did. A company that was out there doing its best at creating things, setting new standards of excellence and providing many thousands of Australian workers with jobs. Were they all wrong?

What was in the Commonwealth Bank's interests to kill off a company that was employing directly or indirectly tens of thousands of people? That had ramped Australian tourism up to a whole new level, winning every local and international award possible for its highest standards of excellence? (Christopher had just received an award from Queensland Tourism for Outstanding Achievement by an Individual.) A company that had created two world-class award-winning resorts and been attracting enormous numbers of visitors and foreign exchange into the country? That had turned the Seven Network into a profitable and successful organization, especially salvaging Channel 7 Melbourne from the trash heap? That had shown constant growth over fifteen years? That had been struck by three combined heavy economic blows but had come up with a workable plan to get back on track?

Now you see why this issue still burns within me. The Commonwealth Bank, the prime financial institution, the bank that should have been doing the right thing by its citizens, put the wooden stake right through the heart of Qintex. It gave it nothing. No funding, no interest payment breaks, no chance to renegotiate loans, nothing. Christopher always maintained that he was told later by an insider that it had taken that action because it had been instructed to shut him down.

Sure, this was the 80s, the decade of greed. This was the time when Alan Bond reportedly stripped $1.2 billion from Bell Resources and drove it into debt to the tune of $662 million. After four years in gaol, he moved to London. It was the decade in which Abe Goldberg's Lintner textile group collapsed with liabilities of over $1.5 billion. He fled to his native Poland. Then there was Bruce Judge's Ariadne group, which went bust with debts of $1.3 billion. He headed off to the south of France. Not forgetting George Herscu's Hooker Corporation, which went into liquidation with debts of nearly $1.7 billion. George dropped out of sight.

Contrary to media folklore, Christopher was prepared to stay on and fight, and fight, until it was fixed. But with the Commonwealth Bank refusing to budge, any opportunity of pulling Qintex out of the fire was lost.

On November 21, 1989, in the Supreme Court of Victoria, Mr Justice Cummins appointed John Allpass and David Crawford of KPMG Peat Marwick

Hungerford as receivers/managers of Qintex Australia Limited and twenty-eight associated companies.

Amanda and I just stared at the announcement. It was mind-boggling, unbelievable. Qintex in receivership? That can't be right! But it was true. The Christopher Skase dream had evaporated.

The crucial point here is that Christopher was the major shareholder. He owned 51 per cent of everything. So anyone who thinks that he deliberately or criminally destroyed the business is barking up the wrong tree. He'd be shooting himself in the foot if he did that, copping worse injuries than anyone else involved. It was always in his interests to keep the company going, to make it profitable, or when things went wrong, to recover things as best as possible. After all, he was doing what was best for the shareholders. And he was the major one!

He was actively guaranteeing everything the family owned, trying to shore up the business, not rape it. Even the most severe of the dubious charges laid against him were only for attempting to shore up the company, not strip it of any assets or funds. What he was accused of, at worst, was only in an attempt to get the company through this nightmare that was rapidly unfolding. He was not shipping money offshore or hiding it in trusts or depriving it of funds, he was just trying to keep the company afloat amid spiralling costs and a toxic business environment.

Here was a man who had spent sixteen hours a day, seven days a week, for fifteen years to build an incredible empire, sacrificing many things along the way so as to build a future for him and 'his girls.' He had built Qintex up from the combination of a $20,000 pot that he and Pixie had put together around a kitchen table, plus some funds from a few investors who had faith in him, plus a hell of a lot of borrowed money. Correct me if I am wrong, but with my limited financial knowledge, borrowing seems to be the only way you can get significant money if you aren't born with it or don't steal it, print it or inherit it. He took some very calculated risks, borrowed because the funding he had wasn't enough to finance what he wanted to achieve and as a result a heck of a lot of people made a lot of money, some far more than others.

No one forced shareholders to invest in Qintex. It was never touted or listed as a blue chip company. It was recognised as an entrepreneurial company with high returns and therefore high risk. But, generally speaking, analysts always liked what they saw. It tendered authorised financial reports to reputable accounting and brokerage firms every year, including Freehill Hollingdale, Pannell Kerr Forster, and McIntosh Hamson Hoare Govett. Right up to mid-1989, Qintex was given a firm recommendation by brokers, analysts, funds managers, tipsters and pundits, albeit within the constraints of being in a high-risk zone.

Look, if you lose at the casino you can't go and blame the management. Similarly, tough as it is, there are no guarantees on the stock market. You put your money down, you climb on board and you embark on the journey. A lot of people took that journey and made a lot of money out of the machine called Qintex. It wasn't what they call a paper shuffling or asset stripping company. It actually did things. It was a company creating businesses or restructuring them to realise their value. Jewellery stores, small hotels, radio stations and rural television stations to begin with, eventually trading businesses up for bigger and better ones, working its way towards world class, industry-leading resorts, putting television networks together and eventually going after MGM/UA.

Here was a simple man with a great vision. The vision of making things happen, of building things, of employing people, of expanding and taking opportunities when they came up. Some didn't like his style. And I am sure some began to fear this incorruptible young man's growing media power. I'm sure Murdoch and Packer weren't too keen on seeing this brash new young media baron disrupting their political power-base set up over generations. But for a lot of people it paid off.

In one survey, 90 per cent of the respondents thought of Christopher Skase as being worse than a child molester, a heroin dealer or an arms runner. I have seen his face published alongside photos of Adolf Hitler, General Pinochet and Attila the Hun. Yes, he could be brutal when it came to business deals, something which I was told about and which I saw first hand later in life. He was tough but fair at the negotiation table, and once he saw a target or dreamed up an idea, he was persistent at not letting it go until it became a reality.

But Hitler? Fair go. Let's put things in perspective. No one lost their lives when Qintex went down. Christopher by far lost more than anyone in the crash because 51 per cent of everything belonged to his family. He never, as was sometimes claimed, stole from the shareholders because he was the biggest shareholder. And most of the other major shareholders were colleagues and friends. The family company, Kahmea, heavily borrowed to finance its controlling interest in Qintex. He invested 99 per cent of everything back into the company to keep it buoyant and vigorous. This is not the action of a man planning to rape or strip his own company.

From what I gather, having spoken to many ex-Skase executives over the years, Qintex, like most growing entrepreneur-based companies, needed to keep acquiring good cash producing assets to fund the non-cash producing ones. This was done every year for fifteen years with solid results, and in fact, the majority of the non-cash producers were starting to generate at least some income, while others had been turned around and sold for solid profits. No one saw 1989 coming with the double killer blows of the pilots' strike and the crippling interest rates. They started to bite hard in the middle of the MGM/UA bid, and it all proved too much.

I met a lot of Christopher's employees during the many years I spent with the family, and the only criticism I ever heard of him was either about his anal-retentive, obsessive attention to detail or his fondness for bestowing dreadful nicknames on people. Sure, there was no doubt he was a control freak who had to maintain majority charge so he could navigate the direction of the company.

On the other hand, he knew everyone's names, their wives' names and their kids' names, and the job they did, and made sure they did it at the highest level they could, to the point of occasionally even dressing incognito and having a poolside hamburger at one of the resorts to check on the quality of the product and service. He was always trying to get people to look their best, be their best and give their best.

Even after all these years, I still fondly remember the 50-year-old security guard accompanying me from a court hearing one day, relating to me how he and his mum thought Christopher was 'Mr Ace' and telling me that if he could help in anyway, he would. Some people knew what was really happening. Real people.

The thing was, Christopher, a thorough gentleman and good company when not at business, was always circumspect about banks. He once told me that a bank is the sort of institution that will gladly lend you an umbrella when it is sunny and then demand it back the minute it starts to rain. That is exactly what happened to him.

Sometimes I don't think he really understood the stratospheric level of the high-stakes game he was playing. I know that sounds hard to believe but behind the tough negotiator and the energetic operator capable of spotting a deal from a mile away, he was in some ways naïve. Maybe just a little blindsided by the extent of the political power-game he had found himself playing in and far too trusting of people, not only outside the building, but those he surrounded himself with. Having established what he thought should be done, he would blithely move on, always looking forward, placing too much trust in people he perhaps should have been more wary of.

It was the hardest lesson of all to learn, and it cost him the lot.

NINETEEN

What to do next? Shocked by their sudden change of fortunes, exhausted by their efforts to save the day and constantly surrounded by a barrage of public vilification and media attacks, Christopher and Pixie decided to temporarily get out of Australia. Not to run away but simply to find some space and time to try and make sense of it all, regroup and start all over again, beginning with the battle to salvage something out of the mess.

Christopher was a smart man and knew instantly that remaining in Australia for the immediate future was suicide. He was all but broke and knew he would be unable to borrow anything locally to pay for the high-powered legal battle that he anticipated coming. But he had to try and get an income to finance it somehow. He wanted to sort out what could be done to get back at least some of what rightfully belonged to the company and therefore the shareholders. Recover, regain, rebuild was the plan. He felt that the best and only way to do that was get out of the blaze of the media spotlight.

In fact, while it is often held that Christopher and Pixie fled straight to Spain, that is not the case. At that stage, they had not even the slightest intention of going anywhere else but London, where Pixie's youngest daughter, Alexandra, was establishing herself and falling in love with a young man named Lawrence Van der Plaat. They arrived in London, set up base camp there and put a team of lawyers to work on the campaign to get the business back.

Long-term, they had no real intention of staying on in the UK; because running parallel with the fight to recover something out of the Qintex wreckage, Christopher began the search for a likely spot where he could start a new resort development. Yes, after all that had happened, he wanted to build resorts again. Why? Well, he figured that that was how he had achieved success before, so why not do it again?

He knew that the UK did not have the weather and the ambience to try something as ambitious as that, so he began examining other locations, including France, Italy and Tunisia. But after several months, he could not find the right spot in any of the places that they had either visited or had been recommended that fitted the Skase resort formula that he had devised over the years. His concept consisted of four major criteria: the location must be no more than two hours from the nearest international airport; it must have clean drinking water; it must have a guaranteed certain number of people incoming; it must have plenty of land to work with. Nor, incidentally, in any of these places was the welcoming mat put out by locals, officials or governments.

Then, Spain came up on the radar. When it was first mentioned to him, Christopher was dubious. He understood Spain to be mainly the playground of the bucket-and-spade tourists, the UK holiday package punters that had been lured by British operator Freddie Laker. An energetic, innovative go-getter like Christopher, Laker had changed the face of tourism, taking the first European charters to Mediterranean holiday destinations in the 1960s.

It was the Laker Airways concept of cheap tickets—with passengers paying for their own food while sitting in a sparse cabin—that had opened the way for what we now take for granted with airlines such as Virgin Atlantic, easyJet and JetStar. Rather than a Butlin's holiday camp, the working man could now take the family to exotic Spain or Portugal, rent a cheap seaside apartment, sit back and enjoy the sunshine. But, like Christopher, Freddie drew the wrath of the establishment, in his case, the major airlines and the government regulators or as he used to call them, 'bums and gangsters.' His airline collapsed in the 1980s.

Although he admired Laker's style, Christopher figured that bucket-and-spade Poms were not his market. They were already well serviced by Costa Brava in the north and Costa del Sol in the south and wouldn't be able to afford the five-star level of resort accommodation he had in mind. He also concluded that the upmarket tourist he would be chasing was already well catered for at places such as Marbella, one of Europe's most exclusive holiday locations.

Then the idea of the island of Mallorca came up. The suggestion came from George Hamilton, the American actor with the permanent suntan, a body of film work dating back to the 1950s and the most perfect set of teeth I have ever seen.

While he had appeared in *The Godfather III* and *Roots*, George had also starred in *Eight Heads In a Duffle Bag* and *The Happy Hooker Goes to Washington*. That's the sort of guy he is. I met him a few times and his self-deprecating sense of humour is part of an engaging personality. He's an intelligent guy, very funny, super smooth, excellent with people. When he surfaced during the negotiations for MGM/UA—all sorts of Hollywood types began hanging around when they saw a new owner at the desk—he quickly became a good friend of Pixie and Christopher. Don't worry, while he gives off the air of the layabout playboy, George is no slouch when it comes to business either. He has successfully supported his career with a chain of tanning salons, a line of skin care products and regular appearances on the chat-show circuit.

George flashed his signature smile and said, 'What about Mallorca?' The holiday isle off the eastern Spanish coast had not entered Christopher or Pixie's minds, and at first they weren't rampant with enthusiasm. But George had travelled a lot and rated it very highly. A second and confirming opinion came from Tim Stranack, a high-end property lawyer with Christopher's London legal firm, Baileys, Shaw & Gillett, which had acted for George for many years. Tim had also spotted Mallorca's commercial opportunities.

If you were looking for somewhere to take yourself away from the glare of the rest of the world and resurrect your career in a beautiful setting, you could not go past Mallorca or Majorca, as it is also known, or Maiorica in the early days. It has all the traditional attributes of the Mediterranean lifestyle: the glorious sunshine, the marvellous blue skies, the churches, the cobblestones, the vino, the restaurants. It is the largest of the four major Balearic Islands, the others being Menorca, Formentera and the party island, Ibiza. At the crossroads of the Mediterranean, it is surrounded by Spain, France, Italy, Tunisia, Algeria and Morocco. Over the centuries, it has been invaded, plundered, conquered, controlled or colonized by the Phoenicians, Greeks, Carthaginians,

Romans, Moors, Turks, Italians and various marauding pirates.

Its capital Palma is a striking city, rising up from behind an amazing cathedral, La Seu, set on the waterline. Parts of it have the broad charm of Barcelona while others, such as the old town, feature closed-in alleyways and lanes that harbour bakeries, eateries and gift shops. There are galleries, museums and retail stores, promenades and theatres. Ancient stone buildings reside side-by-side with art nouveau villas, a feature being their fabulous entrances, breathtaking doorways behind which can be seen magnificent patios.

The added beauty is that because it lies about two hundred kilometres off the Spanish coast, it doesn't have quite the same underlying tensions brought on by terrorism, separatism and the ongoing battle to retain European Community significance. Mallorca is far more relaxed. It marches to the beat of its own drum.

So, with Errol Flynn having spent a lot of time there hiding from Hollywood on his beautiful yacht Sirocco, why not time for another Aussie invasion?

'Just go and have a look,' both George and Tim urged. Christopher and Pixie did, and they fell in love with it. After staying briefly in Palma, they eventually discovered a delightful spot on the southwest tip of the island called Puerto Andraitx, also known as Puerto Andratx, or Port d'Andratx in the traditional language, Mallorquin. At that time, it was a fishing village starting to develop into a quality tourist spot.

While this was all happening, Christopher and Pixie were in constant touch with us. Charlotte, our daughter and their first grandchild, was nearing her first birthday, and they wanted to know everything about her and how she was getting on. While we had been overwhelmed with a very sad feeling for Christopher and Pixie because their years of hard work had gone down the drain and they were now being hated for it, we had to get on with our lives. When they first went to London and then settled in Spain, I continued working and Amanda mixed part-time work with looking after Charlotte. Then, and I will never forget this phone call, Christopher and Pixie rang us up one night and after the usual preamble made us an offer out of the blue. 'Throw everything in,' they said. 'Come over here and live and work with us on Mallorca!'

It came as a hell of a shock. What an idea. What a gamble. What a decision. Over the next few days, Amanda and I had a lot of discussions about the pros and cons of leaving our Sydney lives and heading to Spain. On the one hand, why should we leave? My job as a film technician was going extremely well. With Brownie's help and guidance, I was building up my own cache of equipment plus the reputation to go with it. We had developed a lovely little home out of what had once been the ultimate bachelor's crash pad. We were enjoying parenthood and the suburban lifestyle.

On the other hand ... well, Christopher and Pixie were family, they had been through a dreadful experience and needed help and support. Besides, who knew what life would be like in a totally new set-up on the other side of the world? And it would be good for them to play a more significant role in Charlotte's life. You have to appreciate that film industry life is not conducive to a long and happy marriage. At the time, the generally accepted odds of us making it to our second anniversary were about 500/1. After a lot of talk over several days, one night over a bottle of red we decided that, yes, we would give it a go for six months. They were thrilled when we rang them and told them.

We decided, however, that we would keep our house in Sydney with a tenant in place, who turned out to be one of my sisters, Jane, and that our major personal items would be put in storage. We did this in case things didn't work out and we would have something to come back to. As well, the deal I worked out with Christopher for the work contract was a good one, with all costs being covered, including relocation.

In September 1990, Amanda went across with Charlotte as the advance party to set things up. My sister Kate—Amanda's great friend and who had been Charlotte's nanny for her first year—went along to support her. In October, I finished up my film industry commitments, my last job in the game being on a very expensive Singapore Airlines commercial shoot in Germany. We were the first commercial airliner to land at Schoenefeld airport in East Berlin after the Wall came down.

I had two final weeks as a film technician, working up to twenty-four hours a day, playing hard and working harder, filming in spectacular locations such as the mind blowing Sanssouci Palace in Potsdam, the former summer retreat of Frederick the Great, as well as along the now breached Wall, with the Berlin Hells Angels as security. Lotsa fun. You would be crazy to leave it, but I did. I gave away all the equipment I had with me, said goodbye to all my mates and then boarded a two-hour flight into a totally new life. A life I could not possibly imagine.

A life in SkaseWorld, where truly there was never a dull day.

TWENTY

One of the long-held myths that needs to be busted is the belief that once he got to Spain, Christopher Skase never returned.

That is not true. For the first two years after the Qintex collapse, he made regular trips back to Australia to make court appearances, confer with bankers, talk to the Government, negotiate with financial authorities and meet with anyone else that was involved in the company and the aftermath of its failure. It has to be understood that when he left Australia the first time, no charges had been laid against him. The receivers had simply taken everything from him.

True, there were times when he sought a deferment from travelling back to Australia. This was usually on one of two grounds. First, because of his medical situation. His main problem at that stage was a painful back injury, a disk protrusion, although I believe he may also have been unwittingly suffering the first symptoms of the emphysema that was to cause him so much trouble later. And secondly, Mallorca was now the place where he was creating an income, and therefore, he could not suddenly drop everything and take off every time another charge was laid to come to a hearing on the other side of the world.

Either way, these delays were often for only a week or so, and he always advised the courts of his situation via his lawyer, Geoff Harley of the highly respected law firm Clayton Utz, in Australia. These deferments were always readily accepted by the courts, much to the dismay of the yellow press and others. Sometimes he came by himself; sometimes I came along with him. And then there were occasions when it was just me who came out to resolve a business or legal issue.

As it turned out, the medical problems then associated with his back and his lungs which, while debilitating for him and irritating to those wanting to see him, did not give any real indication of the drama and tragedy that would follow. Besides, what he witnessed each time he returned to Australia, particularly how poorly he was being treated, would have made anyone sick.

After each visit, Christopher always returned to Mallorca, which was home now for the family and the only potential source of income. There, he prepared himself as best as he could for the battle Down Under. He used to use the phrase 'war chest.' That is, garnering every extra dollar he could and putting it away to fund the legal battles and the great fight back in Australia. 'At least from here, we are in a position to take them on and re-establish ourselves,' he would say. The trouble was, the response to him flying back into Australia became increasingly more chaotic and confusing.

Try as he did, he could not stop the fire sale conducted by the receivers. The Qintex jet was sold for about $2 million, the Brisbane Bears were despatched for an undisclosed price and the two regional Queensland television stations, SEQ8 Maryborough and MVQ6 Mackay, fetched a little under their original purchase price of $71 million. The two Mirage hovercraft, which provided guest transport from the airports to the resorts, realised about $4.8 million.

Sale of the yacht Mirage III sparked a huge dispute over who actually owned it as Qintex had bought the struggling Lloyds Ships when it was building the boat. What an irony that was! He'd salvaged the company and saved jobs and now it was being flogged off by the receiver. There were accompanying stories of Lloyds employees complaining that they had lost their jobs or got no compensation, blaming Christopher, yet he had saved the place from collapsing in the first place. One even laid the blame for his wife's miscarriage at the feet of Christopher. It was the determination of the boat's value and who was the owner that set off a chain of events that were to cause Christopher as much, if not more, grief than anything else.

The Lloyd's liquidation hearing began in the Queensland Supreme Court before Judge Miller on March 19, 1990. Christopher did not appear when called as a witness, having sent a message from London that he had European flu and that he would appear when he was better. He did so on March 27.

He was later summoned to appear in the Brisbane District (Magistrates) Court on September 11, 1990, but failed to do so. This time round, a warrant for his arrest was issued. A second warrant was also issued in the Supreme Court for failing to appear at a Queensland Corporate Affairs Commission inquiry. He sent a message via solicitor Geoff Harley, outlining problems with his back and advising the court he would fly in from Mallorca on September 17. This was accepted and agreed to but not widely reported.

Christopher arrived in Brisbane on September 16 for another Lloyds hearing and the next day, September 17, was charged with another incident entirely—the assault of a *Sunday Mail* photographer, Nathan Richter. This was as a result of an incident, described as a 'violent scuffle,' that had occurred nearly a year earlier, on December 29, 1989, during a media scrum at Gold Coast Mirage. Christopher appeared in Southport Magistrate's Court on September 21, and the assault charges were laid. He was freed on bail on the basis that he would appear in court again in February, 1991.

That scheduled appearance was postponed when he could not appear due to his bad back. A medical certificate issued in Mallorca reported that the disk protrusion would require surgery. When he eventually did arrive in Australia for the assault hearing in May of 1991, there was another wild media circus, this time at the airport. Things got very badly out of hand as reporters and photographers closed in and shoved microphones and lenses in his face and shouted questions. It was an appalling performance by these so-called professionals. It appeared to me to be more than just the customary vigorous attempt to get their story. I reckon they were dying for one of us to react, and I have to say I very nearly did. It is a horrifying and threatening situation and one you can't really imagine until you are caught up in it.

A few days later, on May 27, Christopher appeared at the courthouse over the Nathan Richter assault charges. Just as the trial was looking like the farce that it was, an even more astonishing and unprecedented scenario unfolded. A team from the Australian Securities Commission turned up, bursting into the courtroom like something out of a movie, their belligerent behaviour not much better than that of the media.

The judge was shocked as they crashed through the door, marched up to Christopher and charged him with two corporate law breaches. Despite the efforts of our lawyer Shane Herbert and the protestations of the outraged judge—'How dare you enter my court like this!' he remonstrated—they arrested Christopher and dumped him in a cell for two hours. It was an experience he vowed he would never endure again. Little was he to know! He was released when Pixie's dad, Keith, who had earlier sold the family's home in Kew and had shifted with his wife to Queensland, put his new house up as surety. Bail of $100,000 was granted.

One of the two ASC charges was of 'improper use of his position as a director of Qintex' under the Queensland Companies Code, imputing that he had used his position as a director to gain advantage for himself. Well, from my perspective, it would be hard not to make a decision that doesn't benefit yourself when you are the 51 per cent owner.

On reflection I think that that shocking day in court was the moment our lawyer Shane, so outraged by what he had witnessed, swore a lifelong allegiance to Christopher. It was also a major turning point. The ASC requested that Christopher surrender his passport for thirty-six hours pending a hearing in Brisbane. A few days later, on June 13, Christopher declared himself bankrupt and handed his passport over to his appointed trustee-in-bankruptcy, Neville Pocock, of chartered accountants Bentley's.

It was alleged that Christopher had personal debts of about $172 million. That figure still comes up in any discussion about him to this day. These were personal guarantees, given by either or both Christopher and Pixie at the banks' request to lending institutions for loans to

Kahmea, the Skase family company. They were guarantees supporting Qintex. After the collapse and subsequent receivership, these were called in, and of course based on the fact that everything he owned had been tied up in Qintex and it was now gone, he couldn't make good on them. This was all in publicly available documents and everyone involved knew the facts but the public was just never told.

Neville Pocock returned Christopher's passport within twenty-four hours, which shocked some people. But Pocock pointed out to critics that Christopher had met all the conditions and undertakings and that he needed to return to Mallorca, because that was now the location of his business, his only source of income. A couple of weeks later, an attempt by major creditors, mainly the banks, to have Pocock forced out as Christopher's trustee-in-bankruptcy was beaten on a vote. But under intense external pressure from the banks, he resigned on July 24 to be replaced by two bank appointees—Max Donnelly and Des Knight of accountants Ferrier Hodgson. In September, for whatever reason, Knight quit.

The aftermath of the Qintex collapse now went down two distinct paths. Max Donnelly, as the sole trustee-in-bankruptcy, launched himself into zealous pursuance of Christopher, and the receivers set about selling off the assets, the key one being the Seven Network.

Christopher fought hard to stop them from disposing of Seven. He believed it didn't need to be sold. He pointed out that it was solvent, turning a nice profit, getting good ratings, holding the rights for money-earners such as the tennis and the VFL/AFL and looking forward to the 1992 Barcelona Olympic Games. He proposed that it be the engine-room of a new, leaner Qintex, the focal point of a scheme to battle the company's way out of receivership. Trim things back, batten down the hatches, see the tough times through, he said. Many embattled companies had done that before, and it could easily have been achieved by Qintex. The solid foundations of the Qintex assets are still there to this day.

But, sell it the receivers did. They did this by taking the five-station network and incorporating it into a separate entity, selling it for $485 million, plus penalties. According to Christopher, what was realised through this manoeuvre was a pittance, an absolute bargain basement deal, his estimation being that that was about half its market price. His figures showed that the network had an actual book value at that time of $900-plus million. The book value of one of the stations alone, ATN-7 in Sydney, was $422 million. Selling the network at that sort of figure would have enabled Qintex to pay off most of its debt, restructure the rest and keep functioning, albeit missing one of the jewels in the crown. He always said that if that sale of the network by the receivers to the banks was not illegal, then at least it was immoral.

It was all done in an astonishing amount of time, too. In March 1991, the Australian Broadcasting Tribunal had been notified by the receivers that all offers for the Seven Network had been rejected by the thirty-two banks who held security over Qintex assets. Yet in June, the receivers announced that it had been sold. And here's the ironic bit. Guess who they sold it to? The banks!

There it went, the main cash producing asset, sold for bugger-all to the banks, who held security over it. Not even for what they were owed and certainly not for what it was worth. Nice job, everyone, really looked after the shareholders there, huh! The shareholders should have been baying for blood.

This situation was made even more galling by the fact that the decision to sell it to the banks was made by the banks and receiver, the receivers having been installed in that position by the banks in the first place! And guess what the banks did with it? Fifteen months later, they on-sold the asset in a public float to which the original Qintex shareholders had no entitlement. It then emerged in the allocation of shares following the float that the controlling stake rested in the hands of News Ltd with 14.9 per cent and Telecom Australia (Telstra) with 10 per cent, who were described as 'strategic partners.'

You have to laugh, don't you? Somehow, from the time the receivers took control until fifteen months later when it was off-loaded, it had become so valued by the public that the share float was closed one week early when it was over-subscribed, with some estimates putting the value at $1 billion.

Why was Telstra, a government-owned and funded corporation responsible for the overall development of communication facilities in Australia, buying into a privately owned network? The answer is, Telstra was making its move into pay television, which would ultimately see them owning 50 per cent in Foxtel, in a joint venture with News Ltd.

Christopher also felt that the on-selling of the asset via the public float was not in the best interests of anyone, particularly the Qintex shareholders, of which he was the major one. His lawyers Shane Herbert and Tony Morris both agreed, saying that there was probably the opportunity for the shareholders to take out a case against the receivers and sue them for damages. Following the Government's changes to the rules, the advice

Christopher received was that he had to be present in Australia to launch that sort of legal action.

The sale of the Qintex properties went along the same lines, too. The two Australian Mirage Resorts were sold out at what Christopher described as a ridiculous price. Despite his protestations, Qintex's 51 per cent controlling interest was sold quickly to Nippon Shinpan for $148 million, nearly $300 million below Qintex book value. Two years earlier Christopher had sold the minority 49 per cent non-controlling interest of the three Mirage resorts, including the Princeville Mirage Hawaii, to Mitsui and Nippon Shinpan for $433 million.

The remaining 51 per cent of Princeville was sold at a huge loss to Mitsui and Nippon Shinpan, and Christopher always used to ask, 'Why?' He estimated the loss to the Qintex shareholders on that sale alone was $50 million. I was present when he repeated this often stated belief during the television interview with Derryn Hinch.

Now owning 100 per cent, Mitsui and Nippon Shinpan then on-sold 51 per cent to Japanese brewer Suntory within less than thirty days.

We could only watch from afar and in dismay as the former Qintex empire was dismantled for what Christopher considered peanuts. It was a painful experience, certainly for me but especially for Christopher, who dubbed those in command the 'vengeful receivers' and who in his eyes were ripping the company to shreds with little or no regard for the shareholders.

They did it in style, too. At one point, following Mitsui and Nippon Shinpan declaring they had a preference for an American buyer, a party of seventy flew up to stay at Mirage Port Douglas to assess it prior to sale, their all expenses paid weekend coinciding with a Super Skins golf tournament.

The Skase family owned 51 per cent of Qintex shares, so it was in their interests to get the best return for shareholders and not sell things off cheaply. Christopher was the only one fighting for the shareholders. He and Qintex objected strenuously to the sale via their lawyers, but the opposition camp—a mix of receivers and liquidators, debtors and officials, bankers and wankers, all represented by an army of gowned, be-wigged and very expensive lawyers—just started throwing more law suits at us.

I say 'us,' because while I had never worked for Qintex and I was still living in Australia when the company collapsed, I was soon drawn into the situation through the family connection and later became totally involved when I moved my family to Spain. This was my first close-up observation of the dog-eat-dog corporate and political jungle and of the combination of forces that seemed hell bent on Christopher's destruction. For a happy-go-lucky grip from the film industry, it was a very nasty eye-opener.

The time and effort we spent fighting crap legal bullshit was just unbelievable, but on our limited budget against their cashed-up war machines each time we came up with an answer or a solution or a way of doing it so that it would benefit the shareholders, we would be hit with another lawsuit. We used to ask ourselves, 'I wonder what this week's will be?'

Another distressing element of the case was how the amount of money allegedly 'stolen' from Qintex mysteriously escalated over a period of time. From what was originally described as 'no pots of gold' and 'no missing millions,' a figure of $12 million suddenly materialised, then $32 million, then $50 million. Yet the Qintex books were publicly-listed company documents. It would not have been hard to determine if there was missing money or not and draw up documents as proof.

To this day, I have never seen one documented piece of evidence suggesting that Christopher took anything like $12 million out of the country, let alone $50 or $100 million. I'm willing to bet the public and anyone else interested have never been shown anything like that either. Rightly or wrongly, we eventually got the feeling that the Government, which was funding trustee-in-bankruptcy Max Donnelly, was more than happy for Christopher to be occupying the front pages and thus distracting readers from whatever crisis it happened to be dealing with at the time.

There were other cases lodged, too, proposing that money had been incorrectly handled. But they all collapsed. Of all things, one challenge was about the honeymoon trip that Amanda and I enjoyed on our ten-day journey on Mirage III after the famous Wedding That Reduced The Groom To A Shambles. The receivers and the trustee-in-bankruptcy tried to show that the cost for this had been paid for by Qintex and was therefore not a legitimate business expense. But the whole exercise was ultimately shown to have been paid for by Christopher, privately and legitimately, and the case was thrown out of court. But how petty was that? And what did that cost the shareholders and the taxpayers? We felt so much of this saga was a complete waste of court time and taxpayer and shareholder money.

They seemed to want Christopher penniless and unable to fight, and they would have succeeded if people like Tim Stranack, Tony Morris, Shane Herbert and others had not donated their time so freely. After working for a while with Shane, Christopher likened the remarkable Queens Counsel to the famous US lawyer, F. Lee Bailey, the legal eagle who was part of the team that got O. J. Simpson off the hook. Bailey also successfully defended Dr Sam Sheppard on the charge of the murder of his wife, which formed the basis of *The Fugitive* television series, so Christopher was elevating Shane to very high status indeed. He turned out to be a genius that provided remarkable support, advice and help, fiercely representing us in court against the toughest of establishment forces. As time wore on, what he observed in the whole Skase/Qintex saga—the lies, the antagonism and the shifting of the goal posts by the legal and business establishment to suit their ends—led him to the point where he told me that it not only disgusted him as a lawyer but also made him question the entire legal system.

It had been via Gold Coast solicitor Bill Potts, later to become Queensland Law Society President, that we had come across Shane. The first time Christopher and I went to meet him, in Des Brooks' apartment on the Gold Coast, we expected to be greeted by the typical middle-aged QC in conservative suit and horn-rimmed glasses, sporting a leather brief case, with Vivaldi playing in the background. Instead we were greeted by this cool young dude with a battered school satchel containing a blank pad, a Walkman, and half a dozen cassettes including an Angels album. It was an interesting first impression.

This was prior to the hearing of the charge of Christopher allegedly assaulting *Sunday Mail* photographer Nathan Richter.

Ultimately, this case was never finalised. 'Sphincter' as we later dubbed him, was a jumped-up newspaper photographer always crawling around in the bushes, hiding behind fences and coming on to private property, trying to take photos of people under intense stress. And he just wouldn't leave when asked to do so.

The day the 'violent scuffle' happened at the Gold Coast Mirage, the receivers had been appointed just a month before, plans were being made to sell off the assets and Christopher and Pixie had just gone through the sale of Bromley, their beautiful house in Brisbane. So it was an extremely difficult, disheartening period for them. And Richter went one step too far, poking his camera everywhere and clashing with people, as everyone pushed, shoved and grappled to get their stories and photos.

Christopher never went back into court to face those charges, and it was never proven one way or another whether he did it. I can tell you now, there is no way he should ever have been charged in the first place. At no time was Christopher within three metres of him and the journalist with him.

Indeed, here is the ultimate proof that Christopher did not assault Nathan Richter.

I did …

TWENTY-ONE

A huge amount of photos were taken, footage shot and words written by an intrigued Australian media about La Noria, the old Mallorcan farm property that Christopher, Pixie, Amanda, Charlotte and I made our home in the fishing village of Puerto Andratx.

The story of how we came by it is intriguing enough in itself, beginning with the fact that we bought it from a company that was represented by a bloke that was straight out of old-school Russian royalty.

His name was Prince Zourab Tchkotoua of Georgia. Pronounced 'zoo-rab chook-a-tour,' his moniker sounds exotic and his background certainly matched it. Just plain 'Zou' to his friends and business confidantes, he was a displaced Russian aristocrat pursuing life outside communist rule in accordance with how his royal predecessors once lived. He was a claimant to the throne of Georgia, part of that post-Revolution group of royals out of favour in their own country who used their moneyed education and acumen to get into business, particularly finance and property development. Growing up in this somewhat unreal world resulted in Zou becoming best mates with Juan Carlos, the King of Spain.

Juan Carlos's grandfather King Alfonso had been sent to exile in Italy with the proclamation of the Second Spanish Republic in 1931 and while General Francisco

189

Franco proclaimed he had set up rule after the Civil War as a reinstitution of the monarchy, he sidelined the next in line, Juan Carlos' father, the Count of Barcelona. Juan Carlos then became king in 1975 two days after Franco's death.

The thing was, he was educated at the same school in Switzerland as Zou, their friendship continuing on in adulthood to the point where Juan Carlos became the godfather of Zou's son, Igor. Although based on the mainland, the Spanish monarch traditionally spends each summer at the royal residence on Mallorca, so the relationship between Juan Carlos and Zou had continued to flourish over the years. Juan Carlos had defied the long-term wishes of Franco to maintain the authoritarian regime and had led the way for a transition to democracy. With his easy-going style, he was the exact opposite to the way the brutal Franco had run the country.

I always loved the story Zou used to tell about the time that the king, an avid motor cycle enthusiast, was out riding one day without his security detail when he spotted another biker who had run out of fuel. With his full-face helmet on, Juan Carlos takes the rider to get fuel and only when he removes his helmet prior to departure does the biker realise who has just saved his arse. The Spanish loved their king, and I could see why. He was so down-to-earth.

On a professional level, Zou was on the board of trustees of the health care advocacy group, the Kovacs Foundation, and Juan Carlos was its honorary patron. Zou had set up his business headquarters in an incredibly stylish set of offices overlooking the Paseo Maritimo district, one of the most exclusive addresses in Mallorca's capital of Palma. His local links had been strengthened when he had married Marietta Salas, from one of the old established Mallorcan families, who bred beautiful Arab stallions on their magnificent property in the rural municipality of Esporles. This place was breathtaking, so much so that in more recent times Aussie celebrity chef Curtis Stone chose it for his marriage to actress Lindsay Price.

On first meeting Prince Zourab Tchkotoua of Georgia, you had to be impressed. He was physically imposing at probably six foot eight, or 203 centimetres, with rather hawkish features but softly spoken, a thorough gentleman, the epitome of good manners and education. Business-wise, he was an amazing character. His main focus was on property development and entertainment all over the island, including its only gambling house, the Gran Casino Mallorca. He had three major projects under way when we met him: one was an expansion and revamp of the casino, a second was a new resort at the beachside location of Camp de Mar, and a third was overseas, a resort at San Luis Obispo in California.

He came into the picture when Christopher was checking out Puerto Andratx, on the bay adjacent to Camp de Mar, for a property to live in that might also have a bit of potential to develop. Enter Cecelia Sandberg, an extremely well connected Danish lady working for Kühn & Partner, a major real estate agent marketing high-end properties on the island, particularly for the Germans who saw Mallorca, just a two-hour flight away from Munich, as the perfect holiday retreat. She suggested Christopher look at a property in the area.

At first, his selection of Puerto Andratx (pronounced 'p-wear-toe and-ratch') had us all puzzled. In those days, it was just a tiny little fishing village on the southwest corner of the island that only came alive in summer when the tourists turned up. For the other nine months, it was deathly quiet. The road to it from Palma was not much more than a single lane track, the forty kilometres or so trip sometimes taking hours to negotiate, winding its way through coastal villages and bucket-and-spade tourist resorts, the accommodation choice of walkers clad in brightly coloured polyester shell suits. I had only just arrived in Spain when Christopher was scouting the place, and I remember sitting with him aboard a hired boat, patrolling its waters offshore, thinking, 'Where is he going with this?'

As he peered optimistically towards the little village, I thought, 'Is this the sort of place that the king of the five-star luxury resort should be considering? For starters, where's the beach?'

Also on board the boat that sunny day were Christopher's two guests, rock impresario Glenn Wheatley and his main client, singer John Farnham. The three had developed a strong relationship over the years. Glenn and his wife Gaynor had holidayed at Port Douglas while John had performed at Expo '88, which had been exclusively covered by Channel 0, then owned by Qintex. John had also been a guest at the opening of the Mirage resorts, ultimately occupying one of the premier golf-front villas at Port Douglas.

They had come to Mallorca to see how Christopher was getting on and what, if any, opportunities were available on the island. Both were at the height of their powers at that point. John was basking in his *You're The Voice* comeback and Glenn was rebuilding his stable of talent and so I don't think they shared Christopher's enthusiasm for Puerto Andratx. After the inspection trip, they got off the boat, had dinner with us, left the island and we never saw them again.

However, and this was one of Christopher's innate skills that I was to witness many times in the years to come, he had the ability to pick potential long before anyone else. He somehow knew that Puerto Andratx was going to be the next biggest thing on Mallorca, a prophecy that was to be ultimately proven by the figures. Around that time, I began looking at getting a place for Amanda, Charlotte and me. A typical two-bedroom or three-bedroom home. The figure then was of the order of $100,000-plus, already out of our league. Would you believe, by 1997 the little village had boomed so much that those same homes were going for a million dollars plus! A ten-fold increase in seven years. He was right on the money.

Christopher, however, wanted something more substantial than a two-bedroom home. He was after a property that would house our two families, double up as a business headquarters and have development potential. A local real estate agent—called Sid, from Sydney, what a small world—felt that La Noria might be a good fit. And so in conjunction with Cecelia, Big Sid, a larger-than-life character with a heart of gold and with whom we all remained good friends until the end, introduced us to its owner, Zou. Or at least, at that stage, we understood him to be the owner.

After an inspection of the property, Christopher concluded he liked what he saw. Although rundown and in need of a lot work, it was in a great location, on a street called Carrer Cala D'Egos, about two blocks back from the waterfront and near the Puerto Andratx Yacht Club. A deal was struck. To start with, we simply rented La Noria, but crucially Christopher took a punt. Written into the rental agreement was a fixed-price option for us to purchase the property two years down the track. If we chose to go ahead and buy when the lease was up, we would be paying the 'now' price even though, presumably, it would have increased in value across those two years.

To counter the minimal rent we were paying, we also committed to undertaking improvement works on the property at a pre-arranged schedule. If at the end of the two years we did not take up the purchase option, we would not only have to leave the house but also forfeit all the improvements we had done. Depending on how things panned out over the agreed period, we could come out either very happy winners or extremely sad losers. It was a gamble but that is how Christopher did things and it certainly gave us the incentive to work hard.

Once we moved in, we set about improving the place. We dug holes and rebuilt fences, slashed the grass and tidied the grounds, fixed up the garden beds and poured barrow after barrow of manure on them. Four local builders were brought in to renovate the main house. But of course, we needed cash coming in, not only to pay for the improvements but also cover our rent and provide us with something for the two families to live on. This is where the business skills of Christopher came to the fore. He offered Zou a consultancy service to help him with the design and development of the master plans for his three projects—the Gran Casino Mallorca upgrade, the Camp de Mar resort and the San Luis Obispo project in California. No matter how badly things had ended up in Australia, one thing that could not be taken away from Christopher was the fact that he had a proven track record as a creator of world-class resorts. The award-winning Mirage projects were testament to that. The experienced Zou quickly recognised this talent and took Christopher on board, although not all his in-house team happily accepted this appointment. They had been quite successful with their own four-star format and weren't overly welcoming.

Christopher in turn brought on board two of his most trusted experts—Des Brooks, the architect that had designed the Mirage resorts in Australia, and Mac Hunter, who had been involved in the design of the golf courses. Along with ex-Qintex professionals, plus locally-sourced engineers, water consultants, finance people and so on, a very high calibre team was pulled together. On a daily basis, we worked with Zou's two personal assistants, Carmen and Catalina, who were excellent to deal with and invaluable in helping us find our way through a completely new and sometimes strange business environment.

Then came the real stroke of genius. Rather than being paid fees for the consultancy work, Christopher suggested a two-tier payment system. First, Zou would pay us only minimal expenses to keep us going. Second, he would only honour our invoiced fees for our work when each of the three projects went to the next stage and the money started coming in.

Zou agreed to this and so each week we would submit our invoices to him—from Christopher, from me, from the architects, the engineers, the water consultants and so on—for the time we had put in and work we had done. Zou would take these invoices and stash them away, thus building a stockpile of debt he owed to us. In turn, he would simply give us enough money to fund the running costs of our office or cover one-off things for which we simply didn't have the cash at the time, such as the odd airfare. Most of this we would pay initially via my trusty Gold Amex card, which was always in a state of near meltdown.

In this way, he made sure we had enough to keep going while constantly accruing debt to us. He didn't mind. Like a lot of operators, despite his involvement in big projects and his royal connections, he was not flush with cash.

This came about because there was a great respect between the two men. From the moment they met, Christopher really liked Zou, and Zou, a very straight-down-the-line guy, liked Christopher. He appreciated what we were doing and the way we were going about it and so treated Christopher and the rest of us very well. But Christopher was also a very clever, hard-headed businessman who never did anything by chance. He always had the next step brewing in the back of his mind.

So in between creating concepts for Zou's projects, we continued working on La Noria, both on sprucing up the buildings and grounds and, importantly, reconfiguring its zoning with a view to its redevelopment. When we arrived most of the property was zoned 'rústico' (farmland), with the remainder zoned 'uni familia' (single-family dwelling). With the help of local architects, we put together a petition to the Mallorcan council to rezone the whole lot into uni familia in keeping with the surrounding properties. This immediately increased its value, our first real gain in maximising the opportunity. We were still renting it, the fixed price option was yet to be taken up and yet its value had increased overnight.

Then over time I successfully petitioned the council to rezone the whole lot from 'uni familia' into 'multi familia' (multi family), which was what we needed for a major tourism redevelopment. While these rezonings involved a huge amount of paperwork and seemingly never-ending dealings with the local government, they dramatically increased the value of La Noria.

After two years, the deadline arrived for the purchase option to mature, and we either had to come up with the deposit or vacate the property and forfeit all the improvements we had done. The thing was, we literally had no money. Not a problem. Christopher came up with the next part of the grand plan he had been hatching. He said, 'Zou, for our deposit on La Noria, how about this? Don't pay us the accumulated fees you owe us for our work on your projects. Instead, write those invoiced debts off as our deposit.'

It was a masterstroke and showed his capacity to think outside the square. Starting out with practically nothing, through our hard work, thrift and skill, we were now able to put down a deposit on a million-dollar property without writing a cheque or handing over cash. And already it was worth far more than the agreed price! Not only that, we had had cheap rent for two years.

All along I had been wondering why we were carefully generating all these very detailed invoices and which I had to meticulously file and keep. Invoices from Mac Hunter, from the architects, from me, from the water consultants, from everyone involved, for the work on Zou's projects, even Larrabee.

Larrabee was our name for Lawrence Van der Plaat, the young man who had entered the scene via becoming the boyfriend of Alexandra Frew in London. Alex was the youngest of Pixie's daughters, and it was to her place in the UK where Pixie and Christopher had first gone after the Qintex crash.

Lawrence was unemployed, so Christopher decided to give him some work, first in London and then in Spain. To be fair, he was only about twenty-one, he was bright, he was well presented and he was generally a good businessman and seemed ambitious. But soon, because of the muddled way he did some things, and his almost dyslexic use of the English language in written form, we extended his name from Lawrence to Larry to Larrabee after the bumbling agent in *Get Smart*.

So there we were, all dutifully putting in the paperwork, and I could never work it out until Christopher said to me one day, 'Get all those filed invoices together and give them to Zou. That's what he owes us ... and that's our deposit on La Noria!'

That was Christopher Charles Skase at his best. Like a chess grandmaster, always half a dozen moves in front of everyone else. I am sure that this whole idea had been in the back of his mind right from the very start.

TWENTY-TWO

After that stunning turnaround, the process then began to finalise the purchase of La Noria from Zou or as it turned out, from an unknown vendor buried in a series of offshore companies.

In the build-up to all this, speculation had started to quietly grow amongst us as to who actually owned the place. Zou was the man Christopher was dealing with and initially to all intents and purposes the property seemed to belong to him. But after a while we started to think that it might actually belong to his good friend, King Juan Carlos!

A clue to this was that we had seen photos of the king pictured inside La Noria. We started to feel that the monarch might have been the owner or part owner of the property, with the title held at arm's length through offshore trusts and Zou being the front man. We never really did find out, and given our situation, it didn't seem prudent to be asking questions.

The monarch's summer residence, Marivent Palace, at Porto Pi on the western side of Palma is very private, surrounded by huge walls and extremely well-guarded. Everything is strictly controlled by the Spanish Royal Household's Guardia Civil team, and it certainly was in those days because of the then ongoing threat of terrorist attack by the Basque separatist group ETA. Before the family turned up each year, security knocked on every door of every residence in the vicinity to check out who was living there and to ensure there were no suspicious characters around. Even the section of the beach that the palace fronted onto was cut off from the public. You couldn't get into the palace without an invitation and/or an appointment and undergoing a rigorous security check at the gate. There was one occasion when an extremely well-organised ETA attempt to assassinate Juan Carlos during the highlight of the sailing season, the Copa del Rey (the King's Cup), was thwarted at the very last minute.

Yet, such was his friendship with Juan Carlos, Zou was the only person on the island who could drive up to the palace and the twelve-metre high wooden gates would immediately swing open and the guards would let him go straight in. When someone has that sort of influence, you don't ask too many questions. Besides, while the Spanish can be flamboyant and generous and funny, they can also be very abrupt when you try to dig things out. They shrug, turn away and say, 'It's none of our business and certainly none of yours.'

In many ways, however, the veil of secrecy that we never quite penetrated assisted us in getting the property. Whoever owned La Noria, it was made patently clear that they wanted a buyer who would be discreet; someone who would not discuss the sale, the price or any aspect of the deal with anyone else. A newly arrived group of Australians with no connections and who were happy not to rock the boat fitted the bill perfectly.

To protect the set-up, keep things private and avoid tax implications, it was determined Zou's people would set up a structure for the purchase—that was okay, we trusted him—and that the property would be bought by an offshore entity. So a company called Karess was set up in the Caymans, which in turn bought another company in the Caymans, which in turn bought a company registered in Ireland called Kyle, which in turn owned La Noria S.A., which owned the property.

We never actually found out who owned Kyle. It was a locked-down title, run by a legal firm in Switzerland, which was reluctant to let prying eyes see the trustees' names on it. Even though I had been appointed the administrator of Karess and of La Noria S. A. and, therefore, I was the legally appointed representative of the company that owned the property, when I had to go to Zurich to sign the documents, I didn't find out much. The appointment was at the office of a fiduciary, a word I had never heard of before in my life. In my best and only suit and with a fresh haircut, I turned up at the appointed address, a little doorway that led into a tiny room with spartan furniture and fittings. It was my first real outing in any form of representation and I felt pretty good about that but it was a very secretive and quite strange journey.

Zou's company, experienced in this sort of structuring, played a significant role in setting all this up and getting the sale organised. But as smart as Christopher was and despite knowing a lot about company structures and trusts, he never got to the bottom of who ran Kyle and who really owned the property in the first place. Was it Zou? Was it his old school chum, the King of Spain? Was it both of them? Maybe someone else entirely? We never did find out.

At the heart of this was the fact that the main shareholders in Karess, the new owner of La Noria, were Pixie's four daughters: Amanda, Kate, Felicity and Alex. After the Qintex crash, Christopher vowed that he would never hold anything in his own name ever again. He never had another bank account after he left Australia—he'd seen what doing that had done to him—so everything he did on this project was to be held in trust for the girls, while he would simply live on a wage. 'I'm doing this for the girls,' he would say constantly. 'It's all for my girls,'

Christopher now jumped to the next step in his grand plan. He used the property as collateral to borrow money to make life more liveable for us and to expand operations. The original fixed price had been AUD$1.7 million. We had it valued and then borrowed as much as we could against it. We went to the bank and took out a two-year, pre-paid interest loan of $1.9 million. At long last, we had some real money in our hands.

Pulling this together involved much paperwork all around and getting banks and valuers on side, but it was eventually done. This was the beginning of our 'blue books' system where I would gather all the paperwork for a particular project and bind it in a file with a blue cover featuring the gold-embossed logo of our company name, Los Nomadas Resorts Pty Ltd. We had decided on that name after many, many nights mulling things over and trawling through English and Spanish dictionaries and encyclopaedias in those pre-Google days. We liked the idea of 'los nomadas,' which is Spanish for 'nomads' or 'travellers.' It embodied our situation and so Des Brooks designed a logo of three horsemen to go with it. In the ensuing years, the gold embossed blue books for the many projects we were to get involved in became an integral part of our daily lives.

That was because Christopher was a genius on preparation, meticulous in his attention to detail, his object being to have everything so well-prepared that questions and discussions were kept to a minimum and the deal with any potential lender or financial investor would be done quickly. Anything that anyone would want to know, the answer would be in the blue book. They were works of art, those books, full of spread sheets, graphs, projections, legal documents, surveyors' reports, architects' plans, details on rates of return and so on. You name it, it was in there. If we were dealing with a bank, he would have virtually done the bank manager's work for him before the meeting started and he would love him for it. 'The answer is in the blue book,' Christopher would reply when asked any question about the deal. And it would be.

The bank deal on La Noria was an 80 per cent mortgage, 100 per cent debt funded. Because the interest was pre-paid out of the loan, we didn't have to worry about that and the bank always felt comfortable with us. Having the interest already paid, it didn't have to look at us again for another two years.

We got off to a flying start. By the time we had to pay the fixed price option of $1.7 million, the property was already valued at $2.2 million, so we were half a million dollars in front straight away. Property was really heating up in Mallorca about that time because, with talks of a single European currency bubbling, the Germans were finding the island paradise the perfect place to offload, or perhaps even launder, any spare deutsche marks. So it was a very good investment from the word go.

Having now got some money in our hands, we then sorted out our financial arrangements with Zou. Anything that we owed Zou, we paid him in cash. In turn, we cancelled out anything that Zou owed us. Then every two years, as real estate prices went up and the value of the property was further boosted by our improvements and rezonings, we would have it revalued and borrow more against it.

A key to the scheme was the pre-paid interest component. It was an interest-only loan so we always borrowed extra from the bank to pay the interest for the two years. For example, if it was $2.2 million that was being borrowed, we actually took $2.4 million. The extra $200,000 was placed in a separate blocked interest account and the bank drew the interest payment down from it automatically every month. So the bank was very happy. They knew the interest payments were secure and that they did not have to worry about the prospect of us defaulting.

At the end of the agreed period, we would have increased the value of the property by more than enough to cover the fact that we were going back to refinance it again. By then, in a flourishing market, the property had gone up another huge amount on what we were borrowing, and we were offering them interest up front, so why would they say no to another bite of the cherry? We would show them evidence of the work we had done and the plans of the work we were going to do. They could see it was all going along nicely and so they would arrange a new valuation and a new mortgage and it would all roll on again.

The property was always 100 per cent debt funded, and Christopher made sure everything was done for the company that owned it. La Noria was never 'his' or 'hers' or 'ours.' It initially belonged to Karess for purchase requirements but was then divided among the creditors— that is, the shareholders. Any money that came out of the loan was put back into two areas. First, keeping the company alive, which was on a pretty tight string, and second, doing more works on La Noria to further increase its value and put us in the position to borrow more down the track.

Even the agreement with Banca March, the bank that funded it, was a tribute to Christopher's negotiation skills. 'Smoke and mirrors' was one of his favourite sayings. 'If the banks think you have money, they'll lend it to you. But if they think you are broke, they won't give you a cent.'

The deal was also a credit to Zou working hand-in-hand with him. Zou had very strong connections with the bank we were negotiating with, the March family being one of the oldest Mallorcan dynasties. Zou also supported us in the negotiations because quite frankly I think he wanted to dispose of the property with a minimum of fuss and as quickly as he could. He had had it up for sale for quite a while, deals had already fallen through several times and so we felt sure he didn't want to go through the whole process of putting it on the market again. He was keen for us to get it.

Running parallel with this was the formation of Los Nomadas Resorts Pty Ltd, which had the rights to do any work on La Noria to redevelop it as a resort and of which I was appointed the administrator, a director and a shareholder. Here again, Christopher showed his talent for getting around the ticklish problem of not actually having any funds to work with. Anyone who had worked on Zou's projects to that point and had tendered invoices to him was given equity in Los Nomadas. Therefore, Mac Hunter, the architects, the financial people, the water consultants, the engineers, the girls and me, we were all given an interest in Los Nomadas, depending on our input, and therefore a percentage in any outcome of the work on La Noria. All these shareholders were given security over La Noria on the proviso that they were able to take out their equity at any time and leave.

Everyone who was involved in this scheme showed a lot of faith. They knew that they weren't going to get paid up front for the work they had done. All they knew was that they were entitled to their percentage and that in time they would eventually get their money out if things panned out okay. The amount of their investment was directly in proportion to the amount of time and work that they had put in. The more work they had done and the more invoicing they had tendered, the bigger percentage they owned in the company and, in turn, in La Noria, and therefore the more they would eventually get out of it when the work to turn it into an upmarket hotel was finished and it was sold. Just when this would happen was open to speculation.

The concept was such a success that things began to snowball, and ultimately, outside shareholders were brought in when more funds were needed for development of La Noria and other properties. A few of these investors were from Australia. Generally, these were people who wanted to be discreet and did not want to be publicly associated with Christopher, so we never discussed or mentioned names. They came in through offshore entities and had their own tax set-ups, so we could never really say who they were.

That is how, from starting with virtually nothing, we got on our feet in Mallorca. That is how Christopher got us a roof over our heads and the means for us to sustain something of a life on the island. It was a brilliant deal, an incredible coup, showing his genius at work. In a consummate example of his ability to think up a solution and massage it into reality, he had created something virtually out of nothing.

Control of La Noria had been taken up by the nomads with no money!

You gotta give the guy points for balls and brains.

TWENTY-THREE

Y ou have no doubt heard of the Three Tenors? To help us with the renovations at La Noria, we brought in the Four Builders.

The Four Builders—Enrique, Sindo, Ambrosio and Diego—worked for Porto Fornells, Zou's construction company. They were such funny guys, sort of like the Three Stooges in slow motion or O'Reilly and his gang of layabout builders in *Fawlty Towers*. They had a very Mediterranean approach to work. They would turn up when they wanted to and immediately kick off the day with a traditional 'bota bag' or skin full of wine. Then one would be despatched to get preparations under way for the focal point of the day—lunch. He would take the food over to an old wheelbarrow converted into a barbie and get the coals burning. Then they would smash through some work, have a drink and light up a smoke. This would be followed by a break for lunch amid much talk and laughter.

After that, they would get another wineskin going, they would smoke and then they would work some more. Then they would have another drink. And on and on it would go. Sometimes, rather than having a barbecue, they would go off site for lunch and not return. Their tools would still be sitting there for the rest of the day. Then they would turn up at eight o'clock the next morning as if nothing had happened. Lunch had somehow got extended, as it can so easily in Spain.

The Four Builders loved their wine but agua sucia, or dirty water, was also one of their favourites. Brandy and sambuca, I think it was, one glass enough to blow your hat off. They were long-time friends, with one of them, Diego, a bachelor and the other three married. As can happen in Spain, the married trio all had wives named Mari-Carmen. Our little daughter Charlotte got along really well with all of them, and they used to play with her and tease her in between smoking, drinking and working. She was only a toddler then, and it was the beginning of her pathway to speaking fluent Spanish.

Because my grasp of the language was rapidly becoming the best amongst all of us at that time, I did the translating, and the Four Builders and I became very good friends. Christopher would do all the yelling about how he wanted the job done, and I would translate and transform what he had said into something that would get the desired result without upsetting them too much. In between the drinking, the smoking and the laughing, they worked hard and they worked well. They did a great job.

As well as describing us as 'lazy fugitives' for staying in the same place for ten years, the media loved to play up the image that La Noria was some sort of grandiose Spanish palace. It was often written up as a multi-story castle with large palatial rooms centred on a resort-size pool and tennis court amid hectares of exotic, flourishing garden. The view that Señor Skase was living in luxury in his hideaway Spanish mansion became the order of the day and was quickly written into folklore. Fair enough, it made great headlines and good luck to them. But none of these hacks was ever inside the place to take a good look around and get an accurate picture.

A *Sydney Morning Herald* correspondent, Eric Ellis, was one of the first to turn up and try and make a name for himself. I think he claims to have 'found' Christopher on Mallorca. It was Ellis who dubbed La Noria the 'grande hacienda' and who went on about the 'five-story grand tower' and 'servant's quarters that are at least as big as a normal suburban Australian house,' plus other colourful claims. From a fractious meeting with us, plus hanging around the outskirts of the property and chatting up a local gay hairdresser, he concocted a typical report of questionable accuracy for his readers. To his credit, he did quote Des Brooks as saying, quite correctly, that La Noria was 'ramshackle.' But then added that, 'Mr Brooks obviously hasn't visited La Noria for some time.' Christ, we'd only made it just liveable! Fair enough?

This bloke had pestered us at dinner one night, fronting us at a local restaurant, demanding an interview. Christopher, quite rightly, said that he would not talk to him unless he knew who he was, who he was reporting for and where he was staying on the island. He refused, so we told him to go. We never saw him again, and I think he still dines out on his pathetic efforts.

The only media people to actually see the interior of La Noria were two from Australia—Derryn Hinch, then hosting his own television current affairs program on Channel 10, and John Laws, then on 2UE—plus two from the island, Jason Moore, editor of the local paper, the *Majorca Daily Bulletin,* and his chief reporter Humphrey Carter. Over time, Moore and Carter probably had more access to La Noria and Christopher as they were actually reporting the truth, something the Australian press seemed unable to find.

Carter helped organise the Laws meeting with Christopher twelve months before he died, but the Sydney shock jock got pilloried for his supposedly 'soft-cock' approach during the interview, in which Christopher apologized to investors for what had happened. 'I would like to say,' Christopher told Laws in July 2000 on Foxtel, 'in respect of all of the shareholders of Qintex, who lost money as a consequence of what occurred in 1989, for that I am sorry.

'I feel that as the captain of the ship I let them down. Unfortunately, there were events that occurred that we could not foresee, but notwithstanding that, this is my apology. It stands and it is without qualification.'

Hinch did a more straight up and down interview in 1993, which gave Christopher a chance to explain how he saw he was perceived.

'Within the legal fraternity, which obviously is at the cutting edge of this business, there is a general view that I have had the very rough end of the pineapple,' Christopher said.

'I think that within the business community, those people who have been involved or were involved in any form, would share a similar view.

'I think Joe Blow (the man in the street) has a very negative view. He believes that I have been successfully portrayed as a financial fraudster and that I have run away with a bucket load of money. When the fact is, my entire fortune of one hundred-plus million dollars is all still inside Qintex.

'The receivers know that, the banks know that, even the old aunties at the ASC know that.'

Hinch put it to him that some people perceived him as a cross between Gordon Gecko and Ronnie Biggs.

'Those sorts of comments hurt, for very obvious reasons,' he replied, pointing out that one, a fictional Wall Street character, and the other, a petty criminal turned Great Train Robber, 'never built anything.'

'The assault on the sincerity of my beliefs, the assault on the integrity of what was built and the way it was managed, that's what hurts,' he said. 'And it's been very difficult to withstand that hurricane.'

With so few reporters getting inside, the image of La Noria as a palace was based on observations from the outside, particularly photos shot from the roadside that always highlighted a large, four-story tower at one end of the house. The tower added bulk and height, giving an impression of size and grandeur. People concluded that the tower must have contained some sort of staircase leading to an observation deck looking out over the island. In fact, it was hollow and contained only pumping equipment, a ladder and several large bins used to store water. It was nothing but a water tower.

It had a huge tank at the top that constantly leaked and pipes leading down to one of the most complex, over-engineered and expensive desalinisation systems ever devised. It drew up bore water from a well, held it in a series of holding ponds and then ran it through a bank of membranes in a reverse osmosis process to make it useable. It was my nightmare as I was always in there fixing and adjusting it. It was brilliant when it worked but a pain in the arse when it didn't, which was most of the time. Water, of course, is a precious commodity on an island and the idea of having your own desalination plant was brilliant, but it was so costly to run and so time consuming, that at the end of the day it was cheaper and more efficient to buy local water, even though it was nowhere near the quality of the stuff we produced.

The reason for the tower becomes clear when you learn that the name of the property comes from 'noria', a device used in Spain to raise water by a series of buckets on a revolving wheel, usually for irrigation. The name also derives from the Arab 'naura.' It stemmed from the days when La Noria was a much larger, stand-alone farming property. We believe the original wells were dug by the Arabs when they controlled the island, and the story goes that there was a tunnel extending out from the base of the well to provide a rapid means of escape when the next tribe of invaders landed, as happened regularly over the centuries.

La Noria had been a significant property on Mallorca in the old days. At one point, it comprised about a third of Puerto Andratx, but over the years, successive owners had sold off chunks. By the time we got there, it had been reduced to 2.2 hectares, or about five and a half acres, and was virtually a run-down hobby farm. There were four buildings—the large main house; the smaller 'casita'; a third house providing accommodation for the 'posaderos,' the live-in domestic couple looking after the property; and the chicken shed or 'casa de pollo,' as we called it in our pidgin Spanish.

The casita had once been the main homestead. It was about four hundred years old and in many ways, in terms of efficiency, it was ahead of its time. It had walls that were a metre thick that provided excellent insulation plus a space underneath where the animals could thrive. It was self-sufficient for water with a well dug beneath the building that kept the water cool, plus a drainage system that included collecting the roof water. This system stemmed back from the days of the Moors. It was ingenious and estimated to be eight hundred years old.

The main house was decked out in typical Spanish stucco and had fairly thick walls and low doorways, giving the impression of being bigger than it actually was. The photos made it look massive but inside it was narrow and constrained with tiny rooms, most of which were only four metres by three metres. From my understanding, it had been built in the 1950s or 60s as a summer house for the then owner, a French count. It would have been cutting edge when it was constructed, but by the time we moved in, it was showing its age and was pretty much unliveable. There were three levels, plus the water tower, and while this sounds impressive, being a summer house its main features were a very large indoor/outdoor lounge area and a quite massive veranda.

The majority of the house on the ground floor was all garage, boilers and water pumps, with a servants' kitchen and three servants' bedrooms that were like little dog boxes. On the next level, it had been set up as one big lounge room with a veranda along the front, which was beautifully done, plus a relatively small master bedroom and an even smaller guest room. All this was serviced from below by an ancient dumb waiter. On the upper level, there was another large bedroom, opening on to the roof terrace. Add the water tower—made to that height because the water was pumped up to the top and then gravity fed down to the rest of the property—and that was it. It had bad plumbing, poor heating from an antiquated wood-burning boiler, no air conditioning and with its heavy walls and high windows, it was always cold, especially in winter. Overall, it was a pretty dreary place.

The much-vaunted luxury swimming pool that the media went on about? It was a converted water tank done in the 1970s. The famous tennis court? A half-court with fake grass set up for paddle tennis. The sweeping gardens?

Sure, there were a couple of nice old beds including some beautiful roses around the house, a lovely ancient cacti area and a couple of massive bougainvillea growing on the main building. But the majority of the property was fields of almond trees separated by crumbling dry-stone walls, rusting equipment left over from the halcyon days, and dusty stables that once housed long-gone horses.

In a perfect world, you would have knocked the whole lot down and started again. But we didn't have the money. Instead, as part of the deal with Zou and the banks, we did it up. We took out all the pump rooms and boilers, turned the downstairs into a lounge room and kitchen/meals area, converted the lounge room upstairs into a bedroom and fixed the other bedrooms up. We improved the interior by taking down some internal walls and expanding the living area. Even then, there was not the broad expanse of space that you would expect in a house of that size. Its narrow, L-shaped layout made it look twice as big in photographs as it actually was.

But I will gracefully admit it was better than our original accommodation when Amanda, Charlotte and I had made the big decision to move to Spain. When we first arrived on Mallorca, we moved in with Christopher and Pixie in an apartment complex called the Anchorage. With five of us in a two-bedroom flat, I was beginning to ask myself whether I had made the right decision in giving up our happy and successful life in Sydney. I had left behind what I had set up over ten years at a time when I was at the top of my field as a film technician, working on premier productions and earning excellent money. Over the years, I had become a source of industry fascination and speculation because of my connection with Christopher, both on his way up and on his way down, but people had been generally supportive of me.

Sure, I copped crap from some of the more jealous types, particularly when Qintex was flying, but when things started to unravel most people in the game would simply corner me at a party and ask what was going on and how the crash was affecting me and Amanda and then wish me the best of luck.

Even when Christopher came across the opportunity to rent La Noria, Amanda, Charlotte and I lived in the main house only for a short time along with Christopher and Pixie. I hated it. It was like staying in a holiday house full-time. That might sound idyllic, but any couple who has done that with a toddler for a long time will appreciate that it can become a very wearing existence for all concerned.

Once Christopher had locked in contracts to do the renovations, we all moved into the smaller casita and lived there while the Four Builders fixed up the main building. This was worse! The casita, the original property home, had only two bedrooms, both upstairs. Christopher and Pixie were in one, and we were in the other, all sharing the one bathroom, which comprised the rest of upstairs. The ceiling was barely two metres high.

Downstairs, what had been once a stable had been converted into a kitchen and living/meals area with a fireplace. The two families were jammed together again, and we were stuck there for months while work was being done on the main house. Amanda and I eventually reached the point where we had to get out; we could not stand living with Christopher and Pixie any more. It was unbearable for Amanda, pretty shit for me, and not much fun for Charlotte. I don't think Christopher and Pixie were all that happy about the arrangements either. As had been the situation when we were all in the main house, it was like living with your parents.

But where to go to? Amanda and I simply could not afford to go off site and rent a place, and the posaderos' house was still occupied by the live-in couple left over from the days of Zou. Then Christopher came up with the solution—the chicken shed! He said to us one day, 'Why don't we spend a bit of money doing up the casa de pollo and turn it into a place for you guys?'

It was only a little cement-block building. There wasn't much room, and as you can imagine, being a disused chicken shed, it needed a lot of cleaning up. But it was separate from the other buildings, so it meant we would not be rubbing up against each other all the time. Seeing as Christopher and I were committed to working together, it made sense to give the two families their own space. It also meant that once the main house was renovated and Christopher and Pixie moved back in there, we could set up the casita or the posaderos' house as an office to run the business.

So, in between working on the main house, and smoking and drinking and laughing, the Four Builders started to fix up the chicken shed too. God bless them, they cleaned it up, they washed it down, they rendered the walls, they configured two bedrooms and they put a tiny little extension on the front to give us a lounge room. The extra space was really appreciated because the ceilings were only about fifteen centimetres higher than we were. Then, when they took the old kitchen fittings out of the main house, rather than throw them out, they cut them down to size and installed them in the chicken shed to give us somewhere to prepare our meals and make life more bearable.

As a gift, they decided to install a special fireplace to make our new home even more comfy. It was entirely their idea and their project, painstakingly handcrafted out of fake sandstone rendering. As Enrique put it, 'The señor and the señora, they live in the big house with all the flash things, at least we can make for you the nice fireplace.' That fireplace always remained a special part of our little casa de pollo. They were fantastic, the Four Builders. They loved us, and we loved them.

So now, the Larkins family was living in a converted chicken shed. A bit of a ramshackle place, maybe, cramped and funny and filled with second-hand bits and pieces. But it was clean, it was comfortable, and above all, it was ours and was separate from the main house where Christopher and Pixie were living.

Alas, not everything that the Four Builders turned their hand to necessarily worked out for the best. The chicken shed had been built in a corner of the property close to one of the dry-stone boundary walls. The wall was about the same height as the back wall of the two-metre high shed and stood about half a metre away. By creating a false wall at either end of the shed, the guys attached it to the boundary wall. This seemed a good idea, giving the place a bit more solidity.

But when it rains in Mallorca, it often buckets down in a deluge style, like it does at places like Cape Tribulation or Tully in Queensland. One night, not long after we had moved in, the rain pounded down and Mallorca copped something like one hundred and eighty millimetres, or about seven inches, in twelve hours! We had gone to bed early and slept blissfully through this, only to wake up in the middle of the night to the sound of a waterfall in our bedroom. Amanda shouted, 'What's happening?' and as I stepped out of bed to find out what was going on, I felt my foot disappear into about twenty-five centimetres of water. The whole house had been swamped. Clothes, furniture and baby toys were floating past us.

Crashing around in the darkness and sloshing through the water, I got outside to discover the cavity between the shed and the fence was full of water. It was a huge two-metre bath, brimming to the top. The drainage system that the guys had put in had not been adequate enough, and the water was now pouring into the house through the entire length of the back wall. I raced around the yard, found a sledgehammer amongst their tools and smashed a hole in the wall to let the water out. It was like breaking a dam, the water cascading off the property and out into the street. It took us days to dry everything out and get organised again.

Another night, exactly the opposite happened. The casa de pollo caught on fire! The rats had eaten through the wiring, causing a short and starting a blaze. We were lucky to get out, but the ensuing conflagration burnt half our little house. We had to get it all cleaned up and painted yet again.

These were just some of the many traumas that were part and parcel of living at La Noria, the 'fabulous mansion' as the media used to call it. There was always something going wrong, particularly in the main house. The fucking water machine, the heating, the pumps, the electricity, shit like that failed repeatedly.

One morning, after we had been there for quite some time, Christopher and I went over to start work as usual at our office, the converted posaderos' house. We had a well-established routine. Christopher worked on the ground floor, because by then walking up the stairs was hard work for him, and I had my office on the first floor. We set about getting our day started—him downstairs making a phone call and me upstairs turning on the computer, the printer and the fax.

It was eight o'clock in the morning and a bit of a storm had been blowing overnight and through the morning but it did not seem to be of any great significance. However, when I opened the shutters, suddenly there was this incredibly loud noise, like nothing I had ever heard before in my life. A huge explosion, as if a bomb had gone off. It was immediately followed by a stunning sheet of blue light that filled the room, like a dazzling special effect out of a sci-fi movie. It was something I had never experienced before. A fraction of a second later, there followed another loud bang, absolutely deafening, which I recognized as a monster clap of thunder. The place had been directly hit by lightning.

After a few seconds, I shook my head, recovered my bearings, and realised that apart from a ringing in my ears and the shock of the noise and light, I was fine. But everything in the office had gone off. All the machines were dead; no lights were on. Nothing.

I raced downstairs to see if Christopher was okay. There he was, lying on the floor about three metres away from the chair he had been sitting in. He was dazed and confused and holding the side of his face. Still silent and befuddled, he dropped his hand away from his face to reveal a huge burn mark on his cheek in the shape of the handpiece of the phone! He had placed a phone call and then the lightning strike had hit.

I helped him get up and regain his composure and then we began to look around to see if we could get the office operating again. There was not much chance of that. The strike was so strong that it had blown all the power points out of the walls. They had been fired across the room like rockets and lay smashed into smithereens on the opposite side.

It was an amazing sight. But then we walked outside to find even more devastation. The electrical wires that connected the four buildings had all disappeared. Lengths of street-wire cable, industrial strength and the thickness of a thumb, had been liquidated into little puddles of smoking molten rubber and copper on the ground. The cables, all on telegraph poles, had been strung a hundred and fifty metres from the office up to the casita, a hundred metres across to the main house and a hundred and fifty metres down to the casa de pollo. In one almighty bang, the vast majority had melted.

Every appliance that was plugged in—anywhere on the property, not just the office—was cactus. It didn't have to be switched on, just plugged in—computers, televisions, fridges, toasters, irons, ovens, microwaves, washers, stereos. Every single appliance in each of the four buildings had been torched! Inoperable.

Pixie, Amanda and Charlotte were up at the main house and despite the shock of everything, were okay. It was the most amazing sight I have ever seen, but thank Christ, the property was fully insured, being a requirement of our rental deal, and everything was later replaced or repaired.

The truly lucky escape was that of Christopher with the burn on the side of his face. It turned out that when he had made the phone call he had been put on hold, so he had lowered the phone from his ear down to his cheek. We reckon that had he been holding the phone to his ear, the strike would have fried his brains. I can only imagine that some of you reading this now are thinking, 'Well, that would have saved us a lot of money and trouble.' Me too, sometimes.

Like I said. Never a dull day.

TWENTY-FOUR

One bright sunny morning Christopher Skase answered a knock at the door, and standing there was a smiling German couple, kitted out in hiking clothes. They were holding a white puppy.

They could only speak German and Christopher could only speak English, so the conversation took a while to get somewhere. But after some time he worked out that they had found the little stray 'bitser' in the woods nearby and wanted to either find its owner or at least get someone to take it off their hands. Christopher ultimately agreed and took the puppy from them. From that day on, she never left us. She wasn't overly bright but she turned out to be an unbelievably good watchdog and Christopher grew to love her. Her name started out as Maxine and then morphed into Max and finally Macca.

Pixie, more of a cat person, showed some initial reticence. But Macca, with her stupid grin and seal-like eyes, won her over too. So much so that after a year or so, and having seen Macca chase off a journalist or two trying to sneak onto the property, Pixie decided dogs weren't so bad after all and suggested we should get another one as company for Macca. So, as a present, Christopher went into town and bought the cutest little black and white husky you have ever seen.

Yes, a husky. On a Mediterranean island. Obviously this little pup had genetics more attuned to pulling a sled in the Antarctic but she was on Mallorca all right and we soon fell in love with her. Pixie called her Decca. She was much smarter and prettier than Macca, with an engaging personality. Such was her impact that soon two more huskies were added, Nina and Lara. Then over the next couple of years, a husky/malamute cross, Niebla, followed by another tiny husky, pure white with blue eyes, called Nieves. Beautiful dogs one and all, and Christopher showed his love for them, but secretly I am sure he treasured Macca the most.

Surprisingly, these dogs could handle the Mallorcan environment pretty well, partly because the island has a genuine four-seasons climate that includes quite cold winters. From out of nowhere, following that simple knock on the door one day by a passing hiking couple, we now found ourselves providing a happy home for Macca the stray, five huskies, a large tribe of cats and a Chow Chow puppy for Charlotte.

But we awoke one morning to find that the dogs had escaped during the night and had returned covered in blood. Later that day, we were provided with a very graphic explanation of what had happened. We opened the back gate to find six very dead breeding chickens hanging on a string. A fairly blunt warning had been given in the old Spanish way. We expected a follow-up shotgun blast into a window at any time, although it never came. But we recognised that we had now upset the locals and so began working hard at rebuilding and reinforcing both the ancient property fences and our links with the community.

The idea of fixing the fences was to keep the dogs in. The funny thing was, the media hacks hanging around the perimeter of the property thought it was being done to keep them out. It was to become a never-ending nightmare. No matter what we did or what sort of solution we devised, the dogs would still get out. They would dig tunnels under the dry-stone walls, they would rip steel mesh wire fencing apart with their teeth, they would simply barge through the wooden slats we had fitted to block holes. They would do anything to get out. Normal relationships with our neighbours eventually resumed, but we were always on tenterhooks.

There was an upside. The dogs proved handy in shielding us from the media hordes who by now were haunting La Noria in search of any morsel of scandal, particularly about Christopher's health, that they could beat up within an inch of its life and then despatch to their hungry readers and viewers back in Australia. We were becoming the original reality television family!

But with the dogs around there was certainly never any need for us to install security cameras or high-tech surveillance equipment. When intrepid reporters or cameramen spotted a pack of robust teeth-baring huskies, led by the indefatigable Macca, loping towards them on the perimeter of the property, they usually moved quickly back and kept at a distance. Apart from the generally accepted rules of people being able to maintain their privacy, I guess that is why a lot of the media coverage was done long range from outside the property over the years and why so much of it was wrong.

So life went on inside La Noria—the good, the bad, the ugly, the occasionally crazy. At one point, when our finances were struggling and the planning of our various resort projects had slowed, the ever-wandering mind of Christopher, always on the lookout for an additional income stream, decided we should go into the fresh juice business. So he had citrus trees delivered, hundreds of them, mainly to produce oranges, each about fifteen centimetres high. Weeks were spent digging holes, planting trees and installing irrigation pipes.

As I sweated away on the end of a shovel in the boiling Spanish sun, all I could think was that it was the most tortuous, ridiculous project I had ever been involved in. I used to look at him further down the row, gently patting the soil around a newly planted tree, and think, 'Orange juice? Where is that mind of his going?'

We stuck at it and we created a lovely citrus orchard and the trees grew and they looked great and they were still there when we left. But we never made one glass of juice from them in all those years. By the time they matured, we were too involved in other more serious matters.

So, you see, it was not an easy lifestyle. You never knew what was going to happen next during our fourteen-hours-a-day, Monday-to-Saturday working week. And Sunday? That was spent discussing what had happened during the previous six days. It was often very tough, and we were always operating under a lot of pressure as we battled to make a living for ourselves while combating attempts from Australia to take Christopher home and destroy our lives. But there was always something new to learn. And we did it all on a shoestring. Throughout the vast majority of this period, all we had was a pair of Apple Macs, an Apple printer, a fax/phone and a couple of mobiles, and yet on that modest set-up we not only survived but also kept the Australian Government at bay for more than ten years.

That was SkaseWorld. Never a dull day for a Skase Cadet.

TWENTY-FIVE

When we took up residence in La Noria, we briefly inherited the property's posaderos. In Spanish tradition, the posaderos—it literally means 'inn-keepers' or 'hosts'—are a live-in housekeeper and builder/handyman, generally a husband and wife team. The woman does the cooking and cleaning and the man looks after the grounds. It was a great way to keep older Spaniards employed and housed.

Carmen and Tolo, who had been the on-site posaderos for Zou when he owned the property, had been at La Noria a long, long time and knew the place inside out. When we moved in, Zou agreed to leave them with us for three months while we found someone to take their place. They were a lovely old couple, they did their job well and they spent a lot of time with Charlotte. They also helped us look for replacements, which proved more difficult than we thought it would be. We interviewed Spanish couples, we considered Filipino husbands and wives, we looked at all sorts of alternatives, but we could never really find anyone that could fit the bill. We preferred to keep Carmen and Tolo as they were gorgeous. In many ways, they wanted to stay too but they were loyal to Zou and he had other plans in mind for them. When the time came and we finally had to let them go, a young Spanish couple from the mainland, Manny and Lali, came on board.

At first, they were fabulous, and Amanda and I got along well with them. We could converse with them only at a very basic level. They helped us with our Spanish; we helped them with their English. They worked well around the place and seemed a good choice. Until we started to realise Manny had a very serious drinking problem. He would get quite violent when he got on the piss, and Lali would say, 'Help me, hide me, Manny is on the rampage again.' He would angrily stride around the property, bottle in hand, making nasty threats until the grog fully took over and he passed out. The next day I would take him aside and talk to him and calm him down a bit, and he would apologise and promise to mend his ways and we would continue on happily for a while until his next outbreak.

Then, one time when I flew back to Australia with Christopher—I think it was for the Nathan Richter assault hearing where they locked him up—we got a phone call in the middle of the night from Pixie and Amanda saying that Manny had totally lost it and that they and Charlotte and Barry, the gay interior designer, and Lali were all locked in the casita while Manny was running around outside with an axe threatening to kill everybody. It was all going haywire with people in hysterics and urgent phone calls going backwards and forwards from Mallorca to Australia.

Eventually Christopher got on to Zou, who in turn delegated one of his top lieutenants, Johnny The Fixer, to sort things out. Now, with a name like that, you would expect some serious action to follow. Sure enough, Johnny The Fixer had been Zou's main man in Algeria when he had interests there. He had handled a lot of dealings for both Zou and the king, in what must have been difficult times during and after that country's battle for independence from the French. He was an interesting little character. Very suave, very calm, very cool, like Humphrey Bogart straight out of *Casablanca*.

To resolve the problem of drunken Manny on the loose with an axe, Johnny The Fixer turned up at the back gate of La Noria with a small army from King Juan Carlos' personal security division! These guys had been chosen from the elite of the Spanish security forces with each of them having a special set of skills. They were not averse to disposing of someone quickly, silently and efficiently.

On arrival, Johnny The Fixer opened the boot of the car to reveal a display of weapons suitable enough to put down a significant revolution in a sizeable African country. While he set up operations at La Noria, I was despatched back from Australia to try and put a lid on things.

When Manny spotted the boot full of weapons, even a nut-case like him realised that the odds were now stacked in Johnny the Fixer's favour, and instead of calling the shots, he was now in deep shit. Manny disappeared, taking off in his car. The king's men gave him a bit of a fake chase right up his tail for a few kilometres just to make sure he got the message that if he was smart he would leave the island. Which, wisely, he did.

When I got back, Johnny the Fixer's guys were still floating around, and you knew from the minute you met them that they were not people to fuck with. Like SAS operatives, they never looked at you when they were talking to you; their eyes constantly moved, looking out for danger.

With her husband having shot through, poor old Lali was shipped back to wherever it was that she came from, and that was the last we ever heard from her or Manny. I discovered later that darling Barry, despatched to the casita to look after the girls as Manny ran around outside with the axe, had been more hysterical than they were.

After that disaster, we decided that we would not hire any posaderos to look after the property and that Christopher and I would do the job instead. But the pair of us taking over proved to be a bad mistake. La Noria was nowhere near its original size, but it was still a small farm with a lot of buildings to be maintained, gardens to be kept and things to be done on a daily basis. We simply couldn't do it properly while still working at getting development projects going. The worst thing that happened under our regime was that the gardens suffered badly. The beautiful roses caught a disease, some sort of mould or parasite, which wiped them out no matter how hard we tried to stop it. People tried to help us with suggestions and treatments but nothing worked and all the roses died.

We went back to looking for posaderos and finally discovered the solution under our noses. Now, I earlier mentioned the Four Builders who were working on the property—Enrique, Sindo, Ambrosio and Diego. The working, smoking, drinking guys, the four funny men, three of whom had wives called Mari-Carmen.

Once they had completed their work on the main house and the chicken shed, the property still needed to be cleaned up. The four of them would not come at that, saying it was not their responsibility and that they needed to be elsewhere. Christopher was a very tough businessman and negotiator, always pushing the deal and

230

stretching it until he got what he wanted, usually without having to pay. The stand-off ended when Enrique's wife, Mari-Carmen—one of the three Mari-Carmens—offered to do the clean-up and came in and did it. After that, she never really left. She elected to stay on, first as the gardener then as a solo posadero, even though she did not live on the property. She would come in at 7.30 every morning, work throughout the day, both in the main house and in the gardens, and each night go back to her own home in the village of Andratx, where she and Enrique had a little apartment.

Enrique was the consummate, toothless, chain-smoking, alcoholic house builder. He was well named. His surname was Casas meaning houses, and the English derivation of Enrique is Henry. So as his full name was Enrique Casas, we affectionately dubbed him Henry Houses. He continued to do some work around the property and despite his enthusiasm for the bottle, he and his fantastic wife Mari-Carmen proved indispensable.

Our relationship developed so well, the pair of them invited us to dinner one night in their tiny apartment in Andratx. They originally came from Galicia in northwest Spain, well known for its incredible seafood and a beautiful light white wine, so we hopped into several samples of that while Mari-Carmen fed us a whole series of local delicacies, a highlight being pig's ear. Christopher and I were the only ones game enough to have a go at it. I've been around a bit, and I can just about tackle anything put in front of me on a plate, but it was the most inedible dish I have ever come across. It was like eating skin-coated plastic. However, it was a wonderful, funny night out in the tiny little apartment, getting absolutely pissed on Galician wine with Amanda and

Pixie in hysterics as Christopher and I battled to eat pig's ear.

At La Noria, Mari-Carmen did a bit of everything. She cleaned the house, she did the garden, she swept and tidied up, she kept an eye out for visitors. She was a tough little thing, a tiny little mite, hard as nails. She was energetic, sharp and feisty as all get out. She took no bullshit. She and Christopher forged an incredible bond despite the fact that she didn't speak a word of English and he didn't speak a word of Spanish. That was one of the most intriguing aspects of the whole Mallorca experience. In all that time, our ten years on the island, Christopher never mastered more than a few words of Spanish, and Pixie was not much better.

We tried to help him. My Spanish wasn't too bad and it improved over the years but I couldn't get him to mimic even the most basic phrases. So we brought in a teacher called Anne Kay, but after a while, the lessons became a shambles. It was funny in one way, but the truth was it was unproductive and he was hopeless. We were wondering why he was getting nowhere, staring at his Spanish book but not catching on. Then one day I took a peek over his shoulder and discovered that he had a business document hidden inside the pages of his text book and was reading that. We gave up after that.

To get his point across or inform people of a decision or seek information or get out of a predicament, Christopher employed one of two options. He either relied on my skills as an interpreter or on the talents of Charlotte, who learnt the language as a toddler parallel with learning English, went to the local schools and still speaks it fluently.

There were some memorable moments when Christopher would be demanding in English what he wanted from Mari-Carmen and she would be telling him in Spanish that there was no way he was going to get it and neither had a clue what was going on. But it never ended in tears because Christopher had taken a liking to Mari-Carmen from the moment they first met and vice versa. They would yell at each other, yet they loved each other. She became an important part of his life over the years, all of our lives in fact, looking after the house and gardens, caring for the dogs and filling Charlotte in on Spanish customs, stories and old wives' tales.

She would walk with Christopher when he would take the dogs out, acting like a security guard. God knows, no one would approach him when Mari-Carmen was riding shotgun. The dogs might have been dangerous, but Mari-Carmen was the one you had to look out for. She was a very staunch defender of Christopher, particularly when the chips were down and was right there by his side, his faithful protector, through everything until the day he died. She would yell at Amanda, chastise me and castigate Pixie. She particularly hated how much shopping the girls did. She would scream at Pixie. 'You buy too much!' Amanda was so scared of her, she would come home from shopping and try and run down the driveway and hide the bags before Mari-Carmen could spot her.

This devoted little lady was only paid a basic wage, and even when there were times when we couldn't pay her, she would turn up anyway. When Christopher was in gaol and we simply had no cash, she would still arrive every morning saying, 'Doesn't matter, I'm not here for the money, I'm here for the family.' She was a tough little cookie and the most incredibly loyal person who was devastated when Christopher became ill and died.

If he couldn't handle a second language, Christopher wasn't very good with machines either. Like a lot of go-ahead, decision-making businessmen, he was a total technophobe and was very reliant on others when it came to running equipment. He couldn't get a video player to work. So when it came to discussing what my role would be in the business, it was agreed that initially he would be the brains of the outfit, and I would answer the phone, be the receptionist, type every document, send and receive every fax, be the mail boy and the coffee maker, take the photos and do all the banking. I drew the line at wearing a skirt, but it meant that I was au fait with everything that went on.

In the meantime, he kept on thinking about where I would be most useful in the business in the long term. That was typical of him, even at that small scale and now operating in an environment far removed from the corporate mammoth known as Qintex. With his typical Virgo anal-retentive approach, he loved to analyse everyone's strengths and weaknesses and put them in a box and label it. He would examine their skills, study them under pressure, try them out with little tests and then categorise them.

After a while, off the back of my schoolboy French, my Spanish got good enough for me to be able to understand what the locals were saying, and in turn, they even got to understand me. So I spent more and more time by his side in meetings, ultimately moving on to representing us at many of the bank and business dealings, lawyers' briefings and government discussions that he set up. I also learnt more about operating a computer and started to write and design brochures and creating all the detailed financial projections for the hotels and golf projects on Microsoft Excel, before moving on to

Quark Express to produce the blue books outlining our proposed developments. In short, I became his right-hand man, abandoning the film technician's tee-shirt with the sleeves ripped out and wearing business suits to show my status and add a bit of strength and integrity to my case.

My early days working in the weird and wonderful world of business produced results that could be best described as 'mixed.' Whenever I got a figure wrong or missed the important point of the deal or screwed something up and there were roars of laughter around the table, it made me realise just how good Christopher was at it. Under pressure he would not get excited or anxious or flustered, rather he would slow down and think a few steps ahead of everyone else, like a chess master. He once told me he could do three things better than most people—hold his breath underwater for a very long period; maintain facts, images and statements in his photographic memory; and observe absolutely everything that was going on around him, due to his high spatial awareness ability that is evident in only 1 per cent of the population. He used to add that he didn't necessarily do that well at school, even though he was in the top stream of students at Caulfield Grammar, because his mind was on other, bigger things. Whatever he achieved during his education, everyone recognised even then that he was definitely going somewhere.

As we embarked on a program of property development on Mallorca, separate companies were set up to represent the different assets as they were purchased, because each property had its own portfolio of lenders, guarantors and shareholders. In typical style and perhaps to provide some discretion for investors, Christopher named the companies after songs by his favourite singer, Roy Orbison. Names included *Blue Bayou, Beautiful*

Dreamer, My Claudette, and so on. Crazy it might sound, but that is the way he did it.

As his all-round main man, I always felt comfortable working with him. He hid nothing from me, neither from the past nor the present. As I dealt with every scrap of paper and phone call and sat in on every meeting, I knew we weren't doing anything wrong or using hot money or creating dodgy deals. I also had access to all the facts, both past and present, because when it came to our battle with Australian authorities, I was handling every document from our side, the government side and the lawyers' side. I was also the only signatory to all bank accounts, so knew every transaction and balance on a daily basis. Nothing escaped my gaze over all those years. So I can tell you, there was no funny money, no hidden accounts, no trust funds, nothing. I used to say to friends and family, when they queried me on why I had thrown my lot in with a man that was now despised in Australia, 'If you think I could possibly hang around a guy for this long who was supposedly ripping off shareholders or taking the last dollars out of the purses of little old ladies, then you don't know me very well.' That sufficed for most people who knew me. And if you knew my mother! She would have slapped me if I had. I have been accused of many things over the years but dishonesty was most certainly not one of them.

He was relentless, pushing everyone very hard, especially himself, and you just had to try and keep up. We weren't operating from palatial headquarters, either. At first, our office was the dining room table in the main house. Then we used the casita, the original house on the property for a while. Then finally, for most of the time we were there, we ran everything from the posaderos' house. Christopher had the bottom floor, because there were fewer stairs for him to negotiate with his progressing emphysema and crook back, while I had the two rooms, office and copy/fax room upstairs.

For the first couple of years there was just the two of us. Then temporary staff came and went as required. Eventually, two lovely hard-working women, Sylvie and Doreen, were employed as things got busier and the companies needed a real secretary and translator who could accurately relate what was being said or written in Spanish. Sometimes what we took as the literal translation did not tally up with what was actually being said and meant.

After a while, it quietly dawned on me that Christopher was obviously trying—albeit, I feared, to no avail—to train me up to look after 'his girls' if anything happened to him. I was going to be the Man Of The Family when he was gone. I didn't envy him his job of coaching me, but unfortunately, I was the only option at the time apart from the increasingly more suspect Larrabee. You will recall, I mentioned Larrabee was the nom de plume we gave to Lawrence Van der Plaat, the young man who had come into the family via becoming the boyfriend of Alexandra Frew when she was living in London and who Christopher employed.

I didn't consider he was ever going to move up the line and get the job of looking after the family, if only for the fact that none of us could stand the degrading and pompous way he spoke to Alex. As events turned out, he went the other way.

Nevertheless, we had some good times. At that point in time, Puerto Andratx was still a small, quiet village for nine months of the year, followed by three months of summer madness when the tourists arrived. These days, a freeway runs along the southwest coast from the capital,

Palma de Mallorca to Puerto Andratx, but up to the early 1990s, the connection was principally a rustic single/dual lane highway and at peak times, what is now a thirty-minute drive could take hours, so it was still fairly self-contained.

In typical Mediterranean style, the village moved at its own leisurely pace, a rhythm that had been developed over centuries. It had a beautiful fishing port waterfront and a harbour at which were moored astonishing craft—huge, luxurious sailing and motor yachts worth millions. Mixed in with the traditional fishing trawlers and small craft of the still functioning fishing port, they provided a breathtaking sight. Peach-coloured villas hung off the headland cliffs overlooking the sparkling blue Mediterranean. The beautiful people sat in the restaurants and watched the world go by. It was magic.

TWENTY-SIX

L ike just about any village, town or city, if you arrive from foreign shores and set up camp, you will eventually make your own way through persistence but you will never really truly become a local, no matter how long you stay and what contribution you make. This was particularly so on Mallorca. A lot of Mallorquins got to know us quite well, a lot knew us in passing, and a lot did not have the remotest idea that we existed.

To some, 'the Australians' were a somewhat exotic group, to others, just another foreign family trying to make their way. Some understood that Christopher had come to Mallorca to escape some sort of dispute with the Australian Government while others simply viewed him as just another adventurer that had arrived to make a new life, just like thousands of others over the centuries. Either way, they were mainly discreet, said very little and let us get on with our lives while we let them get on with theirs. Over the years, we tried hard to play the game, stick by the rules, adopt the local customs, keep our head down and blend in.

We soon got into the daily cycle of Spanish life. The rhythm of shopping at the local supermarket, buying our meat at the butcher, who became a great friend over the years, selecting fresh rolls at the baker, choosing fresh fruit and vegies, some of which were grown locally and a lot of which were brought in. The greatest pressure was on Amanda trying to come to grips with life in a small village on a smallish island in a foreign land while we raised our little girl.

It was a struggle in the early days, but when we discovered the Pre-Escolar school in Bendinat, things started to fall into place. I say thank God for Luis and Isabel, the ex-priest and former nun who had left the church for the love of each other and their love of children, and who had set the Pre-Escolar up. By then in their sixties, they were a warm, welcoming couple devoted to the best interests of their tiny students. Charlotte spent two happy years there, picking up Spanish, then went to Colegio Madre Alberta, a terrific Catholic school for girls run by the nuns. She was one of the very few foreigners getting a local education, but we preferred that to sending her to an English-only school. We wanted her to be part of the local community and found out later that Colegio Madre Alberta was a highly respected school where the island's young women of tomorrow were sent because of its excellent educational standards and encouraging environment. Charlotte studied there until Year 9 and then had stints at the American International School and the Baleares International School before we had to leave the island.

By going to a Spanish-speaking school at such an early age and being daily involved in conversation with Mari-Carmen, the Four Builders and other visitors to La Noria, Charlotte became remarkably fluent not only in Spanish but also the local language, Mallorquin. As tiny as she was, she was quite often used by us as a translator, and after a while, she got to the point where she used to ask, 'What language do we speak at school? And what one do we speak at home?' Or, 'What am I speaking now?'

She started dreaming in Spanish, eventually became Spanish to all intents and purposes, and the Mallorcans took to this little girl dressed in her local school uniform and speaking with them so comfortably. She became known as Shirley Temple for her mop of curls, although she could never quite fully understand why the Spanish always wanted to touch her hair. By the time she arrived back in Australia, she could speak in seven languages fluently.

Christopher and Charlotte had a very special relationship; the whole world came to a stop for him whenever Eggy, as he called her, or Eggy Thompson in the fuller version, entered the room. The name came from some mysterious character called Eddy Thompson on a television commercial. I never did quite understand it. In turn, she called him Tissy, her childlike shortening of Chrissy, from Christopher. The Great White Hope was Christopher's other nickname for Charlotte, indicating how he hoped things would pan out long term, after I, the Man Of The Family, had done my job. So Charlotte's education was always given top priority by Christopher.

Spain, of course, is a very Catholic country. They hold festivals at the drop of a hat, particularly for the Virgin Mary in varying forms, as well as celebrating Christmas, Easter and saints' days in general. Long, winding processions of priests, altar boys, nuns and the faithful slowly carry statues, photos and relics through the streets in front of adoring, reverential crowds. Christopher and Pixie loved the colour, drama and devotion of the events on Mallorca and enjoyed watching Charlotte's response, particularly to the blessing of the animals, where everyone in Andratx, Puerto Andratx and surrounding villages brought their horses, donkeys, chickens, goats and pets to the main street for the parade. They also loved the boat parade with the Virgin Mary, and even though they saw it many times, they were blown away each year by the Three Kings arriving by sea on an old fishing boat and then riding their horses through the throng of locals with the children up to the church, on a small rise behind the main thoroughfare, where they would give out presents. They would call the children up by name to hand out presents left there secretly earlier by their parents.

There were good times and bad times, happy days and sad days, barbecues in the balmy island air and the tough slog of working all day to make some money to keep it all going in a strange land while maintaining the fight back in Australia. The working day would usually climax with the Christopher Skase piece de resistance, the barbecue. The barbie was his favourite social and relaxation outlet, and he would fire it up four or five nights a week after a fourteen-hour day in the office at the bottom of the property. He loved his work, and it was always a challenge to get him out of there. As evening came on, Pixie would harass him until he would begrudgingly stagger up from the office, often between eight and ten at night. Sometimes, when he was proving particularly difficult to shift, she would resort to sending Charlotte down to drag him out, tempting him with the offer of drinks or 'dinks' as she called it.

'Tissy, come on,' she'd say. 'Come and have dinks.'

It was a very effective ploy because he could never resist Charlotte. 'Dinks' was an important daily ritual for him, and it was great to watch the bond develop between him and our little daughter as they poured out everyone's selections. Some nights 'dinks' might go on for a while, and after about the fifth call from Pixie, Christopher knew it would be time to call stumps.

So, he'd come up from the office hand-in-hand with Charlotte, and they'd make Jack Daniels Black Label and soda for him, a soft drink or juice for Charlotte and a beer or glass of red wine for me. The girls by now would have been onto their second bottle of wine, having sat around the table for ages waiting for him to come up and cook dinner because he wouldn't let anyone else do it. No one was allowed to touch anything until he arrived. Then, with his JD and soda in hand, he'd start another chapter in his search for the perfect hamburger. That was his dream, his goal, his desire to cook the best burger in the world. Everything had been taken away from him, but he was continuing this seemingly impossible mission all on his own.

Sometimes he'd throw on a piece of steak or some sausages but by and large it was hamburgers. He loved them, they were his favourite food, his culinary obsession. And when he had cooked them and plated them up and we had started to eat, he would quiz us on how good they were, asking for a ranking. 'Is it a ten?' he'd inquire. 'Eggy, Pixie, is it a ten?' I don't think we ever scored him a ten. I think had he got a ten, he would have tried for an eleven.

Occasionally someone would visit us from home, faraway Australia, which meant the hamburger judging panel could be expanded. Christopher's mum and dad, Audrey and Charles, came by and so did my mum Maureen and Amanda' sisters, along with other family and friends. These were fun visits, but very emotional as we increasingly realised that we were becoming more and more isolated from our homeland and more and more victimised and that any link or visit was to be treasured.

Two of Amanda's sisters, Kate and Felicity, came across for Christmas lunch one time, and it all started out well and good. The scene was set with a somewhat unusual centrepiece for the decorations. During her travels, Pixie had picked up an antique Chinese sedan chair, the sort of thing used to carry emperors around. She had placed Santa in the seat and done it all up, creating a most bizarre scenario. From the beginnings of good cheer, things ramped up rapidly to the point where Pixie was at one end, pissed, dribbling all over the table telling stories no one wanted to hear while Christopher was down at the other end with his party hat on and two thin grissini bread sticks stuck up his nose pretending to be a walrus. Amanda and I were stoned, everyone else was tanked and it was one of those Christmases that was a heck of a lot of fun but typically turned into a bit of a shit-fight. Those events often started off well but flared into a row because we were under so much pressure, living in a far-off land, trying to succeed but always having the thought in the back of our mind that it could end very suddenly if an extradition attempt succeeded or Christopher's health deteriorated. That year, the New Year's Eve party also went pear-shaped and nobody spoke to each other for days afterwards.

TWENTY-SEVEN

O nce a week Amanda, Charlotte and I would be invited to go out for dinner with Christopher and Pixie. We would usually go somewhere casual in the port and enjoy a bottle of wine and a meal that would cost us maybe $50, as Spanish eating out is pretty cheap. It was a luxury for us, and our first choice would be to go down to the waterfront and dine at one of Mallorca's most popular restaurants, Miramar. This was a favourite of Christopher, owned and run by the island's celebrated maître d', Juan San Juan.

Or we would have a few drinks at places like Tim's, run by an expatriate Pom and a favoured watering hole of the English ex-pats and tourists. Or my personal favourite, the fabulous Mitj y Mitj, a cool little bar on the waterfront with a fantastic view across the harbour to the headlands that form the spectacular entrance to the port. From a seat at that bar, you could take in one of the most beautiful sunsets in the world, dancing across the bay entrance and changing in angle and brilliance as the seasons changed. It also happened to be the place where all the dope smokers hung out, with full police knowledge and acceptance. As they once said to me, 'When we fix everything else, then we'll get on to the marijuana users.'

The Puerto Andratx harbour is absolutely stunning, the blue water lapping against broad thoroughfares, a

245

marina containing yachts worth millions of dollars, amid fishing jetties and busy restaurants and bars. The beauty of it all was that the strip along the waterfront and the town square was friendly and safe. If we were dining outside, we never had to worry about Eggy when she was running around and playing in the gathering twilight, even if she temporarily drifted out of sight. There was always at least one grandmother keeping an eye on all the kids. It was that kind of place.

And, yes, as many people do back home, after a long hard week hunched over the computer or sitting in on lengthy meetings, there was the occasional Thank God It's Friday piss up. One of these led to my determination to tackle pacharan, a potent Spanish firewater. Pacharan, or patxaran in Basque, is a brain-numbing, ball-slamming liqueur made by soaking sloe berries in aniseed spirit, coffee beans and vanilla pods for several months. This forms a lethal concoction with an alcohol content of at least 30 per cent and probably a lot more. Only the brave, foolish and heroic tackle pacharan, it being held very seriously in Spanish folklore that to eat the actual berries after the soaking process will cause you to go mad. But, hey, I'm crazy enough to try anything once. We were at a place called Meson Los Geranios, and it was the same night that Christopher fell backwards off his chair and then walked straight into a No Standing sign as we left.

I ended up with a hangover that was ten times, no, wait, twenty times worse, than the one I accrued after the Wedding That Reduced The Groom To A Shambles. Unfortunately, it just happened to be that all four of us were summoned next morning to attend the National Police station to confirm that our residencia papers were in order. What a long morning that was.

If mates were coming through town, we would take them to places like that, but if a potential investor needed to be wined and dined, we would wheel him off to the casino. The Gran Casino Mallorca was fabulous, spectacular, featuring one of the best show rooms in Europe. If we were bringing a client to show the place off as an example of what we could create, Zou would make sure we were given the red carpet treatment. We would be welcomed like kings and given the best seating and the best table service. That was my favourite time, going to the casino for the dinner and the show, a really flash night out. The best part was that Zou would pick up the tab.

If we wanted to impress clients with simply a drink or two, we would take them to Abaco, a bar in Palma. This place was astonishing. It was built in an old palace with huge timber doors at the entrance, and once you walked through, you were transported into an amazing world. A baroque boudoir with low-slung tables surrounded by plush, ornate couches, armchairs and cushions on which lounged Mallorca's beautiful people and high-end tourists. Around the walls hung an eclectic collection of medieval and modern artworks and sculptures, many of them with startling, provocative imagery, and from the ceiling dangled elaborate lengths of silk. There was velvet everywhere, classical music booming through the speakers, with one of the most striking symbols being a gigantic table groaning with fresh fruit and flowers, which somehow flowed seamlessly onto the floor. The impossibly high ceiling and ornate staircase only added to its appeal. The breathtaking décor summarised the taste of Sebastian, the gay guy who ran the place and his very camp staff. It was exclusive, extremely expensive and very difficult to get into, and so we usually only took our best-bet investors and financiers there.

Despite his complete lack of Spanish, Christopher had managed to impress Sebastian. I think his style and his links with Zou might have played a role in that. We would walk up, there would be a hundred people outside waiting to get in and we'd be selected and marched straight through the big front doors. With all of us in tow, Sebastian would walk over to where half a dozen people would be sitting on couches around a table having a drink and a chat, and just chuck them off. 'Move! Vamoose!' he would shout, waving his arms. 'Go.' They would get up dutifully and leave to find another spot while we would sit down, feeling quite embarrassed. We'd occupy the 'primo' spot in the house with the rest of the customers looking at us as if to say, 'Who the fuck do these guys think they are?'

In between these social moments, I was not only becoming an important part of the business but also getting very close to Christopher as we were spending just about every waking hour of every day working together. It was virtually a 24/7 job, because he was mechanically dyslexic, totally technologically inept and I was on permanent call to come over to the main house at any time night or day to get the heater to work or sort out a problem with the video player.

We reached a point where I sacrificed my credit rating so as not to have to sell anything to pay off my Amex card, which was now in default and they were chasing me for money we just didn't have. What was I thinking? I was hooked, now well and truly under his spell. But who was I to question a man who had turned a pot of $20,000 into a $3 billion company in fifteen years and whose corporate genius made me look like a small business imbecile? He might have been a hard taskmaster, as anyone who knew him will confirm with you, particularly Amanda and her sisters, but he had presentation and charisma and an ability to get anyone to do anything for him. He was a very likeable man. And even those that didn't like him, they always had great respect for him.

From the early days of working for him, I discovered there were no trust funds or secret multi-million dollar cash stashes. So, the only way we could survive was to devise a project and persuade financiers to back it. As well as presentations to local bankers, we made a lot of overtures to other institutions, particularly Japanese and German, to get money. But as the recession started to bite, especially in Europe and Japan, it became very hard to round up finance and we had to start trying to find risk money at a higher cost. Living in luxury? Awash with cash? Is that what the media told you we were up to? Huh! I can tell you, it was never easy. I was supporting my family on a basic wage, a minimum salary of about $450 to $500 a week, which had to cover everything— food, petrol, things for Charlotte, any outings and all outgoings. I'd gone from earning anything up to $3000 a week down to less than a quarter of that. So we lived a very, very basic lifestyle. There just wasn't the money to flash around or splash up.

My salary was in reality handed out as expenses. Every three to six months, depending on how Christopher felt, I had to submit a line-item budget and justify why I was getting that $500 a week and where it was going. So, there was no chance to save anything; in fact, it was made quite clear that you could not put anything away anyway. Within that framework, $1000 was built into the bare bones budget for an annual family holiday for the three of us. Christopher and Pixie were in the same boat, too.

'We all agree that we take only exactly what we need to live on,' Christopher would say. 'Your real money will come when the projects are done. Until then, every cent has to go into the projects.'

This was in keeping with one of his favourite concepts, called The Hundred, Ten, Hundred Theory. That is, you work a hundred hours a week for ten years and make a hundred million dollars. That was the big carrot of opportunity being dangled in front of us. For those who had put their hand up to play, that was the promise of the future. If you want to join the game, you must work only for what you are going to live on, and you will get your reward out at the back end.

He would tease you with things like that all the time. Another one of his more intriguing lures was a foam ball that he had on his desk. It was a strange looking thing with holes drilled through it, like a Swiss cheese Nerf ball. He used to hold it up and say, 'What does it mean?' People would come up with ideas; that it symbolised eternity, that it meant the world was full of holes, that you could go through one hole and come out the other side a better person, that the possibilities in life were endless, and so on. No one—and many, many people tried—came up with an answer that he considered correct. The trouble is, we will never know, because he died before he told anyone!

Throughout all these busy, inventive, speculative and occasionally crazy times, the real pressure was on Amanda. One of her driving forces to move to Spain was so that her mother and stepfather could play a role in Charlotte's life; that they could spend time with their grandchild and witness and be part of her development.

That was a great idea, and over the years the relationship that developed between Charlotte and Christopher especially was a delight to see. But there was a downside. For Amanda, Mallorcan life was a big, big challenge in those early days.

Here she was, on her own in a strange land with a toddler, not seeing me for twelve to fourteen hours a day up to six days a week and with little external stimulus. There were no childcare facilities, no playgrounds, no mothers' groups. It is hard enough to break into any new society and surroundings, much less when you do not speak the local language to begin with. It was made even more difficult by the strong unwritten social rules that existed on Mallorca in those days and probably still do. If you are not an islander, it's a long, hard battle to get yourself into the system even for a mainland Spaniard and doubly difficult for a non-Spanish speaking Australian.

However, Amanda and I were now totally committed. One of our original provisos that we would come to Mallorca had been that we would rent out our Sydney house and put our non-transportable goods in storage, so we had something to fall back on if we felt things were not working out and we wanted to return home. Pretty soon, though, we had adjusted that plan to help out a member of my own family. One of my sisters needed somewhere to live for a while and so I suggested to her that she rent our place for a nominal fee and I would make up the shortfall. After a while, though, as things were getting tougher in Spain, Christopher made it clear that we were all in this odyssey together and that every available dollar was essential if we were going to survive.

Survival? Money? Much has been said about two Rolls-Royces, a BMW, antiques, silverware, furniture and jewellery, among other things, being shipped out of Australia when Qintex collapsed. Sounds exotic, but in fact the two Rollers were still on leases and all endeavours to sell them in Australia had failed because of the downturn in the economy at the time. There was more chance of them being sold in the stronger UK market, so they were shipped over there, sold, the leases were paid out and that was that. As mentioned earlier, the BMW was Pixie's old car, which was not worth selling and which had been given to Alex for her seventeenth birthday many years before, one of the few times any of the girls got a significant gift. Most of the furniture and belongings were Pixie's from her previous life's journey including two marriages, and as such were not subject to the bankruptcy rulings. Besides, don't think that if by chance any of that stuff did end up back in Australia that the shareholders would have seen any of it. It would have been sold and whacked into the receiver's coffers in a blink of an eye.

Bromley, the beautiful Brisbane house, had been sold, as had Christopher and Pixie's personal apartments within the Port Douglas and Gold Coast resorts, with all the proceeds going to creditors. Not one cent went to Christopher.

I also appreciate that there were numerous stories going around about huge amounts of cash being transferred to Barclay's accounts and money supposedly being transferred to an account in the name of Keith Dixon, Pixie's father. This was an amount that was frequently referred to in the Chase for Skase. The truth about Keith was that earlier in the piece, when Qintex was thriving, Christopher had gifted him and Nancy one million dollars. Handed over long before Qintex got into trouble—around about the time Christopher and Pixie moved from Melbourne to Queensland—it was a family gesture, a way of saying thanks to Pixie's parents for what they had done over the years and ensuring that they would not have to worry about finances in their retirement. As a measure of his commitment to the family, when things went wrong, Keith offered the money, or as much of it as he could, back to Christopher.

That money was the only substantial pot Christopher had to work with on Mallorca. He used that plus support from private investors to try and get his first resort project up and going. Any remaining cash quickly drained away on legal fees, the cost of flying backwards and forwards to Australia plus court and other tribunal expenses. You have to remember, this was three years before he was charged.

Far from being awash with cash and living the high life, we were hunkered down, getting by on what we could afford.

TWENTY-EIGHT

Tiny island that it is, Mallorca has some clearly defined areas. With an eye on the strong English pound, Mallorcan locals and foreign investors have, over the years, turned parts of it into a British home away from home. Magalluf, southwest of Palma, is unbridled Pommy Land. Its watering holes include the Benny Hill Bar, The Pub Britannia and the Titanic Café, where the special is egg, bacon, liver and chips. English lads with tattoos and shaved heads strut along the waterfront in shorts and flip-flops, the big belly floating free so it will bake itself into a red ball in the hot Spanish sun.

There has also been a huge influx of German tourists, who are less bucket-and-spade types and have more cash to spend. In the early days the Germans looked down their noses on Mallorca as a holiday destination. They dismissed it as 'putzfrau insel,' meaning 'the cleaning lady's island.' But once celebrities such as Claudia Schiffer and Boris Becker bought properties there and a huge cover story article in *National Geographic* exposed its charms, the whole image changed, and the top-end German tourists flooded in. They tend to amass around places like C'an Pastilla and Arenal in the southeast of the island to enjoy bush walking, bicycle riding and sailing boats.

Then there is Mallorca proper—Palma, the historic capital of 400,000 people with one of the most breathtaking cathedrals you have ever seen; Manacor, a gritty industrial city in the east and the home of Rafael Nadal; Inca, a leather goods city in the centre; and dozens of other towns and villages with residents going about their daily lives, knocking out a living, making products, growing food, running vineyards.

There is also the 'other' Mallorca, the version that appealed to Christopher and Pixie. The more sophisticated Mallorca—the glorious west and north, where people such as business tycoon Richard Branson invested in magnificent properties. The trip along the west coast, winding around green mountains sloping down to the sparkling Mediterranean, is without doubt one of the most spectacular drives in the world. The breathtaking scenery, villages and fabulous old estates have to be seen to be believed.

This Mallorca includes the harbour at Portals Nous, the mooring site of a Monte Carlo-like flotilla of luxury boats. Magnificent cruisers, some of them forty metres long, with staterooms, spas and permanent crews that spend their days polishing the chrome, hardwood and glass until it gleams in the Spanish sun. Meanwhile, their owners sip coffee amongst the other beautiful people at upmarket Wellies restaurant opposite the pier, having arrived in the Ferrari or the Porsche.

Once he saw all this, Christopher realised that Mallorca was not the sole province of the classic English holidaymaker. He figured he could make a go of something on the island, recreating his up-market Mirage success in Australia. So, after they had been there for about ten months and we were about to come across from

Australia and join them, he plunged into the first development proposal, called Raixa.

The concept was superb as Raixa was one of Mallorca's best-known estates. Originally a Moor farming property called Arixa, it was situated in the municipality of Bunyola, north of Palma and at the foot of the Sierra de Tramuntana. A huge castle had been built on the property in the early 1800s by the then Count of Montenegro, who developed a fabulous private artwork collection and was renowned for hosting social events for kings and merchants. His son, a cardinal, had added a library and developed gardens that were acknowledged throughout the Mediterranean for their beauty.

It was about five hundred hectares, and although the gardens had deteriorated, it was still impressive with vast tracts of almond trees, olive trees, exotic plants, mills and dry-stone fencing. The main palace was at one end with a valley running down the middle leading to a smaller palace, Raixetta, at the other. Although it had been let go, it was still good enough for Agatha Christie's *Evil Under The Sun* starring Peter Ustinov, a great fan of Mallorca, to be filmed there.

Ownership had eventually been secured by a family that had grown so big that the head of the clan wanted to get out. Christopher became interested via a local real estate agent, Jesus Martinez Ortega, and through him began the process of meeting all the right people, principally the Bunyola Municipality, the Spanish Tourist Council and the Mallorcan Government.

Christopher's concept was to build a unique golf course winding naturally through the valley. Play the front nine out to the baby palace and then play the back nine on the return to the main palace. The hacienda was to be redeveloped and expanded in sympathy with its historic design, becoming the focal point of a resort featuring dozens of Mallorcan style villas set into the hillsides. These would be made out of natural stone and overlook the golf course studded with almond and olive trees. A pool, tennis courts and other amenities would round the resort out. It was a great concept.

He sought a partnership with the Bendinat Beach Club, a local development that had been quite luxurious in its day but in recent years had been neglected and was quite rundown, bringing in trusted friend Des Brooks as the architect, along with local engineers and other advisors, to devise a master plan.

Christopher was so optimistic about success at Raixa that he made the bravest move of all. He put down a deposit on the property of $500,000. Non-refundable!

How's that for balls? It was the last of the money he had, too. Some of it came from private investors, but most of it was from cash that Keith had given back from his original million-dollar gift. It was a huge gamble, particularly as we knew that if anything went wrong we would never see the half a million bucks again.

We didn't.

Things had gone really well with the planning, and we were about to start on the actual work when disaster struck. The Mallorcan Government, which controlled all building and development on the four Balearic Islands, suddenly—under pressure from a growing greens lobby—rezoned most of the property. Overnight, they turned 60 per cent of it into a national park.

We were stunned. Shocked. Confused. For a while we thought they were just trying us on. That they were giving these newly-arrived Aussies a bit of a scare just to let them know who was boss and having done that would give way. We set about trying to salvage the project and fought very hard. The estate agent set up meeting after meeting with municipal representatives, government officials and the tourism authority, where we had developed an excellent relationship with its legal officer, Antonio Tarrago.

We had made some very good headway at these meetings and felt Antonio had just about got us across the line when, would you believe, he suddenly died.

That finished that. Christopher requested a delay of a week or two, but with Antonio no longer there to provide a sensible, persuasive link, the government hardened its attitude again and simply wouldn't listen. Our appeal was dismissed, and the project never went any further. We never did see that half a million again, and the kitty was now empty.

We walked right into that one! Did they see us coming and set us up? To this day, I do not know whether they were necessarily against us and did it deliberately or, more than likely, we were simply the victims of bad luck, bad timing and a very lazy bureaucracy. Either way, we lost everything on that project, which was a pity because it would have been one of the most spectacular resorts ever built, and we would have made a motza out of it.

The situation was made worse by the fact that at that time court hearings were being held in Australia, some of which Christopher was able to go back to and some of which he couldn't. As well, the Bankruptcy Act was being changed, with clauses being introduced that were widely referred to as the Skase Amendments, making things even tougher for us.

When Raixa went belly-up, Christopher decided that instead of turning La Noria into a family compound he would now redevelop it into an upmarket hotel with fifty rooms and a hundred and fifty bungalows and sell it. On hearing this, Amanda and I were sorely tempted to call it quits and return to our home in Sydney. Instead, he convinced us to do the exact opposite—sell up everything we owned in Australia and throw our lot totally in with him! He said that we simply had to do it as we could now no longer afford to keep both operations running on different sides of the planet and we needed the cash to keep things going on Mallorca. It was a huge thing to ask of us. The Frenchs Forest property was initially my place and then our home as a married couple, and we had worked so hard to turn it into something pretty special. It had nothing to do with Christopher or Pixie. But by this stage, I was very much in awe of Christopher's brilliance.

Amanda and I privately discussed the situation and agreed that rather than us going back home, he was right in saying that we had to be united as a family and be confident that it would all work out in the end. We determined once and for all that we were going to stay on the island. After sorting the situation out with my sister Jane, who was living in our house at a modest rent, we put it on the market.

We sold it at the worst possible time. It was in the middle of the real estate price slump of the 1990s, and we lost badly on it. At least we were able to pay off most of our debts, including some of our credit cards, but the residue was pumped back into the system that was keeping us all going in Spain.

Far out, what had we done? It was now Mallorca or bust! We had burnt our bridges entirely, including ending my working relationship with Brownie, my best man and great mate, mentor and partner in the film game. This hurt me because I knew it would really affect him as he would have to move his trucks and equipment from the property and find a new base. Unfortunately, this caused our relationship to be irreparably damaged. Only in recent times have we been in touch again.

Quite frankly, I think this is where I started to lose a real perspective on the whole thing. Christopher was such an impressive, persuasive, overpowering personality; he could get people to do things like that. But I didn't begrudge him for it. It had to be done.

A second big decision was that as a group we agreed we would have to abandon our plans of rebuilding La Noria as a family compound and instead go ahead with Christopher's proposal to redevelop it as a resort and sell it off. It was now our only tangible asset and our only way of making any money. And so we began to concentrate on La Noria and our working relationship with Zou. The more I met him, the more I appreciated what a thorough gentleman he was. He was in some ways like Robert Holmes a Court—a very private man, very quiet and polite, who had acquired a similar mutual respect for Christopher.

He was also a kind man and always good to us all with a graciousness and patience that came from being educated in the old ways and moving in very elevated circles. He had a sense of style and class that you could not buy and which came only from being born into it. We regularly discussed business ventures and other financial dealings with him, and I am sure he always believed in the viability of a Christopher Skase comeback. I am sure also that given his relationship with the Spanish royal family he had Christopher's background checked out thoroughly.

So much so that after some presentations and site visits to his various properties, Zou employed us to rework his project at Camp de Mar, the seaside village only about a five-minute drive from Puerto Andratx. It was a large property and he had had some earlier designs done but you could see that they didn't do the site justice. They were only three star, and so Christopher offered to put something together to show him what could be done with it.

Christopher, Des Brooks and Mac Hunter quickly prepared and presented what turned out to be a brilliant concept, a fully integrated five-star resort project based on a Port Douglas style development, but with a strong Latin architectural influence. After careful consideration, Zou contracted us to do the work. We formed a company to invoice our management fees for architectural, engineering, analysis and golf course design services and started marketing it in the financial sector. Naturally enough, Des Brooks was brought in to do the architecture and Mac Hunter to do the golf courses.

Mac was one of those types that was ahead of his time. Then about sixty-five, he would create a course by first walking around the site again and again until he knew every rock, tree and natural feature. Only then would he set about the design, linking and preserving where possible all the natural elements. He was a genius with an impeccable pedigree in the business, his grandfather being one of the famous figures of golf in Scotland, rumoured to have been a significant contributor to the architecture of the famous St Andrews course. Spending time with Mac was always fun. He had a great sense of humour and a brilliant mind. He had turned up in Hollywood when he was young, playing golf with entertainers like Bob Hope and stars like Vic Morrow, teaching the reclusive Howard Hughes how to play the game and becoming head pro at the exclusive Los Angeles Golf Course for many years. He had an amazing respect for Christopher with whom he had worked on the Mirage golf courses in Australia and Hawaii.

Zou also owned a very large piece of property in California in San Luis Obispo, about halfway between Los Angeles and San Francisco. They bred Arab stallions on it, but he wanted us to also turn this into a five-star golf resort. It was going to be big time with two courses the focal point of a fully integrated luxury resort with all the bells and whistles. Over a period of about two years we put together a project for him using local people where possible. We were confident that it would be a classic.

As well, he had options to build an accommodation project on his casino property. Our aim was to try to revamp it, possibly even for an on-sell, by creating a top-quality hotel and bungalow project. The work on all three projects—Camp de Mar, San Luis Obispo and Gran Casino Mallorca—was hard but great fun and a good source of income, stashed away as debt to fund our purchase of La Noria. But we knew that we also had to try and get a project of our own off the ground pretty quickly, or we wouldn't last long once we had finished our work on the Zou projects.

The trouble was, while these projects looked great on paper and Zou was thrilled with Christopher's brilliant ideas and the professional designs by Des and Mac, it was a challenge to find a hotel partner to bring them to fruition. That had been Christopher's key to success at Port Douglas and the Gold Coast, getting an established chain to supply the hotel management aspect. It's best to do what you do well—design and build the project—and then get someone else who knows about hotels to take it over. In Queensland it was the Sheraton, an appointment that had developed out of a business relationship and friendship that had grown between Christopher and Kevin Carton, the Senior Vice President and Director of Operations of the Sheraton Hotels for the Pacific Region. Christopher was impressed with Kevin's professionalism and personal approach, and in turn, Kevin could see Christopher had the vision and energy to make something great. Out of this mutual respect, Sheraton had been the perfect choice for management of the Mirage projects on the Gold Coast and Port Douglas and at Princeville.

As for the Mallorca concept, all the major hotel players—some of the most respected names in the world including Hyatt, Hilton and the German group Kempinski—initially expressed interest in Zou's projects. But at that time, economies all over the world were in varying states of crashing or already crashed, and they all felt that it was not the right moment to expand.

There was a moment when two resort hotshots, Dallas Dempster and Lim Goh Tong, agreed to meet us at the casino for dinner to discuss the projects. Dempster was a Western Australian entrepreneur who had gone into partnership with Lim, a prominent Chinese Malaysian businessman, to establish the Burswood Casino in Perth. Lim had made his name with the famous Genting Highlands Resort & Casino and at one stage was Malaysia's richest man. We knew him only as Mad George from Malaysia. Unfortunately, we got delayed on our way to the meeting and during the hour we were late in arriving for dinner, Mad George lost $40,000 at Zou's tables. Not a good start to proceedings, and so we didn't get too far with them either.

We had worked so hard, created a great team and put together an amazing series of projects for Zou, but unfortunately, the economic recession at the time, in-house Spanish resentment of foreigners and concerns about Christopher's track record combined to undermine our marketing. By now we had drawn the attention of the Australian press, who had discovered where we were and a little of what we were doing and were making consistent attacks on Christopher. While many locals did not get to hear of these reports or ignored them as hot air, they were enough to cause some damage, and this all added up to no funds coming in.

We were in a no-win situation. Any time we took a couple of steps forward, it gave the press the opportunity to belabour the image of the 'stolen money, tycoon on the run' scenario. Every time we got close to financing a deal, the media would be conveniently informed, and we would get hammered in the headlines. A meeting with a potential financier that had been a certainty the previous week would be suddenly called off without explanation. I was actually shown by one banking executive an internal memo from his headquarters stating that anyone involved with Christopher Skase was to be denied access to finance. That was an amazing state of affairs, and you just wonder who had the power and contacts to be able to orchestrate such a blanket embargo on working with us. It would have to be someone very high up the ladder. It was very depressing stuff for the pair of us, but we didn't let on to the rest of the family what was happening.

Christopher and I had made a conscious decision not to tell Pixie and Amanda too much about the projects, the people involved or the financial arrangements. There was a good reason for this. We did it so that they could both legitimately and innocently go back home to Australia at anytime they wanted without compromising themselves or our businesses or our investors or the people who had been good to us. They would be able to say that they quite honestly did not know what was going on.

Our concentration on the job at hand was occasionally broken by some extraordinary visitors. Our gloomy spirits were lifted one time when Christopher's friend George Hamilton turned up at La Noria to see how we were going, accompanied by a blonde with the biggest collagen pumped-up lips you have ever seen. She was a stunner. Her name was Christine Forsyth-Peters, and in those days, she worked in the movie business in story development and has since gone on to her own very successful career as a producer with films such as *How To Lose A Guy In 10 Days.* She had briefly been married to Hollywood heavyweight Jon Peters, the hairdresser turned producer who had made films such as *A Star Is Born* with Barbra Streisand and one of my all-time favourites, *Caddy Shack* with Bill Murray.

Zou also constantly astonished us with the sorts of people he knew. One was a Thai prince, an extremely nice man, polite, intelligent, inquisitive and greatly interested in what we were doing. He went very close to investing in us but eventually bought into a development group on mainland Spain. It was the prince who once told me how to enjoy my golf more, after I had cannoned yet another drive into the trees and began fuming. 'Tony, listen to me,' he said. 'Golf is like sex. Don't worry about how good you are at it, just enjoy it …' Sage advice, and I used to walk away from situations like that thinking, 'How has this happened? Me, an anonymous film technician from the backblocks of Frenchs Forest on first name terms with a prince from Thailand?'

Another of Zou's mates was arms dealer and businessman Adnan Khashoggi, who arrived on Mallorca in his customised DC-8 jet with his beautiful new wife

Shahpari and a brace of bodyguards toting Uzi submachine guns. What a sight that was. It created quite a scene at the airport, but typically Zou and Johnny the Fixer somehow resolved the situation with a few quick phone calls. You didn't know whether to admire Khashoggi for creating such an immense fortune—he was the richest man in the world at that point—or despise him for helping foster so much human tragedy. The wise thing was just to remain neutral and show no emotion or unnecessary rapid physical movement in case one of his bodyguards stuck the barrel of his Uzi up your left nostril. Khashoggi was a thorough gentleman, and we had a very pleasant day touring Zou's projects. Unfortunately, nothing ever came of it.

Ironically, this was around the time when the first Gulf War was launched with the Americans attacking Iraq after it had invaded Kuwait. New Zealand-born journalist Peter Arnett of CNN, a veteran of the Vietnam war coverage, was reporting every night live from Baghdad, much to the anger and dismay of President George Bush Snr. As the images flashed across the screen, Christopher, having a few Jack Daniels and watching Arnett and another CNN reporter, Charles Jaco, present their coverage, would give his own authoritative views on what was happening.

For me, having my wife and little daughter there, it was all a bit too close for comfort. The Americans were using Spain as a base and refuelling their B-52s over Mallorca every night in preparation for their bombing runs on Baghdad. Nothing like that ever happened in our little humble abode in Frenchs Forest. But then again, that was now all gone forever.

TWENTY-NINE

A bit of history for you. Mallorca is still shaped by two significant events. First, in 1229, James the Conqueror, a young Catholic Spanish king, assembled a force of mainly Catalans, sailed across from Barcelona and took Mallorca over from the Muslims, who had controlled it for five hundred years. He then freely handed out houses, property and trading privileges to his main supporters.

Then, three hundred years later Mallorca got swept up in the Rebellion of the Brotherhoods, a peasant revolt against Spain's ruler, Charles V, who had the title of 'Holy Roman Emperor, ruler of the Burgundian territories, King of Aragon, Castile, Naples and Sicily, and son of Philip the Handsome and Joanna the Mad.' Sounds like my kinda guy, huh?

His subjugation of the rebellion paved the way for frequent attacks by pirates, which led to the locals constructing their villages back from the coastline with the mountains behind them so they could defend themselves against invaders.

Across this tumultuous journey there emerged seven key Mallorcan families who to this day still quietly play their role in the island's major decision-making, particularly when it comes to construction, development, social growth and who's in and who's out. As an

Englishman who ran a small gift shop in Mallorca put it, 'If you come here, set up a little business and keep quiet and stay out of their way, they'll leave you alone. But if you want to invest and get into property development, then that's a different matter.'

We certainly learnt that the hard way with the Raixa project. Presumably someone spoke to someone who mentioned it to someone else in the right place. Years later, when we were out of the picture, the zoning was changed back to tourist and a group of local developers began to work on it.

Nevertheless, we weren't going to let losing one battle deter us from continuing our fight in the overall war, even though we had done our half a million bucks cold. So, in addition to the continuing redevelopment and refinancing of La Noria, plus our work with Zou, we looked around for other possibilities.

It turned out that the Mallorcan architects we were using at La Noria had a good working relationship with local banking and construction interests. They said that they had a friend who would do a special deal on a block of unfinished units known as the Apartments in a spectacular location at Puerto Andratx. They said they could negotiate directly with the bank that had repossessed the property a year or so previously. The bank had lost a lot of money on the property and wanted it off its books.

The architects thought that maybe we could fold the Apartments concept, with a mortgage provided by the bank, into the La Noria project. They suggested that if they could help us refinance La Noria and purchase the Apartments, then we would, in turn, appoint them to be the lead Spanish architects on the project to revamp things and produce something special. This would

270

provide them with not only the chance to make a bit of money but also gain them a bit of kudos and local credibility. This type of relationship was happening a lot in Spain in some shape or form in those days and no doubt still does.

We agreed on that, the deal was done, and we now had both La Noria and the Apartments under our control. We set about making a project that would incorporate the two elements. The tricky part—and why the bank wanted to offload the property—was that there was a weakness in the original design. The Apartments did not get the sun all the time. At certain times of the year, they were in shadow all day.

This, of course, was quite a flaw in a place like Mallorca where how sunny the day was going to be was the prime topic of the morning conversation. Typically, Des Brooks and Christopher came up with another unique solution—using the strengths of one project to cover the weaknesses of the other and vice versa. For example, the lack of sun at the Apartments at certain times of the year could be covered by shuttling guests from there around to La Noria, where there was year-round sun. In turn, the strength of the Apartments property was that it had waterfront views, which La Noria did not. However, the Apartments did not have direct access to the water, and we knew that for the property to work successfully, it really needed that. The solution lay in a house directly in front of the Apartments, abutting the water, which had been vacant for some years. We tracked down the owner and offered him a long-term, fixed-rental contract with an option to purchase at any time at an agreed price over three years. We figured that once we got control of the house, we would not only gain direct access to the water but also could turn it into some sort of club or communal facility for guests at both the Apartments and La Noria.

The lease contract for the house stated that as part of the deal someone had to occupy it and maintain the property. Initially, Rob Guthrie who was the landscape architect, project manager, site manager and God knows what else of the whole show moved in. The much-loved Rob, universally known as the Gentle Giant because of his imposing size and quiet demeanour, was a good choice as he had brilliant skills as a botanist and resort landscaper. Part of his commitment came from his respect for Christopher because he had worked for him at Port Douglas and the Gold Coast where he had created the award-winning gardens.

Having created major projects all over the world for big-money clients and achieved international acclaim in places such as Malaysia, he did a great job moving our project forward under difficult circumstances. However, after a year or so, we simply couldn't pay the big man anymore, and as he was missing his family, he moved back to Australia and ran into a few pressing problems he had to resolve.

When the call went out for a suitable replacement, Amanda and I jumped at the opportunity of moving into the house. We figured that residing there would be a refreshing change from living in La Noria's chicken shed. Besides, although we got along well with Christopher and Pixie, this move would get us out of living daily in SkaseWorld. We reckoned it would give us some respite from his continuing, almost obsessive drive to restore his fortunes and provide us with a bit of our own autonomy. So we agreed to be the tenants. We had a lot of fun in the house beside the seaside in the summer, but few of the services worked properly and in winter it was freezing.

272

In our search for funds to inject into the projects, we were introduced to a man named R. E. (Ronald) Burton, who had inherited a cool $100 million or so from the sale of his father's huge cable and wire business. Short in stature and maybe just a little bit boganish, he was known universally as the Monkey, although he was soon renamed within our circles when little Charlotte's pronunciation turned that into the Munty. At the end of the day, he turned out to be a financial white knight, refinancing the Apartments with a 100 per cent mortgage, which freed up some working capital for our projects in general.

That was the thing about Mallorca. You never knew just who you would meet next. One of the more extraordinary characters was Howard Marks, the world's biggest hash and marijuana dealer in the 70s and 80s, who later titled his autobiography *Mr Nice*. He had lived on the island with his family until his arrest and extradition by the US Drug Enforcement Agency, where he was sentenced to thirty years in maximum security. But he got out after seven and came back to Mallorca.

I met Howard and his wife Judy the day he arrived back in Spain. I was having dinner with Amanda and English lawyer Steven Garfield and his wife Angela in a little Japanese restaurant in Palma when Howard and Judy walked in. He instantly recognised Steven, who I think had been involved in his case. We had a quick introduction and a few laughs and then wound up seeing them regularly around the island. Howard and I always had a lot in common to talk about, and I was in awe of him, a bit like a groupie at a rock concert. As Goodreads put it, he had the voice of Richard Burton and the looks of a Rolling Stone.

Charlotte went to school with one of his kids, and I remember having a Sunday lunch one day with Amanda, Charlotte and half a dozen friends in Mallorca's most popular family restaurant, C'an Pedro in Genova. It was heaving with a couple of hundred people, and when Howard and Judy and the kids arrived, he caught my eye and gestured that he was going to come over and say hello. I was thinking how cool this was with everyone staring at him. As he got to the table and put out his hand, I was going to shake it, but then realised he was actually passing me a huge three-paper hash joint that he was smoking. I was a bit surprised and oscillated between saying no thanks and looking like a wimp or grabbing the joint and having a toke. I went with the second option, took a quick couple of puffs and handed it back. I was not sure if this was some sort of test, but, hey, I was in awe of the man. On another occasion, I stumbled into the middle of a BBC documentary he was filming outside the fabulous Wellies restaurant in Portals Nous, the owner of which, Geoff Kenyon, had spent time in gaol for his association with Howard.

Mr Nice had an incredible presence wherever he went. He openly smoked joints the entire time after his return to the island, and the Spanish authorities just didn't seem to care. I am sure this stemmed from the fact that he only ever dealt in hash and grass, never powders or pills. It was sad to read of his death in early 2016.

Meanwhile, as I was constantly on the ground working on our projects and also understood Spanish, I kept agreeing to be nominated as the administrator and/or shareholder of all of these companies. There had been a lot set up because many different people had different shareholdings in different projects. The lawyers explained that my nomination was all perfectly legal and also helped justify the modest wage that I was drawing.

One of these companies had been set up to create a project on a fabulous property in Valldemossa, a picturesque village north of Palma. In the hills close to the west coast, Valldemossa is in one of the prettiest parts of the island and over the years had been home to many famous people including Michael Douglas, Dudley Moore and in the 1830s Polish composer Frederic Chopin and his French lover, Amandine Lucile Dupin, better known as the novelist George Sand.

It is said that Valldemossa is the most visited village in Mallorca, featuring the Royal Carthusian Monastery, the King's Palace, a beautiful cathedral and an apothecary, where you can see the old ointments and balms used to improve the health of the monks and villagers. It is five hundred metres above sea level, and the monastery cells open up onto beautiful gardens that look out over the valley. The vertical precipices remind you of the Blue Mountains. When you take in this view, you understand more about Mallorca. Over the centuries, the locals have built and worked with the hills, not against them.

While the Apartments deal was crawling along, it was decided we should go after the Valldemossa property, which had just come on the market. It had been partly built, had stalled and had been repossessed by a Scandinavian bank, which was looking to get out of it discreetly. The contact that had led us to the project had stayed at the Mirage Resorts in Australia and had loved them and felt we would do justice to it. He also knew that we would be fairly quiet about the purchase, which was one of the bank's major concerns. They just wanted it off the books for some reason, a theme we often came across over the years.

The project fitted all the criteria for an integrated resort, most of the permissions were in place and there were even some roads and houses with power already built, plus enough land for a championship golf course among the olive groves. It was part of a broader Government-inspired project at the time, the Chopin Urbanization, dedicated to modernising Valldemossa with a sympathetic approach to its history, architecture and culture. We did our due diligence with local architects, who knew people within the local council, and also with the local branch of accountants and financiers, Ernst & Young. There was a lot involved in concluding the deal. Detail, detail, detail. Detail in financial documents, detail in legal briefs and detail in business brochures.

Nothing was left to chance with Christopher. Check, double check, triple check. Then he would check it all over again. We were up against another consortium led I think by another Australian, but the Munty came up with 100 per cent of the purchase price, and at a $7 million price tag for a property with a bank valuation of $120 million, it was a steal, or not, as the case may be.

The local architect on this project was Xim Ozonas. He helped us right from the early days when we were getting La Noria under way, doing all the rezonings we did on it and Raixa and other projects. A wonderful man, very clever, he knew everyone who was anyone on the island, was brilliant with his advice and skilfully represented us in negotiations.

The thing was, Christopher used to drive Xim nuts with his ambition to get things done too quickly. After he had reeled out of yet another meeting, I'd have to have a drink with Xim, calm him down, and say, 'Look, that's Christopher. He didn't mean it, don't worry about it. He just gets frustrated. It's all good.'

Xim was a descendant of one of the original Mallorcan dynasties—his family once owned and lived in the major castle in the town of Andratx and had donated it to the local council—and was very influential in Mallorcan politics, a man to go and see if you wanted to get things done. Yet despite his status, skills, education and connections, he had never been out of Spain. A trip with me to Hawaii and mainland US to see the Princeville and Bel Air projects and then to Australia to have a look at the Mirage Resorts was his first taste of international travel. And one incident proved to be an astonishing revelation for him. We were in LA, staying at the Bel Air Hotel, where Des Brooks had wanted him to see its architectural influence, because La Noria was going to be done in a similar way. Very much bungalow style, with beautiful gardens. That was the thing about Christopher, always think 'best possible.'

We were having dinner at the celebrity-spotting Ivy restaurant in Los Angeles. Christopher had told me to take Xim there to show him the Ivy's country cottage style interior as an inspiration for his work. After dinner I got talking to the Spanish-speaking barman and wound up buying a couple of illegal Cuban cigars, which were probably worth more than cocaine at that time. Xim said, 'Ask him if there is anything worth seeing in town tonight.'

I dutifully did, and he replied, 'Why don't you go up and see the Kinks?'

Well, Xim's eyes lit up. He was a huge fan. But the Kinks had long dropped off the radar. I said, 'What? Are you sure?'

'They've re-formed,' said the barman. 'Their first concert back. At Dan Aykroyd's House of Blues up on Sunset.'

So off we drove to the House of Blues, hoping like hell it was the real thing. When we found a park easily and saw there was no queue at the front, we started to think that maybe it was too good to be true. But as we opened the door, the opening chords of *Lola* blasted through the place. I thought, 'You've got to be kidding.' We walked across the atrium-style building and peered over the balcony. Sure enough, it was no tribute band. Down below were Ray Davies and the Kinks in full cry.

And Xim? I've never seen anything like it. His face lit up, his eyes sparkled, he was jumping around with excitement. An incredible start to his first travel experience.

On the other hand, I was on the road seemingly permanently, and this was around the time I went to Cuba to see if we could do something there.

Cuba? Did I just say Cuba? I know it sounds mad, jumping from the capitalist market of America into the communist world of Fidel Castro. But, you know, those guys, they're like the barman. They speak Spanish, don't they?

THIRTY

W e came across the Cuba idea while working with Zou's people on his San Luis Obispo project in California. While on visits out there, we started to look around to see what other opportunities were on the horizon, not only in the rest of the US but also Central and South America and the Caribbean. Zou had already been involved in projects in Santa Domingo, in the Dominican Republic.

The Cuban project was sited in an area called St Lucia, on the northeast of the island, near Nuevitas in Camaguey Province. It featured a coral reef with twenty kilometres of pristine beach, providing a great setting for scuba diving and other water sports as well as lagoons and pink flamingos. Another Christopher Skase/Des Brooks creation, the concept included lavish accommodation, a golf course, a marina, and a cleverly designed floating casino based from a cruise ship terminal that was part of the property, as gambling was still illegal in Cuba. It was one of the most beautiful golf course projects I have ever seen, and believe me, I got to see a lot of projects in my ten years with Christopher. We were looking at having the Cuba resort up and running by mid-to-late 1990s. I went on many trips there, including one hectic five-day trip with something like four hundred queries to be answered.

Fortunately, I found a tour guide who introduced me to the right government representatives. They treated me like a king once they saw the Mirage Port Douglas photos and presentation. Out came the chauffeured Mercedes and the Russian Sikorsky twin-rotor helicopter for transport. I even enjoyed a night at the Tropicana, the famous open-air nightclub where stars like Frank Sinatra and Carmen Miranda used to perform before the Cuban-American mafia in the front row. It was like stepping back in time; it hadn't changed in sixty years with the beautiful showgirls in their spectacular costumes and headgear dancing to the driving Latin rhythm.

Not only that, I got into Fidel Castro's offices. I would have met the man himself, but unfortunately, he was away at the time. Instead, I spoke to one of his right hand men, a Mr Cienfuegos, who had one of those great stories to tell. He had fought alongside Castro at the battle of the Moncada Barracks in Santiago de Cuba in 1953, regarded as the beginning of the Revolution. When Castro swept to power six years later, Mr Cienfuegos—his name means 'a hundred fires'—had been rewarded for his bravery and loyalty with senior postings. I did a presentation to him and his staff, including the Minister for Tourism, and outlined how our plans also included the possibility of doing something in Daiquiri, from where the name of the cocktail came.

I absolutely fell in love with Cuba and its people. The best way to sum it up is by what happened on my second visit there. One day I was being driven in a big old Mercedes from Havana down to Santa Lucia with one of the top people in the tourism ministry, Jose Cruz, or Joe Cross as it is translated. We were out in the middle of the countryside traveling through sugarcane fields about an hour from our destination when we suddenly hit a massive pothole that smashed the radiator and ripped out the sump. We ground to a halt with the sun setting and not a vehicle in sight. There weren't many cars on the main roads in those days let alone on the back roads.

Just as we were wondering what to do next and contemplating a night sleeping in the car, an old wooden horse-drawn cart carrying about twenty cane farmers came over the hill on their way home after a long day in the fields. Before we knew it, they were towing the old Merc into town! And while the guys at the garage got to work devising a solution with what they had on hand—just like the old Aussie bush mechanics used to—the rest of us sat around drinking the local workers' rum, Puerto Principe. It is one of the best rums I had in Cuba and only about a buck a bottle. Dangerous. After a few, I had the courage to ask the group why everyone supported Castro so much.

'Everyone I meet loves him,' I said.

One of the farmers asked me if I had children, and I replied that I had a five-year-old daughter. Then he asked, 'If she was very sick, what would you do to save her life?' Obviously my answer was, 'Anything.'

He then explained that under the previous Batista regime, 'If your child or family member was sick, no one gave a fuck. If you weren't part of the elite, he or she died!'

Under Castro every single Cuban had the same access to the same level of excellent health care. It was similar with education, made available to all Cubans up to Year 10 and then in senior years allocated on merit not dollars. I came to the conclusion that Cuba was in many ways a Garden of Eden, and many times while visiting there, I seriously questioned my capitalist view of the world.

We were negotiating with the Cuban Government for management rights for existing hotel properties to help offset any costs we would incur and to negotiate a better deal on the land we were interested in, as this was a common scenario in Cuba at that time. While my treatment by the locals was fantastic, I was a bit freaked out by the Cuban-American mafia, a group you don't really want to muck around with. They had had a controlling interest in running the island before Castro took over. Now, from what I could see, while the balance of power might have changed, they were still pretty active, specialising in smuggling Cubans into Mexico and Florida at a pretty hefty price. They were very skilled at extracting the costs from their clients. I was even covertly warned not to touch any properties that had been owned by these powerful groups prior to the revolution. I was politely told that if Castro fell, then these people wouldn't fuck around issuing a lawsuit to get their property back. Instead, someone resembling a character out of *Scarface* would just arrive at the door with an offer that would be too good to refuse. It was certainly food for thought.

Our involvement with Cuba eventually got side-tracked by the famous Chase for Skase extradition battle with the Australian Government. But I became so enamoured with the place that along with Amanda, as President of the Parents Committee at Charlotte's Mallorcan school, I organised the donation of gifts to the school at St Lucia near where we were planning the resort. One time I took two hundred kilograms of pens, pencils, writing pads, Chupa Chups and other stuff on the plane with me. This was achieved with the fantastic help of the check-in staff at Iberia Airlines who dropped the excess baggage charges when I explained what I was doing.

The school was so appreciative I was not only welcomed with a formal reception but also an impromptu choir performance. The entire school sang the Cuban national anthem to me while I stood next to the statue of Jose Marti, a Cuban founding father who fought for its independence. It's all on video and still brings a lump to my throat. It was hard to believe something so simple could mean so much to so many people. It probably provided me with more credibility in Cuba than anything else I ever did there and opened doors I could normally only dream about.

After all the heavy duty dialogue and top level negotiations we had conducted over the years, a simple gift of some stationery and basic school supplies proved the best karma of all.

THIRTY-ONE

One day, to our horror, Christopher and Pixie got abducted—and not by Australian authorities seeking to get them back home, either. It was an amazing set of events, which has rarely been related before.

It all came about because in our early days on Mallorca, while we were waiting for our permanent residency to come through, we had to do regular visa runs to get our passport re-stamped to allow us to stay on. Every three months, Amanda, Charlotte and I would have to leave Spain, go to another country for a short period and then re-enter. Christopher and Pixie had to do the same, but they were one step ahead of us and were getting closer to permanency. By then, they only had to do it every six months.

Over the years, too, as our perilous money situation improved, we would occasionally put a few dollars together and simply get away from the island. We had to do it; otherwise, we would have gone mad. We would go to France, Holland, the UK, any place that was cheap and convenient. Once, Amanda and I went to England to stay with Alex and her boyfriend Lawrence but the Gulf War had started and after one night of watching it unfold, we wanted to get out of there because the situation was getting tense. There were tanks at the airport and continuing threats to blow London up.

Another time we went to Gibraltar, catching the ferry across from Mallorca to Valencia and then getting a car and driving south. We stayed for a day or two and then came back via Seville to Mallorca. It was all very simple, gave us a break from La Noria and ensured we could continue to reside in Spain. The thing that sticks in my mind about Gibraltar is that once you cross the border, the main road from Spain into Gibraltar passes through the international airport and actually crosses the runway. Every now and then, the bells ring, the boom gates come down and the cars wait until a plane lands or takes off, and then the gates go up and the cars are allowed to continue through. Amazing.

Then one year, late 1991, our scheduled visa runs coincided with winter, and seeing as Charlotte had never seen snow, everyone thought it would be a great idea to go to Switzerland. So we bought a package deal and the five of us flew off. The plan was to go up to Interlaken, the famous skiing and holiday spot, and show Charlotte the snow and the mountains. We also wanted to show her Heidi's cottage, the little house highlighted in the book about the Swiss girl living in the Alps with her grandfather. First stop was Zurich, a city Christopher and Pixie had spent a lot of time in during the Qintex years. They loved the city, its culture, the architecture and the chocolate shops—all things that we had heard about and which they were going to show us. We checked into a hotel at about ten o'clock in the morning and Christopher and Pixie said, 'We're going to go and get the train tickets to Interlaken. We'll be back in an hour or two.'

So we sat and waited. And waited, and waited and waited. And it got to midday, one o'clock, two o'clock, three o'clock.

We started to get anxious. We didn't have any mobile phones so we couldn't ring them direct. We rang reception and did our best to find out what was happening, but they knew nothing. As every hour went by, things got more puzzling and frightening.

About six o'clock, they both appeared at the door looking like they had been mugged. Pixie was in tears, her clothes were crumpled and her face was all red. Christopher was totally dishevelled. He looked like he had been living on the streets for six months. We were so relieved to see them but very distressed at the condition they were in. They told us that they had entered the Zurich railway station, which is a huge place with several levels, and had taken the escalator down to the ticketing zone.

Then their amazing story unfolded like this: Just as they are stepping off the escalator, out of the blue, a group of several men and one woman suddenly lunges at them. Two of these men grab Christopher and crash-tackle him to the ground, while the others grab Pixie and pull her away. It is a crazy scene.

Now, this could be a mugging. But also around that time, there had been stories circulating that the Australian Securities Commission was looking at ways to get Christopher back to Australia and kidnapping was not out of the question. So Christopher thinks he is being abducted by Australian authorities and starts screaming and fighting back, trying to get out of their clutches.

Pixie, understandably, weighs in as well. She pulls away from the man and woman holding her and tries to get the attackers off Christopher, all the while screaming for people to help them. So she is crash-tackled to the ground, too. She then feels a horrible stinging sensation as capsicum spray is blasted into her eyes.

Then they are separated by these people—who at this stage have not shown any form of identification or said anything to indicate why they are doing this, certainly not in English—and are dragged off in separate directions. They are still screaming for help as they are being taken away, but of course even though it is a crowded railway station, no one wants to get involved.

They are taken out of the railway station, bundled into separate unmarked cars and driven rapidly through the back streets of Zurich. At this point, they are both convinced that they are going to be spirited back to Australia or held God knows where for ransom. Finally, the cars pull up outside a place that looks like some sort of warehouse—it certainly has no indication that it is a police station or federal building—and they are bundled inside. Then they are stripped naked. And thrown into separate cells.

It is an amazing turn of events, a physically hurtful and quite degrading experience. Finally, the questioning begins, and it starts to unfold as to who these people are and what is going on. They reveal themselves as undercover policemen. They are convinced Christopher is a well-known European criminal who is a master con man, a man much wanted throughout several countries for committing millions of dollars of fraud. It appears that these undercover policemen at the railway station had spotted Christopher, became convinced he was the man they were after, called for backup and knocked him and Pixie down.

So they begin accusing him. 'You are this man. We know who you are. You have committed fraud all over Europe.'

Christopher is replying, 'I am not him. I swear.'

This goes on for several hours, with both being grilled separately, until finally somebody works out that they have the wrong bloke and that they have made a big mistake. A few scant apologies are given, they hand Christopher his clothes back, and tell him, 'Your wife will meet you around the back.'

He finds Pixie; they fall into each other's arms and make their way back to the hotel.

When they came up to our room, Pixie was very distraught from the emotional shock and physical attack, which had left her face all burnt. After a lot of discussion, we went up to Interlaken, but as you can imagine, it wasn't a very happy journey to show the snow to Charlotte as they were both in shock and suffering. As well, Pixie's eye was really hurting her, and she had to have several lots of medical treatment for it. That incident ruined her eyesight. She lost about 80 per cent of the vision in one eye from the capsicum spray, and it never returned. So when we got back to Zurich, Christopher met up with an old lawyer friend, Dr Max, and started a lawsuit against them.

You would think that they would have had very strong grounds for a successful case, but the legal set-up in Switzerland meant that it was very difficult to sue the police. Initially, they tried to fob Max off, but he persisted and then they fought it really hard.

They could not see what the fuss was about. As far as they were concerned, it was just a couple of Australians caught up in things, and stiff shit, they were just doing their job. But Max would not give up, and in the end, the Swiss Government settled out of court, although it was only a payout for the eye damage to Pixie. There were no damages awarded to Christopher even though he had been tackled, belted, stripped and interrogated. If the same situation had have happened in the US, Pixie probably would have become an instant millionaire, charging them with wrongful arrest, physical damage, mental trauma and so on. Instead she got about $40,000, less Max's commission.

That was what we lived on for the next year.

THIRTY-TWO

T hen, something started to really worry us. We began to notice that while Christopher's spirit was willing to take on any challenge thrown up, the flesh was starting to become weak.

At first we put it down to him having the flu or its after-effects. The disk problem in his back had also caused him a lot of inconvenience over the years, and this had flared even more after he left Australia for the final time in June 1991. Several times he tendered medical evidence about his back, delaying him from flying until it got better. Often he would get a week or ten days' delay and after treatment he would be fine to fly.

But one day in early 1992, he was working around the garden of the main house by himself when he suddenly collapsed against the wall. He couldn't catch his breath, he had pains in his chest, he felt very tired and he had no energy. He could hardly move. No one was around, so he propped himself up against the wall and lay there for a while until he got his breath back and then carefully made his way back to the house. After a glass of water and some rest, he came good. He didn't say much about it, and the incident was put down to lingering effects of the flu and soon forgotten.

A few weeks later, while I was painting the outside of the chicken shed and he was working in the garden, he

291

collapsed again. This time, we all rushed to him and he told us that once more he had chest pains and he couldn't breathe. You could see it had really knocked him around as he battled hard to get his breath back. It was quite an alarming sight. We thought he was having a heart attack.

When we got him inside the house and he started to feel better, Pixie insisted that he go and get a medical opinion. Normally, he was like most blokes, putting any trip to the doctor off for as long as he could. This time, he did as instructed. Pixie was the only one to whom he could not say 'no.' Besides, I think that it was such a scary experience, he wanted to find out for himself what was going on.

I didn't blame Pixie for being so insistent because he was only in his early forties. He should have been in pretty good physical shape, and yet, it was obvious he was finding things harder to do than normal. The appointment was made, tests were done, the results came back, a second appointment was made, and from that moment on, our whole world began to crumble before our very eyes.

The doctor asked him had he ever smoked. Christopher said that yes, he had smoked a bit when he was young, but had given it up and now only smoked one or two thin cigarillos a day.

The doctor then asked him if he had ever had asthma. Yes, said Christopher, he had had asthma pretty much all his life, and although he had occasional attacks, it had never been debilitating to the point of ruining his day-to-day lifestyle or becoming life threatening. He could handle it.

The doctor then asked a question from the far depths of left field. 'With the surname of Skase, are you of

Nordic or Scandinavian stock?' he said. 'Can you trace that lineage back through your forebears?'

This had Christopher on the back foot for a second. Why would he want to know about something like that? After a moment or two, recalling what family members had said over the years, he replied that yes, he was. Skase is from the Old Norse surname Skjotr, meaning swift or fleet, and the name can be found among many Norfolk and Suffolk families as a result of Norse settlement of the east England seaboard.

'Why do you ask?' said Christopher.

'Because you have Alpha 1 Anti-Trypsin Deficiency, an inherited disorder. People of Nordic or Scandinavian stock have a propensity for it.'

'And?'

'Alpha 1 Anti-Trypsin is a protein that protects the lungs. If you are deficient in it, you can develop lung disease, usually emphysema. That is what has happened. You have got emphysema, not so much from your lifestyle, but the luck of the draw. Your genetics.'

There was more.

'Worse still, you have not only got emphysema, you have got a very, very aggressive form of it. It is virtually eating your lungs.'

Then the clincher.

'Sadly, we can't do much about it, either. It is in an advanced state.'

'Advanced?'

'Mr Skase, you are terminally ill. You are going to die from this. Sooner, rather than later.'

There it was, a sudden, confronting, mind-bending change in his health, virtually a death sentence, all because of his genetics.

He was forty-three.

Of course, this sent shock waves through the house and the entire family. We were all devastated and went into denial. This can't be right! It's just not fair! After his terrible reversal of fortunes, he was beginning a new life abroad. Why, it seemed like only yesterday he had celebrated his fortieth birthday with the party of the century. And now here was a doctor telling a very distraught Pixie, 'Mrs Skase, you realise that your husband's case is one hundred per cent terminal? That it is going to kill him?'

But before too much negativity could take over, Christopher typically went on the front foot and declared he was going to beat it. He had faced big challenges before, and he had won. 'I will win this one too,' he said. The manager in him kicked in and a search was immediately launched to find out what was the best treatment, where it was available and how quickly we could get it started.

This took us all the way from the heat of Spain to the mountains of Switzerland, to a clinic in Davos, recognised for its unique climate that provided relief for patients with lung diseases. Situated on the Landwasser River up in the Alps, the crisp dry air drew patients from all around the world, and at its peak, it boasted more than twenty lung treatment centres. Robert Louis Stevenson, the Scots-born writer of *Treasure Island*, went there when he contracted tuberculosis.

Christopher's condition was extreme. What was happening was that a small section of the lung would die and flake away, leaving the lung wall at that spot paper-thin and vulnerable, ready to explode at any time. When it exploded, the pain would be excruciating, and he would battle to breathe.

After many tests, the clinic concluded there was only one solution to save his life, a double-lung transplant. This was astonishing news. The whole situation had happened so fast. Pixie, Amanda and I were left reeling at the thought that he was now a candidate for major surgery. An operation that was still in its infancy, too. The world's first successful double-lung transplant had been completed only about five years before, in Toronto, so it was still early days and a lot of issues involving tissue rejection were yet to be resolved.

As well, surgery like that was dependent on many factors including finding the right match, so it could take ages to set up. There was no guarantee he would live long enough to have the operation. In the meantime, the doctors wanted him to spend six months at the clinic to stabilize and improve his general situation. Christopher said that he couldn't do it in one long stretch because not only could he not afford it, he had a lot of work back in Spain that needed to be done. Typically, he worked out a plan where he would spend the equivalent of the six months across a longer period of time by attending the clinic one week in every six to eight weeks.

To go for the treatment, he had to fly to Zurich and then take the train up to Davos. But the second time he went, the flight nearly killed him. As the plane descended into Zurich, he felt this enormous jabbing pain in his chest, like someone was stabbing him. He had suffered a pneumothorax. A hole had blown out in his right lung, and it had collapsed.

The pain was incredible, but he figured that if he kept going and caught the train for Davos he would be all right. The train station is at the Zurich airport, so he staggered through the terminal, found his way down to the platform, got on the train and promptly crumpled back into his seat, overcome by the shocking pain and lack of breath. A dear old couple sitting opposite, seeing his distressed condition, held his head out the window of the moving train until he regained his breath. They also rang for an ambulance to meet him. They saved his life.

When he finally got to the clinic, the doctors whisked him into emergency surgery, patched the hole in his lung and reinflated it. Amid all the confusion, he had disappeared off our radar, and no one back on Mallorca knew where he was. Pixie became extremely worried. Was he dead? Had he got confused and lost? Had he been kidnapped? She got on the phone and rang around and eventually found him. She flew to Zurich, hired a car and drove to Davos.

The clinic told Pixie that when the spot on the lung burst, causing it to deflate, he would have been in pain that they could only describe as horrific. It showed that he was tough and had incredible strength of character. They added that if the other lung had burst instead, his left, it would have collapsed on his heart and strangled it. That would have killed him.

When he was feeling well enough, she brought him back to Mallorca, by car. That flight into Zurich was the last time he ever went on a plane. Ever.

Things never really did get better from that point on. He started to develop bullae, little pockets of air that develop within and around the lung and impinge on its effectiveness, severely restricting breathing. They are ugly black things, quite common amongst emphysema sufferers and are very dangerous because they can fill with fluid and become infectious. They are tissue paper thin and are in constant risk of bursting.

Despite all this, Christopher remained optimistic, saying that the double-lung transplant would eventually happen and he would be right as rain. He declared that he refused to accept he was going to die, that he would fight on and that he was going to have a successful operation. He believed that once it was done, with his usual optimism and enthusiasm combined with a bit of luck, he would be on top of things for many more years to come. It was only a matter of finding the right donor. 'To think that someone is walking around out there right now with my new lungs,' he used to say with a smile. 'I hope he's a Kenyan marathon runner.'

Throughout all this terrible time, he always maintained his sense of humour. I used to tell him jokes like, 'What's the worst thing about a lung transplant? Coughing up someone else's phlegm.'

Nevertheless, a serious part of my lifestyle had to undergo a dramatic change. For Christopher's sake, we all decided we could no longer smoke anywhere inside. Trouble was, I was a heavy smoker. So along with anyone else who wanted a cigarette—the Four Builders, or someone helping around the place, or Felicity if she was visiting, or Barry Peters—I had to go outside. There we would be, like sneaky school kids, sheltering from the hot sun, having a quiet puff. Sometimes there would be quite a crowd because lots and lots of people smoked in Spain in those days. We made this decision because we realized that Christopher's lungs couldn't cope with the second-hand smoke, yet at that stage he was still denying that he had emphysema. 'It's all those Spanish doctors,' he'd say. 'It's all bullshit. I've just got to find a real doctor who will tell me I don't have emphysema.'

Indeed, at one point after another car-and-ferry trip to the Davos clinic, their opinion, which all along been very forthright and negative, suddenly became just a tad more positive. They told Pixie, 'You know what? We

297

think he might survive long enough to do the transplant.' But there were not too many people out there who were about to die and who had the blood and tissue type to match his.

In his inimitable style, he refused to let anyone around him dwell on it or get morbid because of what he was going through. He insisted that we remain positive and move on with our lives. But the part that made us all so angry was that he was in a grave, terminal situation, bravely battling a medical condition that would have killed a lesser man, yet he was being made the butt of jokes worldwide.

The prying Australian press used to hang around and take long-lens photos or scrounge so-called exclusive eyewitness reports of Christopher moving around the property or swimming or walking the dog. Shock, horror, the headlines would scream, he's supposed to be sick and dying and look, here he is, walking the dog.

Of course he was walking the fucking dog. That's what patients with emphysema are supposed to do! They are encouraged to swim and walk and do as much exercise as they can. The less active they are, the more likely they are to develop fluid and infection on their lungs and drop dead. The more active they are, the better, and if they can take a dog with them when they are walking, it's a bonus. The press only needed to ask any of the medical people involved to understand the gravity of the situation. Not one did.

Eventually his lungs got so bad that at times he needed assistance to breathe. So he began using portable oxygen bottles and a nebuliser—a facemask and regulator—to facilitate his breathing and ease the pain. Oxygen was now permanently installed in his bedroom and office.

This was no joke or subterfuge. He needed it to assist his breathing, take the pressure off his lungs and survive. He described it as like constantly breathing through a straw. We also used to get special medical concoctions sent down from Davos. These were somewhat experimental drugs that he had to take regularly to try and improve his situation.

The crucial point was that his condition, where the lungs could explode at any time and which had happened to him after he had flown to Zurich, meant that he could no longer fly in an aeroplane. That is gospel. When the Government made it clear it was going to force this issue, I approached every significant air, land and sea transport provider around the world, provided them with Christopher's complete medical record, and asked, 'My client wishes to travel to Australia, and I am attaching his full medical history. Would you carry this man as a passenger?'

They each independently stated that they would not risk carrying any patient suffering from Alpha 1 Anti-Trypsin Deficiency with advanced emphysema and a recent history of a life-threatening pneumothorax because of the high risk of mortality.

I gathered a folio of original, notarised documents from airlines including the Australian Government-owned Qantas, as well as British Airways, Malaysian Airlines, Singapore Airlines and others. I also approached every shipping agent, including premier lines such as Cunard and P&O. It was too risky even for an ocean liner to have him on board, they all said. At P&O, I had to speak to a doctor named Ian Fleming, who informed me that they had been pressured by somebody from the Australian Government to change their opinion from 'no' to 'yes.' Of course, P&O had refused to do such a thing, as I am sure did any others who no doubt were contacted. I thought it was quite ironic that the tip about a clandestine attempt to falsify information had been passed on to me by a medico with the same name as the author of the James Bond books.

I also spoke to a series of medical evacuation specialists, and they supplied the same answer too. Everyone I approached said they would not take him, that they would not allow him to travel for fear that he would suffer an irreversible medical setback or die during the journey.

It was written in black and white, and I can show you the letters if you like. That is why he never came back to Australia. He was not running scared or hiding. After all, we had the same address for eleven years and could be easily found. He wanted to come back to Australia as he had done previously on a number of occasions. He wanted to get back 51 per cent of what was his. He wanted to fight for the shareholders' rights. The passion for that never abated. But quite simply, the journey would have killed him.

THIRTY-THREE

O ne of the oddest aspects of this strange and sorry saga was that in all the years of the Chase for Skase and the search for the alleged missing millions, trustee-in-bankruptcy Max Donnelly and Christopher Skase never met! Their paths did not cross once, which is astonishing when you think about it.

Max was appointed after Christopher had left Australia for the last time in 1991, so they did not even come across one another, say, by chance in a corridor during one of the many hearings.

Now, the duties of the trustee include taking suitable action to determine whether the estate concerned includes property that can be realized to pay a dividend to creditors. Or taking appropriate steps to recover any property. Those sorts of things. And in carrying out these duties, obviously the trustee has to go in search of information. And did Max travel as part of his duties? Yes, he did. He went to places including England, where he interviewed Pixie's daughter Alexandra and Christopher's lawyer, Tim Stranack.

But did he come to Mallorca? No, he never came and knocked on our door.

We felt that at some point Max would have hopped on a plane and come over to talk to the one true source of information, Christopher Charles Skase, who by now was living in Spain. Especially when it became quite clear that Christopher was never going to be able to return to Australia. He was terminally ill, he had the medical opinion to confirm it and he had had the written declarations of every reputable air and sea carrier that they would not take him as a passenger because he was too much of a risk. It would make sense, wouldn't it? It would certainly make more sense than some of the bizarre Get Skase ideas and projects that were coming out of Australia.

One time, Max phoned us at La Noria, but Christopher would not speak with him. He felt that if they were to discuss such a complex situation then they should meet face to face. Another time, I personally faxed Max and his lawyer Tim L'Estrange, inviting them to come to Mallorca to interview Christopher and me. There you go, we laid ourselves on the line. Come and talk to us, for Christ's sake. Bring it on.

The only stipulation was that we be notified of the questions in advance so that Christopher could prepare the proper documentation to provide the answers, as just about all the papers he would need were still in Australia. This was a complex affair, and it would have been impossible to have given accurate answers based on memory, particularly in relation to exact times, amounts of money, shareholdings and so on. It made sense to have the appropriate documentation available to corroborate Christopher's responses. No one could then dispute his evidence; it would all be in black and white.

We also suggested that Max and Tim interview us in collaboration with a Spanish judiciary panel of their own selection plus their choice of translators. Here again, we felt that this was a positive thing; that they would not feel compromised being in Spain and would have access to all the necessary services.

So, there you go. For a list of questions, the price of two return airfares, the cost of some Spanish functionaries, plus the hire of a room for a day or two, Max could have got all his answers.

I never received a reply.

Nothing from Max, nor his lawyer.

By all appearances, available funds were used by the trustee-in-bankruptcy to fly around and stay in hotels but not to come straight to the real and only source of the information being sought. Whatever his idea was, it certainly didn't make much sense to us. I know quite a few people who know Max well, and believe me, he is certainly no idiot.

At one stage, the girls—Amanda and her sisters— were accused of harbouring the missing millions. Fuck me, I have been married to Amanda for nearly thirty years. Today, I sit virtually bankrupt on hard-rubbish furniture in our rented home on the outskirts of Melbourne, with us working our arses off and yet still unable to pay off the credit cards carrying the debt left over from those years. I can assure everyone no missing millions came her way or that of her sisters.

Max also got excited about the $500,000 that was used as a deposit on Raixa, despite the fact I had been told by numerous lawyers that that particular cache of money could not be subject to the control of the banks or the trustee-in-bankruptcy. He also approached an Austrian bank, Österreich Landersbank, which had held the mortgage on the London property, only to find that it had been paid out by the proceeds of its sale.

The Bankruptcy Act was continually being rewritten to encircle Christopher, and the trustee-in-bankruptcy used to send him legal letters demanding that unless a payment of a certain amount of money, usually quite large, was made within a period of fourteen days, his bankruptcy would be extended by a further year. You had to laugh. I think that we reached a point where Christopher would have been bankrupt for eight years. When he originally declared himself bankrupt, the standard period was three years.

As well as his health preventing him from travelling, the other thing worrying Christopher was that while the phrase 'Skase will get a fair trial' was being bandied around by people back in Australia, he didn't fancy the odds anymore. Rather than a fair trial, he feared he would have been railroaded into a hostile, media-heightened kangaroo court, presumed guilty before he even got in the witness box. The press had chased, scrutinised and written us up for ages—most of the so-called 'reports' being either wrong, hysterical or both—and we figured they would have only cranked the 'Skase is guilty' chant up to fever pitch.

Researching the possibility of an appeal based on prejudice, we discovered that up to that point the Chase for Skase story had had more column centimetres of news space devoted to it than any event person or thing in Australian history. Fair trial? He would have had a snowball's chance in hell of getting that. A Media Monitors' study confirmed that the public felt he would not get one. An article in 2000 by Professor Jeff Giddings of Griffith University in the Criminal Law Journal was headed up 'Would Christopher Skase Receive a Fair Trial?'

Besides, Christopher did not see why he should put his life at risk in order to be paraded in front of a hostile judiciary for a civil hearing, as suggested by Giddings, with a questionable outcome. Particularly when he had done nothing wrong. Many serious analysts suggested that he would not have been found guilty of any of the charges or at worst been fined. We were convinced that the charges had been inflated from two to thirty-two to suit Spanish extradition requirements. We understood that when the Government asked Spanish authorities if two were enough, it was made clear to them that they were not sufficient, and that there would need to be lots more charges and lots more funds involved to warrant them having a look at it.

Lawyer Shane Herbert always maintained that at least twenty-six of these charges would have been thrown out in the first five minutes of any trial. They were for payments made by Qintex on behalf of Kahmea, the family company, for things like floral arrangements at Bromley and the two Queensland apartments, repairs to properties, the booking of hire car companies for private use, payment of utilities and so on. All these things had been done as per the group's accounting practices set up over the previous fifteen years. At the end of each financial year, Qintex would invoice Kahmea for the full amount owing and Kahmea would pay the amount in full and then the next accounting period would start. These charges, under the Queensland Companies Code, came about because the companies had been put into receivership prior to the end of that financial year, and therefore, the usual legal and transparent accounting procedures had not been completed. This had not been taken on board by the authorities.

Christopher was always notifying the ASC of any movements he made, and always complying with their requests at all times where possible. The only thing he was guilty of was being caught between a rock (the pilots' strike, the high interest rates, the Foreign Investment Review Board rulings and an Australian Broadcasting Tribunal inquiry into the group's media assets) and a hard place (MGM/UA) and, despite his best efforts, being unable to find the cash to scramble out of it. You don't think he drove everything deliberately into the ground, do you, just to ruin the lives of the shareholders? Why would he? He was the major shareholder!

But it had become quite clear that things were going to come to a head and that moves were being made for proceedings to extradite him. Our recovery and rebuild plans were constantly being interrupted as all this loomed, although Christopher kept up his trips by ferry and car to Switzerland for treatment for the emphysema. Due to his progressing condition and inability to travel by air anywhere, I was left to handle our overseas projects. For example, once a month or so, I would fly out and have meetings with architects, government bodies and Zou's people in California and/or Cuba.

With the storm clouds looming, we decided that it would be also prudent if I went back to Australia in November 1993 and attend a scheduled extradition hearing before a judge in Brisbane. Our hope was that I could fully explain to the court why Christopher could no longer travel back to Australia and that any ideas of an extradition should be dropped.

Around about this time, Pixie's youngest daughter Alex took flight from her London home to seek refuge in Mallorca from Larrabee. Remember Larrabee? Lawrence Van der Plaat, her boyfriend who had been doing some work for us in England and Spain? Alex said he had been showing off, playing the tough guy, claiming that he had hand-written notes, photos and other documents about Christopher, Qintex and God knows what else, which he had obviously been photocopying since he met her, and said he would use them against her and us. A row had also developed over her car, the old BMW.

Who did this guy think he was? It was hard to work out why he had become such a trouble-maker when we always thought he was clever enough to make it in his own right. I felt that he was such a pathetic loser, that having pity for him would have been better than feeling hatred for him. After a while, we also began to call him the Not-So-Talented Mr Ripley, from the Jude Law film.

Fortuitously, Bill Jones, who had done some security work for Christopher and who was on one of his regular trips from Australia to visit his wife's family in Germany, phoned Christopher in Mallorca to see how he was going. When he heard what was happening in London, Bill offered to go over and see what he could do to help. This was a generous gesture from Bill to Christopher, who could no longer fly there himself, and it was certainly not done under Christopher's orders like some hired hit man, as Larrabee would infer. Bill simply went to Alex's London flat to retrieve some of her belongings, only to discover that Larrabee had bizarrely barricaded himself and Alex's terrified female flatmate inside. Bill and a couple of people, including Channel 10 cameraman Brett Stanton, who we had met during the interview with Derryn Hinch, had to sort things out, forcibly removing Larrabee from the premises.

So Alex sought a Court Order from the West London County Court against Larrabee. He was ordered to give the car back and return other goods. He undertook to put the registration back into Alex's name and not to cancel the insurance policy on the car before the date of change of the registration. The insurers were then directed to pay Alex any refund due. Larrabee also undertook to return some photographs taken from her apartment.

As well, he undertook not to write to, telephone or visit Alex, and that for a period of three months he would not 'assault, molest or otherwise interfere with the plaintiff.'

With that surreal and nasty state of affairs running in the background, we began amassing evidence about Christopher's health that I could take to Australia to present to the extradition hearing. Christopher had been unable to fly since he had suffered the pneumothorax, the collapsed lung, on the plane as it flew into Zurich. He, therefore, justifiably feared that if he was subjected to the forced air pressure of an airline cabin on a long journey again, it would similarly blow a hole in his lungs.

As well as the responses from the transport providers, which I outlined earlier, saying that they would not take him back to Australia, evidence was also sought from a range of doctors. This included the opinion of those handling Christopher's case in Switzerland, headed up by his treating specialist Professor Tulio Medici and in particular Urs Lagler, Professor of Pneumology at University Hospital, Zurich, an acknowledged world expert in lung disease and the respiratory system. This was vital as Professor Lagler had been directly employed by the Australian Government to examine Christopher on their behalf and give an expert opinion on whether he could travel to Australia or not.

In that capacity, Professor Lagler had demanded Christopher go and see him in Zurich. Christopher had gone there as instructed by ferry and car and an examination was conducted. The professor had then reported to his commissioning employer, the Australian Government, that in his opinion, although Mr Skase looked physically well externally, for the foreseeable future it was too dangerous for him to travel overseas. You would think that would carry some weight, wouldn't you? They had requested the top man in the field to report back, and that is the answer he gave them, that Christopher was unable to travel. There you go; even the Government's man supported the assessments that we were relying upon.

I flew in for the hearing, my emotions swinging from the fleeting feeling of high optimism to long periods of sheer dread. Once our legal team began presenting our case on the first day in court, the feeling of dread took over permanently. To begin with, we suddenly found ourselves facing a new judge, not the one who had been handling the case up until then. Justice William Pincus had been in charge up to that point and was the judge who had allowed Christopher to keep his passport. He had continually stated that any argument that had been put to him that Christopher's passport be taken away did not stand up legally. 'I was bound by the law to restrain him from leaving only if there were some good legal grounds,' Justice Pincus said after Christopher died. 'There weren't any.'

He also pointed out that Christopher had come back to Australia regularly after he had let him keep his passport. He willingly allowed Christopher postponements for health and other issues, which Christopher honoured by returning to Australia each time at a new and agreed date.

Attorney-General Michael Lavarch agreed later that no blame could be accorded Mr Pincus, a former President of the Bar Association and recognised by his peers for his outstanding honesty and acutely perceptive legal mind. 'He called it as he saw it at the time,' Lavarch said, adding that it was 'fair to say' that at that stage Christopher had done all the right things and had maintained contact with the Director of Public Prosecutions. Lavarch conceded that Christopher 'had always been present' when needed at particular proceedings. This, from the man who was instrumental in the initiation of the Government's Chase for Skase. But these comments did not get a lot of media coverage in Australia at the time.

Then on the morning of the trial, we looked up at the bench to discover that Mr Justice Pincus was no longer there. He had been replaced by Justice Eric Pratt, who right off the bat declared he wouldn't accept any submitted material from our side. This was an astounding view. Surely we had the legal and moral right to provide whatever evidence we considered appropriate to support our case? We had brief cases full of evidence, notarised testimonials, transcripts and other data supporting our view.

Okay, fair enough, if it had been dismissed after examination, we would have accepted that. But to hear that it would not even be taken on board was, we felt, a denial of natural justice. Shane strenuously urged the judge to reconsider his decision, outlining the depth of the research that had gone into the material and its importance to our defence. After considering Shane's representations, the judge finally said something along the lines of, 'All right, I will admit it. But I will treat it with the merit it deserves.' He then looked down his nose at our material like it was a dead rat and pushed it aside.

And into the witness box came, would you believe, Larrabee!

Yes, Larrabee, Lawrence Van der Plaat, Alex's now ex-boyfriend, had abandoned the family and crossed to

310

the other side. He had worked with us as part of the old company named Halcyon, long since disbanded, and had lived the high life with Alex in London after meeting her in 1989, including attending the premier of the James Bond film, *Licence To Kill,* with her, Christopher and Pixie. He had even accompanied Christopher and me on the trip to Australia in September 1990 when Christopher was charged with the ridiculous Nathan Richter photographer assault charge and was one of a group of people who had helped me restrain the Sphincter.

Now, Larrabee had turned Government witness.

THIRTY-FOUR

F ollowing his England court appearance a few months earlier in which orders had been made against him to ensure Alex's safety, Larrabee's 'evidence' to the court in Brisbane turned out to be a tired, flimsy collection of hearsay, tittle-tattle, documents he had somehow managed to lay his hands on about resort developments, claims he knew something about offshore funds being transferred and scraps of conversation he'd picked up.

At one stage, he alleged that after Christopher had recovered from the collapsed lung incident he had supposedly said, 'There's no way the fuckers are going to get me now,' and had opened a bottle of Krug supposedly taken from Mirage III years before. What a lot of crap. That did not happen. Christopher was not drinking at the time; he was too ill and could not mix alcohol with the medicines he was taking.

Larrabee also claimed he had overheard a phone conversation in which Christopher said that he had somehow corrupted Professor Lagler's testimony. Apart from the sheer unbelievable nature of this claim and an appalling attack on the integrity of a world expert, this, in anyone's terms, was inadmissible evidence. Firstly, it was hearsay. Secondly, it was the word of a 21-year-old with a grudge versus a respected Professor of Pneumology. Yet, it was accepted. Larrabee also said that he overheard another conversation in which Christopher is supposed to have said that he was going to flee to the Dominican Republic. Little did he know how wrong he was with that as some Government agents were to discover later, much to their chagrin.

With Larrabee sprouting like some sort of all-knowing font of truth and our material cast into the shadows, Christopher's lawyers, Shane Herbert and Tony Morris, advised me to get out of town and fly back to Spain that night, even though this was only the end of day one of a planned four-day trial. 'From what I have seen today, in three days' time, they are going to issue an extradition order against Christopher for sure,' said Shane. 'And they may well detain you in Australia as some sort of surety. So, if I was you, I would leave the country right now.'

I had no reason to doubt his advice. When I had asked him on the first morning of the extradition hearing what I should or should not say to the judge, he surprised me by saying, 'I'll leave that up to you.' He was acknowledged as a skilled defence lawyer and had represented quite a few heavyweight clients over the years but said he always played by the rules and never coached witnesses. This was, he said, because he firmly believed that within the environment of the law if you did not play it straight then the system could not function. He was so good at his job that when fellow lawyer Tony Morris was asked much later if he had any regrets about his career, he said one of them was that he hadn't taken greater advantage of the opportunities he'd had 'to see Shane Herbert in action before a jury.'

Shane and Tony, a similarly brilliant young QC, made a great team—Shane, pugnacious and tough, and

Tony, relaxed and smooth. It was Tony, an expert in constitutional law, who later successfully challenged the Government's tactic of adding the Skase Amendments to the Bankruptcy Law and making them retrospective. He was among the first to say that the extradition process was a shambles, telling the then Attorney-General Daryl Williams that the Chase for Skase was a 'waste of taxpayers' money.' We understood that Williams was seriously considering calling it off at that point but for whatever reason eventually decided that it should keep going.

Shane and Tony trusted and believed in Christopher, as did everyone who really knew him and the facts. Their defence of him was more out of a sense of justice rather than money. After all, they received no payment for the entire time. But they paid heavily for their commitment and loyalty. They later received death threats, including one letter warning them that their lives would be snuffed out like that of the anti-drugs crusader who had disappeared from a Griffith car park in the 1970s and was never seen again. 'Drop Skase or you'll end up in the mincer like Don McKay did,' said the sinister note. We also got some pretty sick letters about Shane, containing all sorts of strange references to rape and torture.

The only thing Shane got from Christopher was a promise of some more work if it came up in the future. As it turned out, and this adds poignancy to Tony's regret that he never did more work with Shane in court, because a couple of years after this case, Shane was killed in a motor accident. I am not alone when I say he died in mysterious circumstances that have never been fully explained.

I am sure a lot of what Shane did for Christopher was because of his own character and upbringing. He was a man who always played within the rules and was not tolerant of injustice; he defended heavy hitters but always within the defined rules of law; he won cases because he was a brilliant lawyer with an incredible mind and a good person who believed in his clients. But by the end of our first day in court, what he observed not only disgusted him as a lawyer but also made him question the entire legal system to the point of declaring he was thinking about dropping out of it forever. Shane said it was becoming increasingly apparent that there was no way we would win this case.

After listening to his advice to get out of the country, I sat down and considered my options. On the one hand, I felt obligated to stay on, show my loyalty and do the job I had flown over to do, and that was represent Christopher. This was a crucial hearing, and we had put in a lot of hard work to come up with what we thought was a strong case. On the other hand, all our carefully compiled evidence was being dismissed out of hand. The prosecution team seemed to be able to change the rules whenever it suited them and were being backed by the usual hostile press coverage.

Unbelievably, an extradition order was also going to be issued against Christopher for not turning up for a hearing that had not yet been held. It was now January, and the hearing was set down for mid-March. Strange justice, methinks. Was this setting a stunning new legal precedent, a sort of court-order pre-emptive strike? That anyone could be arrested in case they wouldn't do something they were supposed to do in the future? Or was this just a ploy to keep Christopher away from trying to stop the fire sale of the Seven Network, which was looming on the horizon? Guess which one I was voting for?

To top things off, I was also getting the distinct impression, rightly or wrongly, that those leading the Chase for Skase were wanting to keep me in Australia to have a hold over Christopher. After seriously considering both sides, I felt Shane's opinion that I leave Australia as soon as possible was the right advice. I decided to get out.

However, in the annals of great theatrical escapes, it was not exactly the cleanest departure ever contrived by a fleeing individual. To start with, I discovered to my horror that there was no available flight direct from Brisbane to Spain. Instead, I had to take a plane from Brisbane to Cairns, stay there overnight, fly out of Cairns early the next morning to a European destination, and then catch a flight from there on to Spain.

I booked the tickets, and to his credit, Tony Morris drove me to Brisbane airport in time to catch the late-night 'milk run' flight to Cairns. All good so far.

Wouldn't you know it, the next morning, exhausted by everything that was going on—and perhaps having had one or two bevvies the night before to settle the nerves—I slept in at Cairns and missed my morning flight to Europe. Damn! Damn! Faaark! I had to get on the phone and very quickly scramble an alternative, because I knew the minute I failed to turn up at court that morning, I would immediately have an order for my arrest placed on me.

After checking with every airline, the best alternative presented to me was to fly from Cairns to Sydney, get a flight from Sydney to an Asian destination, and then go on to Spain from there. All this had added crucial time to my departure and, as I began my next move, to my horror I spotted my photo plastered all over the front pages of the newspapers! There I was, like a wanted criminal, with an accompanying story about how the court was seeking to detain me. Sitting in the taxi, I had to keep my head down and try to remain as calm as possible.

By the time I got to Sydney airport, the picture was everywhere and my stomach was really churning because I figured that the word would now have been passed along the chain of command and that when I handed over my passport for inspection the computer would light up like a poker machine and go bat-shit. I did not feel any better when I spotted people sitting next to me or standing within metres of me, reading the paper with my face all over the front page.

But if there is a higher authority in the mighty universe, he or she stepped in for me that day. Precisely at the time I entered departures, some sort of glitch, apparently a Christmas virus joke, struck the computers and the whole system crashed! They had to revert to manual check only. 'Be calm,' I told myself, as the officer checked my documents. 'Stay still, don't fidget or look around, don't say anything stupid.' And suddenly I was on my way. Was I relieved when the plane door slammed, the engines fired up and we began backing out of the terminal.

When I made it home and briefed Christopher on what had happened, he was furious at how our evidence had been treated with such disdain. He fired off an angry fax saying that the approach of the Australian Securities Commission and the Federal Government ranged between 'the illegal and the unethical.' He said that our legal team had been constantly frustrated in its attempts to admit relevant evidence, that we had been thwarted in our efforts to bring forward expert medical witnesses, and that our proposal that a panel including trustee-in-bankruptcy Max Donnelly come to Mallorca so we could present our case to them had been totally ignored. 'Enough is enough,' he wrote.

We then went into defence mode. Our first move was to go to Spain's Supreme Court and provide notarised, officially translated documents outlining the thirty-two charges laid against Christopher. We explained each of the charges clearly and advised the Spanish judges that, in the next week or so, they would receive an extradition request from Australia based on these charges. We requested them to review the documentation and the charges and to please give us an opinion based on Spanish Law. The judges studied them, and they concluded that the charges did not constitute any offences under Spanish jurisdiction. We felt a bit better about that. Would this be the end of the story?

Not on your life. When the extradition request from the Attorney-General's office finally arrived in Spain without any accompanying detail, it implied that Christopher was wanted for something like a hundred million dollars of fraud. Fraud? This was shocking. This had never come up before and most definitely was not any part of the thirty-two original charges. But typically it was indicative of how we were being treated. We had never changed our story once, yet they were changing theirs constantly.

We were stuck, the Spanish lawyers deciding we could not do anything until the anticipated accompanying material, which would provide more explanatory detail, came across from Australia. Under international law, it would have to arrive within forty days of serving the warrant. The trouble was that under extreme pressure from Australia, the Spanish authorities would want Mr Skase to be close at hand—for that, read gaol—until the documents arrived. Christopher figured it might be time to stay out of sight. He and Pixie went into hiding.

The glamour couple, once seen in the right places, now took up residence incognito in a series of safe houses—apartments rented by me in various parts of Mallorca under different names. The days of dining out at the best restaurants around the world were now a thing of the past as they relied on me to provide the daily takeaway food run, along with the medicine for his emphysema and anything else they needed to make life bearable. In between I was rushing everywhere, doing the rounds of the lawyers, keeping the home fires burning at La Noria and trying to keep the projects on track. For a while police loomed on the horizon and I was personally questioned two or three times but eventually left alone and allowed to get back to keeping Christopher and Pixie hidden while helping him prepare his defence against the extradition order.

Documents, documents and more frigging documents! How the legal system thrives on paperwork. Documents, hundreds of them, written, checked, summarised and copied to Christopher while he worked hard in secret compiling his own defence. It turned out it was all pretty much a waste of time as we eventually discovered that an extradition hearing is only conducted to determine if what you are being charged with in the original country is also a crime in the country you are staying in. It's got nothing to do with being able to defend yourself against the actual charges. Hence, the necessity for the government to use the word fraud.

Then dawned the morning that Mari-Carmen came rushing in to tell me that Spanish Interpol had arrived at La Noria armed to the teeth—the incident I outlined in the Prologue of this book. 'There are many of them, Señor Tony,' she said. 'Many. With guns.'

Such a big pack, bristling with armaments, searching the place, it was certainly a matter of overkill to arrest a harmless, unarmed businessman. But the underlying notion was that they were going through the motions. That they knew I had hidden Christopher and Pixie away somewhere, and if they really wanted to, they could find them. The message was implicit, 'Tell him to keep low and go about his business quietly, and we'll get on with more important things, okay?'

The thing was, would someone like Christopher Skase be able to do that?

THIRTY-FIVE

T he answer to the burning question turned out to be 'no.' Out of the blue, despite the broad hints dropped by Spanish Interpol to stay under cover, Christopher suddenly decided to come out of hiding and give a media interview.

To this day, I don't know whether it was a good thing or a bad thing, seeing as we had got the message from the police to lay low. But you could understand why he wanted to do it. He was very sick and was frustrated by the ways things were going. He was angry with the already trumped-up Australian Government charges now being stunningly inflated to ridiculous levels such as the non-payment of flower deliveries. After a further series of incredibly defamatory stories appeared, he decided with the support of our local legal adviser that he had had enough and wanted to get his side of the story out into the public domain.

The lawyer, well-known Mallorcan solicitor Tony Coll—pronounced 'coy'—contacted Matias Valles, an investigative journalist with the local newspaper *Diaro de Mallorca*. Matias was a hard-nut professional who had tangled with many local and international authorities and departments over the years, including the CIA, in pursuit of stories like ours. The candid interview, outlining how we were being railroaded by what we considered a devious, lying Australian Government, was conducted amid the relative safety of the front lawn of the house of Stephen Garfield, an English lawyer then based on Mallorca and who did a lot of work for us. He and his wife Angela and kids were good friends of ours.

But while Christopher may have got some satisfaction from getting his story out, the interview backfired badly. After their soft-glove search of La Noria, Spanish Interpol now made it clear they were not happy with Christopher suddenly appearing in broad daylight. As they had implied to me, they would have preferred him to stay out of the limelight permanently and not draw attention to himself. The new message passed on to me was that they were far from pleased and that now he either fronted or they would come and pick him up.

After much deliberation, Christopher decided to come out of hiding and give himself up. This was partly done as a result of the Interpol demand and partly on the advice of Tony Coll. The feeling was that if he put himself before the courts, he would almost certainly get bail. He could then go back to La Noria and continue the fight against Australia's extradition request which, by all reports, looked like it was going to fail.

So, on January 31, 1994, accompanied by the family and Tony Coll, he walked into the court at Palma and turned himself in. A short hearing, basically controlled by the prosecution, followed. They repeated the false fraud accusations and said they wanted him held in custody until the arrival of the official documentation within the allowed forty days.

The result? We lose! No bail.

What a stunning blow. Don't forget, this was a sick man suffering from a terminal disease—he appeared in court with the nebuliser to assist his breathing, especially in this stressful situation—and the last thing we wanted was for him to be taken away from his daily medication and his special diet. A request was made for arrangements to have him placed in a situation where he could receive appropriate treatment. After much discussion and representation, including a visit to the forensics department, Tony Coll and I pushed to have Christopher placed in custody in the secure wing of the Palma General Hospital, as opposed to the old, overcrowded, and soon to be condemned main prison on the city's outskirts.

To be placed in the hospital, Christopher had to go for a forensic medical examination in, of all places, the mortuary, located in the basement of the court complex. The medicos said that the results of that would determine whether he would be sent to either the hospital or the prison. Neither destination was all that appealing, but at least in the hospital, he would have some sort of treatment for his illness. After being examined amongst the dead bodies in the mortuary, Christopher was advised he was ill enough to be sent to hospital, where he would stay under guard while legal preparations began on both sides for the upcoming extradition hearing. But first there would be a short stay at the prison. So he was taken up there, while I raced around like a meth addict, getting all the documentation from and to the relevant authorities to finally get him released to the secure section of the hospital. I spent some time at that gaol during all this and believe me it was frightening.

All this was getting tougher and tougher on Pixie. Not only was Christopher sick and getting sicker, but now he had been taken away from her and his whole future was at the mercy of the courts. To begin with, she and I were only allowed to visit him twice a week and for twenty minutes maximum at that. Worse still, the

Australian media was constantly hanging around, trying to get in to see him and bothering staff and patients to dig up any scrap of information. She felt powerless to stop them.

To try and put an end to all that, she decided her views should be known too. She called a press conference at the Son Vida Hotel in Palma and read a prepared statement outlining how the doctors at the hospital were doing all that they could to prevent any further deterioration in her husband's health. She added: 'As a consequence of the intolerable pressures of recent months, his chronic emphysema has worsened and his respiratory function has deteriorated. My family and I are gravely concerned that he may have suffered further irreversible damage to his lungs.'

She said that although 'forces of evil' were conspiring 'to effectively murder my husband,' she and Christopher would continue the fight until justice was achieved. She blasted the initial information sent by the Australian police to Spain as 'inaccurate, inflammatory and misleading' and 'yet another example of the bias directed against him.' With tears in her eyes, Pixie concluded, 'My husband is very weak and asks that you desist harassment of him, doctors and other patients at the hospital.' At least she felt better, but the runaway Chase for Skase train was well and truly roaring down the tracks now.

As we feared, the extradition documents took the full forty days to turn up, and the date for the hearing was finally set down for July 19, 1994. The Supreme Court, the Audencia Nationale, which normally sits in Madrid on the mainland, announced it would come across to Mallorca to conduct the proceedings in Palma because it had studied all the medical and forensic evidence over a number of weeks and, unlike Australian judicial authorities, accepted the opinion that Christopher could not travel anywhere by plane or ship. This was only the second time in Spanish history the Supreme Court had agreed to relocate a hearing away from the capital, showing that its understanding of the gravity of Christopher's illness was certainly at a more profound level than that of Australian legal authorities.

The downside was that the announcement of this history-making relocation got picked up by the Spanish press. Up until then on the local news front, the story had been bubbling along just below the surface, but now the Spanish media ran hard with it and it started to explode. Pixie's pleas for an end to media harassment were not only ignored, there was even more activity around the hospital.

In the lead-up, two overweight, sweaty and obviously well-paid Australian doctors who had never met Christopher before arrived in Palma to give their considered opinion. They landed with twenty or so other very badly-dressed people toting their First Class Qantas baggage tags and staying at the most expensive hotel on the island. Welcome to the Prosecution Holiday Team, in town to barrack for the Aussies and back up their leader, Queensland barrister Ian Callinan, QC.

Callinan, who later became a High Court judge, was listed as the only official Australian legal representative as far as the court was concerned, although curiously he was not allowed to speak at the hearing. We were never sure what the rest of them were there for, other than presumably enjoying the hotel pool and emptying the mini bar.

The hearing at Palma's imposing court house got off to a controversial and somewhat crazy start. We understood that Dr Felipe Renom, the government-sanctioned medico in charge of Christopher at the hospital, would be one of the first to give his evidence. After all, he had been treating Christopher on a daily basis for the preceding six months. You would think he would be a pretty important witness when an application to remove his patient from his care and take him out of the country was to be discussed, wouldn't you? Yet he was conveniently left off the list of those scheduled to appear. Obviously, the prosecution did not want him to speak because they knew he would give evidence that they did not want to have aired in public.

As things turned out, this was typical of what they did to any witness that they considered potentially hostile, including medicos with international reputations for their work on lung diseases. They either left them off the list or trashed their reputation. If I hadn't witnessed this first hand, there's no way I would have believed it if somebody had told me.

We were shocked when we looked around the courtroom and realised Dr Renom was not there. There was no stopping Larkins. Leaving three rather puzzled judges from Madrid staring stone-faced down from their bench, and the Aussie Aussie Aussie Oi-Oi-Oi Prosecution Team looking a little bemused, I hustled out of the chamber, ran through the corridors, slipped out the imposing front door, raced down the steps and took off on foot to get our prized witness. No time to try and get a cab and work my way through the traffic. Running through Palma in 40-degree heat, I pounded along the city streets and up the tree-lined Paseo de Born to the Hospital General de Mallorca to get Dr Renom to come down to the court and appear. I have never run so fast in my life, weaving around pedestrians and dodging traffic. When I got there, I had to sprint through the endless corridors to locate him. Between the heat, the anxiety and the adrenalin pumping, by the time I stood in front of him my previously pressed black suit and ironed white shirt were now soaked in sweat.

Taking some time to catch my breath, I begged him, urged him, pleaded with him, to come and appear in court. He was puzzled on hearing that proceedings were now under way and miffed at not having been officially summoned in the first place, but when I implored him further, he eventually agreed to come. After sorting out his patients for the day, he hopped on his motorbike and headed off to the courthouse, with me following on foot, getting soaked in even more sweat and arriving ragged and exhausted.

Despite the fact that he had not been on the list, the court accepted Dr Renom when he got there, and it was comforting to hear someone telling the truth. He outlined his role in Christopher's detention and treatment, giving a clear assessment of his true situation. He publicly stated his view that Christopher's location was the worst place in the world for him, going into lurid detail about how the spots on his lungs were constantly being reinfected. He and the staff were doing their very best for him, he said, but Mr Skase should not be there.

It was clear-cut, concise and knowledgeable evidence. Certainly more of a handle on the situation than that of the two Australian doctors despatched to give their considered opinion. They based their medical assessment on observations of Christopher through a thirty-centimetre square glass window through two sets of doors. He told me that they never actually put their hands on him; that they never physically examined him.

Some testimony! But typical of the Australian Government approach. In fact, Dr Renom's boss, Dr

Salazar, the head of the hospital, had earlier called me into his office one day when I was visiting Christopher and told me that a representative of the Australian Government had contacted him. We believed that this was a bloke who had been sent over to 'sort things out' and who was hanging around the hospital like a bad smell.

Dr Salazar also told me that someone from the Australian Government had tried to illegally introduce documents into the system denigrating Christopher. He said that they had tried to sway his opinion on Christopher's health issues and had actually asked him to come up with an assessment that was more in keeping with the Australian Government view. Isn't that a disgrace, conspiring to potentially kill him in flight? Here was the government trying to influence another country's medical personnel, to get them to make it sound like it was all a lie and state that Christopher was fit enough to come back to Australia and stand trial. They got the answer they deserved. Dr Salazar told me that he had told them to 'shove it.' Subsequently, sources told us that the government then accused him of being on our payroll! What a terrible, damning false accusation, typical of their tactics. He never buckled.

The accusations continually flew that Dr Renom and Dr Salazar were being paid by us. Nothing could have been further from the truth. We never offered money, and they most certainly never asked. It was a classic example of the sort of shit we had to put up with, and the so-called journalists are equally to blame for reporting this crap in the biased and slanderous way they did.

Throughout the entire time Christopher was in the hospital, Dr Renom and Dr Salazar had been writing to the court every couple of weeks saying, 'Please, this man must be taken out of here.' Their view was that being locked up in that place was killing him. They said the conditions and environment were totally the reverse of what was needed for a person in his situation to remain healthy and alive. They warned that the hospital-grade superinfections he kept repeatedly getting in his lungs were irreversibly destroying him. Several times in the lead up to the hearing, we had petitioned the court with those letters and reports to seek his removal from the hospital, but our appeals had been rejected. Each time, the Australian legal team would strongly object to our application, making it obvious that they did not want him released; they wanted him to stay right where he was. This was despite the opinion from the Swiss doctors that he would never be able to travel anywhere anymore.

The really galling part was back in Australia, the receivers and the banks, having transferred all value of the Seven Network away from Qintex shareholders into a temporary holding company, had now floated the assets on the stock exchange, offering them to the public at half the value of Qintex's listed book worth.

Christopher considered this an act of disgraceful, unprofessional, unnecessary bastardry. If ever there was a time that he wanted to jump on a plane and get back home, it was there and then. But he couldn't. It would have killed him. He had to sit in a hospital gaol on the other side of the world and cop the news that his 'baby' had been sold for peanuts. It became pretty obvious to us that the Government and the receivers were intent on keeping him off air while Qintex was being butchered.

Despite our successful efforts to get Dr Renom into the witness box and his evidence of the actual state of affairs, the Prosecution Holiday Team made sure Christopher was not going to get justice, trotting out as their key witness, would you believe, Larrabee! 'He told me he would do a runner if they gave him bail,' Larrabee was quoted as saying. Did anybody think to ask him when he was supposed to have heard this, seeing as he had not seen Christopher for well over a year and long before the extradition scenario had even surfaced?

Did the great Larrabee have ESP? Did they put him up to it? Or were they just willing listeners? It still makes you wonder about the rest of it.

The trustee-in-bankruptcy and many Government agencies working on the extradition loved Larrabee. At times he had federal police assigned directly to him, and he was flown in and out of Australia with expenses and accommodation provided, ironically even staying at the Sheraton Mirage Port Douglas with his minder. It was almost rock star treatment. I am not quite sure who paid for what or who he was being protected from, except maybe himself. Larrabee loved the attention, and it appeared that all he had to do to keep it happening was to tell the trustee-in-bankruptcy or whichever government department what he claimed to know and offer his story every now and then to the media, which eventually led to the publication of his tale in a book.

Not a bad life if all you have to do is massage the truth, and that seemed to come naturally to Larrabee. Why, he even had the gall to do a television interview wearing a cardigan and tie of Christopher's that had been left in Alex's apartment!

Unemployed for more than a year prior to his newfound five-star lifestyle as a witness, he had become a bitter and twisted ex-lover of Alex with an obvious grudge. But he had become a valuable government mouthpiece in court and in the press, his testimony appearing to be given far more weight than the evidence tendered by highly respected international shipping executives, evacuation specialists and medicos including a professor of pneumology recognised around the world for his experience as a lung specialist.

In reality, despite his big claims, know-all Lawrence Larrabee, the Not-So-Talented-Mr-Ripley Van der Plaat, knew fuck-all. Largely because there was fuck-all to know. After they used him up, the authorities finally dumped him and from then on only the gutter press ran with his unfounded ramblings.

Nevertheless, from our perspective, the damage had been done. As a result, our consistent efforts to secure bail were knocked back and what we had all thought would be an overnight stay at the gaol turned into almost twelve months of hell. I don't care what anyone else says, but the treatment of Christopher Charles Skase for that year was an absolute disgrace. The twelve months in the hospital gaol killed him. He was stuck in a tiny room twenty-four hours a day, basically in solitary, with no light, no fresh air, no stimulation, no chance to even do a bit of exercise to stop his muscles from wasting.

He was seriously ill, his treatment for emphysema in Switzerland had been curtailed and his lungs were sustaining more damage. Despite the fact that he was on a rotating schedule of the strongest antibiotics for the entire time he was incarcerated, the maximum allowable doses they gave him didn't help much. The dead bits of lung would simply seep out due to no blood flow and reinfect him.

He picked up infection after infection, another big risk being the likelihood of getting tuberculosis from the TB patients that kept coming and going in the hospital gaol. It was just so sad to see him like this. The concerned Spanish doctors who were treating him were begging the authorities to have him sent home to La Noria and held there under house arrest, if only for the fact that they feared they would have a dead man on their hands.

It was said by some people that his time spent at the hospital actually enhanced his chances of survival. That's bullshit. In fact, he was there against all sound medical advice, except for that proffered by those on the prosecution money train, and the damage that was done to him there was irreversible. The room was like that of a 1950s mental asylum, a bare gaol room within Palma General Hospital with one fluorescent light. It was a two-bed room, and although he was on his own whenever possible, his co-prisoners over that time included drug addicts, guys suffering from pneumonia or dying of AIDS, and even one with suspected tuberculosis. These not only put him at the risk of infection, but they used to steal his medicine at the drop of a hat. He could hardly move, he got very little simulation and he didn't have much support other than his medical care.

Naturally enough, I visited him every day, once we were allowed to, even though technically we were only supposed to visit a couple of times a week. After a while, I was in there up to four times a day, a circumstance that developed because right from the first day I spoke to the guards in Spanish, made it clear to them that I was not going to cause problems and generally befriended them.

As time went by, it made me both sad and angry to see the way Christopher was being treated. Nevertheless, to his credit, he hung in there, even finding some level of amusement in the characters that paraded past his bed day in and day out, many of whom he gave nicknames, such as the Walker, the Pacer and so on.

The Australian Government wanted it both ways. While the local doctors used to say that he should be moved to better surroundings on the island, Australian authorities would have none of that. It was either 'send him back to Australia or keep him there.'

What a disgraceful action by a morally bankrupt Australian judicial system egged on by a media intent on the demonization of Christopher. Was this simply to silence his protestations about the Seven Network public float?

THIRTY-SIX

While Christopher was hanging on to dear life in prison, Amanda and I were left to attempt to run things back at La Noria, supported by anyone who could give a hand. Many did. They appreciated what we were going through and pitched in.

Amanda had it really tough. She was trying to look after Charlotte and keep the family together without much help from me, as I was spending twenty hours a day working on the extradition case in one form or another, dealing with the numerous daily disasters around the house, maintaining a level of 'Pixie control,' keeping the resort projects on the move and conducting after-hours meeting with all sorts of characters offering all sorts of information in all sorts of bars. The days just stretched on and on into each other, with Christopher stuck in the hospital and us trying to keep things going.

In all, from the time when he was arrested and then finally let out of the hospital gaol, it was a total of three hundred and eleven days. For me, that was three hundred and eleven mornings waking up after barely four or five hours of sleep, thinking, 'What the fuck is going to happen today?' It was like a Tom Clancy thriller with a new blank page staring back at you at every sunrise. Shit really did happen. There was a fire in the laundry, a fire in the nearby hills, things being stolen, Mari-Carmen complaining, dogs being sick, dogs escaping, dogs going on more killing sprees. The dogs! They killed cats, they killed chickens, they killed goats, they killed partridges. These dogs were not fussy. I spent a lot of time having to deal with the owners of late lamented animals, regularly finding small carcasses strung across the fence as a note of warning.

Pixie did her best to help where she could, but she was steadily going crazy through either a lack of information about Christopher's situation or getting news she didn't want to hear. She would top it up daily with a combination of gin-and-tonic and wine to try and keep some semblance of sanity. Not a lot of fun for me to cope with at the end of a long slog each day. Our urbane solicitor Tony Coll and I started hiding in little bars just to get people off our backs and give us a few minutes' sanity away from the madness and the pressure.

I used to tell Pixie that any lack of news was the same for the rest of us. No one had much to tell, the law in most countries moves slowly, and in Spain its movement is almost glacial. We were doing the best we could, putting in bail application after bail application, which were all being rejected. In response, a hysterical Pixie would oscillate between heaping praise on our 'wonderful legal team' and wanting to 'fire those useless fucking lawyers.' How do you sack someone you are not even paying? Her mood used to depend greatly on the angle of that day's major press article written by some drunken would-be journo sitting in a hotel with room service, cable television and a good imagination. Not a bad way to make a living, even if it is at someone else's expense

It was not only an emotionally and physically exhausting time but also draining on our limited financial resources. The Government reckoned we were paying off doctors and others? Ha! We couldn't even pay our lawyers. One day Tony Coll called me in and said that seeing we could no longer actually pay him for his services then from that point on I would have to meet him in his 'other' office, a bar/restaurant called the Diplomatic located directly opposite the back entrance to his 'real' office. Only three doors up from the magnificent La Seu cathedral, the Diplomatic was the gathering spot for the business and legal community in Palma. We met and talked to everyone. Lawyers, journos, politicians, high-powered businessmen and even a bishop one day. A lot of work was done at our clandestine meetings there; the beauty being that the Aussie press never discovered us. Tony also taught me how to make a genuine martini. It was the mark of the man that he would only drink martinis that he had actually made himself. I might point out that the Diplomatic was not his only watering hole. He had a bar in every quarter of Palma, where he was greeted with enthusiasm and warmth, his circle of contacts quite mind-boggling. Whatever drinking establishment we would go to, he would simply go behind the bar and mix us both a martini.

Christopher used to call Tony the Magician and the name fitted him perfectly. He was an ex-boxer who had built up his own legal practice through study, hard work, a great knowledge of the law, a brilliant ability to find the solution and a classy, gentlemanly approach. He knew everyone in town, and he tackled a broad range of jobs, including working for Zou as his business lawyer. He wasn't committed to one particular speciality, and so both his real and his other offices were always humming. He epitomised the Spanish culture—relaxed and patient, courteous and cultured, but showing energy, aggression and flair when needed.

However, his Spanish blood started to boil after a while when he began developing a growing dislike of Christopher. Not so much Christopher the person, but rather Christopher the case. This was partly due to Christopher's general frustration with people who couldn't immediately come up with the right information when it was requested. He liked an instant answer on request. But this was a complex, difficult operation, and most of the paperwork was on the other side of the planet. He couldn't always get what he wanted straight away.

As well, in Spain, if there is nothing to tell you, your lawyer doesn't come and see you. In Christopher's mind, his lawyer should have been visiting him once, twice, three times a day in order to keep him briefed and to discuss new options. This was a deep, abiding difference in their relationship, a disagreement in philosophy that flared regularly. I was often involved in some serious conflict management, I can tell you.

But perhaps as a favour to Zou, and maybe because he and I were having a bit of much-needed fun together amongst all this shit and maybe because he didn't want to lose his drinking partner, Tony kept working hard for us, often taking me along to meetings and introducing me as his assistant.

I was certainly glad of his commitment one day when I got caught well and truly in the crossfire. Christopher had been ordered to go to Juaneda Hospital, a private clinic, for an examination by a court-sanctioned medical team. But before this could happen, the Australian doctors suddenly turned up, ambushing the hospital in what was obviously another illegal attempt by the prosecution to manipulate things. They demanded that they be allowed to examine him. This was against all protocols as Christopher kept trying to tell them in his weakened state. 'You have no authority,' he said. And they didn't. But they kept persisting. Things were looking pretty grim until I called Tony on the mobile, and he turned up just in time with the police to put an end to it, with the pair of them dispatched, a stern warning from the authorities ringing in their ears.

Although Tony was handling the overall brief, another lawyer had been brought in to represent Christopher at the preliminary extradition hearing. This was Enrique Calomarde, a Valencia-based lawyer who had been involved in the Raixa property deal. His nickname, Kitchen Chicken, came from his difficulty to display any difference when pronouncing the English words 'kitchen' and 'chicken.' We prepared the fuller case for the actual extradition proceedings with Luis Rodriguez Ramos, from Madrid and known as the Professor. It was a huge, complex effort. Tony Coll was handling all of the groundwork in Palma while coordinating with Enrique in Valencia and Luis in Madrid and at the same time keeping our UK-based property lawyer Tim Stranack in the loop.

We made several trips to Madrid to meet with Luis to try and ascertain whether the Australian charges were in the same categories under Spanish Law. Luis always believed that they were not and attempted to pursue this angle. A translator became very important during these meetings in Madrid. My Spanish was not too bad at conversational level, but when it came to talking about topics such as extradition and emphysema at the legal level, I risked getting into more strife than Kitchen Chicken did with his English and therefore needed help.

Christopher and I had to do as much as we could ourselves because we were not paying most of the lawyers or not paying them full fees. Luis for example had generously agreed to a fixed fee of about $10,000, which was covered by donations from many, many people. Although Christopher was suffering a lot of pain and constantly under heavy medication, he did not want to miss a beat. He would insist on having everything explained to him on an hourly, if not, half-hourly basis. This could be difficult at times because there was an ever-present throng of journalists hanging around, continually harassing us and trying to glean something, anything, to beat into a story. They generally hung out at a nearby café, where Charlotte took the story to a whole new level one day when she, as only a curious little school preppie could, slipped a coin into one of the joint's poker machines, pressed the button and won the jackpot.

The Australian media were only doing their job as best they could, and I understood that, if you could call publishing only selected legal and medical evidence a good job. I could never understand why they were not focusing on the corrupt, behind-the-scenes Government activity associated with this story. When I put this to Chris Reason, from the Seven Network, he replied that that was not the story that his superiors were interested in.

Some of the reporters that turned up might have won awards around the world for their efforts, but on Mallorca they took the tactics of getting a story to a new low. One of their nastiest techniques was to corner any locals supporting us and put it to them that they were only helping us because we were paying them. That was so far from the truth it was ridiculous. People were helping us because they were showing a bit of compassion and they believed in us. And based on the Australian performance thus far, they quite rightly felt something was odd about the whole thing. No wonder the media hardly got any genuine news from anyone who really knew what was going on.

So eventually they resorted to making things up. One tactic of television crews was to have the sound technician and the story producer stand with anti-Skase placards to flesh out the thin crowd while the cameraman filmed the raging 'mob' outside the court. Good one, guys. Must be at the top of your show reel, I'm sure.

Another was to shoot bogus film in a different location and pretend it was an on-the-spot report from Mallorca. The finest example of this spurious 'journalism' was a story by Channel 7's *Today Tonight* reporter David 'Sluggo' Richardson and his producer Chris Adams.

Going for the big guns in terms of crucial evidence, they devoted most of the segment to, yes, Larrabee, who dutifully trotted out his usual half-baked bullshit. If you watch the video, Sluggo and Larrabee are seen ambushing Christopher near La Noria as he walks the dogs, asking the usual questions about money and making snide remarks about how he has put on weight. Then, Richardson tells the viewers that following that confrontation, Christopher has used his connections with Mallorcan authorities to block them and seize any video they have taken.

'Within minutes, Skase had road blocks in place,' Sluggo says to camera. 'Every car coming from his village to the capital was searched.' And later he says that there 'were hotels searched looking for us.' There is more about how difficult it was for them to finally get off Mallorca.

'The incredible thing is just how much clout this guy has on this island,' adds Sluggo.

He and a passenger are heard mumbling, 'Roadblocks, roadblocks,' as they drive around and footage is shown of officers shifting traffic stanchions. The report also says that Van der Plaat and producer Chris Adams copped 'an equally hot reception at the airport.'

With the camera showing him at the wheel, Richardson says furtively, 'Outta here!' plants his foot and drives off. All very dramatic, making it look like Christopher has the Mallorcan constabulary in his pocket.

However, in a revealing expose later on *Media Watch*, Sluggo was caught out, dead cold, as having fabricated the segment about attempts to block his crew and retrieve the tapes.

'We don't believe a word of it,' says *Media Watch* host Stuart Littlemore.

Littlemore goes on to show that the footage involving the cars was not shot on the island of Mallorca, but 200 kilometres away, on mainland Barcelona! Background buildings in shot are of the Barcelona theatre precinct. The 'B' on car number plates confirms that the cars are in Barcelona, not Mallorca.

And the killer blow? Littlemore adds that the officers in uniform that Richardson says are police setting up roadblocks in Mallorca, are in fact simply urban guards arranging traffic flow in Barcelona.

The story's 'veracity' is further confirmed by the final shot in the program. They cut back to Larrabee—ah, dear old Larrabee—and Sluggo asks him, 'Do you think Skase would be surprised we got away?'

And Larrabee says, 'Surprised? Pissed (meaning pissed off) would be the word.'

Oh, give me a break.

Channel 7 was caught with its pants down and an embarrassed *Today Tonight* was shown up to be what it is, a program of the lowest common denominator. It was a typical report of the times, deliberately setting up a scenario to tell blatant lies, showing the depths to which the media would descend in order to scramble a story together and the contempt with which they held Christopher.

As it turned out, the intrepid Sluggo was suspended by the network for a month. I'm surprised he kept his job at all. But then I guess nothing really should shock me about the media. Sluggo is still turning out his crap for *Today Tonight* but I note with some small satisfaction that not only is the footage now a YouTube favourite, but in 2008 his trumped-up story was included in a Top 20 show about the 'best' fake reports ever aired on television!

So you can see, with that standard of reporting swirling around, after a while I became sort of semi-stunned each morning reading the daily online bullshit press output. We had picked up quite a bit of local notoriety via the Spanish and English daily papers, but they were just as wide of the mark as their Australian counterparts, mainly being fed 'factual stories' by the Aussie playwrights.

Nevertheless, despite the lies, we started to gain support from the local community, even the police and the hospital guards, who knew something was not right. Friends and family rallied as the situation was obviously going to go the distance. Staff and regular diners at our favourite restaurants, such as Miramar, Los Geranios and Wellies, were all behind us.

Every now and then, to Christopher's delight and surprise, I would organise with the guards to let me bring in extra food and drinks, often provided by local restaurants. For example, we might bring him a nice juice or smoothie to start the meal, or one of Pixie's fresh, healthy salads to boost it, or a warming hot chocolate to finish it off, soothe his nerves and help him get some much-needed sleep. Towards the end, I would smuggle in a late-night coffee laced with rum to help him try and drift off.

When Sebastian at Abaco, the exclusive bar in Palma, found out that Christopher was in gaol, he was one of the first ones to say, 'Look, don't worry, we'll organise it. We'll get the Italian restaurant, Giovanni's next door, which I know is one of Christopher's favourites, to deliver meals two nights a week. And the little tapas place around the corner, it will deliver meals another couple of nights.'

'But you can't do that, can you?' I said. 'He's in gaol!'

'Ah, Tony, it's easily organised. This is Mallorca.'

Wonderful as the gesture was, I politely declined. But I could not stall the efforts of Juan San Juan, the stylish maître d' of Miramar. I was driving past his place on the waterfront at Porto Andratx one day when he ran out, flagged me down and asked, 'How's Christopher doing?'

'Juan,' I said. 'It's a nightmare.'

'What's the food like?'

'Well, it's prison food. It's pretty ordinary.'

'Come back tonight, and I'll have something for you to take in.'

When I returned that evening, he was standing there with a silver serving dish. He pulled off the cloche to reveal a magnificent spread of Christopher's favourite—baby leg of roast lamb, special potatoes done with garlic, tomatoes, beans, the whole deal.

'Here, take this in,' he said.

I thought to myself, 'How the heck am I going to take this into a prison?' Imagine rocking up to Long Bay

346

or Pentridge with a leg of lamb on a silver tray and saying you have it for one of the prisoners?

I said to him, 'Juan, this is beautiful, but I can't walk into the gaol with this!'

'Don't be silly. You'll be fine. A man has to eat!'

So I carefully took the dish with me, drove into Palma, parked the car and walked into the hospital with the beautiful smell of roast lamb wafting throughout the corridors. The aroma was incredible, and people were coming from everywhere to find out what was going on. Juan proved to be right. On duty were Javier Castañon, who we called Blue Eyes for obvious reasons, along with the Butcher—that was his other job when not on guard duty—the two most approachable and reasonable guards, who I had befriended. They immediately saw the funny side of it and let me take it in. This was despite the fact that Juan had given me a pair of knives and forks wrapped in serviettes. Imagine, taking two knives into a gaol!

I walked into Christopher's room, placed the silver tray on his bed and theatrically revealed the leg of lamb. 'Da-dah!' He just thought it was fantastic. After all the shit he had been through, after all the pressure he had been under, after all the treatment he had undergone, after all the pain he had been suffering, to be treated like a king by someone who knew the real Christopher and who trusted and admired him, made him feel pretty special. Juan had not missed a beat, either, giving me two sets of cutlery, so the pair of us sat on his little metal bed and tucked into this thing. The other prisoners came out of their cells, drawn by the beautiful aroma, and it turned into a little party.

The madam from a local brothel, who had been locked up across the corridor and who was being visited by a couple of her girls, and the four boys in the cell opposite were hanging off the doors, just begging for bits and pieces from the plate. It was a funny, bizarre crazy moment, and I kept thinking of Juan's simple explanation of why it had to be done. 'A man has to eat.'

Javier Blue Eyes, one of the two guards who let us in that night, was a great man, and it was a wonderful gesture of him to let us do something like that. He was an officer with an impeccable record and well respected within the Spanish National Police, part of a roster of eight who worked in pairs guarding the hospital in eight-hour shifts, around the clock. Javier was one who quickly took a liking to Christopher. Quite often in the early days, he would come and have coffee with me, and I would explain everything about Christopher's situation to him. He was the most incredible guy, his compassionate approach perhaps partly stemming from his own personal challenge. His beautiful young wife was suffering very badly from multiple sclerosis.

Over time we became quite friendly with Javier, but his approach was to ultimately have a damaging effect on his career. At one point, when Christopher was very frail and looking like he was going to die, he said that all he wanted to do was see his dogs. I explained this to Javier, and he said he knew of an alleyway near the hospital where Pixie could discreetly bring the dogs in one day. He said that there was a back stairwell out of the building and a door that very few people knew about that connected with the alleyway. 'Why don't you organise it one day when I'm on?' he said. 'Bring the dogs in the car, and I'll organise for Christopher to be taken down the back stairs so he can go and pat them.'

While the area he was talking about was secure, he would be actually taking Christopher out of the gaol environment. Only a few metres, but this was a risky thing to be offering. We knew that doing this would be of no benefit to Javier whatsoever, in fact it might cause him trouble. But being the caring man he was, he assured us everything would be okay, so I gave him my word that Christopher would not try anything, and we did it.

Pixie and I got Macca the bitser and the four huskies we had at the time and put all of them in the back of the old Merc, drove from Puerto Andratx to Palma and found the little alleyway behind the hospital. It was so tight driving down it, you could not open the doors if you tried. But we got to a little courtyard at the end, and after a few minutes, Christopher appeared at the funny little wooden door at the opposite end with Javier. The kind, gentle guard let the frail Christopher come out and play with the dogs for five minutes. It was a marvellous moment, and sick as he was, Christopher cherished every second of it. There were tears in our eyes, and we were all truly grateful to Javier.

We thought that would be the end of that. But someone in the press found out about it and the story broke. No one is sure how it got out, but one possibility was that two of the very straight guards who always played by the rules, who Christopher called the Doberman and Slim, may have leaked the story. The worst element of it was that the media, no doubt with the Australian Government's pushing, accused Javier of taking bribes from us to let things like this happen.

This beat-up was completely wrong. He had devised this wonderful gesture and other kind things out of the goodness of his own heart, but poor old Javier was punished. He was pulled out of his role at the hospital and rostered to spend his nights standing out in the rain, doing guard duty in winter on the steps of the National

Police Headquarters. It was the most lowly, denigrating job that a person of his experience could be given. A blatant form of punishment—a real, visible and obvious castigation. I used to go and visit him, and he was always cool about what had happened. He never held it against us. But those sorts of things used to really piss me off, journos tearing down people who were simply nice, good-hearted and understanding. The pain and suffering that those deadshits put them through was just incredible and unforgivable. In all that time not only did we never give or were we ever asked for money and I don't think Javier ever even let me pay for his coffee.

Nevertheless, kindness was also shown at the hospital by Sister Felicidad who was the nun permanently attached to the gaol section. She was very well named, translated as Sister Happiness, with her sunny disposition bringing a lot of warmth into an otherwise pretty depressing place. Sister Felicidad used to visit Christopher most days on her rounds. Sometimes she'd sit with him for hours and chat, which was a tribute to the communication skills of them both, his complete lack of Spanish being complemented by her total lack of English.

Whatever she said, it certainly had an impact. Because after some months, Christopher made a decision that some people were shocked by, some didn't care less about, some people said was the worst thing he had done in his life, while others said it was the smartest and most profound. He converted to Catholicism.

In some ways, I was little surprised by this. He had been brought up Christian, in the Church of England I believe. But over the years that I knew him, he had not been a practicing religious person in any way, shape or form. The concept of him going to church or saying prayers or even meditating never entered into the equation. I never saw or heard one instance that indicated that he had some sort of religious or spiritual leaning.

I think that he simply converted because he thought he was dying. It was a genuine fear. Having spent so much time with Sister Felicidad, it was something he could grasp on to. A lot of people in gaol, in desperate straits, turn to religion, if only to keep their head together, and he was a classic case of that. He was fearful of dying, either in the gaol, or on the way back to Australia if they managed to spirit him away. I don't think he received the last rites, but he certainly had a personal embrace of the Church. It was principally Sister Felicidad who encouraged him to accept it. The occasional priest came through the cells, but she was in there every day and he loved her. She got him studying the Bible, reading passages out loud, and she'd sit there with him for a long time, discussing the words and what they meant. Pixie converted, too. But if Christopher's conversion was out of fear, I think hers was out of loneliness and madness.

You can understand why he had a very real fear of death. He was in gaol. He was a prisoner, locked up, albeit in the hospital section. For a lot of time, he was in solitary. I witnessed all this, and I can tell you that he got down to about six stone. He smelt like he was dead, he looked like he was about to die and he had that dreadful, emaciated, haunted look of an AIDS victim on his last legs. He would struggle to pull himself up to sit on the bed, and he was on oxygen twenty-four hours a day, even when he was taken to the bathroom.

This was the real condition he was in when television reporters such as Chris Reason and Hugh Riminton were saying there was 'nothing wrong with him,' which really disgusted me. I'd like to ask them now, 'What were you thinking? Did you not look at him? Did you just disbelieve all those surgeons? Were you accusing those medical people of being on our payroll to suit your stories? While the man was dying, you continued to perpetuate all the bullshit and the lies, just to feed your own purposes. Disgraceful. Just disgraceful.'

I appreciate that Chris was just an ambitious pup reporter at the time, trying to make his mark in a pack containing some pretty big dogs, but later when he himself was diagnosed with testicular cancer, I always wondered how he would have felt if the media had made a mockery of his struggle, like he did of Christopher's. Must ask him one day.

THIRTY-SEVEN

F or months on end, we did our very best to keep up the pressure in this strange international battle for legal supremacy. We would score a few points here and there and win the occasional round, despite Christopher trying to drive it all blindly from a cell with no Spanish and not much understanding of how the Latin legal system worked. Getting bail, the target we so desperately sought, was so difficult to achieve.

True, there were a couple of things I did that were right out there on the legal edge in an endeavour to secure bail. I almost got locked up at one stage for a spot of creative accounting, generating a not entirely legitimate bank draft, employing my newly acquired Photoshop skills. This was done so a payment would appear to have gone through, and the lawyers at Clayton Utz would then release a critical document that we so desperately needed. We had reached a point where they wanted us to pay some of their overdue bills before they would send us the documents, and we simply did not have the money.

It nearly worked, but in the heated follow-up when the bank draft's legitimacy was put under severe scrutiny, the ever-cool Tony Coll used his legal skills and contacts to calm things down and get me off the hook. Funny, I was the one who had actually committed fraud, and international bank fraud at that, albeit for altruistic purposes, not Christopher.

Nevertheless, the court presentations by our legal team were always well within all legal proprieties, unlike the Australian contingent who never ceased to amaze us with their constant pursuit of the case as one of criminal law. In reality, the sole reason for the extradition exercise was that Christopher was supposed to appear at a civil hearing in Queensland. That was all. We used the law to our best effect, but the prosecution used just about every trick in the book in attempting to extradite a man who had never been found guilty of anything and would be facing the distinct possibility of dying if their aims to have him transported were successful.

Our big problem was this: in the eyes of the Spanish judges, the fact that these people were official legal representatives of a democratic Commonwealth country meant that surely they would never stoop to anything underhand, because in Spain being a judge or a high level lawyer or a senior government official means you are occupying a position of respect and professionalism and will act accordingly. The thing was, in our opinion, Australia's legal representatives weren't.

The situation dragged on and on, through hearing after hearing, representation after representation. Many minor moments of victory were saluted, many major moments of defeat were absorbed, many sorrows were drowned, many Tony Coll martinis were drunk. Celebrating one win, Tony and I got absolutely slaughtered one evening. We were congratulating each other on our marvellous skills when I realised time was on the wing and, whether I liked it or not, I had better get myself down to the hospital to tell Christopher the good news before the ten o'clock guard changeover to the straitlaced Doberman and his equally uptight partner Slim.

My reticence to go stemmed from the fact that not only had we been on the turps, but we were not very happy with him at that time. I know that sounds like a departure from the picture of unity that I have been painting so far, but I can tell you the stress of this situation would drive the most unified of teams apart at different stages. During the previous visit, Christopher had been so rude to Tony and me because he couldn't get his own way that we had told him to go fuck himself, adding that we were not going to come back and see him for a week. Now here I was, standing before him only a couple of days later, not so much pissed off, but pissed. I think Christopher's heart must have sunk when I staggered in. Great news that you have delivered, guys, but what a fine example of sober leadership being displayed by my crack legal team.

You see, if Christopher had one weakness, it was his inability to adapt to the local scene. He never learnt Spanish, he never got a proper handle on the Spanish way of doing things and he battled to appreciate that if you wanted to get something done, you had to get down from your ivory tower and mix it with the locals. If that meant numerous drinks in dimly lit bars, so be it. Just as we had done at La Noria, and at the school, and shopping in the village, Amanda, Charlotte and I had become part of the scene at the hospital gaol, getting in and out at will. That's because the guards and staff appreciated that we always spoke in Spanish, that we respected them and the job they were doing and that we were in tune with their rituals and obligations. We knew, too, how important family is to the Spanish.

The clincher for us was Charlotte. The guards spotted this little Spanish-speaking girl in the uniform of Madre Alberta School, a place that played a big role in the life of Mallorcans, and to them that meant we were part of the community. This link firmed up when we started seeing some of the hospital guards dropping their kids off at the same school in the mornings. Before long, guard pairings such as Javier and Camillo, and the Butcher and the Jeweller, were respecting us for what we were doing and treating us like family. In the complex, bizarre and stress-laden atmosphere that we found ourselves in, this was a good feeling and I am forever grateful to those blokes. They were terrific. Unfortunately, this only pissed off the Doberman and Slim even more, so we had to be extremely careful.

Although Christopher could be a bit of a pain in the arse occasionally, the guards who warmed to him began to compare him to Jose Maria Ruiz Mateos, a businessman turned hero whose wine export company had been taken away from him by the Spanish Government in the early 1980s. Mateos was gaoled for fraud and embezzlement but never gave up on his fight to regain his life and his dignity. He was eventually acquitted.

To be compared with the great Mateos was a huge honour, especially as Christopher could be in such varying moods during visits. Sometimes we used to think that maybe he was losing it. I suppose you could not blame him as he was, after all, dying. And what a way to go. Living death in a hospital gaol cell, surrounded by patients that were either terminally ill, zonked out or barking mad. Some of the crazies that came and went through that place would have you doubled up with laughter at their antics one minute and then rigid with fear the next. A lot of these were druggies or AIDS victims or both, so Christopher had a clearly defined rule for incoming inmates, 'This is my side of the room; that is yours. This is my medicine; that is yours. Let's not mix anything up.' Try as hard as he did, that did not stop him from catching infections, and he continually struggled to get on an even keel. He would get over one infection and then be reinfected or pick up a hospital grade superinfection.

It was a sparse, soulless hospital room with two windows. One was small and opaque, high up the wall, which let light in but did not let him look out. The other looked straight into the guards' room, from where they could stare at him 24/7. No stimulation whatsoever. All Christopher could do was gaze at a wall a metre away. There was only a cold shower in the bathroom, and he was never let out to exercise. The only times he left that cell were once to go to the dentist for emergency treatment and once for a court hearing. To be stuck away there for nearly a year, suffering excruciating pain, knowing it was killing him, while a hectic legal case swirled around him was inhumane. An absolute disgrace.

Nevertheless, he never lost his lifetime habit of writing down his day's thoughts and observations on the ever-present yellow legal pads, which intrigued the other inmates. As it turned out, all the ones who came in contact with him grew to like him, some even writing to him from the main prison when they were taken back after their health had been restored.

I used to smuggle in a mobile phone so he could ring family and friends, not only to say hello, but to beg for money so we could not only fund the general living expenses of the family but pay at least something to the lawyers for the direct costs of the upkeep of the case. The begging became a sore point for me after a while. I reached a point where I could no longer bear ringing people I didn't know and pleading for a few hundred dollars or a thousand if they could. Many did but I just couldn't do it so that's when I began secretly taking the phone into him. He would go to the bathroom and make a few calls and then I'd take the phone back out with me.

Having made his calls, he would then work on the daily budget. Without fail, at the end of each day, line by line, he would calculate with infinite detail what had come in and what we had spent. Talk about being down to our last cracker! By now we had no phones at the house, because they had been cut off for non-payment. The only reason we had water was because the suppliers were nice people. Unbelievably, Carlos from Rojales Water would turn up every week and just give me a knowing wave. The only reason we had electricity was because the power authority had not checked the meter for twelve months, mainly because they could not find it. It had vanished under a heavily overgrown bush. When they finally made a reading and sent us a bill, it took us a long time to pay it off, and they were not happy. That certainly confirmed in my mind that there was no hidden money anywhere. If there had been a dollar stashed somewhere, Christopher would have grabbed it. He was fighting for his life.

As was always the case, we did our best to keep things together, while all sorts of characters came and went and all sorts of things were written up about this weird scene. The local English language paper, the *Majorca Daily Bulletin,* was one of the very few media outlets that genuinely knew what was going on and the only one to cover the story with any real degree of accuracy.

We had met editor Jason Moore and reporter Humphrey Carter a few times prior to the extradition proceedings, mainly socially. But once the battle started to heat up, the *Bulletin* was the only newspaper that actually reported the facts in a balanced manner, quoting the medicos and others in a realistic and compassionate way. Due to this we gave them far more access to our side of the story than anyone else. This pissed the Aussie press off no end.

In the middle of all this swirling drama, a lovely Spanish lady, Monica Fonteseca Santa Maria, was appointed as the translator to help out the media contingent. Amid the daily pressure, at least one good story developed. Monica and Humphrey got together as a couple and married. We were blessed to be able to attend their Mallorcan wedding.

Monica was reading and hearing what the Aussies were writing and saying and at the same time witnessing for herself what the reality was, and I am sure this helped with the balanced reporting of the *Bulletin* right throughout the extradition and beyond. In many ways this educated, sophisticated lady was our only real contact with objectivity to the outside world.

We remained quite good friends with all three of them until our forced departure. Both Jason and Humphrey are still passionately involved with the *Bulletin*—Humphrey as deputy editor and Jason, as managing editor, recently celebrating twenty-five years on the paper.

Piece by piece, people began seeing for themselves that it wasn't our team who were doing the lying, but it wasn't enough to turn the tide. The reality television show was in full swing, and like all good productions, the next few episodes had already been written.

Tim Stranack, our lawyer in London, tried to help out whenever and however he could. He had continued to donate his time to an extraordinary degree despite pressure from his partners to drop Christopher due to lack of payment. Tim was a lovely man who was horrified by the behaviour of the Australian Government and despised the injustice that was being meted out to Christopher. As with most of the legal guys, he never received payment but had faith in Christopher and did what he could. He once told me he thought Christopher's only real crime was not setting up offshore accounts or trusts when things were good. 'He was too honest for his own good,' said Tim. 'He obviously thought Qintex would never fail, and therefore thought, why have a safety net?'

All this was turning my hair a whiter shade of grey, and I was having nightmares and not getting a lot of sleep. I kept waking up from this recurring dream of seeing Christopher being loaded onto a plane by guards and turning to me and shouting, 'You prick, you forgot to fax that document!' Or, 'You forgot to see the fucking lawyer!' Or, 'You said we were going to Madrid.' The ending was different each time, but the theme was the same and it had the same effect. It scared me.

Meanwhile, you never knew what the Australian Government would come up with next. Amid all the dispute about whether he was fit enough to be transported back home or not, a mob of doctors arrived at one hearing and came up with the bizarre suggestion that he could be flown back all the way at sea level. This absurd, impractical concept was deservedly howled down amid roars of laughter from the public and press galleries. It would have been a long trip around Africa.

Nevertheless, the bastards finally got their way. On September 16, 1994, the Spanish Court granted extradition of Christopher Charles Skase back to Australia on the basis of the thirty-two Australian Securities Commission charges laid under the Queensland Companies Code. They ruled that he travel home by sea, along with appropriate medical support. This was devastating news, but although we were initially shocked, the judges did rule against the seven bankruptcy charges, which had been hastily put together and then signed off by a Justice of the Peace in order to boost the Australian Securities Commission's ongoing tide of bullshit. Another example of what we thought was a waste of taxpayer money and shareholder funds.

However, the judges gave the Australian authorities just thirty days to satisfy the conditions, which provided us with a little window of opportunity. Tony and Luis yet again applied to get Christopher out on bail and be allowed to return to either La Noria or a private hospital under strict supervision. This failed because of Larrabee's testimony that Christopher would flee to Santo Domingo if granted bail. How anybody would believe anything he said by now was incredulous.

But unbowed and against all the odds, Tony and Luis then put up an appeal against the entire court order! Would you believe, this suddenly gained a bit of traction. Pixie weighed in, pointing out how bad Christopher's situation was and how his incarceration at the hospital, with no exercise and constantly being reinfected, was killing him. She told how not only had his lungs got worse, but his skin had yellowed, his teeth were loose, his breathing was failing continually, and his hands were constantly trembling. We supported her with new evidence from medicos declaring that he was incapable of travelling, including a report from Dr Luca Peña, Iberia Airlines' medical services head.

Now, while the judges were away considering this new thrust, I went off and nearly killed myself. Not deliberately, I might point out, but it may as well have been. Doing anything up to four return trips a day along the forty-odd kilometres of winding road from Puerto Andratx to Palma had started to take its toll on me. It also had started to take its toll on my old Alfa Romeo Spyder. With terminal rust eating its way through the body and holes in the soft-top roof forcing me to provide an umbrella for any passenger when it rained, it was almost at the end of its life. But at least it was getting me around, and I had become pretty good at handling the twisting road to Palma, which has since been replaced by a freeway.

On this day, however, perhaps a tad over-confident and displaying a bit of extra bravado due to a couple of Spanish brandies and many, many glasses of pisco, the famous Peruvian smack-in-a-glass, I headed out of the port at considerable velocity, decided I needed a change of music, and took my eye off the road when the CD I was fiddling with fell on the floor and I reached down to grab it. I then looked up to see a half-metre high, bluestone-walled roundabout under construction directly in front of me.

Frantic endeavours to either slow down the old Spyder, or turn it, or both, proved unsuccessful. I landed smack in the middle of the roundabout, the car a wreck. As I tried to get out, I felt shocking; my back was aching, my head was spinning and I couldn't move my legs. I was also fearful, because I could smell fuel dripping everywhere and figured I didn't have much time before something really nasty might happen. Mustering every bit of strength, I grabbed whatever I could for support, gave one almighty heave, pulled myself up and rolled out of the old Alfa, which immediately burst into flames.

Now lying face down, unable to move and confused, I groggily managed to locate my mobile phone and call Amanda who was pacing angrily outside Gringo's restaurant in Portals Nous with a tired Charlotte, waiting to be picked up. I managed to explain everything before the ambulance turned up to take me to hospital. They drove me to one place, which wouldn't admit me because I did not have private health coverage, so they dumped me in the hospital next door to the one Christopher was in! How crazy was that?

I had been involved in some perilous incidents over the years, but this time I had really done it. I had broken my back in two places, crushing the T4 and T9 vertebrae, and there was some real concern for a few days that I might never walk again. This was the second time I had broken my back—the first being the horrific motorbike accident while growing up in Sydney. Oh well, another life for Larkins the lucky cat, and another page to go onto my file at Royal North Shore Hospital.

Despite all the medical advice, I threatened to crawl out of bed and check myself out because I was so concerned about what was happening down at the court. The staff told me in no uncertain terms not to move. So, there we lay. Me in the general hospital getting continual CT scans, unable to move from the chest down and constantly hearing the Spanish pronunciation of the word 'paraplegic' floating through the ward. And Christopher just down the way in the secure gaol division struggling to even breathe. The both of us began to think that this really was the end. That all our efforts to fight off the Australian Government had failed. That all the energy we had put into creating a lifestyle in Spain had been wasted. That all the complex deals we had put together, in Mallorca and other parts of the world, had come to nothing. To make matters worse, I was informed that my brother Neil, who had been such an influence on my early life, had died in an unfortunate accident in Australia. And there was no way I was going to be able to attend his funeral. 'Oh, go on, kill me,' I thought. 'Just end it all and do me in now.'

A week later, just as doctors told me that I might be able to walk again with a metal brace fitted for a year, a miracle happened and all our fears were washed away with one stroke of the pen. Our last-chance appeal, fleshed out by Pixie's heart-breaking description of Christopher's condition, was accepted by the judges on humanitarian and constitutional grounds. On December 19, 1994, they ruled 'it is a fundamental function of the Spanish Court, according to Article 7 of the Organic Judiciary Act to ensure the basic rights of persons involved in legal proceedings against them. Pre-eminent among such rights is the right to life and physical integrity and health.'

After nearly a year locked away in a morbid hospital gaol ward, Christopher Charles Skase was free! To go home to La Noria. Not back to Australia.

I don't know if my accident a week earlier and the injuries I sustained affected the decision, but I have never felt such an enormous feeling of relief as that day. All our hard work had come to fruition. All the shit we had copped was now a thing of the past. And the best thing, someone in authority had believed us! We weren't telling lies.

The funny thing was that the day Christopher was released from the hospital, I got out of there, too, although I had to force my way out.

When I heard what time Christopher was scheduled to leave, I harassed the staff to chase up the back brace that was being custom made for me. It was a full metal jacket, a shoulder-to-waist job that I had to be strapped into. But as the deadline loomed, it wasn't quite ready, and I was devastated. I explained to them what was happening and threatened to walk out without it if it was not ready. And God love 'em, they pulled out all stops and with literally ten minutes to spare before Christopher was due to be released they strapped me in. As soon as I got it on, I discharged myself with the medical team's approval and walked the two hundred and fifty metres to where he was being released—in my socks because my shoes had disappeared in the accident.

When I say 'walked,' I mean that with Amanda and Charlotte's support I shuffled that stretch in the most unbelievable pain. But there was no way I was going to miss this. Just as I arrived at the main entrance to the gaol section, Christopher materialised in a wheelchair and, smiling as broadly as we could within the confines of our pain, we were both loaded in to the ambulance, him sitting up and me lying on the floor.

As we drove along, it was amazing, heart-warming, to look up and see his face glued to the window like a kid on his first outing in a car, taking everything in. I will never forget that image.

It seemed fitting, the pair of us trundling down the road together, knocked around but not defeated, when you consider that at one stage he owned a film company that gave the world Laurel & Hardy.

THIRTY-EIGHT

The first few days after Christopher's arrival home at La Noria were ones of incredible relief. After three hundred and eleven days of him locked away in a soulless room, it was great to have him back, even though he was grey, stooped, thin and resembling an inmate of a concentration camp.

You don't come out of a situation like that quite the same as you go in, and he was certainly a different man in many ways—not quite so full of bravado, a little more circumspect, even a touch more humble. He wore his hospital pyjamas for days after he came home. You would think that the first thing he would have done would have been to douse them in petrol, burn them in the back yard and put on a pair of Playboy silks. But he stuck with the prison issue PJs for quite a while, maybe as an indicator to others that he was making a transitory move back into the real world from an environment that had been absolutely surreal but which nevertheless had kept him alive through a very debilitating illness. I never did find out.

Pixie was over the moon that he was home and so were Amanda and Charlotte. I was obviously very happy, despite having to spend the next six months, twenty hours a day, lying horizontal on a rock-hard Lilo on the floor in my full metal jacket while trying to keep up with what was happening on the business front. But I was probably more relieved than anything else that all our hard legal work had come to fruition, and this seemed to make the pain easier to deal with. The health issue—that it was too risky for any attempt to take him back to Australia—which we had hammered so hard because we knew it was true, had finally been acknowledged. Acknowledged by the Spanish judiciary, the Audiencia Nacionale, that is, to the point that there was no right of appeal against their blocking of extradition. But not acknowledged by the Australian authorities or the Down Under gutter press.

Oh, no. Their view was still quite the opposite, and they did not give up the attacks. They insinuated that we had bribed the Spanish authorities, the health commission, the doctors, the hospital people and others who had given evidence. These were disgraceful attacks on every aspect of Spanish integrity. How anyone could have believed this rubbish is beyond comprehension. It was staggering.

We did not mind that they would savage us. We were used to it by then and nothing could hurt us or shock us anymore. But it was fucking unbelievable that they would attack and viciously slander people who had done nothing but their professional job. And as usual, although he was emaciated, grey and wandering around in prison-issue pyjamas, the Australian authorities and media painted him as running, jumping, doing handstands, smoking cigars and swimming to the mainland and back each morning.

After many months' rest and slow recuperation, Christopher gathered us all together and promised a re-establishment, a new start to life, a new beginning. Everybody was variously elated, exhausted, shattered or hung over, but we regained our focus. Money was borrowed from relatives, friends and associates, including developer David Stein, who had sold Christopher the Dana Point property in California and who was now coincidentally doing a six-star hotel project on Mallorca. With the great support of people like these, we started to pick up on the projects again, such as the Apartments and Valldemossa and, after nearly a year, a new one that landed in our laps just as I was starting to be able to move around again, on the island of Saint Martin in the Caribbean. Because of the circumstances, Christopher had very little to do with this plan. He had never been to Saint Martin and obviously would now never make it, and he had not met our main contact there, Lillian Hutchence.

Lillian was an Australian who described herself as a business consultant and who, according to the grapevine, was an agent for the CIA. Yes, we moved in interesting circles at times and met extraordinary people with amazing backgrounds. There was more. She told me she had worked in aerospace in hometown Sydney and was now based in Colombia, South America. She had contacted us in association with a bloke called Bob Pritchard, who had been Kerry Packer's marketing guru for the World Series Cricket launch and who had been good friends with Christopher. The message was that she was acting as the agent for the sale of a five-star golf resort and casino project and wanted to know if we were interested.

While working for the CIA, Lillian had become linked to the property through a rather eccentric bloke named Jean-Louis Andreux, a French blueblood who had been kidnapped by rebels while on a business trip to Colombia. She had somehow secured his release—I never asked how, you just knew it was something that you did not want to know—and in turn he had gratefully told her that he knew of a resort project up for sale and that it would do a lot of people the world of good if she could help him find a way of organising its disposal.

After Christopher was settled back in at La Noria, I flew to Los Angeles and then on to the Caribbean with Lillian to inspect the property. We then went on to Paris to pick up the sales prospectus. I could see straight away that it was a fantastic opportunity, something we could not let go by. But where to get the seed money to get things under way? Into the breach stepped an old American mate of Christopher's, Wonchai Wally. I could give you his full name, but I think it is best that we just leave it at that. Wally was an urbane, Harvard-educated, very experienced hand at finding money, and Christopher had used him in the past when looking for finance. Once he flew over to Saint Martin and saw it, Wally fell in love with the project and decided to work pretty much full time on getting the deal done.

Wally and I started spending a good part of each month in the Caribbean, going over the resort again and again with a fine tooth comb, studying the existing buildings and the golf course land, while looking around for potential investors and financiers to help buy it and finish it off. This led us into one of my more bizarre SkaseWorld adventures. At one stage, Christopher organised Wally and I to meet up with the Munty—New Zealand investor Ron Burton, who had helped refinance the Apartments—to encourage him to invest in it.

The meeting was set for New York when Wally and I were passing through on one of our regular trips to the Caribbean. Through my frequent dealings with Air France and a resort called La Samana on the French side of Saint Martin, I was offered an invite to the ultra-exclusive Club 21 in downtown New York. It was virtually impossible to get in without a contact or invitation back then and probably still is. Every President except George W. Bush has dined there and just about every actor of note.

Wally and I decided we should take the Munty along to impress him. Long-term clients have their acknowledged tables at Club 21, and at some point after a swag of very nice French red, Wally noticed that where we were seated had a brass plaque reading 'Fred Trump & Dick Flanagan. Their Table.'

Wally told the Munty that he knew Fred Trump, one of the richest real estate developers in New York and had organised finance deals for his son Donald and that that was how we got the exclusive dinner booking. It was total bullshit but the Munty fell for it. Donald was a big mover and shaker in the property scene then with the Trump World Tower under construction. Just think, Christopher Skase and Donald Trump, what a combination that would have been! We never figured Donald would go on and rock the political world like he has.

Wally got down to business, outlining the Saint Martin project's financial prospectus and other detailed aspects to the Munty, and I got bored and somehow got talking to two gay guys at the next table. They loved the fact that I was 'an Aussie' and the three of us wound up having lots of very nice champagne and lots of giggles and a bit of harmless flirting. Basically, I was just glad for the company.

Then, fuck me, when our bill arrived—and it was pretty substantial by anyone's standards—one of the gay guys simply leaned over and took it from the waiter and told him he would take care of it! He then produced his Gold Amex and paid for the lot. It was one of my most surreal moments ever. I reckon I had known these guys for thirty minutes and couldn't thank them enough. The Munty was very impressed, and Wally and I laughed about this night for years after.

Then it dawned on us, we had a lot of work to do. But would this be the project that would save us?

There were some amazing things about this island project; the standout being that the actual property was divided between two countries. Not counties, or councils, or cities. Two different countries. We were told that when our golf course was completed it would mean that on the first hole you would tee off in Holland but putt out in France!

This came as a result of Saint Martin being controlled by the two colonial superpowers for years. It was only about thirty-seven square kilometres, more or less equally split between the two but predominately Dutch. The southern half is part of the Netherlands Antilles and is called Dutch Saint Martin or Sint Maarten. Despite that, France still maintains a toehold. Its side, on the north, is called Saint-Martin and even includes an area called Quarter of Orleans. In this instance, even though most of the resort property was actually on the Dutch side, the French were calling the shots. They wanted the property, then in maintenance-only mode, to be up and fully operational as it was one of the largest employers on the island. Not good for their image. It was being sold by GMF, the gigantic French Government workers' insurance agency, which wanted to get it off its books in a nice, quiet, clean deal.

There was some murky story in the background about two French Government Ministers being killed plus rumours that $140 million had been laundered through the place to help finance an election campaign. GMF wanted to deal with someone who knew about resorts, who would take it over and turn it around, and who would not say much about it. It had been an embarrassment from the beginning, and they just wanted to get out and save face. Where had we heard all that before? More importantly, who do you bring to the table to negotiate everyone's way through a situation like that? Say no more.

He might have been sick, he may have spent nearly a year in solitary under guard in a hospital gaol and he may well have been suffering from an illness for which there was no cure, but the prospect of doing a deal once more fired up Christopher Charles Skase. He got out a single sheet of his A4 yellow paper, did some calculations, got on the phone and started negotiating the price … down.

The old warhorse, he was an inspiration to watch. Calm, diplomatic and with just the right amount of push when needed. Week by week he would prepare himself, take a deep intake of oxygen from his tank and make the call. He knew GMF was keen to sell to us, so he kept patiently pushing the price lower all the time. He was a genius at beating people down. Every now and then, he would almost say it was a done deal and then add, 'Oh, there is just one more issue …' While they pondered that, he would go back to bed and rest up.

Our potential financiers came on board just as he finally knocked the vendors down to an absolute bargain basement price. How's this for a result? Two respected international banks with branches on the island, Barclays and Scotia Bank, had done valuations for me and put it at between $US120 to $US127 million. Lillian had approached us with a heavily discounted asking price of US$86 million. We got it for US$32 million.

Plus, we got a $5 million cash kickback from a Hurricane Luis insurance payout that would be perfect for getting the project up and running. We got our own airline thrown in, too! I kid you not, the bank looking to finance the buy wanted us to take British West Indies Airways as part of the package. Although this was not our real interest, it fitted the vertical integration, and as they had inherited it and wanted it off the books, we thought well, why not? We immediately began thinking about upgrading it and linking it with the major international airlines, including Concorde. As Christopher used to say, always think big.

Was that a deal or what? It was the Deal of the Decade, I reckon. No, wait, the Deal of the Fuckin' Century.

We were happy again for once. It was all good. On day one, we would have already made US$90 million profit, albeit on paper. We started congratulating ourselves and feeling optimistic about the future. Buoyed by this and with a new and more nutritious diet, Christopher began to put on a bit of weight. The grey, stooped concentration-camp look began to slowly disappear, although his laboured breathing was painful to hear and watch.

So, we were going along nicely and could see a reasonable future panning out, still remortgaging La Noria to keep us going and fund work on new projects. But the Australian Government was not going to go away. Oh no. They were mightily pissed off that we had scored a victory over them in the Spanish courts, whereas we saw it as justice. They turned up the heat by using the press to destroy not only Christopher's name but also mine and that of anyone else who worked with us.

The government had a great ally in the media. Those hacks just wrote what they were told or regurgitated an old lie or elaborated on the 'truth' a bit more. We had no way of combating that sort of concentrated bullshit attack, so it wasn't that hard to take us on and fuck us over. After a while, they scored a significant victory. The local Mallorcan banks, which had worked so well with us over the years, crumbled under the pressure and decided not to remortgage the La Noria deal or finance the group further. This was a killer blow, forcing us into selling bits and pieces of La Noria off in stages to cover the mortgage and running costs.

Undaunted—hey, we'd been kicked in the balls many times before and had bounced back—we focused on the other projects in an attempt to make them happen quickly and get some money flowing. Saint Martin in the Caribbean was the obvious one because it was already built, was cash-flow positive without any outlay at all and could be opened within a month.

We were looking at a time-share resort featuring eighty-eight rooms, with a spectacular world-class casino, the finest and largest marina in the Caribbean, a state-of-the-art health and fitness centre, and permits and plans for a championship golf course. Not to mention its own power generators and sewerage treatment plant, all built to the highest standards by a Dutch engineering company. Not only had it survived Hurricane Luis that had devastated the island two years prior, it had been used as the evacuation centre and was one of the few things left intact. Luis was described as one of the deadliest hurricanes in 1995, a year regarded as one of the worst ever for the Atlantic area.

We had spent nearly two years' due diligence on that project, examining the resort from back to front, getting to understand the island and learning to know its people. Along the journey, we dealt with a range of intriguing characters, starting at the top with the Wathey family, the most important but nevertheless controversial clan on Saint Martin. Al Wathey and his wife Rose were heavy hitters in island tourism and politics and became valuable allies. Funnily enough, I met Al in a bar. What are the odds?

Al's name was good in many respects because his father Claude Wathey had attained legend status as the 'father' of Saint Martin. The locals revered Claude for his long-running battles to gain independence, his clashes with the Dutch over their imposition of financial control and his role in transforming the island into a holiday destination. The locals loved to tell the story about the day the Queen of the Netherlands arrived for an official visit. When her plane touched down, instead of heading up the welcoming party, the most important man on the island was nowhere to be seen. Claude had gone fishing! In the uproar that followed, the Dutch Government decided to extradite him back to Holland to give him a lesson in good manners. But after they had loaded him on the plane, half the island's population, led by Al, Rose and the Attorney-General, rushed to the airport. They smashed the boundary fence down, spilled onto the runway and surrounded the plane, preventing it from taking off. In a tribute to his diplomatic skills, Claude calmed the mob down and flew on to Holland to cop his penance.

So, as far as we were concerned, the Dutch maintained a stony silence about the Wathey family, and the French tried to stop us talking to them. Taking the hint, we determined the best thing to do was stay out of local politics and concentrate on a worldwide search for a suitable financial backer. We finally unearthed a genuinely interested party in the Bank of Trinidad. From there, things rolled along and looked good. The bank did six months' due diligence and saw it as a no-brainer. Ernst & Young, the major international accounting firm, did the numbers, met with the bank and told them that it was a goer. Anyone who ever asked to see the blue book, they were shown the whole deal, so at no point could anyone say, 'This is wrong,' or 'I don't understand,' or 'That's not what you told us.' We had all been personally vetted, and everyone had full knowledge of Christopher's background and involvement. All the boxes were ticked. Ultimately, we even had both the French and Dutch governments on our side, despite the fact that we had dared talk to the Wathey family.

So you can imagine how absolutely shocked, astounded and pissed off we were when, two weeks away from finalising the deal, Wally and I suddenly got a phone call requesting us to fly to the Caribbean, where an officer of the Bank of Trinidad sat us down and told us he had called the whole she-bang off!

This was an amazing turnaround of events, an absolutely shocking decision, a bolt from the blue that no one saw coming. When Wally demanded to know why, it all became clear. The bank had had a last minute visit from Australian Government officials who had told them that we were all 'wanted criminals.' No proof of course, but enough to freak out the bank board and make them back out.

Fuck, fuck, fuck! Two years of hard work, seven days a week, during one of the most trying times of my life, down the drain in a matter of moments. We tried to convince them that Christopher had been the subject of civil complaints, not criminal charges, and that his non-return to Australia had been forced by his ill health, which had been legally recognised by the highest court in Spain. And that the rest of us involved in the project were absolutely clean and just doing our job. But the Australian Government had done a great snow job. The Bank of Trinidad could not be swayed.

I was personally devastated, probably more than anyone else, because this was my baby. I loved the place, the project was a ripper and it had been such good fun pulling it all together. When I relayed the news back to Mallorca, everyone was distraught. To rub it in, a Turkish group moved in and bought the property before we could find someone to refinance the deal.

A serious personal side issue of this project was that at one point I got mugged and so badly beaten, people thought I was dead. I was leaving a nightclub at about two in the morning and heading back to my hotel for a sleep to be up for a seven o'clock meeting at Government House. Yes, I know, not much leeway there, but that is the way I did things in those days.

I was walking through an alleyway to the car park when this bloke suddenly appeared from nowhere and smashed me right in the front of the skull with a river stone. Bang! I hit the deck. With blood streaming from my head, I got up to retaliate. Bang, he whacked me two more times. Again, the alcohol and adrenalin kept me going. I somehow fought him off, and he ran away without taking anything from me. The next thing I knew, I was waking up in hospital with forty-seven stitches patching up my head. You can still see the major scar on my forehead to this day. The other two are thankfully hidden under my hairline.

At the hospital, they told me that I had been found by a man who was working as a security guard for the crew of *Speed 2*, which was being filmed on the island at the time. Seeing me looking so bashed up and lying in a huge pool of blood, he thought I was dead. He was so convinced he told the ambulance not to hurry, and they didn't. But when they finally arrived, I started making a few groaning noises. Shocked at this turn of events, they hurried me off to the hospital. I woke up the following morning all stitched up, with a half shaved head, a pounding headache and my face black, blue and very swollen. Looking good, 'Arold.

Just to rub things in, I was in a decrepit old hospital that was about to be shut down through lack of funding. No sheets on the bed, nothing. And when it came to reporting what had happened, for the first and only time on the island, I did not have much luck with a French Government official. He was not only the local representative, he just happened to be the GMF employee running the resort, which was being maintained with a minimal staff. His name was Nick and he was living like a king at the property and I am pretty sure he knew that once we got the resort going his cosy fiefdom would be finished.

Nick accused me of being a drug dealer, declaring that that was why I had been mugged. Fair go, pal. As I have outlined here truthfully, I am a user, I won't dispute that, but dealing was never my scene. He was the epitome of the arrogant frog, made no real effort to find out who had belted me and certainly did not do much to portray the image of Saint Martin being a place that cared.

The genuine, honest, real Saint Martin that I knew so well was revealed by the fact that my wallet with twelve hundred dollars in it was still with me, sitting untouched on a table next to my hospital bed. When I got back home to Spain, with my head the size of a watermelon, I made a donation to that place in immense gratitude. They had saved my life.

I don't know who whacked me that night, and to this day I do not know whether it was a politically motivated warning, a local business threat, a robbery attempt or simply a random attack by some crack head. I did not let that frighten me. I did not run away, and in fact, I kept going back to push things along because I recognised that it was a wonderful island with beautiful people.

When the project collapsed, I could only ruminate that, despite the bashing and two years' work down the drain, I was at least somewhat better off than the two French Government Ministers alleged to have had something to do with the laundering of cash through the resort. Someone told me they were sent on a mission to the Congo, and their plane mysteriously blew up in mid-air, killing them both.

Nevertheless, the collapse of the Saint Martin deal was one of the toughest pills I have ever had to swallow. Without the glue provided by Christopher, the strength he showed despite his illness, I reckon everything would have fallen apart there and then. I used to stare at the ceiling and think, 'What else can happen?' It didn't take long before I got an answer. The idea of a team coming over to kidnap Christopher and take him back to Australia started to gain traction.

THIRTY-NINE

Kidnap him? We had already been through one crazy abduction incident in Switzerland, which had turned out to be carried out in error. Surely a legitimate government would not stoop to grabbing someone off the street and whisking them back to Australia in a bag? Even though, as the way they wrecked the Saint Martin deal showed, they were not averse to playing hard ball. But a bloke rang up Lillian claiming to be an Australian Federal Policeman and offering a large sum of money to have Christopher and me spirited out of the country and back home. After thinking this incident through, we felt it simply could not have been a government representative who had made the phone call. Surely the AFP would have been too shrewd to get involved in a pathetic stunt like that. But Lillian had recorded the conversation, so we decided the best thing to do would be to hand the tape over to Spanish authorities. All hell broke loose. We all got dragged into endless meetings with local police officers and Interpol agents, trying to drill us for more information and assessing whether there was any substance to the threat.

Then there was the kidnap scheme promoted by Andrew Denton. On the surface, this appeared to be not much more than a har-de-har schoolboy joke, designed to amuse his audience and boost the ratings for his Channel

7 show, *Denton*. He set it up as a public subscription, accepting 20-cent coin donations, hoping to make $200,000 to hire an American bounty hunter, Bob Burton, to go to Mallorca and bring Christopher back. Denton apparently told his audience that if Christopher had a problem with the plan, 'He can come here and sue me.'

It's interesting to note how the involvement of Channel 9's *60 Minutes* program in a 2016 kidnapping attempt in Lebanon drew scorn from the rest of the media, from legal spokespeople and from the Government. Yet twenty years earlier the proposal made on Channel 7, Christopher's former network, to arrange the kidnapping of an Australian citizen, still innocent albeit declared a fugitive, from another sovereign nation was a similar scenario. But it did not draw the same wide-ranging criticism. I think Denton stopped when Attorney-General Michael Lavarch, under Spanish diplomatic pressure, did the only smart thing he ever did in this whole sorry saga and told him to cut it out.

I believe that a plan was also devised by a Gold Coast group called the White Knights for Justice, who claimed they had a team of ex-military personnel plus a lung specialist who could somehow get Christopher legally out of Spain.

These schemes might have sounded unrealistic and, in the Denton case, a bit jokey, but when we heard about them, they did not provide us with much fun at our end. The Spanish police pointed out that even if any of these plans did not get off the ground, some nutter might try to copy them. We heard an Eastern Bloc group might even try and kidnap Charlotte as a bargaining chip. We also became the focal point of bizarre death threats and sicko mail, very often addressed to Amanda or Pixie. For a while, we ended up being provided with protection twenty-four hours a day by the Policia Nacional and were told to be very careful, particularly when taking Charlotte to and from school. For many years I was furious with Denton at the way he had put my daughter at such risk for ratings.

Fortunately, nothing ever came of these threats. The kidnap groups backed away when they were told that if they put a plan into action, they would be charged and end up in the slammer. The only people who came out looking good from all this were the Spanish. They were gentlemen and professionals. The Australian authorities looked the rank amateurs we knew they were as we had consistently witnessed their bungling attempts. Nevertheless, business deals were becoming increasingly difficult to develop because of the press coverage plus the time and energy being spent on keeping Christopher alive. The banks, institutions and other lenders were getting increasingly wary about dealing with us. In retrospect, I am sure I would have been, too. I was now the front man and certainly not a Christopher Skase in any respect, unfortunately for many people.

Running parallel with this was a depressing change in the state of Christopher's health. After a brief spurt of improvement, when getting freed from gaol combined with the promised success of the Saint Martin project temporarily buoyed him, he started to struggle again. The emphysema began to worsen at a rapid rate and everyone associated with his case concluded that the damage done while he was incarcerated for almost a year had taken its toll. Being exposed to hospital-grade superinfections, plus the impact of attendant powerful drugs and a complete and utter lack of physical exercise, had battered his body.

After the investigation of all options and much discussion with medicos, we decided to take him to a hospital in Valencia to try surgery that was still in the experimental stage. What choice did we have? The doctors told him he would be dead within six months to a year if he didn't undergo it. From that point on, he pretty much stopped working and readied himself for the surgery.

The doctors also made it quite clear that there were no guarantees as to the operation's success. By this stage, the double-lung transplant idea proposed by the Swiss surgeons had dropped off the radar but developments were progressing on artificial devices. The general consensus amongst the Spanish medicos was, 'Let's operate now and hope for the best that you will last long enough to have science catch up and make you some new lungs.'

Let's not forget that he was still only in his forties. When you're that age and have led an exciting, successful and somewhat tumultuous life and have a lot of friends and family around you who love you and still believe you have a lot to offer, then you grab at any chance that comes along.

Here was the tricky part. Our successful legal appeal against extradition had centred on proving to the Australian Government that Christopher was incapable of travel of any sort. To have this operation, he was going to have to go by boat to the mainland.

We knew that the minute word leaked out about him travelling somewhere, anywhere, we were gone for all money. The press would have had a field day, and the Government would have been banging on our door, trolley and nebuliser in hand, demanding that if he could be shifted across the water from Mallorca to Valencia, then surely he could come back to Australia.

Getting him off the island with no one finding out was not going to be easy, especially with my Spanish, which although effective was sometimes limited. There were a lot of covert phone calls made and meetings held in quiet places. I am forever grateful to a Mallorcan medico called Dr Felipe Nicolau, who was the practitioner who mainly looked after Christopher's emphysema and who stuck with him right through his illness to the end. Dr Nicolau worked for a private hospital, yet he took Christopher's case on for very little money on the basis that he would get paid if things got better. He was the man who did all the research and the preparatory phase and then organised the surgery in Valencia and helped set it up. With his help, I managed to organise a fully-equipped ambulance, complete with a thoracic evacuation specialist, Dr Carlos Busquets, to undertake the journey. I had met Dr Busquets during the extradition trial and had remained in contact with him.

It was one of the great ironies of this whole saga that after years of being pursued by the media, to the point where we could not wipe our arse without being snapped by a photographer or chased by a reporter, we were able to load Christopher into the back of an ambulance parked at the Club de Vela near La Noria, drive it from Port Andratx down to the docks at Palma, take it aboard a Super Cat ferry linking Mallorca with the mainland, sail it to Barcelona, take it off and then drive it 365 kilometres south to a hospital in Valencia, without anyone tumbling to it.

Little of this escapade has ever been put down in print. In fact, when rumours later started circulating and a couple of photos surfaced, we were accused of faking the story. Us? Faking a story! How's that? Where was Sluggo Richardson when you needed him?

So I feel some satisfaction that after all the torment the media put us through, going through our rubbish bins, filming fake reports, and getting it wrong most of the time, they missed the biggest story of all, the scoop of scoops. Bad luck guys. Too much time spent swimming in your hotel pool, surveying the mini-bar and watching cable. Now this really would have been something for the show reel.

I was in the back of the ambulance all the way, and we ultimately arrived at the Quiron Clinic in Valencia, acknowledged as one of Spain's best hospitals, known for its treatment of tuberculosis and other lung diseases. Valencia had become recognised as a city for this sort of work through tragedy. A couple of years earlier an outbreak of severe interstitial lung disease among textile factory workers had resulted in six deaths, the condition becoming known as the Ardystil Syndrome after one of the factories.

Two charming medicos, Doctor Canto and another Doctor Nic, met us and described the upcoming operation in lurid detail. This was not my favourite bit. The photos they showed me of lungs with ugly black spots everywhere were very real and quite confronting. I found out later there were a lot more pictures that made the ones I saw look pretty. In fact, they asked Christopher if they could photo document the whole operation for training purposes. He agreed, and later these were the photos that the Australian press referred to as fake! Unbelievable. They were released by the hospital to counter the ridiculous and slanderous assertions by the media that it was a hoax. Fucking disgraceful.

Before the operation began, they explained that this new idea involved opening his chest cavity with forceps, surgically removing any areas of dead tissue and letting the lung expand back into the cavity left behind. This was an extraordinary and little known fact about the capacity of the lung. Tough as it sounded, we agreed it was a goer. Christopher disappeared on a trolley down the hall, and I sat down to read a few Spanish magazines and wait.

After three anxious hours waiting for news of an operation that was scheduled to last one, one of the doctors came out and told me he had to speak to me urgently. After a large brandy—for him, not me, I might point out—he told me that they had discovered that Christopher's lungs were full of some strange material, not unlike coral, that they had never seen before. One lung wasn't quite so bad, but the other was full of this stuff. After further consultation, they continued with the operation and removed what they could from the bad lung, also taking out as many bullae as possible. These are nasty bubbles or cavities, ugly black things that develop on the lung wall and reduce its efficiency, causing a lot of pain. Worse still, they constantly threaten to blow out at any moment, like an over-inflated balloon.

The real concern was the unidentifiable substance that had hardened the lung up to the texture of something like the Barrier Reef. The prognosis was not good so I asked the doctor not to tell Christopher the whole story. I felt we would have a better chance of him overcoming the illness if we held the really bad news back from him, kept him positive and generally encouraged the feeling that everything would be okay in the end. Having set that up, I went and had a few drinks, thinking the worst.

We stayed in Valencia for six days while they monitored him and until they could satisfactorily remove the three garden-hose sized suction tubes poking out of his chest draining fluid into clear plastic containers on the floor. It looked like something out of a bad horror movie, particularly with me watching on from the balcony outside his room through the full-length window smoking a cigarette. How very Spanish of me. Mind you, most of the doctors smoked too.

Once the tubes were removed, we readied ourselves for the journey back to Mallorca. We realised that we had to do it quickly and discreetly before some media hack finally stumbled out of his drug-and-alcohol-induced stupor and worked out Christopher had gone AWOL. Bugger me, nearly two weeks and not a fucking clue.

See, they were good at the easy stuff, like hanging around the property and making our lives miserable, monstering hospital staff at Palma or turning up at scheduled court cases. But not the hard stuff. Not making astute observations, putting two and two together and working out something was going on. The fact that we could get him off the island for two weeks for major surgery without them noticing showed how lax and unprofessional they were. No one thought, 'Hey, we haven't sighted him for days, what's going on?' No wonder they later claimed the whole thing was a fake; they had been embarrassed and made to look the fools they were and had to come up with something to save their miserable careers. We left the hospital in the evening, and this time, due to a favourable timetable, we were able to put the ambulance onto the ferry directly home from Valencia, rather than having to drive back to Barcelona. We arrived in Palma at six o'clock the following morning, greeted by a beautiful sunny day and no one else. Good omen, I thought.

The doctors quietly informed Pixie of the coral-like substance in his lungs, telling her, 'What we found inside, we don't like.' No one ever did determine what it actually was despite a worldwide search for answers. The medicos added that while Christopher had a very strong mind and had shown that he could handle any situation thrown at him, it might be best to stick with my original decision to not tell him of the discovery. So Pixie didn't, not until a long time after.

Whether he knew the true circumstances surrounding the operation or not—he was a pretty smart cookie and must have worked out something pretty serious had gone on under the knife—Christopher attacked his recovery when he got home with the same vigour he did with a corporate takeover. That is, one hundred and ten per cent. He walked when they told him to walk, he swam when they told him to swim, he took all the medicine they gave him and then some. It had a tremendous effect. He gradually started to look better, feel better, sound better and get a bit of his old confidence and flair back. Six months later, one of the medicos pulled me aside and said, 'This man is a tribute to both modern medicine and what a positive mind can do. He should still be in a wheelchair, at best!'

FORTY

F inally, the media noticed that Christopher was visible again. But while the Valencia operation remained a secret for the time being, they typically grabbed a hold of his passionate adherence to his post-operative recovery regime and converted it into a lie. 'See,' they said, 'he's walking, he's swimming, he's getting around, there's obviously nothing wrong with him.' Nobody bothered to check—isn't that what journalists are supposed to do?—what an emphysema patient should be doing if he doesn't want to lose his life before he turns fifty. Exercise, walk, get up, get out, be mobile. Lie flat on your back, he had been told, and your lungs will fill up and you will die. And I can tell you, he did not want that.

Even when they did bother to check and didn't get the answers that suited them, the reporters either defamed or discredited the doctors, specialists, lawyers or government contractors involved. His improvement had come via a combination of medical skill and personal dedication, but any pictures or video of him out of the wheelchair and moving around were accompanied by the story that he had been tricking people, that he had never been all that sick, and that he had consistently fooled the Australia Government by deliberately creating this monstrous façade to avoid facing up to shareholders, prosecutors, courts and anyone else who wanted to have a piece of him.

This was truly the beginning of my hatred for the Australian media. From my experience in Mallorca, you were a bunch of pathetic, unprofessional, lying, cheating bastards. Sluggo may have been your captain-coach but you all played your part in the team by writing or reporting anything to save your own arses and keep the holiday gravy train rolling. In my darkest times, I wished you all had to witness the horrendous demise of a loved one from an incurable disease while being publicly lampooned. The saying goes that you can forgive but you never forget. To be honest, I don't think I have even forgiven you yet.

Across the ten years, I saw a lot of media stuff about Christopher, but bad as it generally was, I have never seen a greater pile of fabricated bullshit than was created on our doorstep in Mallorca and transmitted around the world. Rarely did they ever get anywhere near the truth. They just made up what they thought would comprise a great headline-grabbing story and, seeing as they hunted in packs, tossed the idea around among themselves to make it consistent for the next week's episode. There was never any determination to find out what actually was going on, rather they just ran with the government's Get Skase campaign and did their very best to make it happen. Never once did I see any of them attempt to interview Professor Lagler to ask about the slanderous and defamatory statements made about him by Larrabee and accepted by the Australian judicial system.

The way they hung around the hospital or La Noria or anywhere that we were located was shameful. Not forgetting how they harassed friends, neighbours, business associates and anybody else who had the right to come and see us but who had to force their way through a noisy, nasty gauntlet of hacks to get to the front door. If you saw how bad things were in that prison hospital, how awful he looked when he got home weighing six stone wringing wet, how ugly the photos were of the black bullae on his lungs, how gravely the doctors spoke of the unidentified coral substance that had filled up his right lung, and how a transplant or some sort of artificial lung was his only salvation from certain death, then you would know that any suggestion that he was healthy was crap. Unbelievable. Any family who has been through a medical nightmare similar to this would understand how traumatic a situation it is for all involved, but to additionally have the media and doctors and government officials venting their pathetic opinions was just inhumane.

Enter the one and only Amanda Vanstone, the attractive one, the Minister for Justice. Or as Christopher called her, Mrs Fatstone, after a Peter Nicholson cartoon in The Age which parodied Fawlty Towers. Titled 'Fawlty Lungs,' it featured Christopher as the owner of a 'five-star hotel,' Pixie as Sybil, Manuel as a 'Spanish surgeon' and 'Amanda Vanstone as the maid.' It soon became a family joke where Christopher would sometimes call her by the names shown on the ever-changing sign in the television show's opening credits, such as Mrs Fatty Owls or Mrs Farty Towels.

Having been dropped from the Cabinet and the role of Minister for Employment a few months before, and handed the lesser portfolio of Justice, she now thrust her way into the fray. I reckon she woke up one morning and had a brain wave, the notion of contacting the Spanish National Police and requesting something along the lines of, 'Next time Mr Skase hands in his passport for the required renewal of his Spanish Residencia, please do not return it to him; send it back to us.'

No matter how the directive was constructed and how high our opponents might have considered the stakes were, we reckoned that this was a low blow, a really cheap shot. A person's passport is surely an inviolate possession. We felt the move was illegal and our legal advisor Tony Coll thought so too. Off his own bat he instituted a challenge, proposing that any such attempt would be an unlawful seizure of an individual's most valuable, private document.

Further, we had developed a fairly good relationship with the Mallorcan police over the years. They generally took the view that if we kept to ourselves, didn't break any Spanish laws, blended into the community and contributed to the local economy, then they didn't really want to get involved in some inspired pursuit for documentation being orchestrated from the other side of the world.

So we were a bit disappointed when the court ruled against Tony's appeal and the police dutifully followed Mrs Vanstone's instructions. Christopher did as required and suddenly found that he was a man without papers, persona non grata. Before long, his passport was back in Australia.

On May 24, 1998, at a press conference in Adelaide, Senator Vanstone proudly displayed it to the adoring media, with the word 'Cancelled' ominously stamped under his photograph. But noticeably she was a bit circumspect when making any comment about what would happen next. 'There may well be appeal rights Mr Skase would have if his residency permit is refused,' she said. 'We'll simply have to wait and let the Spanish authorities deal with this as they see fit.'

Three days later when door-stopped at Canberra, she added that 'there are appeal procedures that Mr Skase would be able to take.' And three weeks after that a department press release said that 'the Minister stressed that Mr Skase does have judicial appeal processes open to him in Spain.'

Yep, we were thinking, as the old sports saying goes, 'It ain't over 'til the fat lady sings ...'

Christopher knew of course that now his passport was gone he was extremely vulnerable. The next time Spanish authorities wanted to check his residencia, whether as scheduled or on a sudden whim or under court direction, he would not be able to satisfactorily prove his identity and would be kicked out. So the appeal was really his only next option.

Mrs Vanstone was obviously working on the basis that if he were suddenly forced to move somewhere else, then Australia would be able to extradite him from that third country and they would focus their efforts in that direction.

In fact—and let me just divert here for a moment—I had a quiet chuckle to myself two decades on when, writing as a Fairfax columnist, Mrs Vanstone went into print in 2015 and said the proposal of then Prime Minister Tony Abbott to give ministers the power to take away the passport of any mercenary fighter returning to Australia without following the traditional legal process was 'shameful' and 'unlawful.' She also defended Cardinal George Pell, who is not a fugitive by any means, but did rely on controversial medical evidence to avoid returning to Australia to personally give evidence at the inquiry into one of the most shocking paedophilia scenarios ever to be unearthed.

She wrote about how 'hunting in a pack is very primal' and how Pell was the 'latest to fall prey to this ugly side of humanity.' She wrote, 'Rules go out the window. We go looking, desperately, for blood. We become hunters and if you're the hunted, watch out. What's ugly about this is not just the hunt but how few people care.'

Come on. The scenarios might be different, but the principal is the same. Twenty years on and no suggestion from her that Pell might be brought back to Australia on a suitably fitted-out boat or plane accompanied by medical evacuation specialists, as she so vehemently insisted on should be done with Christopher. When she was the Minister for Family and Community Services and there were cuts to be made to disabled funding, the then Opposition spokesman Wayne Swan said Mrs Vanstone was 'a political hyena,' adding that, 'she just singles out the most vulnerable people in our community.'

All that was achieved by Senator Vanstone's approach to Christopher's situation was to trigger one of the more fascinating sagas of the Chase for Skase—the great passport hunt. It came down to this: Christopher figured that if the ruling Government of his place of birth was going to take his most prized document away from him and virtually declare him a non-person, then maybe it was time to turn his back on the whole country forever.

The point was, by this stage, a massive gap had opened up between 'us' and 'them.' And the 'them' camp had broadened over the years from being simply the Qintex receivers and the trustee-in-bankruptcy to a large amalgam of people and organizations, including the Government, the media, the legal fraternity, the business community, the medical profession and the many others who had decided to stick their oar in and offer their opinion on the situation.

It is sad to have to admit this, but as a family, we had all become very disenchanted with 'them' and Australia generally. Although we were doing it tough in Spain, we were starting to think we didn't really care if we ever landed on the shores of our homeland ever again. A horrible thought, but that is the point that we had reached.

From Christopher's perspective, the solution was simple—regain citizenship, but not necessarily Australian. Simply, citizenship that would satisfy Spanish authorities that he should be allowed to continue living in the country. So, we got on the phone and the internet and began to find out which countries sold legal passports and/or citizenships, which ones would be accepted by Spain, how much they cost and what was involved. One thing in our favour was that in those days quite a few countries, mainly small ones, sold passports as a means of generating income. It was a matter of finding one that would accept Christopher's application and background and do it quickly. The best way to do that was to visit each one personally. I learned later that this plan was not some spur-of-the-moment, knee-jerk response. He had set it in train in advance so that when they did take his own away from him, he was ready to pursue an alternative. This showed the brilliant vision of the man.

So armed with a wad of information on Christopher, including his history, his family, his achievements, his failures, the charges, the press harassment, his medical records, I hit the road or sky, actually.

My first stop was Belize in Central America, tucked under the toe of the Mexican peninsula and on the border of Guatemala. Formerly British Honduras, it proved to be an amazing country, a tropical paradise. It was similar to North Queensland including having a fabulous coral reef, which I was told was second only to the Great Barrier Reef, plus many small islands, a bit like the Whitsundays. As the Poms had controlled it for a century, it had a parliamentary democracy based on the British system, and the main language was English. The hinterland featured fantastic Mayan stone ruins, and the wanna-be developer in me saw it as a potential spot for a resort project.

I was told that for about US$50,000 Christopher could acquire a Belizean passport that was fully legal and accepted around the world. For another US$25,000 he could change his name. It was appealing but far too expensive for us. Not only that, despite the wonderful tourist picture I have just painted, it was a scary place. Guatemalan guerrillas were constantly coming across the border and causing grief, and after I left, gunmen shot dead a tourist on a road I had travelled on only a day before on the four-hour return trip to Belize's capital Belmopan.

Next on the list was Panama on the southernmost part of Central America. My visit got off to quite a start when the ancient Cadillac taxi taking me from the airport to the hotel got caught in a huge downpour, one of the most incredible thunderstorms I have ever seen, worse than anything I had witnessed in Far North Queensland. As we entered a major intersection, the Caddy began to float. There we were, drifting through the red lights like a ship without a rudder. People were stranded everywhere, and my fifteen-minute journey turned into a four-hour nightmare.

Panama City proved to be a beautiful place to visit with great things to see and do but with an underlying notion of tension. Although it had been ten years since the Americans had invaded the country and taken their President and resident drug lord, General Manuel Noriega, off to prison, he was still a popular and divisive topic of taxi driver conversation. As well, the US was nervous about the upcoming end of the Panama Canal Treaty and the scheduled handing of it over to the locals.

Contrasted by some of the most beautiful women I have ever seen in the world, there were a lot of spy types hanging around street corners, sleazy spivs in sports coats and Panama hats, smooth talkers in smooth shoes. I visited lawyers, bureaucrats, Panamanian businessmen and other people and places of interest, but legal passports were not on the list of available items. Not on our budget, anyway. For considerably less, I could have got a not-quite-so-legal one on the spot from one of the shady characters in the top floor bar of the Intercontinental. It was like sitting in a scene from that Geoffrey Rush spy thriller *The Tailor of Panama*. But I thought better of it.

Time to take an evening flight to Caracas, capital of Venezuela, to meet up with a contact we had been given by a friend in Spain. My flight arrived very late at night and all I remember was getting in a taxi and spending the next hour and a half going up a steep hill—up and up and up. Every now and then there would be a cluster of lights in the darkness, but otherwise nothing but blackness and total silence from the driver as we continually went skywards.

Now, Venezuela has never been known as a bastion of security, with kidnapping appearing to be some sort of national sport. The official government statistic in 1998, the year I visited, was that there were fifty kidnappings per year. By 2011, that figure had reached twelve hundred. Add to this that Venezuela also has one of the highest homicide rates in the world, and so after about an hour of silent motoring up a darkened hill, I was starting to get just a little paranoid. Images flashed through my mind of me being bundled out of the car at gunpoint, hooded, taken to a mountain hideaway and held for ransom. A disturbing enough thought, made even more distressing by the certainty that we wouldn't be able to afford the payout anyway.

Then suddenly we arrived in Caracas, the driver took me straight to the hotel, accepted payment with a minimum of discussion, gave a slight smile and disappeared into the night. There I was, safe and sound.

I had two appointments the next day, one at 9 a.m. and one at 2.15 p.m., and then a cab organised to get back to the airport. I discovered that Caracas is a fascinating, amazing city to drive around. The birthplace and final resting place of Simon Bolivar, the independence hero, it is crowded, polluted, boiling hot, jammed with traffic and a bit like the old wild west. In keeping, I discovered that their passports were not 'fully legal' either, which was the last thing we needed. On the trip back to the airport, this time going down the mountain in daylight, I worked out of what the clusters of lights were that I had spotted the previous night. They were shantytowns made of tin, cardboard and mud, crowded with families and clinging to the mountainsides. Caracas may have been one of the most elevated capital cities in the world, but this was the bottom end of poverty. Empty handed, I got into the plane and headed off for the next country on my list, Dominica in the West Indies.

Now, it is very important for the reader to understand that I headed off to the Commonwealth of Dominica, a tiny Caribbean island, a former British colony, with English as its first language and a democratic parliament. It is in the Lesser Antilles, between Guadeloupe and Martinique, and the name Dominica comes from Sunday, the day Christopher Columbus came across the island.

The Commonwealth of Dominica is not to be confused with the Dominican Republic. The Dominican Republic is a much larger country, situated on the eastern half of the island known as Hispaniola, the other half being Haiti. The Dominican Republic has had a long, troubled history of poverty, turmoil and political unrest, so I was not going there. I was landing instead in the Garden of Eden, as the Commonwealth of Dominica tourist brochure assured me.

It turned out to be true, too. I had to fly in via nearby Saint Lucia because Dominica's runway was then too short to take jets, and we had to transfer into a little twin-engine eight-seater for the last leg. Out of the Caribbean blue, there suddenly appeared the coast of paradise about ten metres below—sparkling water, white sand and waving coconut palms. It had beautiful mountains, rare plants, exotic birds, unusual animals and a boiling lake. The population was about 50,000, the lifestyle very relaxed and it thrived on playing a significant role in West Indies cricket.

The Marigot Airport runway had been carved into a working coconut plantation and had a very definite end to it. 'Wouldn't want to overshoot here,' I thought to myself, the nagging feeling stemming from the fact that just a few weeks before my arrival a flight went wrong, killing all eleven on board. But the plane landed safely and taxied right up to the terminal, a shed of about twenty metres by ten metres nestled amongst the palms. I hopped out to a welcome that was warm and an atmosphere that was friendly.

It was Rose Wathey, wife of Al, our man in Saint Martin, who had put us on to the idea of Dominica. She had been born on the island and had contacts there, and pretty soon, I began to see that she had provided us with an excellent opportunity. I met the Tourism Minister and some local lawyers and presented Christopher's case to them, which led to a meeting with the Attorney-General. They were enthusiastic about what I had presented but the business was not finalised that day. Two more trips back to the Garden of Eden were needed and then they finally agreed to issue a passport for Christopher with full knowledge and documentation of who they were giving it to, as well as one for Pixie. Dominica's Ambassador to the UK then flew across from London to Mallorca to interview them, after which he confirmed the approval for the passports, and they were duly issued.

The story did not quite end there. While they both now had passports and therefore identities, they did not have visas that said that they could stay on in Spain. The visa was a separate document that needed to be issued by someone from Spain who was in authority overseas. For example, the Spanish Ambassador, or Consul General, or Charge d'affaires to another country, that sort of thing. What we needed to do was find someone overseas who held that level of position, whose signature would carry the necessary weight back in Spain and who was willing to do it.

It was not easy. I got a lot of knock-backs from representatives that were variously too scared, too lazy, too puzzled or too pissed to put their signature to the documents. But near the end of the journey, good old reliable Wally set me up with a meeting with Spain's

Consul to Jamaica. This man quite happily signed the visas. I could have kissed him there and then, although I refrained. As it turned out, it would have been the Kiss of Death. When the Spanish Government heard what he had done, they recalled him to Madrid.

This whole thing had been surely the craziest journey I have ever undertaken in my life, something straight out of a Marx Brothers movie. As I recall, armed with just a suit-bag containing a couple of clean shirts, plus socks, ties and reg grundies, I had gone from Spain to France to the US to Canada, back to the US, on to Mexico, to Venezuela, to Trinidad, to Dominica three times, to St Lucia, to Panama, to Belize, to Puerto Rico, to Curacao, to Jamaica and then back home to Spain, all in twenty-one days! I would wake up every morning to yet another fax telling me where I was, who I was meeting that day and when and where, what time my flight out of there was and what country I was going to next.

The last leg, the flight out of Jamaica back to Spain, was a nail-biting event with three false starts due to three planes being grounded because of mechanical problems. As I got on the fourth plane, calmed a little by the free drinks offered around because of the delays, would you believe I wound up sitting next to the Spanish Consul who had just issued me the visas! He was now on his way back home for what he thought was a holiday. Little did he know that this was going to be his last as an official representative of his country.

When I got home, I could not praise highly enough the lovely people of the Commonwealth of Dominica. They not only gave us the passports, but they stuck by us when the going got tough. Later, when the Australian Government typically tried to pressure them into revoking the passports, they would not back down.

Dominica was only a little place trying to make its way in the big world and it could have easily succumbed to bullying or compromise by a much bigger nation, but it didn't. God bless 'em!

Then, in one of those glorious, ironic twists, the all-important difference that I outlined earlier between the tiny and beautiful Commonwealth of Dominica, from where we got the passports, and the larger, nastier but similarly named Dominican Republic, from where we did not, suddenly proved to be mightily significant. Certainly for a group of Australian Government investigators hot on my tail.

These highly paid, terribly intelligent, sharp-as-a-tack Department of Immigration geniuses got wind that I would be flying in to pick up the new passports on a certain day. So they lay in wait at the airport, ready to grab me, seize the documents and take me triumphantly back to Australia.

Their only trouble was, at the precise moment I was arriving at the airport of the Commonwealth of Dominica in time for my scheduled appointment, they were laying in wait at the airport of the Dominican Republic …

Wrong airport, wrong country. Sorry about that, guys.

Better luck next time, Mrs Vanstone.

FORTY-ONE

I have said very little about the Palm Farm so far, probably for no other reason than it was the place where Christopher passed away and it has a lot of sad memories for all of us.

It was a property that I had found early in the piece and for which we had great hopes. As far back as when we were looking at doing up La Noria and the Apartments, Christopher said he wanted to have massive palms lining their entry boulevards like he had done so spectacularly at Port Douglas.

He also wanted to get hold of the palms the same way as he had done in Queensland. That is, instead of becoming a customer and buying the trees from a palm farm, buy the whole plantation lock, stock and barrel. You then dig up all the palms, transport them to your required location and plant them. Then you either redevelop the empty farmland or sell it off to an interested speculator. Either way, you get your palms plus the bonus of the land. Not a bad scheme, hey?

So, we had always been on the lookout for the right property. One day I met a man, ironically in Palma, when I was going to a legal meeting. I was photocopying some documents and he was next to me copying a brochure and I couldn't help but notice that it had pictures of palms all over it. So we got chatting, and it turned out his name was Trevor Clarke, an Englishman and successful photographer whose work had included portfolios of major bands such as the Beatles and the Rolling Stones. He had made his money, had bailed out of the rat race and was now living the hippy life in Mallorca. He told me he had a commercial palm farm about five minutes drive out of Andratx, so I took one of his brochures and later showed it to Christopher.

He was most excited. The farm was on about six hectares split into two sections, upper and lower, by a road that ran up the valley at the back of Andratx. Trevor was growing thousands of lovely looking Washingtonia palms on it, all in neat rows and in varying stages of maturity. There were about five thousand trees ranging in height from one metre to four metres, providing everything that we needed. As well, I loved the property from the moment I saw it, particularly its beautiful little sandstone 'finca' or farmhouse. It was ramshackle and run down but very appealing.

The palms were neatly dotted all over the place on terraced plots of land separated by dry-stone walls, and we recognised it was not going to be easy to get them out. Nevertheless, we went ahead with the purchase, structuring a typical Skase deal where Trevor stayed in and kept one third, Los Nomadas took one third and I took the final third in the company name of My Claudette, which had been set up for Amanda, Charlotte and me to hold our interests. The arrangement was another one of Christopher's deferred payment deals, a typical Skase scenario, with an option to buy Trevor out later at a fixed price.

We would sell the palms to Los Nomadas Pty Ltd for the resort developments, then work out what the three owners of the property were owed. We calculated that by the time we had sold the palms to the resorts, boosting the value of the properties, the Palm Farm would owe us nothing. We would then be able to pay Trevor out. He was happy with that because he had a house in Portals Nous that he was developing into a boutique resort project, and we supplied architectural services to him.

That was Christopher's brilliance, his ability to set up a deal like that. He was saying more or less, 'You win, Trevor, and we win, but you just have to trust us and be patient.' His ability to get people to believe in a vision was just astonishing. Long term, Amanda and I would end up owning the Palm Farm at very little cost and would be able to fix up the finca and move into it. At last, we would finally be able to establish a real family home for us and Charlotte on Mallorca.

To do it, we had to get permission to rezone the whole property from agricultural and split it into two titles. We would keep the lower half with the finca on it and redevelop the upper half, building some sort of saleable house or boutique hotel or something like that. Once all that was done, by then La Noria would have been developed, and Christopher and Pixie could either stay on there or move somewhere else. One plan was that they might take over the building that we planned to construct on the upper half of the Palm Farm. There were several options to consider.

The whole thing was a great concept, and while the deal was being sorted out, Amanda and I started knocking the finca into shape. We used to go up there on weekends and have barbecues, do a bit of work and dream about how it was going to become our home. We put an old bed up there, got the fireplace working and tidied up the funny little kitchen. The only drawback was that it had no electricity. None of the valley had power at that time, and that's why property values were much lower than the surroundings.

However, Mallorca was booming, and after we had done the deal with Trevor, the area started becoming very popular with German investors. They began investing huge amounts of money into properties all the way up the valley, turning them into mansions. This confirmed our original thought that it was going to be a good buy right from the beginning. The nearest electricity point for us was only about four hundred metres away, and we were hoping the council would put it through, on the basis of the ever-increasing investment in the area. We also looked at the option of bringing the electricity across ourselves. This wasn't cheap, but it was doable. Either way, power would have greatly enhanced the property's value.

But it all went pear-shaped. We never really got many palms shifted. They proved to be buggers of things to get out of the terraced plots separated by the unforgiving dry-stone walls. It proved to be much harder than we thought. We had to get Rob Guthrie, our landscape architect on other projects, to come down and have a look and work out a way of doing it. Under his guidance, we extricated a few and placed them around La Noria, mainly in pots, just as decoration. But the plan to shift them all to various projects, including Zou's resort at Camp de Mar, never happened. The closest we got to positioning any of them on a work site was to landscape our sales office up at the Valldemossa project.

Ah, Valldemossa. With its ground-breaking plans on a breathtaking site, this should have been the crown jewel in our portfolio. But sadly after we had done all the preliminary work, it started to falter. One of our long-running problems was with the rapidly growing green movement. Through their agitation, it surfaced that there had been an earlier, illegal classification of the property to suit certain environmental standards. The subsequent reclassification, which we felt was unnecessary, proved to be a process that was both time consuming and money wasting. From our perspective, the greenies were revolting in both senses of the word. It dragged on and on, to the point where the project was not worth pursuing anymore.

So from around late 1998 and early 1999, our financial situation started to go into a deathly downward spiral from which we were never to recover. Things had really started to struggle after the Saint Martin deal fell apart—the project that the Australian Government had sabotaged after we had done two years' hard work, by warning off our agreed financier the Bank of Trinidad with export/import trade threats and telling shocking lies.

Emboldened by that triumph, they then embarked on a worldwide campaign to shut down any avenue of finance that we were either pursuing or likely to seek. Lillian Hutchence, who had led us to Saint Martin, warned us that any likely access to finance was about to be blocked, and at first we did not know how seriously to take her. But she turned out to be right. That's the path the government took when it realised that it couldn't extradite Christopher, couldn't get him deported, couldn't get him on tax charges and couldn't stop him from getting a new passport when its agents had spectacularly failed by turning up at the wrong airport in the wrong country to try and arrest me with the documents.

It was a clever, insidious campaign, putting pressure on banks, getting insiders to pull the plug on our financing deals, shut off our credit cards and refuse to renegotiate our mortgages. What had been a certain deal one week would be suddenly terminated the next without any explanation. 'Sorry, don't want to touch it,' they'd say over the phone and hang up. One tactic was to outline to the bank or financial institution how dealing with us might impact on trade negotiations between the two sovereign nations. As we were often seeking offshore funds from banks in small countries, this had the desired effect, such as with the Bank of Trinidad pulling out of Saint Martin.

The situation only got messier and messier. Even reports about the Australian and Spanish Governments wrangling over a trade deal involving oranges impacted on us.

Worse still, Christopher's health was not improving, even though he was working hard on getting better and determined the emphysema would not beat him. To add to our woes, he was becoming more and more removed. He could no longer make it down to his office so he was taking his medical treatment and running the business from his bedroom, where we had his oxygen tanks installed and the lines of communication were starting to falter.

Wally and I were trying to keep things moving but were hitting brick walls everywhere. The light at the end of the tunnel was getting dimmer and dimmer, and we suspected that if anything, it was going to be a train that was going to run right over us anyway.

It ultimately became obvious we wouldn't be able to get dough for anything. Everything ground to a halt. The focus turned to simply keeping Christopher alive.

FORTY-TWO

I t was around about this time that I began to realise that I might have a bit of a drinking problem …

I had begun starting the day with not one, not two, but quite often three carajillos, a heart-starter made from a stiff slug of brandy, roast coffee grains, espresso coffee and lemon. They say the Spanish troops that once occupied Cuba devised it to give them 'corajillo.' That is, courage. Sometimes I bolstered it with a line of good toot from a trusted friend, a wonderful man I always called Al. This was due to his uncanny resemblance to Al Pacino. His other nickname was Don Blanco, or Mr White, for obvious reasons.

I met him when we were planning our brochures and other marketing material for Los Nomadas and were looking for a graphic artist extraordinaire. He turned out to be the one for us, a genius from mainland Spain. But as you can see, he was helpful in other ways. It all began one morning when I arrived at his office unexpectedly, and he thought I was someone else. As I approached his desk, he hastily began covering up a couple of lines he had laid out for whoever he thought was turning up. But I made it quite clear that I wasn't fazed. I just rolled with it, and from that day forward, Al and I had the most fantastic relationship both personally and professionally until I left Mallorca.

Quite frankly, I needed all this stuff to get through the day. The meetings, the disputes, the clashes, the travel, the frantic dashes everywhere, the legal threats, the impossible tasks, the continual pressure to scrape up money, the realisation that no matter how hard we battled, we would lose one way or the other, it was all getting to me. I was starting to lose it and fall apart. Begging people to do things for no payment or telling them that we couldn't pay them 'at the moment' was never my style, but I simply had to harden up and do it. It was a dreadful feeling, constantly organizing people to do things for you for nothing. Christ, can't I have my old movie life back, please? Just tell me where to lay the dolly tracks. Point to where the next set up is. Please.

Just as one example alone, I could not estimate even remotely what the figure would have come to if Tony Coll, Luis Rodriguez Ramos, Tim Stranack and all the other lawyers had actually billed us for the thousands of hours of complex work they did both in and out of the courts.

My God, the wonderful Tim Stranack! An incredible talent in the highest bastions of the British legal system, a partner in one of London's leading property and investments legal firms, a man who against enormous internal partner pressure put his credibility on the line for Christopher. Tim got fuck all for his backing of Christopher. To the contrary, he had his impeccable character called into question by the Government, the Murdoch press and the trustee-in-bankruptcy. Tim Stranack, I can't thank you enough from the bottom of my heart.

Not forgetting all the others that helped us out, such as the fantastic medical people. The doctors, nurses, specialists, academics, they all gave so freely of their time and expertise and devotion to Christopher's cause without ever quibbling about payment. If we could pay them something, we did. But if we couldn't, they just overlooked it and turned up next time or made another appointment or provided the medicine without batting an eyelid. They believed in him, and they were wonderful.

A lot of this came about because Christopher had an incredible ability to not only engage, entrance and encourage people, but also to manipulate them. Consciously or not? I wouldn't dare attempt a guess. But over the years, so many people did things for him and us just because he was who he was and because he had a fantastic way of getting what he wanted. He could get people to do the most extraordinary things and make the biggest of sacrifices, often at their own financial or personal risk, and yet they would never show any resentment. They did it just because he was who he was. People loved him.

But from my perspective, this tumultuous on-going drama was wrecking my marriage. I could no longer separate my work life from my personal life, seven days a week, twenty-four hours a day, even in my dreams, which were mainly nightmares. Where did reality start and the dreams end? It totally obsessed me. I had nothing else in my life. If it wasn't Christopher's health, it was the extradition. If it wasn't a cock-up with one of the local resorts, it was a balls-up with one of the overseas ones. If it wasn't a difficulty with the La Noria mortgage, it was a problem with the building itself. Pixie getting pissed and taking her anger out on everybody, including Christopher. Amanda asking me to please step back a bit and spend some time with her and Charlotte. Spanish Interpol trying to get in; the killer huskies trying to get out. Police, press, television, bankers, creditors, lawyers, governments, builders, architects, investigators, all coming and going, hanging around, banging on doors, threatening, chasing, haranguing.

It didn't seem to affect Christopher like it did me. His ability to handle stress and multiple shit fights without letting it get to him had always been impressive and he continued to maintain some sort of balance.

Me? Soon the morning carajillo was only the beginning. I was drinking virtually twenty-four hours a day so I could stagger through the gauntlet. Every now and then I would think to myself, 'I must make a decision between two options. One, get out of here and get a grip on things. Two, stay and drink myself to death.' Number two always seemed to be the better bet.

By the time the emphysema had gripped him badly, Christopher could barely have a glass of his favourite tipple, Jack Daniels Black Label and soda. Because of the lack of oxygen in his blood, he could no longer drink red wine either. So Amanda and I got into what was left of his cellar, now stored in a garden shed, and started drinking the quality range of wines he had down there, including some Grange Hermitage. A lot of it was badly corked, and sometimes we would have to open three or four bottles before we would find one that was drinkable. But when friends came around, it was great to watch their expression when they would examine the label and say, 'Bloody hell, this is a Grange!' I was always thinking, 'Ah, this is one Max won't get to drink.'

To compound matters, whereas I had been the dutiful and relatively anonymous sidekick, I was now becoming the main man, the centre of attention, the go-to player as Christopher's health deteriorated. The Australian Government started to target me and Amanda, trying to winkle us out of La Noria and back Down Under, presumably as hostages or bargaining chips to force Christopher and Pixie to succumb. We managed to keep them at bay by keeping the place secure—ironic when you consider that people couldn't get in but those bloody dogs could easily get out—and going to ground when they appeared on the horizon. One day they served notices on us by throwing packets of official-looking papers over the wall. We threw them back.

In this isolated atmosphere of fear and loathing, courage and contempt, bravery and bastardry, cool sanity and shrieking madness, we had become unhinged. We had actually started to dislike Australia and Australians. We felt like this because we were living the reverse of what the people at home believed we were doing. While we were embroiled in a chaotic, stress-laden, mind-bending daily battle to survive, they were reading about some cashed-up up bunch of layabouts, lolling by the pool in the Spanish sun. Don't know who that group was, it certainly wasn't us.

The Apartments project had hit a brick wall because of its shadowy position, the greenies were steadfastly delaying Valldemossa and all the other plans were stalling because of the lack of funds. With no access to finance, we started selling off chunks of La Noria to stay alive. As it got smaller in size, this meant it was becoming less and less viable as a resort project. It was a Catch 22 situation. Everything that we once had going was grinding to a halt, and things were turning into a nightmare. I had been on the ground, scampering around, doing my best but realising that we were heading nowhere. I spent days on end with Ernst & Young and the architects and the government officials and the bankers and the lawyers, trying to get things resolved, but deep down in my heart, I knew that we were fighting a losing battle.

The money had dried up, the wheels were wobbling badly and there was not a mechanic in sight. I was hitting the booze hard because I needed to bolster myself to go and face the many people I had to deal with and somehow give the impression all was well. I knew what was in the bank accounts; I knew what was doable and what wasn't; I knew what we were promising; I knew whether we could honour those promises or not. But the situation was rapidly getting to the point where we wouldn't be able to cover anything. This business, this idea, this notion that we were going to build resorts everywhere was not going to happen. It was dead in the water.

Christopher was getting increasingly frustrated and angry, more and more demanding, yelling from his bedroom. He was refusing to face reality, yet I was still dealing with it on a daily basis, face-to-face. It was getting harder and harder, and it was sending me around the bend.

The worst part was that Amanda and I were arguing a lot. Life on the domestic front had become unbearable. I just did not want to go home at the end of the day anymore. I didn't want to see my wife, my daughter or anyone. In early 2000, it all became too much. I sat down with everyone and told them that I was getting out of there. That I was leaving. Going back to Australia.

It was a pretty traumatic announcement during very awful circumstances. But I just had to get out of the place and try and get my head together. I was certain that if I stayed in Mallorca any longer, Amanda and I would have ended up getting divorced, or I would kill myself in a car or wind up in gaol. All were very real prospects at that point. So I just packed up and walked out the gate, eluding the media and everybody else that had been harassing me, and went home to Sydney, leaving Amanda and Charlotte behind.

I had not seen the Larkins clan at home for nearly seven years, and the timing was good. My mum, Maureen, was celebrating her eightieth birthday, and I was having my fortieth. Of course, I stayed in touch with my lovely wife and our beautiful daughter, but things were not getting any better on that side of the world. Life on Mallorca had all but destroyed what should have been the most important thing to me, my family.

When I look back now, I am not proud of myself. While I was trying to drink myself to death on an alcoholic binge in Sydney, Amanda was enduring a living hell in Spain. Can you imagine the scenario? The world's nosiest media and nastiest creditors are permanently camped at the front door; her mother is wandering around the house with a gin-and-tonic in one hand and a bottle of Valium in the other blaming everybody in the world for the predicament they are in bar Mother Theresa; her stepfather is dying but won't give up the ghost or accept that his business has had the gong; her daughter, now in her teens, is witnessing this whole God-awful family implosion first-hand; and her booze-addled husband has cracked under the pressure and fucked off. Thanks for nothing, Tony. Happy fortieth and I hope the weather on the Harbour is good, you fucking arsehole. It was during this time that Amanda lost fifteen kilos and swore her lifelong allegiance to Prozac.

After six months and many phone calls, and a hell of a lot of help and guidance from my wonderful sister Kate, I finally came to my senses. I decided to go back, grab Amanda and Charlotte, get them off Mallorca and try to start a life somewhere where we were not part of the twenty-four-hour-a-day soap opera known as the Chase for Skase. But before I could leave, guess who suddenly reappeared on stage?

Max Donnelly.

Never a dull day.

FORTY-THREE

O n the day of my departure from Australia in November 2000, to go back to my long-suffering wife and family on Mallorca after six months away, I was issued with a summons at Brisbane airport. I had been staying with my friend KJ and his kids Leroy and Jenny at his Palm Beach apartment on the Gold Coast. This was just after his own painful separation and where I finally made the decision to get on a jet and go get my family.

I was about to board the plane when I was stopped at Immigration and two Federal Police officers suddenly appeared by my side with the documents. Trustee-in-bankruptcy Max Donnelly wanted me to appear in court for a bankruptcy hearing and answer questions under oath about Christopher, about La Noria, about Qintex, about everything. 'Max,' I thought to myself. 'Our trusty trustee, where have you been all this time? It's been ten years. We've missed you. Not.'

Funnily enough, despite being handed the summons, I was allowed to catch the plane. The feds seemed to know something wasn't quite right and were incredibly kind and helpful. My luggage had already been loaded on board when they turned up, so I continued to fly out to a meeting in Thailand on my way back to Spain. The assumption was that I would adhere to the summons and come back and make my appearance in court at the

419

required time. When I got to Phuket, I phoned Christopher in Mallorca and explained what had happened. 'Give me a couple of days to work out something, and I'll get back to you,' he said.

Two days went by. Three days. Four days, and no word. I was beginning to think that maybe he could not find a solution, and it was probably best to go back to Australia when I got a phone call from Amanda with the most shattering news. 'He's been diagnosed with terminal cancer,' she said. 'You better come straight back.' It was not his lungs that were going to kill him after all. It was stomach cancer that had been developing slowly and nastily inside him. Damage caused by his awful incarceration in prison, thanks to all the disgraceful press attacks and the government ghouls that would not leave him alone.

This forced me into one final momentous decision. Do I leave Phuket and go on to Spain and see my dying best friend and reconcile with my family? Or do I bow to the summons and go back to Australia for a chat with Max? It would be worth it to return home just to ask him one question. 'Mate,' I could say to him, 'why did you never come to Mallorca to see the two most important players in the game? Why didn't you simply come over and ask us a few questions and find out what really happened? We could have told you everything.'

It was declared that the search by the trustee-in-bankruptcy and the government across more than a decade cost the taxpayer $2.65 million to finance. I think it was more. Christopher thought so, too. I doubt that that figure covers all the court, extradition, ASC, NCSC, and Australian Federal Police costs, plus other costs, many of which may well have been absorbed within departmental budgets.

And what about the dough that was spent on enjoying things like Skins golf tournaments? The cost of people flying to every far-flung corner of the world?

As well, Christopher estimated that about $10 million was spent in disposing of more than one hundred and sixty Qintex companies. That was shareholder and taxpayer money. Just 5 per cent of that would have done me. I would have been a very happy man. It'd be like winning the lottery.

So, there I was in Thailand, pondering what to do. Go on to Spain to see Christopher who was now under an imminent death sentence? Or go back to Australia to talk to Max?

Nah. No thank you, Max. If you wouldn't come and see us when you had the opportunity, why should I put my life on hold to go and see you now?

There was another compelling reason to go back to Mallorca. They wanted me to explain to Christopher exactly what the medicos were saying. As one of the doctors later put it, 'Look, Tony, you are the only one in the family that speaks Spanish well enough to understand what is being exactly said in the medical sense and the one closest enough to translate and deliver that message properly to Christopher. He has got to understand that he is going to be dead within six months. You have to tell him that. You have to try and make him understand that this is it!'

So, accepting that as soon as it became obvious I would not be returning to Australia, a warrant for my arrest would be issued and hang permanently over my head, I pushed onto Mallorca. I rang Amanda and said, 'Look, I'm returning to Spain. I'm still not mentally capable of dealing with it all, but I'm coming back.'

Once I arrived and began to try and get the message through to a disbelieving Christopher that he was now on the final lap, I realised that there was no way I could walk away again, anyway. I was very quickly back in the loop of dealing with doctors, journalists, creditors, lawyers, government and investors, while trying to calm Pixie down and hopefully patch up my marriage. To this day I feel incredibly guilty for abandoning the family and putting even more pressure on an increasingly sick Christopher. However, at the time I really felt it was a matter of life or death for me.

While I had been in Australia, Christopher had made the decision that they would have to leave La Noria and move to the Palm Farm. They had had no real choice. They were out of money, out of time, out of everything. What little was left of La Noria was sold to the neighbours, who had been gradually buying up the bits and pieces as we had been selling them off. They owned apartments next door and wanted to combine the lot and build a hotel on the site, which they did. It is called the Hotel Montport and is still there today.

By the time I got back from Australia, the last of the proceeds of the sale of La Noria had gone into doing up the Palm Farm finca to make it liveable for Christopher and Pixie. It was not flash, but it was comfortable. Typically, Christopher's idea was that they would try and leverage something out of it to keep things going. His plan was to either continue to try and dig up the palm trees and sell them to bring in some revenue or flog off the whole property as a single entity and make a profit. It was a nice place and probably would have sold for a fair slab of cash as by then the market in the valley was pretty strong.

But after a while, I knew that they were just the medicine-induced dreams of a deluded, dying man, and the notion started to form in the back of my mind that perhaps the whole Larkins clan should get out of Spain. Of course, while that idea held some appeal for Amanda, she simply could not leave. The whole situation was too stressful and too close for comfort. Christopher was now going back and forth to the hospital for treatment for the stomach cancer, spending more and more time at the hospital as his condition worsened. I realised that we had to somehow get some cash coming in to keep things going because there was certainly no money being generated by the projects. So, after a break of more than a decade, I went back into the film industry.

I drove into town one day and went and saw Palma Pictures, a company I had been keeping an eye on as it grew into a sizeable local production facility and very quickly had a job. When I showed them my resume, they were so blown away by the level and quality of work that I had done, they put me on the very next day. For the next six months, until Christopher died, I worked solidly with them as a grip in Spain and other parts of Europe. Working three to five days a week not only brought in much-needed money to keep us all alive but was good for me. I was still undergoing heavy-duty stress but enjoyed being back in the game I loved. I was making good money while trying wherever possible to be there for the family and for Christopher. That's how my family survived, how we were able to feed ourselves during those tough times. We shifted into rented accommodation in Andratx, sharing a battered old town house with Jonesy, a friend of Amanda's from her Melbourne days. We knew him well; he was Amanda's longest and dearest lifelong friend and still is and had stayed with us many times over the years. He had come over to help Amanda when I had lost the plot and bailed out for Australia.

And what of Mari-Carmen, our little posadero? She was still working for Christopher. When everyone had moved from La Noria to the Palm Farm, Mari-Carmen had gone along too. She was an amazing woman. She would make her way up from her and Enrique's tiny Andratx apartment every morning to do her job, helping around the place and keeping out the interlopers. She was like a watchdog; no one could get past the gates unless Mari-Carmen gave them the okay. If Christopher felt capable of getting out into the sunshine for a moment, she would walk with him, taking the dogs along, fending off the journalists and anyone else who came near. It certainly wasn't a glamorous job and she was on a minimum wage, so she did it more for the love of him than anything else. She was there until the day he died.

In between my film jobs, I would work with Christopher because the sheer force of his personality made me. He was sick, he was dying, he was in and out of hospital, he was angry, we were down to our last penny and the banks had cut us off. Yet he was still the ultimate optimist, convinced that he was not going to die and that he would make one of the projects come good and he would bank some money so that 'his girls' would be okay. In the meantime, he was writing his book, *Postcard From Mallorca*—published in Spain but unreleased here— giving his side of things.

Then, one day, we knew we had taken the final turn into the home straight. When Christopher had developed the cancer, Dr Nicolau, the very generous emphysema medico who had organised the trip to Valencia for the lung operation, took that treatment on as well without payment, even though he was not an oncologist. I will always be grateful for what he did. But after yet another session at the hospital, Dr Nicolau and the others declared that they could do no more and that Christopher would be sent home to die. They said he could have as much morphine as he wanted to ease the pain because the end was nigh.

Typically, Christopher would have none of this. He still refused to accept the death sentence, stating that he 'was going to beat it, no matter what.' After the medicos and nurses would come in each day to fix his medicine and make him comfortable, he would try and do some paperwork. He was convinced that everything was going to keep going and we would turn the corner. But he started to go more and more off with the fairies as the increased morphine consumption kicked in.

In the last couple of weeks, in a last ditch effort, Amanda trawled through the internet trying to unearth things that might ease his situation. Ideas for cures, alternative treatments, different foods, medicines, exercise, anything that would help. She would make him fruit smoothies and other concoctions that she hoped he would at least be able to swallow and provide him with some nutrition. Or she got him his preferred drink, a McDonald's strawberry thick shake, which involved driving into town and back with a little Esky full of ice. It might have had little or no nutrient value, but he loved it. She spent her days with him, trying to keep him as comfortable as possible while doing all the research that she could.

A lot of local people rallied around to help. We were strangers in a strange land, and the Mallorcans could have very easily abandoned us. But they didn't. They were very good to us. Mari-Carmen kept on working like there was no tomorrow and Juan the gardener continued to turn up each day and do a great job, even though we could not pay him.

By now, however, the vultures had started to circle. The family was subjected to the grotesque, undignified spectacle of the Australian Medical Association lashing its Spanish counterpart for inefficiency and collusion, accusing them of faking the operation, one doctor even going so far as to say it looked like they had sprayed blood everywhere for effect. Backed to the hilt by the bloodthirsty Australian media, some members of the AMA described Christopher's terminal cancer as another ruse to avoid being deported.

This was the most disgraceful display by any so-called professional organization or individual I had ever seen. And over the years, I had certainly seen a fair cross-section. To call in to question the reputation of some of the world's best medical minds just to satisfy a hungry press and their insatiable readers was beyond belief. It still makes me angry when I think about it. He was dying. You could see he was dying. And yet they reckoned he was using it as an excuse to not come home and face the music. We used to talk about how my wonderful uncle, Dr Nicholas 'Uncle Bill' Larkins, a humanitarian and former Secretary-General of the Australian Medical Association, would have turned in his grave at the disgraceful behaviour of the AMA and its members. Maybe they were dyslexic and thought the Hippocratic Oath was actually the Hypocritic Oath. It was during this time that the Australian Government was pressuring its Spanish counterpart to deport him. Nice work.

While the media frenzy raged on, I continued to meet with Christopher when possible, although fitting it in between my film work and his medical regime wasn't always easy. We maintained our working and personal relationship right up until the death knell, by now with nearly eleven amazing years of extraordinary experiences under our belts. Never once did he have a go at me for abandoning the family and disappearing back to Sydney for six months; I think he understood more than anyone what I was going through. Amanda spent a lot of time with him, trying to help him fix his affairs and leave them in an acceptable and orderly way. They discussed Charlotte's final years of school and how he wanted to help, with him vowing to fund her education even after his death, so that she could finish her Spanish schooling, of which he was so proud.

As the bedside scenario worsened, the simmering tension between Pixie and I began to boil over. The situation between the pair of us had been brewing for ages, with lots of strange things going on as we grew further and further apart. Now she went into overdrive, making crazy accusations about drug abuse and physical assault and Christ knows what else, trying to keep me away from the Palm Farm by changing the locks and ordering the others not to let me enter.

I went up there one day simply to collect some paperwork, and Mari-Carmen blocked me at the front door, saying, 'You have been banned from the property.'

'I don't think so, Mari-Carmen,' I said. 'Open the door and I am coming in and I am taking whatever I want.'

'Señor Tony, I do not understand it either, but that is what the señora has told me.'

'Well, you can tell the señora to go fuck herself, because I will do what I want.'

Christopher was so drugged up that he was going along with whatever Pixie said or did, including putting money down on ridiculous, expensive things to dress up the farmhouse when we all knew everything was going down the gurgler. Just before he died, when we owed money everywhere and there was nothing in the accounts and people were coming to me and demanding their dough, I turned around to find that she was buying a new Mercedes! I thought, 'What fucking world is she living in?'

As my name was still listed on the majority of the company documents, I was the one getting hassled for rent, payments to builders, money owing to people who had been helping us and fees to architects, accountants and lawyers. No one was getting paid, and I was the one who had to face them and say, 'Well, sorry, I can't pay you, you know. But on the other hand, Pixie *is* buying herself a new Benz, if that helps!'

Where was she getting the money for it? Did Christopher leave cash to be used for other purposes? Was she pulling it out of the Palm Farm somehow? Which didn't make sense, because from what I could see and knew there simply wasn't the money there. I put my foot down. I said, 'Pixie, what are you doing? This is ridiculous. I'm the one who has to tell all these people that we haven't get any money while you're going to be turning up all over the island in a brand new Merc.' But she took delivery of it.

Then one day, about five o'clock in the afternoon, I woke up with a raging hangover on a mate's couch, having got to bed at eight in the morning after a massive night on the tiles, as you can so easily do in Spain. Amanda and I had had a classic fight the night before while out at a nightclub, and I had stormed off, as was my typical response, and had bumped into this mate. We'd had a lot of drinks and a lot of fun and had gone back to his place, and I had passed out on the couch in his lounge room. I came to life feeling like absolute shit and turned my phone on to hear the message, 'You arsehole, he's dead!'

What a scene. I had just managed to wake in forty-degree Spanish heat with my tongue stuck to the roof of my mouth and pounding cannon noises going off in my head thinking, 'God, all I want to do was die,' and the first message I got reads, 'He's dead.'

I thought, 'Fuck!' Then I thought, 'Hmmm, Larkins, you're not going to be popular.'

I fell off the couch, tidied myself up, grabbed a hair of the dog, rang Amanda and staggered up to the Palm Farm to find everyone in various states of emotional decay. Pixie had lost it. She had been drinking and was very emotional. It transpired that neither she nor Amanda had been in the room when Christopher had died and that fact in particular was clearly distressing her. She been downstairs when he had passed away by himself in his upstairs bedroom. Amanda was at home, and Pixie had rung her and said, 'I think he's dead.' Amanda had grabbed Charlotte and, not being able to find me, had headed up to the farm.

By that stage, Christopher had been staying in bed most of the day as he was very weak. He was requiring a lot of morphine to dull the pain, and he couldn't eat much, only occasionally sipping on one of Amanda's smoothies or trying to get a little bit of food down. On this day, Pixie had gone upstairs at one stage to give him something and began rubbing his back. He was very quiet, and Amanda believes that in effect, Pixie was probably inadvertently reviving him. Pixie said later that he was dozing when she went back downstairs. Later, she went up again only to discover that he had passed away. She had heard nothing. It had all been very peaceful. The stomach cancer had won this battle.

When I finally got there, Pixie was in hysterics while a grief-stricken Amanda was oscillating between wanting to strangle me because of the previous night's episode and

429

urging me to do all the right things. I called the undertakers, went upstairs and helped the nurse dress Christopher in a navy tracksuit and waited for their arrival. When the undertakers turned up, we discovered that the tiny stairway was too narrow to get the coffin up to the bedroom. So we had to wrap Christopher in a sheet and take him down.

It was like something out of *Fawlty Towers* with me playing Basil and the undertaker playing Manuel, bumping this body down the stairs. I now know what they mean by the saying 'dead weight.' Pixie and Amanda were hiding in the kitchen going hysterical, but all I could imagine was the body tumbling out of the sheet, sliding down all the way to the bottom and landing at their feet. That really would have brought everybody undone.

'Manuel' put the body in the coffin, saying he would return the next morning to take it away in readiness for the funeral. He then took out an old plastic comb and started brushing Christopher's hair! While I looked on fascinated, he asked if I thought Pixie would want to say goodbye. A reasonable question, but I nearly lost it. How would I know if she wanted to do that? By then we were barely speaking.

But I did feel really sorry for Amanda who had lost the one, true, solid rock in her life, and for Charlotte, who was devastated that her Tissy was now gone. The famous Friday night 'dinks' sessions were no more. Amanda crawled into the bed in the spare room with Charlotte, Pixie passed out and I was consigned to the couch.

That morning of the day he died, Christopher was still refusing to believe that the end was nigh. He was still trying to save the company. He had even called a meeting for the next day to draw up new battle plans.

It was August 5, 2001. Christopher Charles Skase had passed away a month short of his fifty-third birthday.

430

FORTY-FOUR

We were all shattered. For Pixie, it was the end of her longest and most successful marriage, a partnership that had been based on love and the premise that the young, aspiring business tycoon and the brilliant social butterfly were good for each other. A joint team effort that had enjoyed the highest of highs and survived the lowest of lows. It was a tribute to Pixie's loyalty and love that she stuck it out right to the very end. A climax that was certainly not all joy and light. It was a shocking finale.

For Amanda, it terminated a great period in her life, one where this amazing person had provided her with stability, confidence, guidance, boundaries, belief and a whole lot of love.

For Charlotte, well, it took ages for her to come to grips with what had happened. He idolised Eggy, his little evening 'dinks' partner, his designated Great White Hope, and in turn she absolutely worshipped her Tissy. It broke her heart. She slept with his photo under her pillow for ages.

For me? Well, there had been no one else like him in my life. He had been my mentor, friend, counsellor, buddy, business partner and drinking mate. We had worked side by side for more than ten years, trying to create something out of nothing in the most hostile of circumstances. Yet he never ceased to amaze me with his calm, controlled approach, his sublime business brain, his ideas and enthusiasm, and his determination to bounce back even when things were obviously and absolutely stuffed. He was my inspiration.

But after all the agony we had been through, all the tension and dispute, the threats and challenges, if we thought that at last were going to achieve a level of tranquillity and dignity following his death, how sadly mistaken we were. At eight o'clock the next morning, there was a ring of the bell, and I assumed it was the undertakers arriving to take him away. So I went out to the front gate and there was this massive, heaving mob of journalists. Sure, there had always been a small knot of media hanging around—three, four, five, six usually, maybe more when things looked like they were hotting up. When La Noria had been sold, that dedicated group had simply followed their noses up the hill and had begun hanging around the gates of the Palm Farm.

But now that he had died, the media's logistical response was amazing. He had passed away that previous day, the report had gone out almost immediately and by eight o'clock that next morning, fifty journos had flown in from around the world and had scrambled for every hotel bed in Palma, Puerto Andratx and Andratx. Not only Australian journalists, but Spanish journos as well, because it had become a huge local story by then.

The funny thing was, desperate and aggressive as they were for a story, it was not the media who had rung the bell. Standing at the front of the throng was the bloke who had actually pressed the button. A little Spanish feller. He stepped forward, confirmed that I was Señor Larkins, and then in his capacity as a writ processor for the Spanish Tax Department calmly served me with documents containing thirty charges of tax evasion and fraud! Such exquisite timing. 'Ah, fuck, good morning,' I said, throwing it aside as I marched back to the house.

Not to be outdone by the Spanish Tax Department, the Australian Government duly turned up. They arrived to fingerprint Christopher's body like a common criminal, once again calling into question the integrity of the local authorities, like they had so many times in the past. They had to come and see for themselves that he was actually dead. I knew they were on the way because Spanish Interpol had phoned to tell me. They had developed a real dislike for the Australian authorities and the way they treated their Spanish counterparts.

After a routine and what seemed to be an appropriate enough examination, the medicos then insisted on going further, taking samples to check out the coral substance in his lungs. At the mention of this, other family members and their lawyers started jumping in on the action, claiming they should be running the show, thus turning it into a true bun-fight. And while we were dealing with these, and the corpse and the undertakers, the press was hovering around like jackals, salivating like hyenas, writing whatever they wanted, loving every bit of it.

Obviously good people around us were trying to keep things tempered, to calm things down and keep things rational, but Pixie just lost the plot entirely. By now she had started to fall completely under the spell of James, a very young English lawyer who had earlier been sent down by our London-based solicitor Tim Stranack to work as a translation helper during the extradition hearing. James was married to a Spanish woman and spoke excellent Spanish. He was obviously a very bright young boy and he thought so, too. I called him Rabbit Twitch because of his annoying habit of twitching his nose and top lip up and down in unison, revealing his front teeth just like a rabbit does. He did it the whole time anyone was talking to him, and it used to drive me mad, particularly at round table meetings.

He might have thought of himself as a hotshot, but to me there just seemed to be something wrong about him being there, and the situation got stranger after Christopher died. He started lodging the proverbial Chinese whispers into poor Pixie's ear, and she, suffering so much and not thinking straight, fell for them.

As the chaos rolled on, her behaviour did not improve, and about three days later, I spoke to her for virtually the last time for nearly ten years. This came about because we had all been given express legal advice by our Mallorcan solicitors not to talk to anyone in the media about what had happened. Not to talk to any newspaper reporters, not to talk to any television crews, not to talk to any magazine writers, not to give any stories to anyone. Not even if they offered to pay, despite the fact that we were all broke.

So I was at the wake lunch at El Coche restaurant when I got a phone call from Australia. It was Sue Smethurst, then a senior writer and later editor of *New Idea*, who I knew well. 'Hi Tony,' said Sue, 'the deal's all done, the money is in both Pixie's and James' accounts, and I'm arriving tomorrow with the crew. Will you be picking us up from the airport?'

I was at one end of the table with Pixie at the other. Amanda was to one side of me. As Sue chatted away, outlining how it had all been set up, what a great opportunity it was and how she couldn't wait to get the tell-all story from Pixie, the look on my face must have been priceless. 'Ahh, yeah,' I said politely, 'thanks, Sue. Yep, sure.'

I hung up and let it roll around my head for a minute, just to let it sink in. Then, still white-hot with rage, I hissed to Amanda that I had just discovered that her mother had gone behind our backs, expressly against all the legal advice we had been given, and sold her story. Amanda spat the dummy. Not at Pixie. At me! She told me that, considering the circumstances, it was best to leave it alone. What the hell? I was not going to let that stop me.

I looked down toward Pixie and shouted, 'You! You've done a fucking press deal! You and James fucking Rabbit Twitch! You've both had money put into your accounts!'

I stood up, ignoring Amanda. I was not going to be stopped. 'Fuck me. None of us have got a cent between us. We don't know how we're going to survive, we don't have any idea of how we're gonna get out of this country, and I'm facing thirty criminal charges. And you have gone behind our backs and done a deal that you've already been paid for! That's disgraceful, Pixie, fucking disgraceful.'

Pixie was obviously very embarrassed and instead of discussing it, tried to fob me off. I wasn't going to let her off the hook. 'So, when were you going to tell me?' I persisted. 'I just found out by a phone call. It's a done deal. Come on. When were you going to tell me?'

I got no real answer, and the lunch very quickly dissipated. Pixie and the others went off to the Palm Farm, and Amanda and I went back to our house in Andratx. I had a couple of more drinks, decided that she needed to be told a few more home truths, and stormed up to the farm. I didn't quite kick the door in, didn't smash it or anything, but I certainly opened it with a fair force, marched inside and in front of the small gathering gave Pixie an earful. Which to my mind, was thoroughly deserved after all that time.

The main thrust of my outburst was that I had dedicated the previous ten years of my life to Christopher—well, apart from my six-month stint back in Sydney in my very own *One Flew Over The Cuckoo's Nest* experience—abandoning everything I had going for me in Australia to throw my lot in with him and work with him until the day he died on projects all over the world while we tried to clear his name and get back what was rightfully his, despite all the shit that had been slung at us. And now she had ignored everyone's advice, gone behind my back and sold her story. I concluded by pointing out that it had always been me who had handled the press whenever they were on the island. That I was the one that had always dealt with things like that with people like Sue Smethurst, Derryn Hinch or Helen Dalley at Channel 9. That was obviously why Sue had phoned me. And that for her, Pixie, to ignore the explicit instruction about remaining quiet and to not let me know anything about what she was doing, particularly going with Rabbit Twitch, well, that was unforgivable and I was ropeable. Boom! I let her have it with both barrels.

That is why I was not at Christopher's final farewell.

Yes, he was my best mate. But I refused to go along when the family took a boat ride up the west coast to scatter Christopher's ashes on the sea near the village of Deià, a place he loved. It has lovely little stonework and stucco houses and the surrounding mountains, palm trees and white cliffs sparkle in the sunshine. It's a fantastic spot with wonderful views across the sea. In a poignant ceremony, the family sprinkled the ashes of Christopher Charles Skase onto the blue waters of the Mediterranean and Charlotte threw her copy of *Harry Potter and the*

Prisoner of Azkaban into the water because Christopher had read it with her when I had abandoned them and they both had loved it.

No doubt my decision not to be there seems astonishing, seeing as it was the last rites for a man who had had so much influence on my life. But I refused to go because I still wanted to kill Pixie. True. I could no longer trust myself to be in the same room, on the same boat or in any situation that would mean I would be in close proximity to her as I would have strangled her. For the family's sake, I helped organise the cremation and handled all that side of the proceedings, but I did not go along for Pixie's safety and my own long-term self-preservation.

A few days after our lunchtime clash, she declared she was leaving for England the following morning and walking away from everything. Despite the angry standoff that had developed between Pixie and me, Amanda, still trying desperately to hold the shards of the family together, agreed for her to come and stay with us for her last night! I begrudgingly allowed her to come, but quite frankly, I still wanted to kill her. I calmly sat her down and said, 'On what fucking basis would you do this to me? Run off to *New Idea* like that? Hey? When I put ten years of my life on the fucking line for you? Why would you do that?'

All she could do was sob. No answer, just tears. I said, 'That's fucking pathetic, Pixie. Fucking pathetic,' and went and drank myself to sleep. Boy, was this all going swimmingly.

Look, to be fair, all this sounds dreadful, particularly me attacking her about the *New Idea* story and buying the Mercedes. I will always praise her for her love and loyalty to Christopher and she and I had many, many fabulous times over the years and I guess her actions are understandable in many ways. After all, every one of us had been physically and emotionally put through a wringer and then stretched out on a rack that was then ratcheted up until we could bear the pain no longer. They were the cruellest of times, and she had kind of lost it. I tried to remind myself that I had, too.

Later she took the only bit of cash left out of the disaster, a million-dollar life insurance policy Christopher had had since his days with Qintex. As she was his wife and the sole nominated recipient, she kept the whole million bucks, sidelining Amanda, Charlotte and me in the process. You would have thought she might have considered that as we had all been in this together and that I was now facing thirty charges of tax fraud with an arrest warrant awaiting me in Australia, then we deserved just a little cash which would have gone a long, long way in getting us back on our feet. But she gave us nothing. There was not even an offer of money for Charlotte's education, which was Christopher's dying wish, much less any help to get ourselves or our stuff back to Australia.

In his morphine-induced condition, Christopher had been trying to hide from everybody the fact that the well was completely dry. I knew that anyway. But did I ever really get to know this wonderful but complicated man? You just could never guess what was going to happen next, particularly with so many things having been changed while I had been AWOL having my nervous breakdown.

There was one small lifeline left; some money still owing from a final remortgaging of the Palm Farm. It had been a typical Skase tactic—his plan being that we were going to live on some of it while we used the rest to try and keep the projects alive. Shortly before he died, I flew to Valencia, went to the bank and got the payout—it was a fair slab of cash—and brought it back to Mallorca.

I took a small amount of it and paid the back rent we owed on the town-house Amanda and I were living in, paid something to some of the lawyers that had worked so hard for us and paid back a couple of other people that had been so helpful and who I had assured that they would get money. I don't know how many times over the preceding years I had used the phrase, 'I give you my word, if you do this for me now, I promise you will get paid.' I paid something to as many of them as I could, and the rest of that amount I had taken went toward getting us out of Spain. I could reflect on at least something good that had come out of all this. United in our grief and aware that we were now totally on our own, Amanda and Charlotte and I suddenly found ourselves back together as a family. And as a family, we had to get out of Mallorca; there was no way we were going to be allowed to stay on.

The lawyers said to me, 'Look, these tax charges they summoned you with, they were never really aimed at you. It was another attempt to try and get Christopher on charges through you. So just get out of the country, leave Spain, and we will deal with it. You can't deal with it while you are here, so just leave.'

But the lawyers warned us, and we already knew, that heading straight back to Australia would not be a good idea. Not only would the media chase us, but it would be an especially risky situation for me. I had been told that there was definitely a warrant out for my arrest. It had been issued after Max Donnelly had had me served with a writ just as I was leaving Australia via Brisbane airport; a writ that I had ignored when I heard that Christopher had developed cancer and I was needed in

Spain. The message was clear. The Federal Police would come on board and apprehend me as soon as my plane touched down.

Where to go to, then? Wally stepped up to the plate. 'Mate,' he said, 'I've got this apartment in Thailand. You guys can go and live there for a couple of months.' He had it on timeshare, I think, or on a leaseback deal where he used to live in it for a certain amount of time for free every year. He told us that it was all ours.

So with the last of the cash I had taken from the final payout, plus some frequent flyer points kindly donated by Wally, we bought three tickets for Thailand, where we were to be joined by an Australian friend, our old mate Jonesy again. We took a suitcase each and nothing else and bolted. We had to buy return tickets—under regulations, you weren't able to buy one-way tickets to Thailand from Spain in those days—and so the possibility was still in the back of our mind that one day we might return to Spain. Perhaps I might have to go back and sort out a few things. Who knows? Quite frankly, we didn't know where we might end up.

Pixie left the Palm Farm and went to London, taking all the furniture, her clothes and other bits and pieces in shipping containers. Thinking it was for the best, we shipped everything that we owned over to England with her things as well. It turned out to be not a good idea. Six months later Pixie decided to go back to Mallorca and had all her stuff shipped back to Spain. Then she had it taken back to England and then finally on to Australia!

But she only brought her own stuff home to Australia. She didn't think of bringing any of ours. Everything we ever owned was left in storage in London. All the stuff that Amanda and I both as a couple and as individuals had put together over thirty years. Everything we had taken from Australia to Mallorca; everything we had picked up during the ten years in Spain. All our furniture, kitchen equipment, clothes, tools, golf clubs, art work, mementos, pictures, Charlotte's childhood memories, everything. As I write this, that was fifteen years ago and, would you believe, it is still all over there in London. We have not seen any of it since. Yeah, cheers, thanks a lot.

I headed off to Thailand expecting that Pixie and James would tidy things up by selling off the Apartments and the Palm Farm and paying out the mortgages, and that we would all share in a carve-up of what was left. I expected it wasn't going to be much, but we needed that money to keep us going in Asia and also buy our airfares for the last leg to Australia when we knew that the day would eventually come and we would have to go home and face the music. But Pixie decided that she would go with the brilliant thoughts of James, who I felt had by now determined that he was going to be the next Christopher Skase. He advised her that they should resurrect the projects, get them finished, sell them off and make a profit! This was against all common sense and my advice. I sent her a message, 'Pixie, I've been working on those projects for years, and I can tell you, they have hit the proverbial brick wall. It just ain't going to happen.'

She still went against my objections and the pleas of others. She and James, and one of the other sons-in-law, who also thought he was going to be the next Skase, went ahead with their hare-brained scheme. With their gung ho approach and lack of any local knowledge of the complexities of how things are done, the plan collapsed of course and nothing came of it. I am not sure what happened as I have never been told exactly what occurred. I think that in the end the mortgage on the Apartments was foreclosed, while the Palm Farm was sold, and Pixie just lived off that, going backwards and forwards to London. After the banks and the lawyers were paid out, there would not have been a lot left over from the proceeds. Maybe a hundred, a hundred and fifty thousand dollars. But I think that just got eaten up. It was all gone. Not a thing to show after all that effort and here we were, stuck in Thailand with nothing. No clothes, no food, no money, no income, no airfares. Nothing. Now what happens?

FORTY-FIVE

Just when we thought we were down and out for the count, things turned slightly our way. I was still owed a bit of money by Palma Pictures, and they started dribbling it into my bank account. We live again! Or at least, we were able to start eking out a living. We rented a traditional Thai house in Rawai on Phuket Island and after a while started to enjoy the lifestyle. As long as you didn't mind living with no walls and having snakes in the roof chasing the rats up there, the monsoon whipping up the water and flooding the house, invasions of science fiction-like insects appearing from nowhere, and baby cobras slithering up through the drainage system. In fact, after all the crap we had been through, it was one of the best times in our lives, living by the beach and enjoying the tropical weather.

We got Charlotte into school, although we chose QISP (Quality Schools International of Phuket). As clever as she was, dropping her into a local Thai school just wasn't realistic. I was busy, too, trying to set up a small film production company with a local American who had very good connections with the Thai movie industry. No more worrying about shaky resort projects and hounding media hordes and Christopher's terminal illness. It was all in the past.

But I will admit that I was still hitting the piss pretty hard. I was feeling under a lot of pressure and more than a little alarmed at the thought of what was going to happen to me when I got back to Australia. Gaol probably. The prison joke kept ringing in my head about the old lag saying to his new cellmate, 'Let's play husband and wife.'

Things were not improved when I had a motorcycle accident, badly smashing my left hip and nearly severing my left leg at the knee. There you go, Larkins in the wars again, just like the old times when I was a daredevil kid growing up in Sydney. I said to the local doctor when they were stitching me up that he should ring Royal North Shore Hospital and get my medical files flown over. 'You'll need a jumbo ...' I added.

But I was lucky. I only have a left leg thanks to Jonesy, who arrived at the hospital in the nick of time to convince them not to remove it.

Just about all the money we had left went on the surgery to the point that one day Amanda and I worked out we were down to what we were wearing and what we were carrying. We had a couple of hundred bucks left, or about four weeks of living, and no way of making any more. Kicking goals, 'Arold! Our tropical fantasy could not go on forever. Twenty-five years of hard work by both of us at home and abroad had disappeared down the drain. We simply were not going to survive.

So we started talking seriously about going back to Australia, settling the issue for once and for all and hopefully putting a bit of an honest perspective on the whole thing. But the prospect of talking to the Federal Police really worried me. In my fragile mind, they were going to hurl me in the slammer and throw away the key. One day, having checked myself out of the hospital but

444

still immobilised on the couch, Amanda forced my hand by saying that she was taking Charlotte, getting on a plane and heading back to Australia one way or another. 'You can follow us if you want,' she said. They flew out courtesy of frequent flyer points supplied by Jack Holt, her then brother-in-law, lead singer of the alternative Melbourne rock band, TISM.

With Amanda and Charlotte gone, I hooked up employment-wise with a bloke called Reinhard to keep myself occupied while my leg got better. Best known as RH, he was a former major league ice hockey player, a round-the-world sailor and an ex-drug runner who was now living in Phuket. This all came about because Charlotte's Thai school teacher had asked me to do a substantial favour for a friend, whose husband at the time was in California. The friend turned out to be RH's wife. When he returned from the US, he was very grateful and he and Lck took me under their wing and looked after me until my return to Australia. Thank you, my friends.

I helped RH refurbish and stock a nightclub he was planning to open, including doing a five-day duty free booze run from Phuket to Langkawi and back aboard his former smuggling yacht, a forty-five foot ex-Atlantic Ocean racer.

This period is when I wrote the majority of the notes for this book. After a further six months hanging around Thailand, existing on the smell of an oily rag, living in an old house out in the jungle with six bar girls—now, that's another book in itself—and steadfastly putting the inevitable off, I finally decided I must make my way home. My good friend, Roy Mico, one of my groomsmen at the Wedding That Reduced The Groom To A Shambles, lent me the money to not only pay off some debts I had incurred while recovering but also buy the ticket to get out of there. For that, Roy, I am eternally grateful.

Of course, those in the know say that the Federal Police have plenty of time on their hands and one eye permanently fixed on the immigration computer. I was convinced that as soon as the plane door was opened in Sydney, a team of big coppers would march resolutely down the aisle, yank me out of my seat and arrest me. So much so, that prior to leaving Thailand I phoned home and told everybody not to bother coming out to the airport to pick me up. 'I'll be arrested and taken to court,' I said. On the flight, I did not even bother to fill in my immigration card because I felt it would be a waste of time.

Flying across Australia and with breakfast being handed out, I suddenly remembered that I had a big bud of Thai marijuana in my bum bag that someone had given me at my farewell party the night before I left Phuket. What to do with it? Flush it? Hide it under the seat? Or ..?

I just ate it with breakfast and sort of forgot about it until we landed and I realised I was off my face and about to be arrested by the feds. Yeah, nice work, 'Arold.

But the plane landed and nothing happened. No burly officers coming on board at all. I got off as usual and cruised up to the immigration counter where the man said, 'Welcome to Australia, Mr Larkins, do you have your card?' I explained that I didn't, so he got me to go back and fill one out.

I got through there and reached customs, where again I was treated with a warm welcome and told, 'Have a nice day.' As I was heading to the door, I was beginning to think two things. 'One, isn't this odd? It looks like they're going to leave me alone. And two, now what happens?' Having told everyone to stay away from the airport, I now realized that I did not have any money to get out of there. All I had was about three dollars in Thai baht, having spent the last of my dough in the Phuket duty free on a cheap bottle of vodka and some cigarettes. Well, I figured, I was going to need some sustenance to get me through the drama that was about to unfold.

So much so, when a bloke quietly sidled up to me and introduced himself as a Federal Police officer, I almost fell in his arms and said, 'Oh, thank fuck for that.' It was a response I don't think he was quite expecting. 'We've been watching you since you landed and didn't want to make a scene,' he said.

As it turned out, they were really nice guys who treated me very well. From there, they took me back through the airport, drove me across the tarmac and out via a tunnel to the court, thus avoiding the massive media throng that I found out later had been waiting at the airport. They even let me go outside on to the tarmac and have a nerve-settling cigarette, advising me that if I had some better clothes in my bag that I should put them on as I was about to appear before a Judge of the High Court. Sadly, I had to inform them that I was already wearing my Sunday best!

There was plenty of media at the court, too, but we got around them with the feds escorting me right through the pack, which I really appreciated. It was interesting that in all my dealings with the feds they were nothing but gentlemen and extremely professional in their approach. Unlike their Government counterparts.

After a ten-minute court hearing, I was given the option of going to gaol or attending an interview with, of course, my old sparring partner, Max Donnelly!

'Maxie, you old number cruncher you, how the fuck are ya?'

Well, actually, I didn't say that; I was a little more mellow, aware of the seriousness of it all, as well as being somewhat wasted from the marijuana bud. Fortunately, it was not as strong as the hash I consumed at the Wedding That Reduced The Groom To A Shambles, and I was able to hold my end up with what I felt was intelligence, politeness and consistency. No doubt Max just assumed that my look and behaviour was due to jet lag. It certainly made my time with him a much more pleasant experience than what I had anticipated.

In fact, we had a nice chat for six hours, about the same amount of time he had spent interviewing Amanda on her arrival a few months earlier. During our conversation, I told Max everything I knew, including the fact that there was certainly no money left and that the only sizeable amount of cash floating around from the shards of the Skase empire was the million-dollar insurance payout that Pixie had collected and which was not subject to the bankruptcy provisions. I was going to add, 'And not even you will get your hands on any of that, Max, believe me.' But I thought better of it. All I wanted to do was just get out of there and go and lie down somewhere.

Then, he let me go. That was it. No charges, no warrants, no cautions, no gaol. Nothing. To his credit, Max even gave me the money for a taxi to Roy's place!

Of course to this day I am constantly asked, 'Where did all the money go?' There are several components to the answer.

First, it was consistently reported that Qintex had collapsed with debts of about $1.7 billion. This, in fact, was incorrect. John Allpass, one of the Qintex receivers, was asked on *Four Corners* what Qintex had actually owed at the time, and he replied: 'In round figures, six to seven hundred million owing to unsecured creditors together with certain amounts of bank debt which are also outstanding and will not be repaid because the assets didn't realise sufficient to repay the banks in full.'

That is because, after the stock market suspended trading when Qintex Ltd shares dropped to $1.05 and Qintex Australia Ltd fell to 16 cents, the shareholder equity asset value was absorbed into the level of security debt equity asset value. That is, all the share certificates, with no longer any asset value to support the share price, had become virtually worthless pieces of paper. The capitalised value of Qintex Australia Ltd had been dissipated to a mere $26.8 million and Qintex Ltd's to $25.9 million. Just a few months before the companies had been worth billions.

The creditors holding security over the firm's assets then seized possession of the assets with the aim of selling them and retrieving what they could. The receivers reported that the directors gave their position as having liabilities of $2 billion but assets well in advance of that, worth $3 billion. Yet, the ensuing sale of those assets realised a reported figure of only $1 billion, roughly a third of their estimated value. There is no published material identifying the percentage of secured debt that was paid out from the sale of the assets, but it is known that the main debt syndicate had secured loans totalling $725 million.

It is also public knowledge that after the fire sale of the assets, the unsecured creditors and the shareholders—the last in line—received nothing. Those shareholders included Christopher, who was the majority holder with 51 per cent.

The receivers/liquidators were chasing personal loan guarantees given by either or both Christopher and Pixie over Qintex debt to several financial institutions. These guarantees totalled $171,471,824 'plus interest, plus costs.' They consisted of Nippon Shinpan Company $82,615, 785, by written agreement; State Bank of Victoria/Tricontinental $66,462,358; Wardley $20,800,743; and ANZ $1,592,938. This figure was generally reported as between $171 and $177 million and usually termed as 'personal debts.' Despite coming up with a plan to get the company back on track, Christopher was never given any opportunity to reconfigure things to sort out those guarantees.

Add to this, the unrealised amounts from both the secured and unsecured loans that were written off against taxable income by creditors from the senior debt syndicate all the way down the line to the small business losses later referred to by Peter Reith, Minister for Workplace Relations and Small Business, on their behalf in Parliament, and there was very, very little left. Reith spoke of 'the bloke who is owed $1160' for providing 'plants and services' and 'the bloke who runs a car hire business who loses $462.84' as examples of the 'loads of people in the small business community who had an interest in seeing the full pursuit of Mr Skase.'

Max Donnelly, the trustee-in-bankruptcy had been reported as chasing Christopher for somewhere between $10 and $50 million in cash, plus $5 million worth of assets. After an eleven-year search, he recovered nothing. When it was announced the government would no longer investigate the Skase bankruptcy, one headline read, 'Hunt for Skase millions fruitless.' Later Max stated on ABC radio that the records I provided him with tied in with the records he had. Therefore, there was nothing to recover, and he could only account for it as 'failed development projects and living expenses' with no accompanying detail. I have no doubt that he set out to find the money that he was told was there, did his best to do so and then found nothing, because there was nothing there in the first place.

It's as simple as that. When you consider the situation I have outlined in this book, it takes the focus off Christopher as being the one who took the money and puts it fair and square on a re-evaluation and rearrangement of asset values that pushed everything downwards. It's all fact. Nobody can deny it.

Not only that, at the end of this long and sorry saga, I can only reflect on the views of our lawyer, the late Shane Herbert on the thirty-two charges laid against Christopher. Shane felt that of those, thirty were simply ridiculous and had only been issued to satisfy the Spanish jurisdiction's extradition hearing requirements. The original two charges were the only ones that held any water, one of them relating to the financing behind the purchase of Qintex shares and the other about the authorisation of management fees. Nothing to do with theft or the transfer of funds to offshore accounts.

Of those, one was for something that was actually not committed by Christopher but by one of Qintex's principal in-house lawyers. Christopher always said that to save his own arse, this man had taken immunity from prosecution and thrown him, Christopher, under the bus. But Christopher never criticized the lawyer for doing it as he recognized the pressure the government had put on him including threatening to disbar him. As well, that man had lost a lot in the collapse, too, and needed to survive.

Things officially came to an end on April 3, 2003, when the Attorney-General Daryl Williams released this statement:

> 'I have accepted a recommendation by bankruptcy trustee Mr Max Donnelly to discontinue investigations into the bankruptcy of the late Christopher Skase.
>
> 'Mr Donnelly has recently provided me with a report on the most recent phase of his investigations, which involved telephone conversations with Mrs Pixie Skase and formal interviews with her daughter Mrs Amanda Larkins and son-in-law Mr Tony Larkins. The Larkins returned to Australia last year.
>
> 'Based upon the information obtained from those interviews, earlier investigations, legal advice and legal proceedings in Australia, Spain, the Cayman Islands and the United Kingdom, Mr Donnelly believes no reasonable avenues of investigation remain to be pursued.
>
> 'On Mr Donnelly's assessment, Mr Skase consumed substantial funds on failed development projects and living expenses. Mr Donnelly believes it would not be cost-effective to pursue what few assets may possibly remain.
>
> 'Subject to new and relevant information emerging that might lead to a recovery of assets, he has recommended that the investigation cease.

'The Commonwealth has provided approximately $2.65 million to fund the investigation and related legal proceedings since 1993, including fees to Mr Donnelly of $310,290.

'Throughout the proceedings, Mr Donnelly's investigations have been hindered by Mr Skase's use of an array of corporate vehicles and trusts. In addition, Mr Skase's former associates were unwilling to assist Mr Donnelly and had to be compelled to do so through the courts.

'The original purpose in funding Mr Donnelly's efforts was to ensure that all legal avenues for the possible recovery of assets for the benefit of the late Mr Skase's creditors had been fully exhausted.

'I accept Mr Donnelly's advice that that position has been reached. However, if further relevant information emerges, the Government would be prepared to consider approving further funding to Mr Donnelly.

'The Commonwealth remains committed to supporting bankruptcy laws and to assisting bankruptcy trustees to perform their statutory duties.'

One simple six-hour chat between Max and me had achieved what more than ten years of expensive investigations, trials, searches, extraditions, threats, disputes and headlines could not.

The Chase for Skase was over.

No one has ever bothered me since.

Weird.

453

FORTY-SIX

Through Lillian, the Australian-born CIA agent who had led us to the Saint Martin property via the mad French prince she had rescued from rebels who had kidnapped him in Colombia—I can't believe I just wrote that sentence, but it's all true—we were lucky enough to meet an incredible man, Georges Huguenot. He was a Swiss banker of the old school, who did a lot of work for the Bank of Liechtenstein, one of the preferred banks of Queen Elizabeth.

Christopher asked me to pick up Georges from the airport one day and bring him back to La Noria where we would do some presentations, site visits and so on. He was one of the most refined men I have ever met, a class act, stemming from his role as a banker for many of the European royal families. When I had the pleasure of driving him home after dinner one night, he asked me, 'Tony, do you know the difference between being clever and being intelligent?'

Right at that point I was so fucked up, angry and wired, I was having trouble determining the difference between left and right, so I said, 'No, Georges, tell me.'

'There are two types of people in the business world,' Georges said. 'Clever and intelligent. Sadly, there are a lot of clever ones, who do what they do for all the wrong reasons, and not enough intelligent ones, who do what they do for all the right reasons. Your Christopher is one of the intelligent ones.'

I tell you that story because that sums up Christopher Charles Skase. He was intelligent, perceptive, a brilliant thinker. His tourism projects were and still are stunning, and I am firmly convinced the industry is a lot worse off for his departure. The man had style, proven without doubt by the Gold Coast, Port Douglas and Princeville Mirage properties, three of the best resorts in the world to this day. He left monuments to himself in the guise of those creations and the Seven Network still shines on. No one can take that away from him. Not bad for a boy who started with nothing.

His entire life was his business and his family; he just enjoyed doing it and was always proud of the people he could help while doing it. Few people get to do what they love doing. He did. He was never doing it for the money, but because he got a thrill out of doing it.

He was an enigma. The hotshot businessman dressed in his Hermes suit by day and the ordinary bloke hopping into his shorts and tee-shirt at night. Standing around the pool with a Jack Daniels and soda with lots of ice, cracking awful jokes, he was such a dag. Cooking his own barbecue was his favourite past time or going on a boat, any kind of boat. It didn't have to be a flash boat; a rubber ducky would do, or a jet ski, or anything that moved across the top of the water. Just being in a boat for a bit of fun. He loved that sort of thing, the simple life.

Yes, he was a control freak, but he had a great sense of humour too, and if he had one real weakness, it was a lack of judging character. He was too nice a guy and got done over by people he should not have trusted.

When we met, I was twenty-five and he was thirty-seven, and he could not have been more welcoming. Over the years he went from being a busy entrepreneur, a man who I saw in the media more than I saw personally, to being my father-in-law (in the context that he was the stepfather of my wife), to being my best mate. We had great times together, particularly out on the golf course, a game that he loved but at which he was not very good. Then again, neither am I. One of his few regrets was that he could never find the right box to put me in. He examined, classified and catalogued everyone else that he met, but he could not find the correct file for me.

I will always remember the magnetism. The incredible charisma. The way he made you feel good and that you could achieve anything. Obviously, as a developer, he was a believer in the capitalist system and therefore he was ultra-conservative in his politics, but over the years he had lots of dealings with politicians from right across the spectrum, and these were usually productive because he treated them with respect no matter what their views were.

If things were not working out the way he wanted or a view was being pressed that he did not necessarily like, he seldom got flustered or angry. Under stress, he only got calmer and calmer ... and calmer. While everyone else would be running around like headless chooks, he would focus on the facts at hand and work out a solution.

I know some people are going to choke on this next statement, but he was the most honest man I ever met. His parents were very straight with the highest of moral values, and he carried that on. Sure, he did some risky things in business, but he had a team of extremely well-paid lawyers and accountants who made sure it was all legal and above board. As Kerry Packer famously said before a House of Representatives Select Committee on

Print Media, 'If anybody in this country doesn't minimize their tax, they want their head read.'

If you check through Christopher's file, you will find he had never fallen foul of the law and until the Qintex crash had never been accused of impropriety in business or in private. For example, he had been offered incentives by the Bjelke-Petersen Government to shift Qintex operations to Queensland. While these incentives were generous, there was nothing dodgy about them. When the Fitzgerald Inquiry later investigated state corruption, Qintex and Christopher came under intense scrutiny, but everything was found to be above board. Indeed, he never even copped a speeding ticket even though he was such a lousy driver.

Look, I worked with Christopher for more than a decade, from October 1990 to August 2001. In that time, I saw every document, sat in on every meeting, sent out every bill and wrote out every cheque. He always made sure things were above board. Had he done anything illegal, it would have worried me and I would have stopped it or left him.

Was there hidden money? No. In my role in Spain, I was a director of all companies. I was privy to every fax, every letter, every invoice and every phone call that came through or went out. I had access to every bank account. In fact, was the only signatory on all the bank accounts. Christopher never had another bank account in his name after he left Australia. No one could put money in or take money out of those accounts without me providing the signature. I can assure you, there was no hidden money.

I think one of Christopher's biggest problems was that he did not come from 'old money.' He was a self-made man, not part of the old-school-tie, the old boys' fraternity, the Melbourne Establishment.

As for him and Pixie, I don't think Christopher chased her because he thought she could be good for him. I don't think it was calculating in the context of him seeing what she could do for him in terms of success, although that is the way it turned out. He was just infatuated.

They worked as an interesting duo. In the Qintex days, he never hid anything from her, he trusted her implicitly, and he told her everything that was going on in terms of the business. In turn, she had full input, offering her thoughts, advice and ideas, although this was always done privately. She never attended Qintex business meetings, nor did she ever take any claim if one of her ideas, presented by Christopher, took off and succeeded. Despite the occasionally sharp tongue and the ego, she recognised that it was important that Christopher took all the kudos.

He would confide in me because we were the only two males within the immediate group, and we gravitated towards each other. He often asked my opinion on matters, starting the conversation with one of the varying names he had devised for me. My full name is Harold Antony Larkins, so like most of the people I worked with in the Sydney movie industry, he would often call me Harold. Or he would look at the shape of my thick, long hair and call me Helmut. Or he would call me Ruprecht, from a very odd character in his favourite movie *Dirty Rotten Scoundrels*; a character within a character in the movie, best described as the result of too much inbreeding within the nobility. It's a nickname I still proudly use.

Recognising, as the years went by and the media attention got more frenzied, that the name Skase was becoming less and less a door opener, he used to adopt the name David Johnston when setting up an appointment on the phone for me to go and see someone about a deal. 'This is David Johnston,' he would say, 'and our Mr Larkins will come and see you.' Sometimes during those meetings when I needed his guidance, opinion or decision, I would excuse myself to make a phone call. 'I'll have to talk to David Johnston about that,' I would say. At other times, I occasionally pretended to be a lawyer or a doctor, not to shake anyone down or do anything wrong or cause anyone harm, just to keep things moving along. We lived in a frenetic situation, and we had to be on top of our game all the time and be prepared to take a few risks and bend the rules to get somewhere, anywhere.

We moved in the upper stratosphere of finance sometimes, even making presentations to Goldman Sachs and Bear Stearns in their World Trade Centre offices, which were later casualties of 9/11. That really struck a chord with me on that horrendous day as I watched it all unfold while working on a film set in Mallorca. I had been in meetings in the same building at about the same time of day as the attack took place.

In the end, it was a funny situation. Over the ten years, starting with practically nothing, we got ourselves involved in travel and hospitality projects worth potentially hundreds of millions of dollars. Top quality projects, five star, not only in Spain but as far flung as the US, Central America, the Caribbean and Cuba. We worked hard on all those schemes, we designed some beautiful resorts and we got many of them well under way. Through Christopher's genius of trading off our skills for expenses, they provided us with a living. Not a great living, but at least with a roof over our heads and food to eat and a bottle of wine at the end of the day. Yet not one of those projects ever actually came to fruition under our control! Some came perilously close, but through a combination of many influences—lack of funds, lack of local knowledge, poor decision-making, unfortunate timing, Australian Government malevolence, Spanish Government intransigence, Mallorcan Government interference, island politics, bureaucratic hold-ups, the constant barrage of media lies, sheer bad luck—we never actually got to the point where we turned the keys to the front door of one or gave it a final polish before handing it over to its new owner. Funny about that. Sad, ironic and disappointing maybe, but in a strange way, after all the argument and dispute that constantly ran parallel with it, funny.

If none of these events had occurred, if Qintex had continued on and made billions, I would have stayed in the film industry. The movie game suited me; it suited my style, suited my personality, suited my character. But the collapse of Qintex changed all that. I said 'yes' when Christopher asked me to come to Spain and help him out, and I was plunged into a world like no other. He could be strong and demanding but I was never intimidated by him and he never tried to intimidate me.

Did I fall under his spell? No, I don't think I did.

Did I ever do things that I didn't want to? No, I didn't.

Was he my best friend? Yes, he was.

He was charismatic, and I don't think that I ever met anyone who had dealt with him who did not think the best of him. He could make people see what he wanted to do and get them excited about coming along for the ride and investing with him and making the vision become a reality.

I respected him in every way. I did not jump on the bandwagon, but I was taken by his honesty and integrity. He was straight as the day is long. That was his problem. If he had been a bit corrupt, he would have been all right. Even his lawyers said that if he had not been so correct and so straight, he would have been a rich man, like Alan Bond and so many of the other entrepreneurs of the 80s and 90s. The problem was he eventually got screwed over, with a little help from some powerful enemies and others who either jumped ship or bailed out.

As my long-suffering wife Amanda said about Christopher during a Radio National interview:

'I no longer care what anyone thinks about him. There is just no excuse, yes, if he was Ronald Biggs, or if he was Pinochet, sure. (But) try and speak to the family and find out what the man's done. I'm terribly sorry, but companies operated the way Qintex operated. Annual reports were handed out every year. Nobody had a problem with it when they were making money, did they? It was not illegally run. People may consider it unethical, but it's exactly the way business was done in that era.'

Thank you, darling, that says it all. We may be poor, but we are happy; and happy with the choices we made!

Throughout the journey in SkaseWorld, there was never a dull day.

EPILOGUE

Oh, 'Arold, you've done it again!

In 2015 I was working on a huge BMW commercial shoot in Melbourne when a bloke came up to me and said, 'Hullo, 'Arold. Last time I saw you, you dropped out of the sky and landed in a fishpond at my feet ...'

Ah, yes, I must confess, that actually did happen. In 1989, as I recall, when we were filming a Camel cigarette ad in a new shopping mall in Cairns. Yet another incident in the sometimes curious, randomly adventurous and occasionally disturbing life and times of Harold Antony Larkins.

As you will have observed throughout this book, using up more lives than the most tried and tested cat, I have survived many precarious situations over the years prompting people who have not seen me in a while to gasp, 'Christ almighty, Larkins, you're still alive.'

The fishpond incident was one of my better ones, although it typically involved my usual downfall formula of too much drink, a scantily clad model and a desperate need to show off.

As we were leaving the restaurant on the upper level, I decided I would impress her with a few moves and raced over to the escalator with the intention of jumping onto the handrail and sliding down to the bottom. But as soon as I hit the rubber rail I got too much grip, went straight over the edge, and fell backwards six metres to the ground.

Mercifully, I landed flat on my back in the fishpond, strategically positioned in the middle of a garden feature near where one of my co-workers Kevin McGrath and a security guard were standing waiting for us to come down and get driven home.

I immediately jumped up and although soaking wet, discovered I did not have a scratch on me. So off I went to a nightclub where, sadly, I was asked to leave when I started dripping water all over the floor. Another day, another Larkins escapade.

But it was good to see Kevin after all these years and have a laugh about incidents such as that, seeing as since returning to Melbourne from Spain via Thailand in 2002 I have had the occasional up, but plenty of downs.

So what has happened since I got back into the country?

Following my six-hour interview with Max Donnelly in Sydney and having been released by the High Court after fulfilling my legal obligations, I spent the night there with a good friend and then flew the following day down to Melbourne. Here I joined my wife and child who had been living in a rented house for six months awaiting my arrival while I recovered from my motorcycle accident in Thailand.

I had arrived not only penniless, with no credit rating, and cards charged to the max, but a further $10,000 in the hole, thanks to a Sydney reporter named Annette Sharp. A *New Idea* story about my Skase experiences had been negotiated by editor Sue Smethurst. But at the last minute Sharp fucked everything. Writing for Fairfax in those days, she got wind of the story, somehow got hold of my number in Thailand from one of my sisters, Lou, by claiming she was a friend, and phoned me in the middle of the night just before I was due to fly back to Australia. I explained my agreement with *New Idea* to her. She assured me that she was great friends with my sister and a close personal friend of Sue Smethurst, and promised faithfully to hold the piece back until the *New Idea* feature was run.

It was then run on October 20, 2002, in the *Sun-Herald* before the *New Idea* article was due for release, which of course instantly wrecked my agreement with Sue. Not only did this action totally screw me financially, it also destroyed my relationship with Sue, who was justifiably furious, as they had advertised it as an exclusive. In one stroke, this so-called journalist had wrecked our family's only chance of getting back on our feet in Melbourne. I am still waiting for her Karma to hit.

I received my first Centrelink payment a few weeks later only to discover it wasn't even going to cover the cost of my cigarettes much less anything else. To add to my woes, I quickly found that I was now living in a city that was not mine, amidst people I didn't know, and not qualified for any sort of employment in my original profession, the film industry. In my eleven-year absence, the introduction of the need for a certificate or a ticket to get a job that I would normally have walked straight into had now made me virtually redundant. Nor did I have a vehicle or even access to one, so my options were somewhat limited. But I needed to find some form of employment and fast.

Then it came to me.

While flat on my back recovering from my injuries in Thailand, I had spent many hours watching one of the few English language shows on television there, a fantastic American program called *Taxicab Confessions*. It was filmed entirely inside the cab with passengers prompted into revealing their innermost feelings about their lives, loves, jobs, sex, habits and aspirations. I figured that getting into an environment like that was right up my alley.

So I signed up for a Silver Top Taxis driver course. Having never lived in Melbourne, it was always going to be a challenge, but I soon began to get a handle on the city and wound up driving for four years. Typically, I worked fourteen hours a night, six nights a week, fifty-two weeks a year, through birthdays, holidays, Christmases, whatever. It didn't matter. I loved it.

The job did not pay well, but the parade of people that jumped in and out of my vehicle provided me with the most fascinating insight into modern society imaginable—black, white, gay, straight, rich, poor, hookers, strippers, rent boys, drug runners, thieves, conmen, judges, doctors, lawyers, corporate cowboys, business Barbies, piss-heads, drug-fucked morons and even the occasional hit-man. Once again, never a dull day. You couldn't put half of what happened inside that cab into a book, on screen or to air; it would be triple-X rated.

Luckily, I got a bit of break when, in a curious set of events, my old mate Wally organised a stint for me to be the owner's representative on a French-run cruise ship named the Paul Gauguin, based out of Tahiti. What was initially going to be a one-month gig turned into six months of pure bliss sailing the sparkling waters of French Polynesia, doing … well, I was not quite sure what I was supposed to be doing, other than wandering all over the boat in a suit looking like I was the owner's representative, keeping an eye on things that I knew very little about and living like a king in the premium suite. The crew variously treated me with respect, courtesy and deep-seated Gallic suspicion. Eventually, the boat was sold, and I actually shed tears the day I had to disembark, fly home and get back behind the wheel of the cab.

Then in 2005, joy of joys, one of my dearest and oldest friends organised for a pal of hers to take me on as a truck driver on the filming of a Stephen King mini-series, *Nightmares & Dreamscapes*, starring William Hurt and William H. Macy, which was being filmed in Melbourne. At last, back in the game I loved and had missed so much.

After this wrapped, I got jobs driving for other productions and eventually bagged the role of second unit transport manager on a big budget fantasy drama, *Where The Wild Things Are*, directed by Spike Jonez. From there I got work as a unit assistant or unit manager on productions such as the fantastic biopic, *Hawke*, the mini-series *Bastard Boys* and long-form series such as the Channel 7 hit *Winners & Losers*. I also was involved in many commercial shoots and reality shows including *MasterChef* and *The Block*.

Then, as only Larkins can, I lost my licence for eighteen months for drink driving. I continued working but this made employment incredibly difficult to find and even when I did get a job I often had to pay someone to drive me there, particularly on the more remote shoots. After a few months, this forced me into my own personal bankruptcy, as I had been unable to keep up the regular monthly payments on the maxed credit card debts I had incurred while trying to keep the family afloat during the previous decade.

As you can imagine, Amanda was really impressed with all this. What can I say? I'm a slow learner.

Fortunately, Amanda had always had a steady job in commercial and retail roles, and this has allowed us to put food on the table and keep a roof over our heads. But it has not been easy and any thought of us buying a home or getting a new car or going on a decent holiday is just a pipedream.

Initially we were in a small, rundown two-bedroom weatherboard in East Hawthorn, which Amanda had organised through an old school friend. This was so we could be close to Charlotte's new school, John Gardiner High School, often referred to as Fight Club Hawthorn. I think poor Charlotte suffered more than anyone during this period of constant change and turmoil. She is now, of course, all grown up, living in outer east Melbourne, happy in her job and loving life.

Then in early 2015, I broke my back for a third time. Oh, 'Arold, when is this going to stop?

I fell off a stepladder during the move to our present place on the outskirts of Melbourne, cracking my back on the unforgiving sharp edge of a heavy chrome and glass coffee table. At first, convincing myself I was okay, I loaded up on high-dose painkillers and high-octane vodka in order to keep working. Then one day the actual fracture let go, virtually paralysing me. I woke up in the most incredible pain, face down on the front lawn a few hours after my last memory. It was now dark, I had no real movement from the chest down and I was unable to make a sound.

Over the next few hours, a few centimetres at a time, I dragged myself to the front door where the dogs alerted Amanda and she found me on the step, absolutely wrecked. Ah, she has such a stress-free life.

After treatment at Frankston Hospital, I spent the next nine months more or less horizontal once again! This time on a fairly hefty cocktail of hospital-grade painkillers. It was during this period of forced nothingness that I decided that I should finally let this book see the light of day. I am now in a prolonged period of recovery and facing the prospect of major back surgery. That is, if my seriously overworked internal organs hold up for long enough.

It'd be a pity for the surgeon to do all that work only to have it all undone by a massive inner collapse. In that situation, most people would ask, 'Why me?' But I would not need to. I already know the answer.

Don't forget to check out the website for full access to all photos, videos and supporting documentation:

skasespainandme.com.au

(Yes, I know, it could be also read as "skases pain and me". Too funny.)

Acknowledgements

A special thanks to Alex Patterson for his in-depth analysis, *A Pilot's Perspective of the Australian Pilots Dispute of 1989,* which provides remarkable insight into an event that played such a crucial role in the downfall of Qintex.

I would further like to acknowledge all the airline personnel, plus the associated small business owners and their employees, as well as the shareholders and everyday Australians who enjoyed the benefits of the tourism boom of the 80s, along with those involved in the broadcasting and other industries that flourished within the spirited economy of the times, but who unfortunately became cannon fodder in 'the recession that Australia had to have.'

Thanks - sadly, posthumously - to the late Catherine Ann Hoyte BA (Hons.) whose 2003 Griffith University thesis *An Australian Mirage* contributed much to furthering my understanding of Christopher's situation. Her encyclopaedic research into the juggernaut that is presented in this book as SkaseWorld helped create a thorough and meaningful time-line of the events leading up to and dictating my life in Mallorca and beyond.

I also acknowledge the massive media coverage that provided a plethora of information about an extraordinary period in our nation's history, an amazing corporate story and a thrilling but occasionally chilling environment that I was plunged into and which kept me prisoner for eleven years.

Reference Material

Reference material used in the development of this book and the chronology of events includes:

An Australian Mirage
Thesis by the late Catherine Ann Hoyte BA (Hons.), Griffiths University
August, 2003
www120.secure.griffith.edu.au

A Pilot's Perspective of the Australian Pilots' Dispute of 1989
Authored by Alex Paterson, former Ansett pilot
Last update, March, 2008
vision.net.au

Credit Losses at Australian Banks: 1980-2013
Research discussion paper by David Rodgers
May, 2015
rba.gov.au

Australia's Experience with Financial Deregulation
Speech by the Deputy Governor of the Reserve Bank
July 16, 2007
rba.gov.au

Outline of the Waterfront Dispute
Current Issues Brief
1997-98
aph.gov.au

Investigation into Control
Australian Broadcasting Authority into Seven Network
Limited
April, 1996
acma.gov.au

Investigation into Control
Australian Broadcasting Authority into TEN Group
November, 1995; April, 1997; October, 1998
acma.gov.au

*Commonwealth v Skase: A matter of life or death or a
nomination for an Oscar?*
UNSW Law Journal Case Note, Volume 18(2)
1995
austlii.edu.au

Would Christopher Skase receive a fair trial?
Jeff Giddings, BEc, LLB, LLM, Associate Professor,
Faculty of Law, Griffith University
2000
www98.griffith.edu.au

My Gratitude

My heartfelt thanks to the many friends, relatives, workmates, business partners and colourful characters who came in and out of my life, particularly during my years in SkaseWorld, and without whom this book would never have materialised.

Particularly to:

- Christopher Charles Skase. Fuck, what a ride. Better than any rollercoaster I know of.

- Pixie Skase. For all the good and bad times. It most certainly was never dull. I hope you find peace and happiness in your golden years.

- My parents, Maureen and Mick Larkins. What can I say? Thank you so much for giving this little Hunters Hill boy every chance to get out there and give life a shake.

- The wife, the long-suffering Amanda Elizabeth (Argenti) Larkins. Can't believe you hung around for so long! You must be a masochist. I do love you and thank you so much for always being there. At least it's never been dreary.

- Our beautiful daughter, Charlotte Caroline Larkins. Thanks for still loving me after everything I put you through; you are my raison d'être. I can only hope that at least it wasn't boring.

- The man known in a former life as Axe. Couldn't have done this without your genius. Those who know you will understand the admiration I have for you and the input you have had into the finished product. Muchas gracias, my friend.

- The Wordsmith, Jacko, who spent most of his golden years turning my rambling thoughts into a readable document and then continually re-working them and finally turning them into what you have just read - all the while, I can only guess, as some sort of pre-heaven purgatory. I can't thank you enough, Señor. This book would never have even gotten off the ground if I hadn't met you back in my taxi-driving days, much less into print without your belief in me and your extreme generosity and perseverance over the years, Amazingly, all on a handshake deal. And to your wonderful wife who has tolerated me and this project for the last eleven years, I send a big hug.

Finally, as a great believer in karma I feel compelled to say: To whom ever I was last time around, I can't express my gratitude enough. And to whom ever I will be next time around, I am so sorry ..!

A Chronology of Events

1940

September 21: Federal Election sees the Coalition, consisting of the United Australia Party led by Prime Minister Robert Menzies and the Country Party, retain Government but requiring the support of two Independent Members.

1941

May 24: Jo-Anne Nanette Dixon (Pixie) born in Melbourne.

October 7: The two Independent Members abandon support of the Coalition. The Australian Labor Party led by John Curtin forms Government.

1943

August 21: ALP under Curtin retains Government at election.

1945

July 5: As World War II draws to an end, Curtin dies and is replaced briefly by Frank Forde and then Ben Chifley.

1946

September 28: ALP under Chifley retains Government, defeating Coalition that includes newly created Liberal Party, founded and led by Menzies.

1948

September 18: Christopher Charles Skase born in Melbourne.

November 29: The first Holden car, popularly known as the FX, rolls off the production line.

1949

December 10: Menzies leads Liberal/Country Coalition to power, beginning an unprecedented run of victories under his guidance in 1951, 1954, 1955, 1958, 1961 and 1963.

1960

July 19: The world's first reported skyjacking is attempted when a Russian-born passenger threatens the crew of TAA flight 408 over Brisbane with a gun and a bomb and demands the plane continue on to Singapore. He is overwhelmed by the captain and first officer and later gaoled.

September 9: Harold Antony (Tony) Larkins born in Sydney.

1966

November 26: The Coalition, with new Liberal Party leader Harold Holt, retains Government.

1967

December: Skase finishes education at Caulfield Grammar, Melbourne.

December 17: Holt vanishes while swimming at Cheviot Beach, near Portsea, Victoria. Country Party leader John McEwan takes over temporarily as PM until the Liberals elect John Gorton as leader.

1968

Skase employed at J.B. Were, starting as a clerk and later becoming a stockbroker.

1969

October 25: The Gorton-led Coalition retains power but the ALP under new leader Gough Whitlam makes significant gains.

1970-74

Skase leaves J. B. Were and sets off to drive around Australia, working at various jobs. Visiting Port Douglas he is so inspired by the tourism potential of the then quiet Far North Queensland fishing village he makes a sketch in the sand of his plans for it. On his return joins Melbourne's morning daily newspaper, *The Sun-News Pictorial*, as a finance journalist and then takes up a similar role in the Melbourne office of the *Australian Financial Review*, gleaning as much as he can about big business and high finance.

1972

December 2: ALP under Whitlam sweeps to power, introducing a raft of social, cultural and economic changes.

1973

February 10: Australia's first casino opens at Wrest Point, Hobart.

October: Organization of Arab Petroleum Exporting Countries proclaims an embargo that will quadruple the oil barrel price seriously affecting international politics and the global economy.

1974

May 18: Whitlam Government retains power, beating Billy Snedden-led Coalition, but with reduced majority.

September 18: Skase joins with three other investors in the formation of an investment company, Takeovers, Equities & Management Securities, or TEAM Securities. One of its companies, Ludbrookes Ltd, a small Tasmanian operation, will later be renamed Qintex Limited.

478

1975

November 11: Whitlam Government dismissed by Governor-General Sir John Kerr.

December 13: Malcolm Fraser leads Coalition to victory.

1976

Skase meets Pixie for the first time at a business function.

1977

December 10: Coalition under Fraser retains power.

1978

Skase leaves TEAM, taking the controlling stake in Qintex with him.

1979

March: Skase and Pixie marry. It is his second marriage, her third.

1979-85

Qintex embarks on a campaign of spectacular growth via acquisitions and mergers in a range of opportunities including media (television stations), hospitality (Leonda Receptions), merchandising (Hardy Brothers jewellers) and property development (the former Victoria Hotel in Melbourne's CBD, which makes Skase his first million.)

1980

October 18: Coalition under Fraser retains power.

1982

Tony Larkins gets into film production, working his way up from driver to technician on films such as *Phar Lap, Burke & Wills* and *Coolangatta Gold.*

1983

March 5: ALP, led by Bob Hawke, wins Government.

June 1: Government introduces the original Prices and Incomes Accord, a centralised system of wage fixing principles known as the National Wage Guidelines, securing all workers a 4.3 per cent pay rise in September.

September 27: Alan Bond's yacht Australia II wins the America's Cup.

December 12: Government floats the Australian dollar, commencing the de-regulation of the financial sector.

December 30: The All Ordinaries Index closes at 743.80 points.

Australia's Standard Variable Home Loan interest rate is 12 per cent.

1984

June: To further de-regulate the financial sector, the Government grants forty foreign exchange licenses while giving the Reserve Bank the power to control domestic liquidity, effectively muzzling the influence of private (foreign) capital flows on monetary policy. Reserve Bank policy is changed to use 'market operations' to influence short-term interest rates initially and ultimately the interest rates that all lenders charge.

December 1: ALP, led by Bob Hawke, retains Government.

1985

February: Government grants banking licenses to sixteen foreign banks and eases controls for the establishment of new domestic banks, further de-regulating the financial sector and accelerating lending competition. Local banks respond by reducing their required security and lowering rates.

March: Qintex purchases 4.23 hectares on Southport Spit, Gold Coast, Queensland, with a view to building a resort.

April 22: Pre-production starts on Paul Hogan film *Crocodile Dundee* with a budget of nearly $8.9m and qualifying for 10BA tax concessions (133 per cent deductions and 33 per cent exemption) as listed in the Rimfire Films Ltd prospectus.

June/July: While working as a technician on *Crocodile Dundee* shoot, on location in the Northern Territory, Tony Larkins meets Ansett flight attendant Amanda Argenti, eldest daughter of Pixie, in Darwin.

September 4: Rupert Murdoch becomes a US citizen enabling the purchase of a 50 per cent stake in 20th Century-Fox.

September: In the first step towards bringing to fruition Skase's earlier dream of making something of Port Douglas, Qintex subsidiary PML (later known as Mirage Resorts Trust) contracts to develop a resort on an eighty-hectare site in the Far North Queensland fishing village.

September 19: Capital Gains Tax introduced on all assets purchased from this date forward.

1986

January 1: Encouraged by Queensland Premier, Joh Bjelke-Petersen, Qintex moves head office to Brisbane.

April 24: *Crocodile Dundee* premieres in Australia.

September 26: *Crocodile Dundee* released in the US.

December 26: Government ownership and control legislation is enacted to aggregate country television viewing audience via three commercial television networks, restrict cross-media ownership and introduce a television operator limit of 60 per cent reach of the national audience.

1987

January 22: Alan Bond purchases TCN9 and GTV9 plus ancillaries from Kerry Packer for a reported $1184 million, consisting of $984 million in cash and $200 million in Redeemable Preference Shares in Bond Media.

January 31: Australia's defence of the America's Cup begins in Fremantle, WA.

February: Northern Star Holdings, an offshoot of Westfield Capital Corporation, purchases News Ltd's stake in Network Ten Holdings for $840 million.

April 1: Formation of the Australian Stock Exchange, amalgamating the existing six independent stock exchanges in state capitals. All Ords closes at 1691.1.

July 11: ALP, led by Bob Hawke, retains Government.

July 24: Qintex purchases ATN7, HSV7 and BTQ7 from John Fairfax Ltd for $780 million with an initial payment of $25 million, as the basis of a nationwide network.

August 22: Tony Larkins and Amanda Argenti marry and go on honeymoon on Qintex yacht Mirage III.

September: Mirage Gold Coast resort opens.

September 21: All Ords reaches an historical intra-day high of 2312.4 points before closing six and a half points lower.

September/October: Tony Larkins works on location at *Crocodile Dundee 2* filming.

October 20: Stock Market crash sees the All Ords index drop 25 per cent from 2052.20 points to 1549.90 points on the worst day of trading recorded on the ASX.

November: Mirage Port Douglas resort opens.

November/December: *Crocodile Dundee 2* wrap party held in New York. The Australian crew celebrates with Paul Hogan and business partner John Cornell who have paid the crew's air travel and expenses to attend.

1988

January 26: The First Fleet Re-enactment Voyage is completed as the 'Second First Fleet' sails into Sydney Harbour, commencing the nation's Bicentennial celebrations. Amongst the celebrating fleet is the Qintex yacht, Mirage III, with family and guests on board.

March 31: Qintex purchases television stations in Perth and Adelaide creating a national network, officially the Australian Television Network, but better known as the Seven Network. It has the potential to reach 66.9 per cent of the national audience, in conflict with the legislated 60 per cent rule.

April-October: Brisbane hosts World Expo 88.

May: Gold Coast Marina Mirage, advertised as a prestigious retail outlet, opens.

May 9: New Parliament House in Canberra officially opened by the Queen.

September: Australian Broadcasting Tribunal announces inquiry into Qintex's television purchases in relation to the 60 per cent rule.

December 23: Industrial Relations Commission president declares a 36 per cent pay rise granted to politicians as 'within the wage fixing principles.'

1989

March 31: Qintex launches $US1.2 billion bid for MGM/UA Communications.

April: Australian Broadcasting Tribunal begins hearings into Qintex's television purchases.

April: Qintex begins redevelopment of Mirage Princeville resort in Hawaii.

June: Australia's Standard Variable Home Loan interest rate reaches a historical high of 17 per cent. Business interest rates, 13 per cent at the start of 1988, reach more than 20 per cent.

August 15: A meeting is held in the Prime Minister's office attended by the PM, Bob Hawke, Sir Peter Abeles (Ansett), Ted Harris (Australian Airlines), Government Ministers Ralph Willis and Peter Morris, and ACTU Secretary Bill Kelty, by phone, to plan tactics for an upcoming industrial campaign declared by the Australian Federation of Air Pilots.

August 18: Domestic air pilots commence working within normal office hours of 9am-5pm.

August 23: Government declares a national emergency, leasing seats on international carriers, waiving landing charges and organising RAAF services to carry domestic passengers. Both domestic carriers shut down and ground aircraft.

September: Westfield Capital sells control of Network Ten to Broadcom for a reported $30 million. Consortium partner Curran Capital Television buys other stations for $185 million.

October 11: Qintex bid for MGM/UA collapses.

October 16: The All Ords index drops 8.1 per cent on, historically, the third worst day of trading.

October 20: Qintex Entertainment Incorporated and subsidiary, Qintex production, file for Chapter 11 under US bankruptcy laws allowing Qintex, as debtor in possession, to formulate a plan to restructure the business. If approved by the court, Chapter 11 allows the debtor in possession to cancel contracts and protect against litigation by imposing an automatic stay.

October 22: The Qintex board refuses to pay Skase's management fee, which is subsequently found to have been paid.

October 22: Australian Stock Exchange suspends Qintex Australia Limited and Qintex Ltd shares from trading. National Companies and Securities Commission announces an investigation into a $32.6 million fee paid to a private management company with a further $9.5 million disclosed later.

October 27: The Australian Federation of Air Pilots offers a return to work and a cooling off period for Christmas, which is rejected by the domestic airlines and the Government.

October 30: Government declares that the pilots' dispute has finished. Tourism industry losses are estimated to be $560 million.

November 2: *Australian Financial Review* carries a $7680 advertisement headed 'Australians support Qintex,' signed by a group of prominent Australians.

November 20: Qintex Australia Limited applies to the Victorian Supreme Court to be placed in receivership owing twelve banks nearly $1.1 billion. By the end of the year Qintex Australia Limited and twenty-eight of its subsidiaries are in the hands of receivers. In the US, Qintex Entertainment Incorporated is in Chapter 11 bankruptcy.

November 21: David Crawford and John Allpass, of KPMG Peat Marwick and Hungerford, are appointed receivers and managers of Qintex Australia Limited and associated companies.

Qintex is one of more than 6100 corporate insolvencies declared during 1989.

December 15: RAAF ceases 'public transport operations.'

1990

January 12: Government re-instates airport landing charges.

January: Skase leaves Australia for Europe, making return trips on several occasions to contest court actions. His London domicile (described as a 'mysterious asset') becomes the subject of much scrutiny. He will later move to the Spanish island of Mallorca.

March 19: Skase appears in the Queensland Supreme Court as a witness in a liquidators hearing involving Lloyds Ships Holdings, builders of the Qintex yacht, Mirage III.

March 24: ALP, led by Bob Hawke, retains Government.

June: Kerry Packer redeems $200 million preference shares plus $25 million owed in interest by Bond Media, seizing control of an expanded Nine Network, declaring $618.9 million capital losses after writing down the broadcast licence value and abnormal losses in September. He declares, 'You only get one Alan Bond in your lifetime and I've had mine.'

July: The Australian economy enters a severe recession.

August 24: Tasmanian Supreme Court appoints Ian Ferrier as liquidator of Qintex Ltd.

September 7: Queensland Supreme Court appoints Robert Burns and Peter Geroff as provisional liquidators of Qintex Group Management Services and two other companies that list Skase as sole director. Burns notes a $3 million discrepancy in the books, which he identifies as an 'accounting problem,' but later emphasises that that does not imply that someone has absconded with the money.

September 11: Two warrants are issued for Skase's arrest after his failure to appear before the Brisbane Magistrate's Court.

September 14: Appointment of receiver/manager to Ten Network after Westpac place Northern Star Holdings into receivership with debts of $455 million. After converting the debt to equity, Westpac emerges with 60 per cent and the Commonwealth Bank 40 per cent of the new entity.

September 17: Upon his return to Australia, Skase is charged with the alleged assault of *Sunday Mail* photographer, Nathan Richter, following an incident on December 29, 1989. National Companies and Securities Commission summons Skase to appear at its own inquiry.

October 14: Amanda Larkins and daughter Charlotte leave Australia to take up residence in Mallorca with Skase and Pixie.

October 22: After completing film work on location in Berlin, Tony Larkins flies to Mallorca to join Amanda and Charlotte.

November 1: Acquisition of MGM/UA is completed by Italian financier Giancarlo Parretti, merging it with his Pathé Communications Corp.

November 8: At a cost of $1.6 billion, the Commonwealth Bank of Australia rescues the State Bank of Victoria following the collapse of its merchant bank arm Tricontinental. Qintex company debt to the State Bank of Victoria totals more than $110 million.

November 29: Treasurer Paul Keating acknowledges the economy's performance, labelling it the 'recession that Australia had to have.' With the banks reacting to falling collateral values, the booming economy built on rising asset prices financed by increased borrowings comes to an end.

December 3: Robert Burns, provisional liquidator of Qintex Group Management Services, auctions art, furniture and silverware assets for $530,000.

December: Skase signs a rental agreement with an option to purchase La Noria, an old farm property in the quiet village of Puerto Andratx on the Spanish island of Mallorca.

1991

January 1: National Companies and Securities Commission replaced by Australian Securities Commission.

January 10: Skase resigns as Qintex Australia Limited chairman.

February 12: The order for the court registry to retain Skase's arrest warrant on file is continued until 5 March.

March: Australian Broadcasting Tribunal notified that all offers for the Australian Television Network (formerly the Seven Network) have been rejected by the banks. The banks and receivers propose that the Australian banks (without cross ownership conflicts) take equity in the network, and foreign banks along with the Commonwealth Bank take $470m equity in a separate company, which will lend money to and collect interest from the network. By converting this equity into a method of finance known as CRUST, the banks are able to avoid this amount being referred to as debt thereby avoiding Broadcasting Act restrictions covering solvency and foreign ownership.

March/April: US Bankruptcy Court orders management change at MGM-Pathé Communications saving the studio from Chapter 7 liquidation under US bankruptcy laws.

April 17: Conversion of Commonwealth Bank into a public company with the first tranche, consisting of 30 per cent shares, issued in September.

May 27: Skase appears in Southport Magistrate's Court on assault charges. The Australian Securities Commission enters the court and issues two charges of misusing his position as a company director. He is arrested and placed in a cell for two hours.

Tony Larkins, who has accompanied Skase to Australia, returns to Mallorca to manage a problem with domestic staff.

June 13: Skase declares himself bankrupt and his passport is surrendered to Neville Pocock, of Bentley's Chartered Accountants, acting as trustee-in-bankruptcy. Within twenty-four hours Skase's passport is returned and he leaves Australia for the last time.

June: Qintex receivers 'sell' the Australian Television Network to THL (Television Holdings Ltd.), a group of bankers and investors, for a reported $485 million.

July 10: Former Qintex treasurer Richard Capps pleads guilty to one of two Australian Securities Commission charges involving inter-company loans enabling share purchases. He is fined $1500 with no conviction recorded. The second charge is dropped.

July 24: Neville Pocock resigns as Skase's trustee-in-bankruptcy.

July 30: Victorian Supreme Court approves the separate incorporation of the Australian Television Network assets, as per the plan proposed in March, endorsing the planned recovery of the network from the Qintex receivership.

August 2: Max Donnelly and Desmond Knight, of Ferrier Hodgson, appointed bankruptcy co-trustees.

August 26: Trustees' public inquiry into Skase's bankruptcy opens in Brisbane Federal Court.

September 24: Desmond Knight resigns as bankruptcy co-trustee. Max Donnelly is sole trustee.

November 29: Skase fails to appear at bankruptcy proceedings. Further warrants issued for his arrest.

December 19: Paul Keating replaces Bob Hawke as Prime Minister.

1992

January 17: The Bankruptcy Amendment Bill, later referred to as the Skase Amendments, is passed into Federal Law, allowing the trustee to extend the bankruptcy period from three years to eight years.

January 22: An action to bankrupt Pixie is commenced in the Queensland Supreme Court seeking to enforce the Victorian Supreme Court's August 1991 order to repay $76.88 million in loans that she had personally guaranteed, jointly and severally, with Skase.

March 11: Brisbane Supreme Court appoints Pat Finnimore and Alan Taylor, of Horwath & Horwath, liquidators of Kahmea.

March 12: Brisbane Supreme Court appoints John Allpass and David Crawford liquidators of seven further companies.

July/August: Skase agrees to submit to interview and formal examination in Mallorca and invites Max Donnelly to fly to Spain.

August 31: Australian Securities Commission lays thirty-two charges against Skase in the Brisbane District Court alleging improper use of his position and the misuse of over $10 million.

Ian Callinan, representing the Commonwealth DPP, and Skase's barrister, Shane Herbert, agree that medical advice tendered to the court precludes Skase's appearance.

September 30: Westpac Banking Corporation reports a loss of $1.6 billion.

October 14: Qintex receivers report that none of the secured creditors who had received proceeds from asset sales (media estimates about $1 billion) had recouped all their money. The report identifies $2 billion in liabilities. The shortfall between this and the directors' asset valuation of $3 billion is described as 'another matter.'

October 28: A warrant for Skase's arrest on bankruptcy charges is refused by Justice Drummond in the Federal Court on the grounds that it is unenforceable.

November 26: Kerry Packer acquires just under 10 per cent of Westpac's capital for nearly $500 million, seeking two board appointments and forcing a debt restructure of the Ten Network.

December 30: Ten Group Ltd consortium purchases Network Ten Ltd from Westpac for a reported $140 million. Canadian corporation CanWest emerges with a 15 per cent voting interest and a 57.5 per cent economic interest for $52 million, which satisfies the 15 per cent foreign ownership requirement. CanWest will later sell its holding in 2009 for a reported $680 million.

December: More than 10,300 corporate insolvencies listed during 1992.

1993

March: Australian Securities Commission charges against Skase are deferred for a year when Judge Brian Hoath accepts the medical reports from experts Dr Villiger, Professor Lagler and Professor Medici that Skase is too ill to travel.

March 13: ALP, under new leader Paul Keating, re-elected.

April 18: Gold Coast based group the White Knights claims it can return Skase to Australia legally.

June: Former Skase employee Lawrence Van der Plaat commences interviews with the Australian Securities Commission in Australia after requesting and receiving 'indemnity from prosecution.'

June 29: Seven Network prospectus with a $2 issue price is listed with the Australian Stock Exchange.

July: Australian Securities Commission interviews Lawrence Van der Plaat in London. He flies to Sydney for 'a few days of protracted interviews' before leaving Australia.

July 31: Seven Network prospectus closes one week early after oversubscription estimates reached $1 billion with institutions seeking $700 million. Of the $600 million raised the public are issued with 35 per cent, institutions 40 per cent and 'strategic partners', with effective control, News 14.9 per cent and Telecom Australia 10 per cent of the shares.

August 12: Seven Network shares begin trading on the stock exchange.

September: Lawrence Van der Plaat travels to Australia for month-long interviews with Australian Securities Commission and the Australian Federal Police before leaving Australia on 1 October.

September 24: Sydney wins the right to host the XXVII Olympiad.

October: Second tranche of Commonwealth Bank shares, consisting of 19.6 per cent, is issued to public reducing government majority holding to 50.4 per cent.

November 24: Australian Federal Police granted seven arrest warrants against Skase alleging a failure to disclose assets to the trustee-in-bankruptcy.

December 23/24: Lawrence Van der Plaat spends 'two intense days' completing statements with the Australian Securities Commission and Australian Federal Police.

<u>1994</u>

January 5: At a special sitting of the Queensland District Court, Judge Pratt, recalled from holiday, commences hearing the Australian Securities Commission charges that had been scheduled for 14 March 1994. Tony Larkins and Lawrence Van der Plaat give evidence. Larkins flees Australia during the course of the trial, to return to Mallorca.

January 9: Lawrence Van der Plaat returns to London.

January 25: Judge Pratt rules Skase a fugitive and issues a warrant for his arrest, paving the way for extradition based on 'dual criminality and ... an equivalent offence in Spain.'

January 25: Australian authorities send Spain a provisional arrest warrant through Interpol.

January 31: Skase is arrested by Spanish police when presenting to police station at Palma, capital of Mallorca.

488

February 3: After a medical examination, Skase is remanded in custody under police guard in the secure wing of Palma General Hospital. He will spend more than three hundred days there.

February 5: In a prepared statement, Pixie pleads for the legal, government and media harassment of her husband to stop.

March 3: Australia's extradition request for Skase is submitted to court in Madrid, alleging thirty-six charges of dishonest conduct, through the provision of false information to independent directors, breach of fiduciary duties and improper use of position under the Companies (Qld) Code. A further six charges alleging failure to disclose relevant information under the Bankruptcy Act are included.

March 14: Judge Pratt remands charges against Skase in the Brisbane District Court.

July 19: Extradition hearing begins on Mallorca with the Australian Government's Spanish legal representative arguing that the allegations constitute 'robbery, even if the defence claimed it was simply a bad financial move.'

September 16: Audiencia Nacional de España grants extradition of Skase from Spain to Australia on thirty-two charges (not the bankruptcy charges) conditional upon travel by sea with appropriate medical assistance.

December 19: Nine judges of the Audiencia Nacional de España overturn extradition ruling on humanitarian grounds, criticising Australian authorities for their failure to clearly acknowledge Skase's health problems. He is released after 311 days under guard in the gaol section of Palma General Hospital and allowed to return to La Noria.

1995

March 1: Australian Attorney-General's Office ceases Skase extradition requests.

March 23: Television presenter Andrew Denton launches a campaign to kidnap Skase under the banner 'Chase for Skase' seeking $200,000 to hire an American bounty hunter. Only $100,000 is raised and the campaign peters out.

1996

March 2: Coalition, led by John Howard, wins Government.

April: Skase lawyer, Tim Stranack, and Alexandra Frew (Pixie's daughter) examined by the trustee-in-bankruptcy in a London private court hearing.

June 8: It is reported that business associate Lillian Hutchence alleges that the National Crime Authority, in meetings arranged by Sydney identity Tim

Bristow, have offered her $50,000 to lure Skase away from Mallorca, to a location where he could be extradited.

July 22: Full privatisation of the Commonwealth Bank completed as the Government sells its majority stake.

October 1: TNT sells its Ansett stake to Air New Zealand leaving News Ltd as manager of the airline.

October: Trustee-in-bankruptcy Max Donnelly's application for further government funding is rejected on the grounds that the search for assets has little chance of success.

October 10: PM John Howard instructs his Attorney-General to investigate the rejection of the trustee-in-bankruptcy application. It is announced that funding will be resumed in November amid reports that the Australian Federal Police could prosecute over an alleged assault of Lawrence Van der Plaat.

November 13: Government provides trustee-in-bankruptcy with further funding.

November: Seven Network's *Today Tonight* broadcasts a story by reporter David 'Sluggo' Richardson and producer Chris Adams, featuring Van der Plaat, which claims that Skase's influence on Mallorca is so powerful he ordered police roadblocks to inhibit their story and implying that they had to escape the island.

1997

March 31: ABC's *Media Watch* exposes the misrepresentations contained in the *Today Tonight* story, awarding it the title 'Barcelona Tonight.' Reporter Richardson is suspended by the Seven Network for a month.

December: The trustee-in-bankruptcy seeks orders to freeze assets in the UK and Cayman Islands. (Later, when no assets have been recovered by early 2000, the focus will be turned onto Tony Larkins.)

December: Disposing of non-core Australian assets, News Ltd sells its 14.04 per cent stake in the Seven Network for $245 million, effectively valuing it at more than $1.7 billion.

December 31: The All Ords closes at 2616.5 points.

1998

March 12: Peter Reith, Minister for Workplace Relations and Small Business, in an answer to a question without notice in Parliament, identifies 'the bloke who is owed $1160' for providing 'plants and services' and 'the bloke who runs a car hire business who loses $462.84' as examples of the 'loads of people in the small business community who had an interest in seeing the full pursuit of Mr Skase.'

490

May 24: Senator Amanda Vanstone, Minister for Justice, publicly displays Skase's passport with the word 'Cancelled' stamped under his photograph.

July: Spanish Government refuses Skase's renewal of his Spanish residency permit, giving him fifteen days to leave Spain.

July: Skase gains citizenship and passport from the Commonwealth of Dominica.

September 7: ABC airs *Four Corners* report in which trustee-in-bankruptcy Max Donnelly claims that he has 'traced about $10 million' and that Skase is currently 'earning at least US$25,000 a month.' Based on this estimate, the Spanish Government begins seeking income tax from Skase.

October 3: Howard-led Coalition retains Government.

November 13: Date of ordered departure of Skase, following earlier rejection of his re-application for Spanish residency with his Dominican passport.

1999

March 1: Skase undergoes lung surgery. Photographs attract the scepticism of Dr Michael Wooldridge, Minister for Health and Aged Care, who says that 'the operations that I was at, looked a little bit different to that one.' Minister for Justice and Customs Amanda Vanstone says Australian medical travel experts have told her that Skase 'could be returned in a much sooner time' than three months.

March 4: Spanish deportation order is suspended.

June 1: Media release from Minister of Justice and Customs, Senator Amanda Vanstone, reveals that the Coalition and Labor Governments have spent $1.45 million and $750,000 respectively in pursuit of Skase.

July: Skase is ordered to leave Spain within fifteen days. An appeal is lodged.

2000

May: Tony Larkins goes home to Sydney for an indefinite break.

June 13: News Corp sells Ansett stake to Air New Zealand.

September 15-October 1: Sydney hosts the 2000 Summer Olympic Games.

October: Article by Professor Jeff Giddings, *Would Christopher Skase Receive a Fair Trial?* is published in Volume 24 of the Criminal Law Journal.

November: Tony Larkins is served in Sydney with a summons for failing to attend a bankruptcy hearing into Skase's business dealings. Larkins exits Australia and returns to Mallorca.

March: Skase loses his right of appeal against deportation, leaving the Court of Human Rights in Brussels as the only way of avoiding deportation.

July: After an independent medical examination, the Spanish Government places a three-month delay on the Skase extradition.

August 5: Christopher Charles Skase dies of cancer, aged 52.

August: PM John Howard indicates the Government would continue funding the pursuit of Skase's assets resulting in Chris Ellison, Minister for Justice and Customs, supporting moves to recoup the 'over $170 million in assets that were lost to creditors.' (This amount appears to represent the $171.5 million that Skase and Pixie gave in loan guarantees to secured creditors.)

August 24: ABC's *AM* reports on the 'supposed existence' of a Skase autobiography, *Postcard from Mallorca - Nightmare in Paradise*. In fact, the book was published by Mallorquina Publishing in 1999, ISBN 84-930916-3-4.

September 14: Ansett placed in voluntary liquidation with PricewaterhouseCoopers.

October: Tony, Amanda and Charlotte Larkins leave Mallorca to live temporarily in Thailand.

November 10: Howard-led Coalition retains Government.

2002

March 10: *The Age* reports that trustee-in-bankruptcy, Max Donnelly, has asked the Australian Government to consider abandoning the chase for Skase assets, questioning 'whether the cost benefit would stack up.'

April: Frequent flyer points, given by a friend, enable Amanda and Charlotte Larkins return to Australia from Thailand. Tony stays behind.

October 20: In a *Sun-Herald* report, journalist Annette Sharp reports that Tony Larkins is planning to return to Melbourne.

October 23: Tony Larkins flies in to Australia, is arrested at Sydney airport, taken to the Federal Court, and then interviewed by Max Donnelly. After six hours' discussion he is free to go.

December 7: Max Donnelly, trustee-in-bankruptcy, announces the end of the ten-year international pursuit of an estimated $10 million Skase fortune during which numerous trails were followed without any asset recovery. He adds that Skase appeared to have lost most of the money in badly planned, disorganised business ventures in Majorca.

2003

April 3: Attorney-General Daryl Williams announces an end to Government funding, conceding that after spending $2.65 million (including $310,290 fees to the trustee-in-bankruptcy) the results were disappointing. One headline covering the story reads, 'Hunt for Skase millions fruitless.'

In an interview on the ABC's *PM*, Max Donnelly reports that he had 'been given sufficient material to be satisfied that the assets have effectively been lost and wasted' and that his concerns over assets in a bank account were quashed by recent 'evidence from various family members' nominating that the records and answers provided by Tony Larkins 'tied in with the various banking records that we were aware of.'

When asked if he was disappointed that he had been unable to recover any assets, he answered that it was 'disappointing' that the original trustee handed back the passport but his 'main disappointment' was that despite the Government's successful extradition proceedings 'the court determined that Skase was too sick to travel.'

August: *An Australian Mirage*, a thesis by the late Catherine Ann Hoyte BA (Hons.), in fulfilment of the requirements of her degree of Doctor of Philosophy, is submitted to Griffith University.

2004

October 9: Howard-led Coalition retains Government.

2007

November 24: ALP under Kevin Rudd defeats Coalition to gain Government, with Howard losing his seat.

2008

May 19: All Ords reaches an all time intra-day high of 6059.5 points.

September 6: The US Government places two government-sponsored enterprises, guaranteed nearly US$5 trillion in mortgage obligations, into 'conservatorship', accelerating a year-long decline in the Dow Jones Industrial Average. The Global Financial Crisis that follows prompts the largest drop in Australian business credit growth since the 1990 recession. (However, figures will later show that the 1990s fall was far longer and deeper than the one accompanying this crisis.)

October 10: The All Ords drops 351.8 points (-8.2 per cent) to finish the day's trading at 3939.5 points, marking the second worst day in its trading history.

December 19: Pixie returns to Melbourne amid misreporting that she had purchased a million dollar house in Toorak.

December 31: The All Ords finishes the year at 3,659.3 points.

2010

August 21: Following election, ALP led by Julia Gillard forms Minority Government with the support of one Green and three Independent MPs.

2013

September 7: Coalition under Tony Abbott wins Government.

December 12: Ex-Minister for Health and Aged Care, Michael Wooldridge, a former non-executive director of Australian Property Custodian Holdings Ltd, the entity managing the Prime Trust investment scheme, is found to have breached his duties as a director by allowing fellow APCHL director Bill Lewski to orchestrate a $33 million payment from Prime Trust for his own financial benefit. Prime Trust had collapsed with more than $560 million in funds under management in 2010 after listing on the stock exchange in 2007.

2015

June 8: Former Howard Government Minister, Amanda Vanstone, now a Fairfax columnist, writes that the proposal of then Prime Minister Tony Abbott to give ministers the power to take away the passport of any mercenary fighter returning to Australia without following the traditional legal process was 'shameful' and 'unlawful.' She writes of her disappointment 'when I see some on my team thinking it is OK for a minister alone to take away a citizen's rights,' chastising 'cabinet ministers in favour of excluding the courts' and arguing that 'the suggestion that ministers alone should be able to, without appeal, take away anyone's right shows a profound misunderstanding of the western democratic tradition.'

December 21: Amanda Vanstone, in a Fairfax column about Cardinal George Pell relying on medical evidence to avoid returning to Australia to personally give evidence at the paedophilia inquiry, says Pell has 'become the lightning rod for all the hatred, anger and resentment that's built up around Australia' and hopes that 'the royal commission on child abuse is out for the truth from everyone - not a blood sacrifice to appease the baying crowd.'

2016

June 30: The All Ordinaries Index closes at 5310.4 points.

Australia's Standard Variable Home Loan interest rate is at 5.1 per cent.

July 2: The Coalition, now led by Malcolm Turnbull, retains Government with one-seat majority.

August 5: Fifteen years to the day after Skase's death and twelve years after the shutting down of the taxpayer-funded search, described in one news story as 'fruitless,' no cash or assets have been recovered.